Complete Greek

Complete Greek

Aristarhos Matsukas

Teach Yourself®

First published in Great Britain in 1997 by Hodder Education. An Hachette UK company.

First published in US in 1997 by The McGraw-Hill Companies, Inc.

This edition published in 2019 by John Murray Learning

Copyright © Aristarhos Matsukas 1997, 2003, 2010, 2014, 2019

The right of Aristarhos Matsukas to be identified as the Author of the Work has been asserted by him in accordance with the Copyright, Designs and Patents Act 1988.

Database right Hodder & Stoughton (makers)

The *Teach Yourself* name is a registered trademark of Hachette UK.

British Library Cataloguing in Publication Data: a catalogue record for this title is available from the British Library.

Library of Congress Catalog Card Number: on file.

ISBN 9781529325003

6

The publisher has used its best endeavours to ensure that any website addresses referred to in this book are correct and active at the time of going to press. However, the publisher and the author have no responsibility for the websites and can make no guarantee that a site will remain live or that the content will remain relevant, decent or appropriate.

The publisher has made every effort to mark as such all words which it believes to be trademarks. The publisher should also like to make it clear that the presence of a word in the book, whether marked or unmarked, in no way affects its legal status as a trademark.

Every reasonable effort has been made by the publisher to trace the copyright holders of material in this book. Any errors or omissions should be notified in writing to the publisher, who will endeavour to rectify the situation for any reprints and future editions.

Cover image © Alamy

Typeset by Cenveo® Publisher Services.

Printed and bound in Great Britain by CPI Group (UK) Ltd., Croydon, CR0 4YY.

John Murray Learning policy is to use papers that are natural, renewable and recyclable products and made from wood grown in sustainable forests. The logging and manufacturing processes are expected to conform to the environmental regulations of the country of origin.

Carmelite House

50 Victoria Embankment

London EC4Y 0DZ

www.hodder.co.uk

Acknowledgements

This book has survived over the last 20 years and has benefited directly or indirectly from many people. Many thanks go to my past editors Rebecca Green, Ginny Catmur, and Sue Hart. This new edition, compared to all other past editions, is a major overhaul especially methodologically and Sindith Custer and Julie Cracco have lent their expertise and talents. Special thanks go particularly to Julie Cracco who has contributed insightful comments and has thus substantially enhanced many parts of this new edition. It would have been an oversight not to mention my students in New York City, Athens, and now in Berlin who have shown me over the years what is important and fun when learning Greek. **Σας ευχαριστώ όλους πάρα πολύ!**

Contents

Meet the author

I have worked as a professional author, translator, and language teacher for over 30 years. I have written more than ten language books with special focus on Greek as a foreign language, including a bilingual English–Greek, Greek–English pocket dictionary and a German–Greek picture dictionary. I have lived more than half of my life away from Athens, my birthplace, first in the US for 14 years, where I studied Teaching English as a Foreign Language (TEFL) and Applied Linguistics, and now in Berlin for the last 14 years. My accumulated teaching experience of Modern Greek comes from teaching adults and college students in New York City, then Athens, and more recently Berlin. My professional experience also includes university teaching in the USA; working as a head of department in a community college in Athens; as a language school director in Ioannina (Greece) and as the translator of three cookery books and two language books. Here in Berlin, I teach Greek in two Community Adult Schools. When not at my desk, I can usually be found in the kitchen, in a bookshop, in a coffee shop, or at a language book fair. I love travelling (having visited more than 20 countries), watching TV (especially soccer), and learning languages (particularly exotic ones).

Aristarhos Matsukas

How this book works

This course assumes no previous knowledge of Greek. The emphasis is first and foremost on using the language, but we also aim to give you an idea of how Greek works, so that you can create sentences of your own. The course covers all four of the basic skills – listening and speaking, reading and writing. If you are working on your own, the audio will be all the more important, as it provides you with the essential opportunity to listen to native Greek voices and to speak Greek within a controlled environment.

Don't expect to be able to understand everything you hear or read straight away. If you listen to Greek audio material, or watch a Greek programme or film, or are able to get newspapers or magazines, you should not get discouraged when you realize how quickly native speakers speak and how much vocabulary there is still to be learnt. Just concentrate on a small extract – either a video/audio clip or a short article – and work through it till you have mastered it. In this way, you'll find that your command of Greek increases steadily.

All the units in *Complete Greek* are structured in the following way:

▶ **What you will learn.** A set of learning objectives identifies what you will be able to do in Greek by the end of the unit.
▶ **Culture point.** An opening passage about a cultural aspect related to the unit theme introduces some key words and phrases.
▶ **Vocabulary builder.** This section, along with the accompanying audio, brings in the key vocabulary you will learn in the unit.
▶ **Dialogues.** New language is presented through a series of recorded dialogues. Each dialogue is preceded by key words and comprehension questions to support your comprehension and focus your attention before you listen.
▶ **Language discovery** questions guide you to consider language points in the conversations. Look to the light bulb icon to discover how the language works, whether it is a grammar rule or a way of saying things. The Language discovery section presents the forms of the language in a systematic way, leading you to construct your own sentences correctly. Exercises allow you to practise and confirm your understanding of the language forms you have learned. Try to do these as you come to them.
▶ **Practice.** A variety of exercises, including speaking activities and role-plays, give you a chance to 'pull it all together' and use your Greek actively and creatively. Some exercises help you to understand written and spoken Greek, but right from the start, you are given specific guidance and models so that you can speak, write, and express yourself.
▶ **Language tips.** Throughout the book, you will find tips on language, vocabulary or culture. This information is given in English to provide insights about life and customs in Greece.
▶ **Test yourself** will help you assess how much you have learnt. Do the tests without looking at the language notes.

▶ **Self-check** lets you see what you can do in Greek. When you feel confident that you can use the language correctly, move on to the next unit.

Study the units at your own pace, and remember to make frequent and repeated use of the audio.

SYMBOLS

To make your learning easier and more efficient, a system of icons indicates the actions you should take:

Read about the culture

Play the audio track

Listen and pronounce

Figure something out for yourself

Learn key words and expressions

Exercises coming up!

Write and make notes

Speak Greek out loud

Check your Greek ability

As you work your way through the course, you will also become familiar with studying on your own, looking things up, and checking your Greek ability.

You can consult at the beginning of the book:

▶ **Pronunciation**: an overview of Greek sounds and a logical starting point.

And at the end of the book:

▶ A **Grammar glossary**.
▶ An **Answer key** to check your answers to the all exercises and self-tests in order to monitor your progress and performance.
▶ A **Greek–English** and **English–Greek glossary**, which includes most of the words used in the course.

ABBREVIATIONS USED IN THIS BOOK

m	masculine
f	feminine
sing	singular

pl	plural
fam	familiar (or informal)
lit	literally

PUNCTUATION

Greek punctuation is very similar to that of English. The only obvious difference is the semicolon (;) which is used as a question mark in Greek! The Greek semicolon looks like an English full stop slightly raised (·).

THE STRESS MARK IN GREEK

A written accent is used in all words of more than one syllable to show where the stress falls, both in the Greek script and in the transliteration. Try to observe this as carefully as possible. Changing the stress can alter the meaning entirely, so pay close attention. No stress mark is used when the word is spelled out in capital letters only. You can read more about 'stress and intonation' in the **Pronunciation guide**.

Learn to learn

THE DISCOVERY METHOD

There are lots of approaches to language learning, some practical and some quite unconventional. Perhaps you know of a few, or even have some techniques of your own. In this book we have incorporated the **Discovery method** of learning, a sort of DIY approach to language learning. What this means is that you will be encouraged throughout the course to engage your mind and figure out the language for yourself, through identifying patterns, understanding grammar concepts, noticing words that are similar to English, and more. This method promotes language awareness, a critical skill in acquiring a new language. As a result of your own efforts, you will be able to better retain what you have learnt, use it with confidence, and, even better, apply those same skills to continuing to learn the language (or, indeed, another one) on your own after you've finished this book.

Everyone can succeed in learning a language – the key is to know how to learn it. Learning is more than just reading or memorizing grammar and vocabulary. It's about being an active learner, learning in real contexts, and, most importantly, using what you've learnt in different situations. Simply put, if you figure something out for yourself, you're more likely to understand it. And when you use what you've learnt, you're more likely to remember it.

And because many of the essential but (let's admit it!) dull details, such as grammar rules, are taught through the **Discovery method**, you'll have more fun while learning. Soon, the language will start to make sense and you'll be relying on your own intuition to construct original sentences independently, not just listening and repeating.

Enjoy yourself!

Become a successful language learner

1 MAKE A HABIT OUT OF LEARNING

Study a little every day, between 20 and 30 minutes if possible, rather than two to three hours in one session. Give yourself **short-term goals**, e.g. work out how long you'll spend on a particular unit and work within the time limit. This will help you to **create a study habit**, much in the same way you would a sport or music. You will need to concentrate, so try to **create an environment conducive to learning** which is calm and quiet and free from distractions. As you study, do not worry about your mistakes or the things you can't remember or understand. Languages settle differently in our brains, but gradually the language will become clearer as your brain starts to make new connections. Just **give yourself enough time** and you will succeed.

2 EXPAND YOUR LANGUAGE CONTACT

As part of your study habit try to take other opportunities to expose yourself to the language. As well as using this book you could try listening to radio and television or reading articles and blogs. Remember that as well as listening to online radio live you can use catch-up services to listen more than once. Perhaps you could find information in Greek about a personal passion or hobby or even a news story that interests you. In time you'll find that your vocabulary and language recognition deepen and you'll become used to a range of writing and speaking styles.

3 VOCABULARY

▶ To organize your study of vocabulary, group new words under:
  a generic categories, e.g. *food, furniture.*
  b situations in which they occur, e.g. under *restaurant* you can write *waiter, table, menu, bill.*
  c functions, e.g. *greetings, parting, thanks, apologizing.*

▶ Say the words out loud as you read them.

▶ Write the words over and over again. Remember that if you want to keep lists on your smartphone or tablet you can usually switch the keyboard language to make sure you are able to include all accents and special characters.

▶ Listen to the audio several times.

▶ Cover up the English side of the vocabulary list and see if you remember the meaning of the word.

▶ Associate the words with similar sounding words in English, e.g. **πέντε** *five* with Pentagon (a five corner building), **έξι** *six* with hexagon (the six corner shape), or **δέκα** *ten* with decathlon (ten different athletics).

▶ Create flash cards, drawings and mind maps.

▶ Write words for objects around your house and stick them to objects.

▶ Pay attention to patterns in words, e.g. adding **καλη-** to the start of a word usually indicates a greeting, e.g. **καλημέρα, καλησπέρα, καληνύχτα.**

▶ Experiment with words. Use the words that you learn in new contexts and find out if they are correct. For example, you learn in Unit 4 the phrase **Καλή όρεξη!** *Bon appétit!* Extend this knowledge with new examples and check if you get it right in different contexts, e.g. **καλός μεζές** *good (tasty) appetizer,* **καλή εποχή** *good season,* **καλό κρασί** *good wine,* or even **καλά σουτζουκάκια** *good meatballs.* All words from these examples come from Unit 4 and it is a great idea for you to experiment with new but possible combinations. Check the new phrases either in this book, a dictionary or with Greek speakers.

▶ Make the best of words you already know. When you start thinking about it you will realize that there are lots of Greek words and expressions which are commonly used in English: **θέατρο** *theatre,* **μουσική** *music,* **σαλάτα** *salad,* **φωτογραφία** *photography,* **ψυχολογία** *psychology* and many more.

4 GRAMMAR

▶ To organize the study of grammar write your own grammar glossary and add new information and examples as you go along.

▶ Experiment with grammar rules. Sit back and reflect on the rules you learn. See how they compare with your own language or other languages you may already speak. Try to find out some rules on your own and be ready to spot the exceptions. By doing this you'll remember the rules better and get a feel for the language.

▶ Try to find examples of grammar in conversations or other articles.

▶ Keep a 'pattern bank' that organizes examples that can be listed under the structures you've learnt.

▶ Use old vocabulary to practise new grammar structures.

▶ When you learn a new verb form, write the conjugation of several different verbs you know that follow the same form.

5 PRONUNCIATION

▶ When organizing the study of pronunciation keep a section of your notebook for pronunciation rules and practise those that trouble you.

▶ Repeat all of the conversations, line by line. Listen to yourself and try to mimic what you hear.

▶ Record yourself and compare yourself to a native speaker.

▶ Make a list of words that give you trouble and practise them.

▶ Study individual sounds, then full words.

▶ Don't forget, it's not just about pronouncing letters and words correctly, but using the right intonation. So, when practising words and sentences, mimic the rising and falling intonation of native speakers.

6 LISTENING AND READING

The conversations in this book include questions to help guide you in your understanding. But you can go further by following some of these tips.

▶ Imagine the situation. When listening to or reading the conversations, try to imagine where the scene is taking place and who the main characters are. Let your experience of the world help you guess the meaning of the conversation, e.g. if a conversation takes place in a snack bar you can predict the kind of vocabulary that is being used.

▶ Concentrate on the main part. When watching a foreign film you usually get the meaning of the whole story from a few individual shots. Understanding a foreign conversation or article is similar. Concentrate on the main parts to get the message and don't worry about individual words.

▶ Guess the key words; if you cannot, ask or look them up.

When there are key words you don't understand, try to guess what they mean from the context. If you're listening to a Greek speaker and cannot get the gist of a whole passage because of one word or phrase, try to repeat that word with a questioning tone; the speaker will probably paraphrase it, giving you the chance to understand it. If for example you wanted to find out the meaning of the word **θέλω** *to like/want* in a statement you hear: **Θέλω μία κόκα κόλα** *I'd like/I want a coke*, you would ask **Τι είναι 'θέλω';** *What is 'thelo'?* or **Τι σημαίνει 'θέλω';** *What does 'thelo' mean?* Of course, before you get the right answer, we're sure that your guessing from this context could have been: *I'd like a coke*, or *I want a coke*, or *I'm having a coke*, or even *I'm drinking a coke!*

7 SPEAKING

Rehearse in the foreign language. As all language teachers will assure you, the successful learners are those students who overcome their inhibitions and get into situations where they must speak, write and listen to the foreign language. Here are some useful tips to help you practise speaking Greek:

▶ Hold a conversation with yourself, using the conversations of the units as models and the structures you have learnt previously.

▶ After you have conducted a transaction with a salesperson, clerk or waiter in your own language, pretend that you have to do it in Greek, e.g. buying groceries, ordering food, drinks and so on.

▶ Look at objects around you and try to name them in Greek.

▶ Look at people around you and try to describe them in detail.

▶ Try to answer all of the questions in the book out loud.

▶ Say the dialogues out loud then try to replace sentences with ones that are true for you.

▶ Try to role-play different situations in the book.

8 LEARN FROM YOUR ERRORS

▶ Don't let errors interfere with getting your message across. Making errors is part of any normal learning process, but some people get so worried that they won't say anything unless they are sure it is correct.

▶ This leads to a vicious circle as the less they say, the less practice they get and the more mistakes they make.

▶ Note the seriousness of errors. Many errors are not serious, as they do not affect the meaning; for example if you use the wrong article (**ο** for **το**), wrong pronouns (**με αρέσει** for **μου αρέσει**) or wrong adjective endings (**άσπρο** for **άσπρος**). So concentrate on getting your message across and learn from your mistakes.

▶ As you progress you will also become aware of **λάθος φίλους** *false friends*. These are words which look or sound like English words, but may have a very different meaning, e.g. **ο χημικός** is not the chemist's or pharmacy, but *the chemist (the scientist)* in Greek (**το φαρμακείο**). The most important thing to remember though is BE BOLD! Getting it wrong at times is a huge part of your learning process and success.

9 LEARN TO COPE WITH UNCERTAINTY

▶ Don't overuse your dictionary.

When reading a text in the foreign language, don't be tempted to look up every word you don't know. Underline the words you do not understand and read the passage several times, concentrating on trying to get the gist of the passage. If after the third time there are still words which prevent you from getting the general meaning of the passage, look them up in the dictionary.

▶ Don't panic if you don't understand.

If at some point you feel you don't understand what you are told, don't panic or give up listening. Either try and guess what is being said and keep following the conversation or, if you cannot, isolate the expression or words you haven't understood and have them explained to you. The speaker might paraphrase them and the conversation will carry on.

▶ Keep talking.

The best way to improve your fluency in the foreign language is to talk every time you have the opportunity to do so: keep the conversations flowing and don't worry about the mistakes. If you get stuck for a particular word, don't let the conversation stop; paraphrase or replace the unknown word with one you do know, even if you have to simplify what you want to say. As a last resort use the word from your own language and pronounce it in the foreign accent.

Pronunciation guide

The Greek alphabet

The Greek alphabet has 24 capital letters and 25 small letters. This is because the letter **Σ** [sígma] becomes a small **σ** in any position of a word except at the end, where it is **ς**. If you have the audio, listen to how the alphabet sounds when recited in Greek. Alternatively, check the names below:

 00.01

Α α	(álfa)	**Ν ν**	(ni)
Β β	(víta)	**Ξ ξ**	(ksi)
Γ γ	(gháma)	**Ο ο**	(ómikron)
Δ δ	(THélta)	**Π π**	(pi)
Ε ε	(épsilon)	**Ρ ρ**	(ro)
Ζ ζ	(zíta)	**Σ σ/ς**	(síghma)
Η η	(íta)	**Τ τ**	(taf)
Θ θ	(thíta)	**Υ υ**	(ípsilon)
Ι ι	(yóta)	**Φ φ**	(fi)
Κ κ	(kápa)	**Χ χ**	(hi)
Λ λ	(lámTHa)	**Ψ ψ**	(psi)
Μ μ	(mi)	**Ω ω**	(omégha)

Greek, unlike English, is a phonetic language. This means that you can read or pronounce any word once you know the alphabet, something similar to German, Italian or Spanish.

It's important to know the difference in the sounds (TH) and (th). The first is used to produce the sound of **Δ δ** as in *this*, *though* or *thus*. The second is used to produce the sound of **Θ θ** as in *thin*, *thought*, or *thug*.

Be careful with two letters that have almost the same name: **Ε ε** (épsilon) and **Υ υ** (ípsilon).

VOWELS AND CONSONANTS

There are 7 vowels and 17 consonants in Greek.

Vowels	Consonants
α, ε, η, ι, ο, υ, ω	β, γ, δ, ζ, θ, κ, λ, μ, ν, ξ, π, ρ, σ/ς, τ, φ, χ, ψ

Two-letter vowels	Two-letter consonants
αι, ει, οι, ου	**γγ, γκ, γχ, μπ, ντ, τσ, τζ**
Vowel combinations	Two same-letter consonants
αυ, ευ	**ββ, κκ, λλ, μμ, νν, ππ, ρρ, σσ, ττ**

The sounds of vowels and consonants in each sub-group above are explained in the following section.

LETTERS AND SOUNDS

In general, remember that all letters have one sound, with a few exceptions: **Γ γ** (gháma), **Σ σ/ς** (síghma), and **X χ** (hi). Otherwise, the vowel or consonant sounds are always pronounced in the same way in Greek, in contrast with English where one letter usually has more than one sound, e.g. *a* as in *mat*, *mate*, *mayor*, etc.

VOWEL SOUNDS

 00.02

Α α	(álfa)	*a* as in *raft*
Ε ε	(épsilon)	*e* as in *met*
Η η	(íta)	*i* as in *inn*
Ι ι	(yóta)	*i* as in *sit*
Ο ο	(ómikron)	*o* as in *lot*
Υ υ	(ípsilon)	*i* as in *inn*
Ω ω	(omégha)	*o* as in *lot*

Here are some examples of vowel sounds:

Α α	(a) **αεροπλάνο**	(aeropláno)	*aeroplane*
Ε ε	(e) **ελικόπτερο**	(elikóptero)	*helicopter*
Η η	(i) **ήρωας**	(íroas)	*hero*
Ι ι	(i) **ιδέα**	(iTHéa)	*idea*
Ο ο	(o) **οξυγόνο**	(oksighóno)	*oxygen*
Υ υ	(i) **υπόθεση**	(ipóthesi)	*hypothesis*
Ω ω	(o) **ώρα**	(óra)	*hour*

Greek vowels can be short or long. The transliteration system used in this course does not show this, since in Greek, unlike English, you will rarely find word pairs such as *fit-feet* or *sit-seat*. Consequently the Greek word **σπίτι** *house* is transliterated as (spíti) although the first (i) is longer than the second.

Remember that **Ηη**, **Ιι**, and **Υυ** have the same sound (*i* as in *sit*). Also, **Οο** and **Ωω** have the same sound (*o* as in *lot*).

CONSONANT SOUNDS

 00.03

Β β	(víta)	*v* as in *vet*
Γ γ	(gháma)	1 *y* as in *yes* or *yield**
		2 1 *gh* as in *ghost*
Δ δ	(THélta)	*TH* as in *this*
Ζ ζ	(zíta)	*z* as in *zip*
Θ θ	(thíta)	*th* as in *thin*
Κ κ	(kápa)	*k* as in *kit*
Λ λ	(lámTHa)	*l* as in *let*
Μ μ	(mi)	*m* as in *met*
Ν ν	(ni)	*n* as in *net*
Ξ ξ	(ksi)	*ks* as in *banks*
Π π	(pi)	*p* as in *pet*
Ρ ρ	(ro)	*r* as in *rest*
Σ σ/ς	(síghma)	1 *s* as in *set*
		2 *z* as in *zip*
Τ τ	(taf)	*t* as in *tea*
Φ φ	(fi)	*f* as in *fit*
Χ χ	(hi)	1 *h* as in *hat*
		2 *ch* as in *loch*
Ψ ψ	(psi)	*ps* as in *laps*

*There is no exact equivalent of this sound in English.

Here are some examples of consonant sounds:

Β β	(v)	**βούτυρο**	(vútiro)	*butter*
Γ γ	(gh)*	**γάλα**	(ghála)	*milk*
	(y)	**γιαγιά**	(yayá)	*granny*
Δ δ	(TH)	**δημοκρατία**	(THimokratía)	*democracy*
Ζ ζ	(z)	**ζώδιο**	(zóTHio)	*zodiac*
Θ θ	(th)	**θέατρο**	(théatro)	*theatre*
Κ κ	(k)	**κιθάρα**	(kithára)	*guitar*

Λ λ	(l)	**λεμόνι**	(lemóni)	*lemon*
Μ μ	(m)	**μουσική**	(musikí)	*music*
Ν ν	(n)	**νοσταλγία**	(nostalghía)	*nostalgia*
Ξ ξ	(ks)**	**ξενοδοχείο**	(ksenoTHochío)	*hotel*
Π π	(p)	**πιάνο**	(piáno)	*piano*
Ρ ρ	(r)	**ράδιο**	(ráTHio)	*radio*
Σ σ/ς	(s)	**σαλάτα**	(saláta)	*salad*
	(z)	**κόσμος**	(kózmos)	*cosmos/world*
Τ τ	(t)	**τρένο**	(tréno)	*train*
Υ υ	(i)	**υπόθεση**	(ipóthesi)	*hypothesis*
Φ φ	(f)	**φωτογραφία**	(fotoghrafía)	*photography*
Χ χ	(h)	**χορός**	(horós)	*chorus/dance*
	(ch)	**όχι**	(óchi)	*no*
Ψ ψ	(ps)	**ψυχολόγια**	(psihologhía)	*psychology*

* The transliteration of the letter **Γ γ** (gh) sounds almost like *y* in *yield* and not *gh* in *ghost*.

** The letter **Ξ ξ** (ksi) sounds like the *x* in *six* or *box*.

Please note that all these transliterations are approximate sounds and only the audio or native speakers can offer the exact sound.

TWO-LETTER VOWELS

 00.04

The following two-letter vowels have only one sound, short or long, depending on whether they are found in a stressed syllable or not.

ΑΙ	αι	(e)	(álfa-yóta)	*e* as in *set*
ΕΙ	ει	(i)	(épsilon-yóta)	*i* as in *inn*
ΟΙ	οι	(i)	(ómikron-yóta)	*i* as in *inn*
ΟΥ	ου	(u)	(ómikron-ípsilon)	*u* as in *put*

The remaining two-letter vowels have two different sounds each:

ΑΥ	αυ*	(af)	(álfa-ípsilon)	*af* as in *after*
		(av)		*av* as in *avenue*
ΕΥ	ευ**	(ef)	(épsilon-ípsilon)	*ef* as in *effort*
		(ev)		*ev* as in *ever*

* It is always (af) and (ef) when **αυ** or **ευ** is followed by any **θ, κ, ξ, π, σ, φ, χ, ψ** letter.

** It is always (av) or (ev) when **αυ** or **ευ** is followed by any **β, γ, δ, ζ, λ, μ, ν, ρ,** letter or any vowel.

Here are some examples of two-letter vowels:

AI	**αι**	(e)	**ναι**	(ne)	*yes*
AY	**αυ**	(af)	**αυτοκίνητο**	(aftokínito)	*car*
		(av)	**Αύγουστος**	(ávghustos)	*August*
EI	**ει**	(i)	**είμαι**	(íme)	*I am*
EY	**ευ**	(ef)	**ευκαιρία**	(efkería)	*chance*
		(ev)	**Ευρώπη**	(evrópi)	*Europe*
OI	**οι**	(i)	**οικονομία**	(ikonomía)	*economy*
OY	**ου**	(u)	**ουρανός**	(uranós)	*Uranus/sky*

TWO-LETTER CONSONANTS

 00.05

The following two-letter consonants have only one sound:

γγ	(gháma-gháma)	*ng* as in *England* (Not as in *engine*)
γχ	(gháma-hi)	*nh* as in *inherent*
τσ	(taf-síghma)	*ts* as in *sets*
τζ	(taf-zíta)	*dz* as in *ads*

The remaining two-letter consonants have two different sounds each:

γκ	(gháma-kápa)	1 *g* as in *go*
		2 *ng* as in *England*
μπ	(mi-pi)	1 *b* as in *boy*
		2 *mb* as in *timber*
ντ	(ni-taf)	1 *d* as in *day*
		2 *nd* as in *end*

The *g*, *b* and *d* sounds occur at the beginning of Greek words, whereas the *ng*, *mb* and *nd* sounds occur within a Greek word.

Here are some examples of two-letter consonants:

	γγ	(ng)	**Αγγλία**	(anglía)	*England*
ΓΚ/Γκ	**γκ**	(g)	**γκολφ**	(golf)	*golf*
		(ng)	**άγκυρα**	(ángira)	*anchor*
	γχ	(nh)	**άγχος**	(ánhos)	*stress*
ΜΠ/Μπ	**μπ**	(b)	**μπράβο**	(brávo)	*bravo*
		(mb)	**λάμπα**	(lámba)	*lamp*
ΝΤ/Ντ	**ντ**	(d)	**ντομάτα**	(domáta)	*tomato*
		(nd)	**μοντέρνο**	(mondérno)	*modern*

TZ/Tζ	τζ	(tz)	**τζαζ**	(tzaz)	*jazz*
TΣ/Τσ	τσ	(ts)	**τσιγάρο**	(tsigháro)	*cigarette*

TWO SAME-LETTER CONSONANTS

The following two same-letter consonants are always pronounced as the one letter consonant.

ββ	(v)	**Σάββατο** (*Saturday*)	*v* as in *vet*
κκ	(k)	**εκκεντρικός** (*eccentric*)	*k* as in *kept*
λλ	(l)	**μέταλλο** (*metal*)	*l* as in *let*
μμ	(m)	**πρόγραμμα** (*programme*)	*m* as in *met*
νν	(n)	**τυραννία** (*tyranny*)	*n* as in *net*
ππ	(p)	**ιππόδρομος** (*hippodrome*)	*p* as in *pet*
ρρ	(r)	**αρρυθμία** (*arrhythmia*)	*r* as in *rent*
σσ	(s)	**γλωσσάριο** (*glossary*)	*s* as in *set*
ττ	(t)	**Αττική** (*Attica*)	*t* as in *tent*

SOME OTHER REMARKS

The following six words have two different spellings: one with the final letter **ν** and one without.

αυτή	**αυτήν**	*her* (personal pronoun)
τη	**την**	*the/her* (article, personal pronoun)
ένα	**έναν**	*one* (indefinite article, numeral)
το	**τον**	*the* (definite article)
δε	**δεν**	*not* (negative particle)
μη	**μην**	*don't* (negative particle)

The grammatical rules for this are as follows:

Keep the final -ν	Drop the final -ν
(**a**) when the following word starts with a vowel (**b**) when the following word starts with one of the following consonants: κ, π, τ γκ, μπ, ντ τσ, τζ ξ, ψ	(**a**) when the following word starts with a consonant other than the ones listed on the left: β, γ, δ, ζ, θ, λ, μ, ν, ρ, σ, φ, χ

When the final letter **ν** in a word is followed by a new word starting with **κ**, **ξ**, **π**, **τ** or **ψ** then the two words sound as one and the corresponding combinations create the following sounds:

έναν καφέ	ν + κ	(ng)	(enangafe)	*a coffee*
τον ξέρω	ν + ξ	(ngz)	(tongzero)	*I know him*
δεν πάω	ν + π	(nb)	(THenbao)	*I don't go*
στην Τήνο	ν + τ	(nd)	(stindino)	*to Tinos*
την ψάχνω	ν + ψ	(nbz)	(tinbzahno)	*I look for her*

Try to ask a native speaker to say them at a normal speed and pay attention to these sound combinations.

STRESS MARK AND INTONATION

You have probably noticed that most Greek examples in this section have a stress mark. This mark is used to show the main or primary stressed syllable in a given word. It always falls on one of the Greek vowels and never on a consonant. It is primarily used with words of two or more syllables, although there are a few exceptions of one-syllable words with a stress mark. This is the case when two words have a similar sound but different function and meaning, for instance, the word **η** meaning *the* without a stress mark and *or* with a stress mark. The stress mark can be used on lower case vowels and only on an initial capital vowel letter in a proper name (names for people or places), for example **καλά** (kalá) *well/fine*, or **Άννα** (ána). No stress mark is used, when the word is spelled out in capital letters only, for example **ANNA** (ána).

Intonation focuses on the rise and fall of the level of the voice, which often adds meaning to what is being said. A statement in Greek is changed into a question by changing the intonation of the voice without changing the sequence of words or adding question words. To turn a statement in Greek into a question the voice should go up at the end of the sentence instead of going down. You should remember that falling intonation is used in statements and rising intonation is used in questions. Question-words such as *do … ?*, *does … ?*, *did … ?*, or inversions like *you are → are you* are not used when formulating questions in Greek.

Two examples to illustrate this point are given below:

You speak English. (miláte angliká) **Μιλάτε αγγλικά**.

Do you speak English? (miláte angliká)? **Μιλάτε αγγλικά;**

You are from Greece. (íste apó tin eláTHa) **Είστε από την Ελλάδα.**

Are you from Greece? (íste apó tin eláTHA)? **Είστε από την Ελλάδα;**

> Stop here and check your memory. Can you list five words found in the two lists of two-letter vowel consonants. Here is a hint: these lists include several related words in both languages.

Practice

Here are some exercises for you to practise. Each question concentrates on a specific feature of the alphabet. When in doubt, you can check your answers in the **Answer key** section at the back of the book.

1 **There are some unique capital letters in the Greek alphabet. Can you provide the answer working horizontally to complete the alphabet?**

A	B			E	Z	H	
I	K		M	N		O	
P		T	Y		X		

2 **There are also some unique lower-case letters in the Greek alphabet. Can you provide the answers working horizontally to complete the alphabet?**

α				ε	ζ	η	
ι				ν		ο	π
ρ		τ	υ		χ		

3 **Some Greek letters look like English but have a different sound. See if you can get them right.**
   a B : (b) or (v)
   b H : (i) or (h)
   c P : (p) or (r)
   d X : (h) or (x)

4 **Lower-case Greek letters can be divided into three groups according to how they are written. We can do the same in English:**
   a letters on the line like *a, c, e,* etc.;
   b letters with risers above the line like *b, d, f,* etc.;
   c letters with descenders below the line like *g, p, q,* etc.

   Can you group the Greek letters accordingly? The first three have been done for you.

group									
a	α								
b	β								
c	γ								

5 Some capital Greek letters do not have an obvious association with their corresponding small letters. Can you complete the grid?

a Γ		b Δ		c H		d K	
e Λ		f M		g N		h Ξ	
i Σ		j T		k Υ		l Ω	

6 Some Greek streets are named after British/American people or places. Try to match the English names on the left with the Greek script on the right.

a BYRON   1 ΚΕΝΝΕΝΤΥ
b HILL   2 ΒΙΚΤΩΡΙΑ
c KENNEDY   3 ΒΥΡΩΝ
d VICTORIA   4 ΧΙΛΛ

7 Most examples in the Pronunciation guide used words that are similar in Greek and English, for instance radio and (ráTHio) ράδιο. Can you remember two sports, two instruments, two countries, and two means of transportation? If you can't remember everything, the box below will help you. You can write in Greek script or transliteration.

> τρένο Αγγλία μπάσκετ κιθάρα
> πιάνο τέννις αεροπλάνο Ελλάδα

8 00.06 Match the words on the left with the words on the right to form word pairs. Check your answers on the audio. If you don't have the audio, check your answers at the back of the book.

a (ne) ναι   1 (domáta) ντομάτα
b (musikí) μουσική   2 (stres) στρες
c (saláta) σαλάτα   3 (bála) μπάλα
d (anglía) Αγγλία   4 (ráTHio) ράδιο
e (golf) γκολφ   5 (óchi) όχι
f (ánhos) άγχος   6 (eláTHa) Ελλάδα

9 00.07 Now practise your pronunciation by saying some names of geographical regions in Greece. Listen to each one first and look them up on the map in your book. One of the regions has not been recorded. Listen to see if you can find which one is missing.

a (atikí) – (nisiá saronikú) ΑΤΤΙΚΗ – ΝΗΣΙΑ ΣΑΡΩΝΙΚΟΥ
b (kikláTHes) ΚΥΚΛΑΔΕΣ
c (THoTHekánisos) – ΔΩΔΕΚΑΝΗΣΟΣ
d (vorioanatoliká nisiá eghéu) – ΒΟΡΕΙΟΑΝΑΤΟΛΙΚΑ ΝΗΣΙΑ ΑΙΓΑΙΟΥ
e (thráki) – (samothráki) ΘΡΑΚΗ – ΣΑΜΟΘΡΑΚΗ
f (makeTHonía) – ΜΑΚΕΔΟΝΙΑ
g (thesalía) – ΘΕΣΣΑΛΙΑ

h (ípiros) – ΗΠΕΙΡΟΣ

i (évia) – (sporáTHes) – ΕΥΒΟΙΑ – ΣΠΟΡΑΔΕΣ

j (kendrikí eláTHa) – ΚΕΝΤΡΙΚΗ ΕΛΛΑΔΑ

k (nisiá ioníu) – ΝΗΣΙΑ ΙΟΝΙΟΥ

l (pelopónisos) – ΠΕΛΟΠΟΝΝΗΣΟΣ

m (kríti) – ΚΡΗΤΗ

Did you pick up the word for *Greece* (eláTHa) **Ελλάδα** and the word for *islands* (nisiá) **νησιά**? They will come in handy later on.

(kalí epithichía!) **Καλή επιτυχία!** stands for *good luck*! Now you are ready to move on to the first unit. Do not worry if you haven't remembered all the details. That will happen in due time with your efforts to follow the conversations and texts of the upcoming units. Rome was not built in a day! That is to say that you should not be putting pressure on yourself before, let's say, Unit 15! But even then, there is still a long way to go...

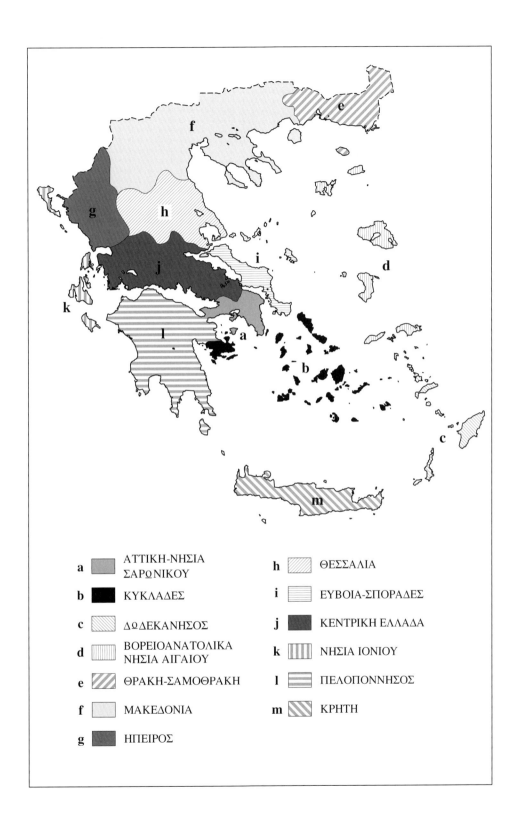

a	ATTIKH-NHΣIA ΣAPΩNIKOY	h		ΘEΣΣAΛIA
b	KYKΛAΔEΣ	i		EYBOIA-ΣΠOPAΔEΣ
c	ΔΩΔEKANHΣOΣ	j		KENTPIKH EΛΛAΔA
d	BOPEIOANATOΛIKA NHΣIA AIΓAIOY	k		NHΣIA IONIOY
e	ΘPAKH-ΣAMOΘPAKH	l		ΠEΛOΠONNHΣOΣ
f	MAKEΔONIA	m		KPHTH
g	HΠEIPOΣ			

Γεια σου!
Hi!

In this unit you will learn how to:
▶ *ask for and give personal information.*
▶ *introduce people.*
▶ *greet people and say goodbye.*

CEFR: (A1) *Can understand and use greetings and farewells. Can introduce oneself. Can ask and answer questions about personal information, place of origin and place of residence. Can produce simple phrases to describe personal details.*

Χαιρετισμοί και αποχαιρετισμοί *Greetings and farewells*

You have probably heard the expressions **γεια σου!** (yásu) *hi* (informal way of addressing people you know) and **γεια σας!** (yásas) *hello* (formal way, for people you don't know, or for addressing more than one person). They are both expressions used every day by young and old alike. The word **γεια** (ya) comes from **υγεία** (ighía) *health* and the expression actually means *health to you!* There are three other meanings of this expression: *goodbye* – when leaving, *bless you* – when sneezing and *cheers!* – when drinking.

Although **γεια σου, γεια σας** or simply **γεια** (yásu-yásas-ya) can be used throughout the day, Greeks use other greetings and farewells too, such as **καλημέρα** (kaliméra) *good morning*, **καλό μεσημέρι** (kaló mesiméri) *have a nice siesta!* **καλό απόγευμα** (kaló apóghevma) *have a nice afternoon*, **καλησπέρα** (kalispéra) *good evening*, **καλό βράδυ** (kaló vráTHi) *have a nice evening* and **καληνύχτα** (kaliníhta) *good night*. **Καλημέρα** stands for both *good morning* and *good day* in English.

---

1 Several greetings or farewells contain the prefix **καλο-** or **καλη-**. What does this mean?
2 What is the difference between **καλησπέρα** and **καλό απόγευμα**?

Vocabulary builder

ΧΑΙΡΕΤΙΣΜΟΙ ΚΑΙ ΑΠΟΧΑΙΡΕΤΙΣΜΟΙ *GREETINGS AND FAREWELLS*

1 01.01 **Listen to the greetings and farewells and repeat. Then listen again and complete the English translations.**

Καλημέρα!	*Good morning!*
Καλησπέρα, κυρία Μαρία!	*Good _____ Ms Maria!*

Καληνύχτα, δεσποινίς Ελένη!	Good _____ Miss Eleni!
Χαίρετε, κύριε Κώστα!	_____ Mr Kosta!
Καλό απόγευμα!	Good _____!
Γεια σου, Νίκο!	Hi Niko!

 2 01.02 **You are asked to say appropriate greetings and farewells to certain people. Speak first and then listen and check your answers. At the end listen again and repeat after the speaker.**

    a Say *hello* to Petro.

    b Say *good day* to Ms Andoniou.

    c Say *good night* to Toula.

    d Say *have a nice afternoon* to Soula.

ΧΩΡΕΣ *COUNTRIES*

 3 01.03 **Listen to the names of some countries and repeat after the speaker.**

η Ελλάδα	*Greece*
η Αγγλία	*England*
η Ιταλία	*Italy*
η Ισπανία	*Spain*
η Γαλλία	*France*
η Γερμανία	*Germany*

ΠΟΛΕΙΣ *CITIES*

 4 01.04 **You are going to hear the names of some cities in Europe. Listen carefully and repeat. Listen again and match the Greek and English counterparts.**

a	η Αθήνα	**1**	*Liverpool*
b	το Λονδίνο	**2**	*Berlin*
c	η Θεσσαλονίκη	**3**	*Athens*
d	το Βερολίνο	**4**	*Rome*
e	η Ρώμη	**5**	*London*
f	το Λίβερπουλ	**6**	*Thessaloniki*

ΓΛΩΣΣΕΣ *LANGUAGES*

 5 01.05 **You are going to hear the names of some languages in Greek. Listen carefully and repeat after the speaker.**

Ελληνικά	*Greek*
Αγγλικά	*English*
Ιταλικά	*Italian*
Ισπανικά	*Spanish*
Γαλλικά	*French*
Γερμανικά	*German*

Conversation 1

ΠΩΣ ΣΑΣ ΛΕΝΕ; *WHAT'S YOUR NAME?*

 NEW EXPRESSIONS

🎧 01.06

πώς (pos)	*how (what)*
Πώς σας λένε; (ois sas léne)	*What's your name? (lit. How are you called? or How do they call you?) (fm./pl.)*
με λένε (me léne)	*my name is*
Αα! (a)	*Aha! (Oh, I get it!)*
και (ke)	*and*
Από πού είστε; (apó pu íste)	*Where are you from?*
είμαι (íme)	*I am*
τη (v)	*the (f)*
Από ποιο μέρος; (apó pyo méros)	*From which place? or Where exactly?*
εσείς; (esís)	*you? (How about you?)*

 01.07 *Tim and Mary Johnson are a young British couple both with one-year work placements in Greece. Tim works for a bank and Mary is an archaeologist.*

1 Listen to the conversation that Mary has at a party. Does she speak to a Greek person?

Mary	Γεια σας! Πώς σας λένε;
Jean-Pierre	Γεια σας! Με λένε Jean-Pierre Depardieu.
Mary	Πώς;
Jean-Pierre	Jean-Pierre Depardieu.
Mary	Αα! Και από πού είστε;
Jean-Pierre	Είμαι από τη Γαλλία.
Mary	Από ποιο μέρος;
Jean-Pierre	Από το Παρίσι. Εσείς;
Mary	Από την Αγγλία. Από το Λονδίνο.
Mary	(yásas) (pos sas léne)?
Jean-Pierre	(yásas) (me léne Jean-Pierre Depardieu)
Mary	(pos)?
Jean-Pierre	(Jean-Pierre Depardieu)
Mary	(a) (ke apó pu íste)?
Jean-Pierre	(íme apó ti ghalía)
Mary	(apó pyo méros)?
Jean-Pierre	(apó to parísi) (esís)?
Mary	(apó tin anglía) (apó to lonTHíno)

2 Now read the conversation and answer the questions.

    a Which country is Mr Depardieu from?

    b And which city is he from?

    c Which country is Mary from?

    d And which city is she from?

3 Listen again and pay special attention to the words that run together. Practise speaking the part of both speakers and pay particular attention to your pronunciation.

Language discovery 1

1 Listen to the conversation again and find the Greek expressions for the following phrases. Then find the small words (articles) in each of the expressions. How many different articles did you find?

    a I am from France. _____

    b I am from Paris. _____

    c I am from England. _____

    d I am from London. _____

2 Go back now to the New Expressions list and find the corresponding article for these places. Nouns, which are naming words referring to persons, concepts, or objects, are given in the new expressions lists always with their article. Can you notice any similarities or differences?

    a France _____

    b Paris _____

    c England _____

    d London _____

    e …from France _____

    f …from Paris _____

    g …from England _____

    h …from London _____

3 There are three question words in this conversation. What are they?

    a Which? _____

    b How? _____

    c Where? _____

Learn more

1 PERSONAL PRONOUNS

The personal pronouns (words for *I, you*, etc.) are not usually used with a verb in Greek. If you go back to the conversation again you can find two forms of the verb *to be*: *I am*: **είμαι** and *you are*: **είστε** without any personal pronouns! All verbs in Greek consist of a stem and an ending. The form of the ending tells you whether *I*, *you*, *we*, etc. are performing the action, namely here the endings **–μαι** for *I* and **–στε** for *you*. If somebody would like to emphasize the person saying or doing something, then the personal pronouns can accommodate the verb forms: **εγώ είμαι** or **εσείς είστε**. The translation remains the same: *I am* and *you are*.

2 VERB ENDINGS

A verb normally expresses an action or a state. As stated above, in Greek you need to learn which endings to put on the verb for each pronoun because the pronouns are not always used. The form of the verb that you find in a dictionary or glossary is called the infinitive. In English, one has to look up the verb *to be*, this is the infinitive, whereas in Greek the verb **είμαι** is its corresponding counterpart. That means that each Greek verb in the first person singular of simple present tense can be both the infinitive dictionary form **είμαι**: *to be* but also the first person singular of simple present tense **είμαι**: *I am*! More notes and examples will follow.

3 BASIC WORD ORDER

Sometimes the order of words in Greek is different than in English but at other times it's the same. At first, it can help to learn phrases as single 'chunks' and not worry too much about the different parts. One example from our first conversation is the following question:

Από πού είστε;   *Where are you from?*

Try learning that as a chunk rather than word for word translation: *From where are (you)?*

Conversation 2

ΤΙ ΓΛΩΣΣΕΣ ΜΙΛΑΤΕ; *WHAT LANGUAGES DO YOU SPEAK?*

 NEW EXPRESSIONS

 01.08

Τι γλώσσες μιλάτε; (ti ghlóses miláte)	*What languages do you speak?*
Μόνο Ιταλικά. (móno italiká)	*Only Italian.*
Αα! (ah)	*I see!* (lit. *Aha!*)

01.09 *Tim and Domenico meet at a party and have a short conversation.*

1 Listen to their conversation. What do they talk about?

Tim	Γεια σας! Πώς σας λένε;
Domenico	Domenico Di Capo.
Tim	Τι γλώσσες μιλάτε;
Domenico	Ιταλικά.
Tim	Μόνο Ιταλικά;
Domenico	Μόνο Ιταλικά.
Tim	Αα!

Tim	(yásas) (pos sas léne)?
Domenico	(Domenico di Capo)
Tim	(ti ghlóses miláte)?
Domenico	(italiká)
Tim	(móno italiká)?
Domenico	(móno italiká)
Tim	(a)

2 Now read the conversation and answer the questions.

    a Which phrase does Tim use to ask Domenico his name?

    b How does he find out how many languages Domenico speaks?

 3 Listen again and pay special attention to the words that run together. Practise speaking the part of both speakers and pay particular attention to your pronunciation.

Language discovery 2

1 What are the three questions in Conversation 2? Read them out loud one by one then listen again to compare your pronunciation.

2 What are the following punctuation marks in Greek? Do you notice any differences?

    a full stop _____

    b exclamation mark _____

    c question mark _____

3 You may have noticed that Greek words, when written in lower-case letters, carry an accent over one of the letters. Try going over the last two dialogues and find all one-syllable words. What do you notice?

One-syllable words without an accent	One-syllable words with an accent

Learn more

1 ASKING QUESTIONS

It is easy to ask a question in Greek; just remember that the pitch of your voice goes up at the end of the statement. In this dialogue you hear the same phrase twice; once as a question and once as a statement:

Μόνο Ιταλικά.	*Only Italian.* (when the pitch of your voice goes down at the end)
Μόνο Ιταλικά;	*Only Italian?* (when the pitch of your voice goes up at the end)

You will be pleased to know that to ask questions in Greek there are no changes in word order as in English, such as *you are*: **είστε** – *are you?*: **είστε;** or the addition of extra words, such as *you speak*: **μιλάτε** – *do you speak?*: **μιλάτε;**.

The English semicolon (;) is the question mark (?) in written Greek. The Greek semicolon is a mark we do not use in English; it is a raised full stop (·).

2 STRESS MARKS

When written in lower-case letters most Greek words contain an accent sign over one of the letters to show which part of the word is stressed. This simple approach was introduced in 1981. Previously there were five different accent signs and you may still see these on old street signs or in old books.

Some important points for you to remember are:

1 The accent will always fall into the last three syllables, e.g. last syllable: **ε-σείς**, one syllable before the last one: **μό-νο**, or two syllables before the last one: **α-πό-γευ-μα**.

2 Most one-syllable words have no accent, e.g. **τι, σας, και, το, την**. Some question words though do take an accent, e.g. **πώς** or **πού**.

3 Words written only with capital letters carry no accent, e.g. the name **ANNA** but when written in lower case, then the accent is found before the capital **Α: Άννα**.

Conversation 3

ΕΙΣΑΙ ΙΤΑΛΟΣ; *ARE YOU ITALIAN?*

 NEW EXPRESSIONS

 01.10

ο Ιταλός (o italós)	*Italian* (n) (origin)
Από ποια πόλη; (apó pya póli)	*From which city?*
το Μιλάνο (to miláno)	*Milan* (n)
αλλά (alá)	*but*
τώρα μένω στην Αθήνα (tóra méno stin athína)	*now I live in Athens*
εγώ (eghó)	*I* (first person)
όχι (óchi)	*no*
ξέρεις; (kséris)?	*you know* (here, *do you know?*)
δυστυχώς (THistihós)	*unfortunately/I am sorry but …*
Πώς σε λένε; (pos se léne)?	*What's your name?* (infm./sing.)
εσένα (eséna)	*you*
ή (i)	*or*

8

01.11 *Mary and Antonio get chatting at the party.*

1 Listen to the conversation then answer the following. What do they talk about? Try to answer this without looking at the text.

Mary	Γεια σου! Είσαι Ιταλός;
Antonio	Ναι, είμαι!
Mary	Από ποια πόλη;
Antonio	Από το Μιλάνο, αλλά τώρα μένω στην Αθήνα.
Mary	Εγώ είμαι από το Λονδίνο. Ξέρεις Αγγλικά;
Antonio	Όχι! Δυστυχώς! Μόνο Ιταλικά και τώρα … Ελληνικά!
Mary	Πώς σε λένε;
Antonio	Αντόνιο. Εσένα;
Mary	Μαίρη ή Μαρία.
Antonio	Ωραία. Γεια σου, Μαίρη.
Mary	Γεια σου, Αντόνιο.
Mary	(yásu) (íse italós)?
Antonio	(ne íme)
Mary	(apó pya póli)?
Antonio	(apó to miláno) (alá tóra méno stin athína)
Mary	(eghó íme apó to lonTHíno) (kséris angliká)?
Antonio	(óchi) (THistihós) (móno italiká ke tora eliniká)
Mary	(pos se léne)?
Antonio	(antónio) (eséna)?
Mary	(méri i maría)
Antonio	(orea) (yasu meri)
Mary	(yasu antonio)

2 Now read the conversation and answer the following questions.
  a Which city is Antonio from?
  b Can Antonio speak English?
  c Mary says her name in two different ways. How?

3 Now listen to the conversation once again and practise speaking the part of Mary.

Language discovery 3

1 Read the conversation again. What are the Greek words for the following languages? Do they all have the same ending?
  a Greek _____
  b Italian _____
  c English _____

Did you come up with the ending **–ικα** for all of them? It is good to know that most words for languages end in **–ικα**.

2 Provide the Greek translation of the following two questions. What differences do you notice in the words written in Italics?

   a From *which* place? _____

   b From *which* city? _____

It is good to know that **ποιο** agrees with neuter nouns (here: **το μέρος**) and **ποια** with feminine nouns (here: **η πόλη**).

3 Some words have more than one form, as in the exercise above, but many do not. Search for the following words in the conversation without looking them up in the new expressions. Can you find all of them?

   a now _____

   b but _____

   c nice _____

   d yes _____

   e no _____

   f or _____

   g I _____

   h unfortunately _____

   i only _____

   j and _____

4 01.12 Listen to the following words and decide if what you hear corresponds to the sound /i/ as in *pin* or an /e/ as in *bed*?

	είσαι	είμαι	πόλη	μένω	εγώ	ξέρεις	δυστυχώς
i as in *pin*							
e as in *bed*							

	Αθήνα	Λονδίνο	Αγγλικά	Μαίρη	ωραία	σε	Αντόνιο
i as in *pin*							
e as in *bed*							

5 How many different spelling alternatives did you notice for the sound *i* as in *pin* or for *e* as in *bed*? _____

Learn more

1 EIMAI *TO BE*

Notice the different forms of the verb **είμαι** in the following phrases:

Και από πού είστε; Είσαι Ιταλός;

Ναι είμαι. Εγώ είμαι από το Λονδίνο.

Only one example makes use of a personal pronoun. Which one?

Did you decide? We hope you went for the last one with the pronoun **εγώ**!

Now look at the statement and the question forms of the verb **είμαι** in full.

είμαι (íme)	*I am*	**είμαι;** (íme)	*am I?*
είσαι (íse)	*you are* (infm)	**είσαι;** (íse)	*are you?* (infm)
είναι (íne)	*he/she/it is*	**είναι;** (íne)	*is he/she/it?*
είμαστε (ímaste)	*we are*	**είμαστε;** (ímaste)	*are we?*
είσαστε/είστε (ísaste) (íste)	*you are* (fm)	**είσαστε/είστε;** (ísaste) (íste)	*are you?* (fm)
είναι (íne)	*they are*	**είναι;** (íne)	*are they?*

You use **είσαι** when talking to one person that you know well, or when he or she is younger than you; this is the 'informal form' (infm.). However, when you use **είσαστε** or **είστε** for one person, it is probably out of respect (with an older person, higher social status and so on) or when you address more than one person; this is the 'formal' (fm.) or plural form.

2 SAYING *YES* AND *NO*

In Greek, as in most languages, you can answer a question fully or give a shorter answer. Look at the following example and the possible answers:

Είσαι Ιταλός;   *Are you Italian?*   **Ναι, είμαι Ιταλός.**   *Yes, I am Italian.*

                                      Ναι, είμαι.   *Yes, I am.*

                                      Ναι.   *Yes.*

Or you can even give a silent answer by tilting your head forward a couple of times.

Soon you will learn other ways of saying *yes* such as **μάλιστα**, **αμέ** and **πως!** with their corresponding uses.

The opposite of **ναι** *yes* is **όχι** *no*. This is often confusing to the ears of many foreigners because the Greek word for *yes* **ναι** sounds like the English *no*. Notice also the head nodding, when speaking to native speakers, that usually accompanies a Greek *yes* or *no*! People do not move their heads from left to right but actually up and down!

3 THE VERBS *LIVE/STAY* AND *KNOW*

Verbs (i.e. words expressing an action or state such as *go*, *be*, *eat* as stated before) are conjugated in Greek. This means that you put endings after the stem of the verb. (The stem is the simplest form of a word, i.e. without any ending, such as **μεν-** *live*, and **ξερ-** *know*.) The function of an ending is to identify who is doing the action. Notice the different forms of two common verbs: **μένω** *I live* and **ξέρω** *I know* from our last dialogue.

μέν-ω (méno)	*I live/stay*	**ξέρ-ω** (kséro)	*I know*
μέν-εις (ménis)	*you live*	**ξέρ-εις** (kséris)	*you know*
μέν-ει (méni)	*he/she/it lives*	**ξέρ-ει** (kséri)	*he/she/it knows*
μέν-ουμε (ménume)	*we live*	**ξέρ-ουμε** (ksérume)	*we know*
μέν-ετε (ménete)	*you live*	**ξέρ-ετε** (ksérete)	*you know*
μέν-ουν (ménun)	*they live*	**ξέρ-ουν** (ksérun)	*they know*

4 THE DEFINITE ARTICLE

You have already learnt in this unit some different words for the word *the* (the definite article). Now answer the following questions.

1 **Give the three forms of definite article:**

    a _____ for masculine nouns.

    b _____ for feminine nouns.

    c _____ for neuter nouns.

2 **Give the correct definite article for the following nouns.**

    a _____ Ιταλός (m) *the Italian*

    b _____ πόλη (f) *the city*

    c _____ μέρος (n) *the place*

3 **Greek definite articles are also used with proper nouns (words which have a capital letter, like first names, city names, or country names). Complete the following:**

    a _____ Αντόνιο

    b _____ Μαίρη

    c _____ Αθήνα

    d _____ Λονδίνο

    e _____ Αγγλία.

4 **When the article follows the preposition από** *from* **it changes its form. What is the word for** *the* **in the following sentences?**

    a Είμαι από _____ Αγγλία.

    b Είμαι από _____ Λονδίνο.

    c Είμαι από _____ Γαλλία.

5 **Likewise, the article changes its form when it is with the preposition σε** *in.* **What is the word for** *the* **in the following sentences?**

    a Μένω _____ Αγγλία.

    b Μένω _____ Λονδίνο.

    c Μένω _____ Γαλλία.

Practice

1 **See if you can cope with some typical situations that you might encounter in Greece.**

    a You have been introduced to a young Greek woman. Ask her name.

    b You have just seen a friend in the street. Say *hello* and ask him how he is.

    c You meet your boss in the street. Say *hello* and ask her how she is.

    d You have just arrived in Greece and you want to find people who speak English. How would you ask: *Do you speak English?*

2 **Match each question to its most appropriate answer.**

a	Ξέρετε Ελληνικά;	**1**	Από το Μιλάνο.
b	Είστε Ιταλός;	**2**	΄Οχι, από την Ιταλία.
c	Είσαι από την Αγγλία;	**3**	Ναι, ξέρω.
d	Από ποια πόλη;	**4**	Ναι, είμαι!

3 **Rearrange these lines to make a short conversation. Then try reading both parts out loud.**

a Μαρία Πέτρου.

b ΄Οχι, μόνο Ελληνικά.

c Καλημέρα, πώς σας λένε;

d Μιλάτε Αγγλικά;

4 **Complete the dialogue using the English prompts. Practise speaking both parts.**

Ο Νίκος	Γεια σας! Πώς σας λένε;
You	**a** *Say your name.*
Ο Νίκος	Από πού είστε;
You	**b** *Tell him which country you are from.*
Ο Νίκος	Από ποιο μέρος;
You	**c** *Tell him which city/town you come from.*
Ο Νίκος	Τι γλώσσες μιλάτε;
You	**d** *Say which language(s) you speak.*

5 **How many words can you recognize from Unit 1? Match up the words on the left with those on the right. The words in brackets might help you.**

a	εγώ	**1**	health (hygiene)
b	λέξεις	**2**	languages (polyglot)
c	υγεία	**3**	only (monopoly)
d	γλώσσες	**4**	city (metropolis)
e	μόνο	**5**	night
f	πόλη	**6**	me
g	νύχτα	**7**	words (lexicon)

 6 01.13 **Read the following new words and expressions. Listen to the following conversation and find the missing words. Then listen once again and practise speaking Robert's part out loud.**

Ρόμπερτ (róbert)	*Robert* (m)
Να σου συστήσω (na su sistíso)	*Let me introduce … to you*
το Λίβερπουλ (to líverpul)	*Liverpool* (n)
δεν το ξέρω (THen to kséro)	*I don't know it*
η Θεσσαλονίκη (i thesaloníki)	*Thessaloniki/Salonica* (f)

Mary	Γεια σου, **a** _____.
Robert	Γεια σου, Μαρία.
Mary	Να σου συστήσω την **b** _____.
Robert	Γεια σου, **b** _____! Είσαι **c** _____;
Helen	Ναι, είμαι. Εσύ;
Robert	Εγώ είμαι από την **d** _____.
Helen	Από ποιο μέρος;
Robert	Από το Λίβερπουλ. Το ξέρεις;
Helen	Όχι, **e** _____ το ξέρω!
Robert	Εσύ, από πού **f** _____;
Helen	Από τη Θεσσαλονίκη.

> Ελένη   δεν   Ρόμπερτ
> είσαι   Αγγλία   Ελληνίδα

7 01.14 **Listen to the following words, decide if what you hear corresponds to the sound /a/ as in** cat, **or /e/ as in** bed.

/a/ as in cat   /e/ as in bed

_____   _____

_____   _____

_____   _____

_____   _____

> λένε   ναι   ξέρω   με
> να   αλλά   από   σας

8 01.15 **Listen to Conversation and complete the missing words.**

Mary	Γεια σου! **a** _____ Ιταλός;
Antonio	Ναι, **b** _____!
Mary	Από ποια **c** _____;
Antonio	Από το Μιλάνο, **d** _____ τώρα μένω στην Αθήνα.
Mary	Εγώ είμαι από το Λονδίνο. **e** _____ Αγγλικά;
Antonio	Όχι! Δυστυχώς! **f** _____ Ιταλικά και τώρα … Ελληνικά!
Mary	Πώς σε λένε;
Antonio	Αντόνιο. **g** _____;
Mary	Μαίρη ή Μαρία.
Antonio	**h** _____! Γεια σου, Μαίρη.
Mary	Γεια σου, Αντόνιο.

> ωραία   αλλά   πόλη   είμαι
> εσένα   μόνο   είσαι   ξέρεις

9 01.16 **How many different greetings or farewells do you hear? Make a list.**

_____

_____

_____

_____

_____

_____

⁉ Test yourself

1 Write the Greek for the following words.

   a hello _____   **f** where _____

   b bye _____   **g** yes _____

   c good _____   **h** no _____

   d from _____   **i** with _____

   e here _____   **j** near _____

2 Can you remember the following phrases from this unit?

   a What's your name?   **f** Do you speak English?

   b Where are you from?   **g** I live in…

   c From which city/town?   **h** I'm staying at …

   d From London, England.   **i** It's near.

   e My name's…   **j** I don't know.

3 The following five phrases use the informal way of addressing people. Can you change them into formal Greek?

   a (pos se léne)? Πώς σε λένε;

   b (apó pu íse)? Από πού είσαι;

   c (pu ménis)? Πού μένεις;

   d (milás angliká)? Μιλάς Αγγλικά;

   e (yásu) Γεια σου.

SELF CHECK

	I CAN. . .
⚪	. . . greet someone around 10 a.m. or 5 p.m.
⚪	. . . use appropriate farewells around 2 p.m., 6 p.m., or 10 p.m.
⚪	. . . exchange name information.
⚪	. . . ask people where they are from.
⚪	. . . also tell them where I am from.
⚪	. . . ask people where they live.
⚪	. . . even tell them where I live now.
⚪	. . . ask people what languages they speak.
⚪	. . . also tell them the languages I speak.

Τι κάνεις;
How are you doing?

In this unit you will learn how to:
▶ *engage in 'small talk'.*
▶ *enquire about each other's health.*
▶ *count from 0 to 10.*

CEFR: (A1) *Can address people with names and titles. Can ask how people are and react. Can ask and answer questions about personal details. Can engage in 'small talk' when meeting people.*

Ονόματα και τίτλοι στα Ελληνικά   *Names and titles in Greek*

We have already seen in Unit 1 that *Mr* **κύριος (κ.)**, *Mrs* or *Ms* **κυρία (κα)** and *Miss* **δεσποινίδα (δίδα)** are used as courtesy titles in Greek. The word **κύριος** (when you talk indirectly about someone) changes to **κύριε** (when you address someone directly). The words **κυρία (κα)** and **δεσποινίδα (δίδα)** do not change.

Δόκτωρ ή Διδάκτωρ (Δρ.) *Doctor/Dr* is a title attached to the name of medical doctors or professionals with a PhD, EdD, or LLD. **Μεσιέ** or **Μαντάμ**, as *Monsieur* and *Madame* in French, are used less and less by the new generation. What is interesting and different is the use of **κ.**, **κα** or **δίδα** with the first name of a person only (such as **κ. Γιώργος** *Mr George* or **κα Μαρία** *Mrs/Ms Maria*) as a semi-formal form that does not exist in English.

Not only the title but also the name that follows can have changes when addressing men. Notice the differences in the following examples: **Ο κ. (κύριος) Παπάς είναι από την Ελλάδα.** *Mr Papas is from Greece.* **Κύριε Παπά, τι κάνετε;** *How are you doing, Mr Papas?* **Ο γιατρός Πέτρου είναι πολύ καλός.** *Dr Petrou is very good.* **Γιατρέ, από πού είστε;** *Where are you from, doctor?*

---

1 There are many Greek names that have a similar first part (prefix). Some examples are: **Θεόδωρος, Θεοφάνης, Θεόφιλος** or **Αριστοτέλης, Αριστείδης, Αριστοφάνης, Αρίσταρχος**. Can you guess what **Θεο-** and **Αριστ-** mean?

Vocabulary builder

ΡΩΤΩ ΠΩΣ ΕΙΝΑΙ ΚΑΠΟΙΟΣ *ASKING HOW PEOPLE ARE*

1 02.01 Listen to some alternative expressions when asking how people are. Then listen again and repeat after the speaker.

Τι κάνεις, Κώστα;	*How are you doing Kosta?*
Τι κάνετε, κύριε Ράπτη;	*How are you Mr Raptis?*
Πώς είσαι, Άννα;	*How are you doing Anne?*
Πώς είστε, κυρία Πέτρου;	*How are you Ms Petrou?*

ΑΠΑΝΤΩ ΠΩΣ ΕΙΝΑΙ ΚΑΠΟΙΟΣ *ANSWERING HOW PEOPLE ARE*

 2 02.02 Listen to some alternative expressions when answering how people are then listen again and repeat. Now match the Greek and English counterparts.

a	Πολύ καλά. Εσύ;	**1**	Not so good! How about you?
b	Καλά, ευχαριστώ. Εσείς;	**2**	I'm also fine.
c	Έτσι κι έτσι. Εσύ;	**3**	Very well. And yourself?
d	Άσχημα! Εσύ πώς είσαι σήμερα;	**4**	Fine, thanks. And you?
e	Κι εγώ καλά είμαι.	**5**	Awful! How are you doing today?

ΜΕΤΡΩ ΑΠΟ ΤΟ 0–10 *COUNTING FROM 0–10*

 3 02.03 Listen to the numbers from 0 to 10 a couple of times. Then listen again and repeat.

μηδέν	*zero*
ένα	*one*
δύο	*two*
τρία	*three*
τέσσερα	*four*
πέντε	*five*
έξι	*six*
εφτά	*seven*
οχτώ	*eight*
εννιά	*nine*
δέκα	*ten*

Conversation 1

ΤΙ ΚΑΝΕΤΕ; *HOW ARE YOU?*

NEW EXPRESSIONS

 02.04

Τι κάνετε; (ti kánete)	*How are you? (pl./fm. form)*
Τι κάνεις; (ti kánis)	*How are you doing? (sing./infm. form)*
καλά (kalá)	*well, fine, good, OK*
Ευχαριστώ, εσείς; (efharistó esís)	*Thank you/Thanks, and you?*
Λίγο κουρασμένος (lígho kurazménos)	*a little (bit) tired*
Αλλά γιατί μου μιλάς στον πληθυντικό; (milás ston pilithindikó)	*Why are you talking to me in a formal way?*
το λάθος (to láthos)	*the mistake* (n), *false*
ο/η συνάδελφος (o/i sináTHelfos)	*colleague (m/f)*
συνάδελφοι (sináTHelfi)	*colleagues (m/f) (pl.)*
όλοι με φωνάζουν (óli me fonázun)	*everybody calls me (people call me)*
εντάξει (endáksi)	*all right, OK*

02.05 *Mary Johnson meets her Greek colleague Γιώργος Παπαδόπουλος (Yórghos PapaTHópulos) at the Greek Archaeological Society lounge.*

1 **Listen to the conversation carefully a couple of times without looking at the text. Can you hear the two different ways the question** *How are you doing?* **is asked? Which of the two speakers uses a less formal version of** *How are you doing?*, **the man or the woman?**

Mary	Γεια σας, κύριε Παπαδόπουλε! Τι κάνετε;
Γιώργος	Γεια σου, Μαίρη. Τι κάνεις;
Mary	Καλά, καλά. Ευχαριστώ, εσείς;
Γιώργος	Κι εγώ καλά είμαι. Λίγο κουρασμένος, αλλά γιατί μου μιλάς στον πληθυντικό;
Mary	Δεν ξέρω! Δεν ξέρω καλά Ελληνικά. Είναι λάθος;
Γιώργος	Όχι, δεν είναι λάθος … αλλά είμαστε συνάδελφοι. Όλοι με φωνάζουν Γιώργο.
Mary	Εντάξει, Γιώργο …
Mary	(yásas kírie papaTHópule) (ti kánete)?
Γιώργος	(yásu méri) (ti kánis)?
Mary	(kalá-kalá efharistó) (esís)?
Γιώργος	(ki eghó kalá íme) (lígho Kurazménos) (alá yatí mu milás ston plithindikó)?
Mary	(THen kséro) (THen kséro kalá eliniká) (íne láthos)?
Γιώργος	(óchi) (THen íne láthos) … (alá ímaste sináTHelfi) (óli me fonázun yórgho)
Mary	(endáksi yórgho) …

2 **Read the conversation and try to answer the following questions.**

   a What's the first name of Mr Papadopoulos?
   b Who is a little bit tired? The man or the woman?
   c Which word stands for OK in Greek?

 3 **Listen again and pay special attention to the words that run together. Practise speaking the part of Mary and pay particular attention to your pronunciation.**

Language discovery 1

1 **Complete the negative particle** *not* **in these three phrases. Would you assume that its word order comes always before the verb in Greek?**

   a _____ ξέρω!
   b _____ ξέρω καλά Ελληνικά.
   c Όχι, _____ είναι λάθος.

2 There are two different words for the pronoun *me* in the dialogue. Can you first find the words and then think about their word order in relation to the verbs they refer to? Do you have a perfect match in both languages?

   a _____ μιλάς (English: _____)

   b _____ φωνάζουν (English: _____)

3 The conversation makes use of formal and informal language. Can you figure out if the following phrases are formal or informal and think for a second if the verb form or other key words help someone to switch from formal into informal language?

   a Τι κάνετε;

   b Ευχαριστώ, εσείς;

   c … αλλά γιατί μου μιλάς στον πληθυντικό;

   d Εντάξει, Γιώργο.

4 The Greek letter υ has interesting pronunciation alternatives. Listen to the dialogue very carefully once again and find seven words with three different alternatives.

/i/ as in *pin*	/u/ as in *put*	/f/ as in *foot*
_____	_____	_____
_____	_____	
_____	_____	

Learn more

1 THE NEGATIVE PARTICLE *NOT*

Note that the negative particle **δεν** *not* is always placed before the verb in Greek: **Δεν είμαι κουρασμένος** *I'm not tired.* **Δεν ξέρω καλά Ελληνικά** *I don't speak good Greek.* **Δεν είναι λάθος** *It is not wrong.* The last letter from this particle is often dropped when the next word starts with one of the following consonants: **β, γ, δ, ζ, θ, λ, μ, ν, ρ, σ, φ, χ**. We suggest that you can always use **δεν** instead of **δε** especially in your early attempts of using Greek. The particle is often so quickly pronounced with the verb following, that not too many native speakers will be aware of which form you have used!

This negative particle is also placed before pronouns that come before the verb. Be careful with this word order that is different to English. Notice the following examples:

Γιατί δε μου μιλάς; *Why don't you speak to me?* **Δε με λένε Γιώργο.** *My name's not George.* **Δε με φωνάζουν Νίκο.** *They don't call me Nick.*

As said above, the negative particle **δεν/δε** is used when a verb follows. If there is no verb, the word **όχι** is used instead. Notice the examples:

Μιλάω Ελληνικά, όχι Αγγλικά! *I speak Greek, not English!* **Με λένε Γιώργο, όχι Νίκο!** *My name's George, not Nick!* **Όχι τώρα!** *Not now!*

2 ASKING *HOW ARE YOU DOING?*

There were two different ways of asking this question in the dialogue above: **Τι κάνεις;** and **Τι κάνετε;**. The language makes a clear distinction when addressing one person informally,

Γιώργο, τι κάνεις; or one person formally, **Κύριε Γιώργο, τι κάνετε;**. The latter verb form, **κάνετε**, can also be used when addressing more than one person, formally or informally. Just keep this in mind, because it applies to all Greek verbs.

Τι κάνεις; and **Τι κάνετε;** are only two ways of enquiring about somebody's health; here are some examples of other expressions commonly used:

Singular (Informal)	Plural (Formal)	
Τι κάνεις;	**Τι κάνετε;**	*How are you doing?* (lit. *What are you doing?*)
Πώς είσαι;	**Πώς είστε;**	*How are you?*
Πώς πας;	**Πώς πάτε;**	*How's everything with you?*
Πώς πάει;	**Πώς πάνε;**	*How's it going?*

Here are some common answers:

καλά	*well*	**όχι (και) πολύ καλά**	*not very well*
πολύ καλά	*very well*	**ας τα λέμε καλά**	*I guess I'm all right!*
έτσι κι έτσι	*so, so*	**άσχημα**	*bad, awful*

In Greek you probably won't often hear **ευχαριστώ** *thanks* at the end of the reply.

3 THANKING SOMEONE

Ευχαριστώ *thank you/thanks* and **ευχαριστώ πολύ** *thanks a lot* are the two most common expressions for thanking someone. **Χίλια ευχαριστώ** *many thanks* literally means *one thousand thanks*.

Παρακαλώ *You're welcome* and **τίποτα** *don't mention it* are the two most common responses. **Παρακαλώ** is a useful word in Greek; it has many meanings depending on context:

Please when asking for something.

Hello when answering the phone.

Come in when answering the door.

What can I do for you? when talking to a customer in a shop.

Take a seat when pointing to a chair.

What did you say? or *Pardon?* when asking someone to repeat something.

Conversation 2

ΕΙΜΑΙ ΚΑΛΑ, ΕΣΥ ΠΩΣ ΕΙΣΑΙ ΣΗΜΕΡΑ; *I'M DOING FINE, AND YOU, HOW ARE YOU TODAY?*

 NEW EXPRESSIONS

 02.06

Εσύ πώς είσαι; (esí pos íse)?	*How are you?* (sing./infm.)
σήμερα (símera)	*today*

έχω όμως (écho ómos)	but I have/I have though
πέντε μαθήματα (pénde mathímata)	five classes (courses)
Πω! πω! (po-po)	Wow!
Ποιος κάνει το πρόγραμμά σου; (pyos káni to próghrama su)	Who arranges (makes) your schedule?
Το ξέχασα! (to kséhasa)	I forgot that!

 02.07 Mary strikes up a conversation in a corridor at the Polyglot Institute Πολύγλωττο Ινστιτούτο (Políghloto Institúto) with the director Γιάννης Αντωνίου (yánnis andoníu).

1 **Listen to the conversation carefully a couple of times without looking at the text. Can you hear the two ways used to ask** *How are you doing?*

Mary	Καλημέρα, κύριε Αντωνίου! Τι κάνετε;
Γιάννης	Καλημέρα ά Μαρία. Είμαι καλά, εσύ πώς είσαι σήμερα;
Mary	Καλά, έχω όμως πέντε μαθήματα σήμερα!
Γιάννης	*(laughing).* Πω! πω! Ποιος κάνει το πρόγραμμά σου;
Mary	Εσείς, κύριε Αντωνίου!
Γιάννης	Α, ναι! Το ξέχασα!
Mary	(kaliméra kírie andoníu) (ti kánete)?
Γιάννης	(kaliméra maría) (íme kalá) (esí pos íse símera)?
Mary	(kalá) (ého ómos pénde mathímata símera)
Γιάννης	(po-po) (pyos káni to próghrama su)?
Mary	(esís kírie andoníu)
Γιάννης	(a ne)! (to kséhasa)!

2 **Read the conversation and answer the questions.**
   a How many classes does Mary have today?
   b Who makes her class schedule?
   c What has Mr Antoniou forgotten?

 3 **Listen again and pay special attention to the words that run together. Practise speaking the part of Mary and pay particular attention to your pronunciation.**

Language discovery 2

1 **The dialogue makes use of the word** *you* **twice. Can you find the two different forms?**
   a you (singular/informal) _____
   b you (formal/plural) _____

2 **There are four question words introduced in the first two dialogues. Can you find them?**

   a Who? _____

   b What? _____

   c How? _____

   d Why? _____

3 **Two verbs were fully conjugated for you in Unit 1: μένω and ξέρω. Three more verbs, κάνω** *do/make*, **φωνάζω** *call/name* **and έχω** *have/possess* **are introduced in this unit and are conjugated exactly the same. Can you find the missing forms of the verbs below without checking the previous unit?**

μέν-ω	κάν-ω	φωνάζ-_____	έχ-_____
μέν-εις	κάν-_____	φωνάζ-εις	έχ-εις
μέν-_____	κάν-ει	φωνάζ-ει	έχ-_____
μέν-ουμε	κάν-_____	φωνάζ-_____	έχ-ουμε
μέν-_____	κάν-_____	φωνάζ-_____	έχ-_____
μέν-_____	κάν-ουν	φωνάζ-ουν	έχ-ουν

Learn more

1 INTERJECTIONS

Interjections are words that give flavour and emphasis to a statement or question, something like *Wow! Ah! Oh! Hm!* The translations of these words probably wouldn't help you much. It is best to use your imagination and try them out. In the first two units you came across: **Αα! Α! Πω! πω! Χμ! Μπα!** denote understanding, admiration, uncertainty, and surprise in the corresponding contexts. If you have a Greek circle, pay close attention to how native speakers use those words. This list will increase in the units to come, so start looking out for these interjections.

2 VERBS AND CORRESPONDING PRONOUNS

As already said, Greek verbs are usually without their corresponding pronouns since the verb endings help someone understand who is doing or receiving the action. These personal pronouns (words like *I, you, he, they*) are part of English because the same verb form can be used with different pronouns, e.g. *I have, you have, we have, they have*. In Greek, these four verb forms are completely different, e.g. **έχ-ω**, **έχ-εις**, **έχ-ουμε**, and **έχ-ουν**. If we also add the **έχ-ετε** for the form *you have* (plural/formal) then we realize that it takes some time to do this brain retraining with the Greek verbs and their endings or even their corresponding pronouns. To sum it up, keep in mind that although Greek has corresponding words for these pronouns, they are normally left out and mostly used only for emphasis. Notice now the verb **έχ-ω** fully conjugated with all corresponding pronouns. Be careful how the words with the letter (**υ**) are pronounced differently, including **εσύ**, **αυτός** and **έχουμε**.

02.08 You are going to listen to the conjugation of the verb to have in its present form. Listen to it a couple of times and then try to repeat after the speaker.

Singular		Plural	
εγώ έχω	*I have*	**εμείς έχουμε**	*we have*
εσύ έχεις	*you have*	**εσείς έχετε**	*you have*
αυτός έχει	*he has* (m)	**αυτοί έχουν**	*they have* (m/m+f)
αυτή έχει	*she has* (f)	**αυτές έχουν**	*they have* (f)
αυτό έχει	*it has* (n)	**αυτά έχουν**	*they have* (n)

The pronoun *they [It]* has three forms for masculine, feminine and neuter case. For example, **αυτές έχουν** means that only a group of women has something. The pronoun **αυτές** automatically excludes groups of men (or masculine nouns in general) or groups of kids (or neuter nouns in general).

Conversation 3

ΔΕ ΘΥΜΑΜΑΙ *I DON'T REMEMBER*

 NEW EXPRESSIONS

 02.09

χαίρομαι που σε ξαναβλέπω (hérome pu se ksanavlépo)	*I am glad to see you again*
δεν το πιστεύω! (THen to pistévo)	*I don't believe that!*
Πώς πας; (pos pas)?	*How are you doing? How's everything?*
πολύ καλά (polí kalá)	*very well, pretty good*
πόσες μέρες; (póses)?	*How many days?*
Έχω τρεις μέρες στην Αθήνα (ého tris méres stin athína)	*I have been in Athens for three days* (lit. *I have three days in Athens…*)
Νομίζω τέσσερις (nomízo téseris)	*I think four*

 02.10 *Domenico Di Capo, an archaeologist, meets Μαριάννα Αγγέλου (Marianne Angelou), a Greek archaeologist who spent three months in Italy last year. They meet at the National Archaeological Museum.*

1 **Listen to the conversation carefully a couple of times without looking at the text. Can you find these two statements?**

   a I don't believe it! _____

   b I don't remember. _____

Marianne	Γεια σου, Ντομένικο. Χαίρομαι που σε ξαναβλέπω. Πώς είσαι;
Domenico	Γεια σου, Μαριάννα. Δεν το πιστεύω! Σε ξαναβλέπω στην Αθήνα. Πώς πας; Είσαι καλά;
Marianne	Είμαι πολύ καλά. Εσύ πώς είσαι;
Domenico	Καλά, πολύ καλά!
Marianne	Πόσες μέρες είσαι στην Αθήνα;
Domenico	Έχω τρεις μέρες στην Αθήνα … Νομίζω τέσσερις … Χμ! Δε θυμάμαι.
Marianne	(yáasu doméniko) (hérome pu se ksanavlépo) (pos íse)?
Domenico	(yásu mariána) (THen to pistévo) (se ksanavlépo stin athína) (pos pas)? (íse kalá)?
Marianne	(íme polí kalá) (esí pos íse)?
Domenico	(kalá) (polí kalá)
Marianne	(póses méres íse stin athína)?
Domenico	(ého tris meres stin athína) (nomízo téseris) (hm)! (THe thimáme)!

2 Now read the conversation and answer the following questions.

    a Does Marianne know Domenico from before?

    b Are they both fine?

    c How many days has Domenico been in Athens already?

 3 Listen again and pay special attention to the words that run together. Practise speaking the part of Marianne and pay particular attention to your pronunciation. At the end, switch parts and practise again.

Language discovery 3

1 There are three new verbs in this dialogue which comply with what we have learnt so far regarding verb endings in verbs like έχω, κάνω, or ξέρω. Can you find them?

    a think _____

    b believe _____

    c see again _____

2 There are also three verbs in this dialogue that do not comply with the verb endings we have learnt so far. Can you spot them? One hint that might help you: the verb ending is not –ω!

    _____, _____, _____

3 If you have solved the mystery in the previous question, then you should have no problem completing the following three statements:

    a The personal pronoun for I is _____ in Greek.

    b Many Greek verbs denote this pronoun in the ending _____.

    c Some Greek verbs denote this pronoun also in the ending _____.

4 The verb **βλέπω** means *I see*. **The prefix ξανα was used in the dialogue with this verb. Its meaning resembles the English prefix** *re-* **in certain verbs, e.g.** *redo, remake,* **or the word again following a verb. Can you expand this to the following verbs? All verbs come from Conversation 3.**

   a I'm glad again _____

   b I believe again _____

   c I see again _____

   d I think again _____

   e I remember again _____

5 **The numbers 3 and 4 used in this conversation are a little bit different compared to those you have learnt in the Vocabulary builder earlier in this unit. Can you guess why that happens?**

Learn more

1 THE NUMBERS 1–10

 02.11 Conversation 3 introduced the numbers 3 and 4. Here are the numbers 1–10 for you. Listen carefully and repeat after the speaker.

  1 **ένα/μία/ένας** (éna/mía/énas)   **6** **έξι** (éksi)

  2 **δύο** (THío)   **7** **επτά/εφτά** (eptá/eftá)

  3 **τρία/τρεις** (tría/tris)   **8** **οκτώ/οχτώ** (októ/ohtó)

  4 **τέσσερα/τέσσερις** (tésera/téseris)   **9** **εννέα/εννιά** (enéa, eniá)

  5 **πέντε** (pénde)   **10** **δέκα** (THéka)

When you count, you can use the words **ένα**, **τρία**, **τέσσερα**. The numbers 1, 3 and 4 have different forms because of grammatical rules, **ένας συνάδελφος** *one colleague* (m), **μία μέρα** *one day* (f), **ένα μάθημα** *one class/lesson* (n). The numbers 7, 8 and 9 have two different forms; the first one is often used in formal Greek and the second one in everyday, informal Greek. Many Greek numbers are hidden in English words! Can you find which numbers are hidden here: *decathlon, octagon, hexagon, Pentagon, trigonometry, duo, duologue,* or *duel*? Study and learn the numbers by heart.

2 INDEFINITE ARTICLES

The indefinite article (*a* or *an* in English) is expressed by **ένας**, **μία** (**μια**), or **ένα** in Greek.

ένας κύριος	*a gentleman*
μία μέρα	*a day*
ένα λάθος	*a mistake*

The words **ένας** (m), **μία** (**μια**) (f) and **ένα** (n) can also be used as the numeral *one*:

ένα λάθος means *a mistake* or *one mistake*.

More details will follow in later units.

3 VERBS ENDING IN –MAI

One group of verbs that you have learnt so far includes **ξέρ-ω, έχ-ω, κάν-ω, φωνάζ-ω**, etc. What is common to these verbs is that they have the same conjugation, i.e. all verb endings are the same. The third dialogue in this unit introduced a new group of verbs ending in **-μαι**, including **χαίρο-μαι** *I'm glad*, **θυμά-μαι** *I remember*, **εί-μαι** *I am*. This new group also needs special attention, especially in its conjugation. Except for the verb **είμαι**, only learn by heart the first and second person singular, to begin with, since these two verb forms are used in questions or answers in everyday language. Keep this table for future reference and come back to it as often as necessary. These three verbs are fully conjugated for you now.

 02.12 **Listen and repeat the verb conjugations after the speaker.**

Singular	Plural
εγώ είμαι / θυμάμαι / χαίρομαι	**εμείς είμαστε / θυμόμαστε / χαιρόμαστε**
εσύ είσαι / θυμάσαι / χαίρεσαι	**εσείς είστε (είσαστε) / θυμάστε (θυμόσαστε) / χαίρεστε (χαιρόσαστε)**
αυτός είναι / θυμάται / χαίρεται	**αυτοί είναι / θυμούνται / χαίρονται**
αυτή είναι / θυμάται / χαίρεται	**αυτές είναι / θυμούνται / χαίρονται**
αυτό είναι / θυμάται / χαίρεται	**αυτά είναι / θυμούνται / χαίρονται**

> **TIP**
>
> Have a short break now. The three dialogues include many new words and it will take some time to learn them. It is helpful if you want to improve your pronunciation to listen to these dialogues often without the text. Concentrate only on the intonation and general message of each dialogue rather than individual words. Be satisfied if you can follow part of the conversation. This actually resembles real-life situations where we cannot look up what a speaker says and of course we do not understand everything at the beginning.

 Practice

1 **See if you can react to the following situations:**
   a You are asked about your health. Say that you are very well.
   b You want to ask: *How about you?* (infm. and fm. form)
   c You would like to enquire about κ. Μαύρος's health.
   d You are asked to join a group of people. Tell them that you are a little bit tired.
   e In the beginning you will forget a lot. How do you say *Oh, I forgot that!*?
   f How would you tell someone that you have only been in Athens for two, three, four and five days?

2 Match each question with the most appropriate answer.

a Τι κάνεις;   1 Είμαι καλά, ευχαριστώ!

b Είναι λάθος;   2 Νομίζω έξι.

c Τι κάνετε, κύριε Αντωνίου;   3 Όχι, δεν είναι.

d Πόσες μέρες είσαι εδώ;   4 Καλά, εσύ;

3 Rearrange these lines to make a dialogue.

a Καλά, πολύ καλά. Εσύ;

b Δεν ξέρω. Έτσι κι έτσι.

c Πώς πας; Είσαι καλά;

d Γιατί τι έχεις;

e Είμαι λίγο κουρασμένος!

4 Translate the English into Greek in the following dialogue:

Γιώργος	Γεια σας! Πώς σας λένε;
You	a *William Jones, but everybody calls me Bill.*
Γιώργος	Α! Ωραία! Από πού είστε;
You	b *From England, but please be less formal.* (lit. *why are you speaking to me formally?*)
Γιώργος	Δεν ξέρω. Δε σας ξέρω καλά! Από ποιο μέρος είστε;
You	c *From Liverpool. How about you?*
Γιώργος	Από τη Θεσσαλονίκη. Πόσες μέρες είστε στην Ελλάδα;
You	d *I think only two or three days.*

5 Match the words on the left with those on the right.

a όλοι   1 institute

b πρόγραμμα   2 national (ethnic)

c πολύγλωττο   3 museum

d ινστιτούτο   4 centre

e άγγελος   5 schedule (programme)

f εθνικό   6 archaeological

g αρχαιολογικό   7 all (everyone)

h μουσείο   8 polyglot

i κέντρο   9 angel

6 Can you recognize some of the words you have already learnt? Find as many words as you can – horizontally, vertically and diagonally – of two, three, four and five letters.

Ο	Ε	Σ	Υ	Π
Μ	Η	Χ	Μ	Ε
Ω	Ν	Ο	Ω	Ν
Σ	Π	Α	Σ	Τ
Κ	Υ	Ρ	Ι	Ε

7 02.13 Listen to the words and match them to their corresponding sound. If you want, you can first use the words in the box and then listen and find out how they sound.

/i/ as in *inn*	/o/ as in *or*
_____	_____
_____	_____
_____	_____
_____	_____

πώς	κοντά	μόνο	είναι
κύριε	όμως	τρεις	στην

8 02.14 Listen to Conversation 3 in this unit again and fill in the missing words. If you don't have the recording, try to fill in the gaps from the words in the box.

Marianne	Γεια σου, Ντομένικο. **a** _____ που σε ξαναβλέπω. Πώς **b** _____;
Domenico	Γεια σου, Μαριάννα. Δεν το **c** _____! Σε ξαναβλέπω στην Αθήνα. Πώς πας; Είσαι καλά;
Marianne	**d** _____ πολύ καλά. Εσύ; **e** _____ **b** _____;
Domenico	Καλά, πολύ καλά.
Marianne	**f** _____ μέρες **b** _____ στην Αθήνα;
Domenico	Έχω τρεις μέρες στην Αθήνα … **g** _____ τέσσερις … ! Δε **h** _____.

θυμάμαι	νομίζω	είμαι	πώς
χαίρομαι	πιστεύω	είσαι	πόσες

9 Translate the cartoon.

Ξέρει κανείς αγγλικά; [kséri kanís angliká]?

? Test yourself

1 Write the Greek for the following ten words.

a thanks _____ **f** but _____

b Greek _____ **g** excuse me _____

c tired _____ **h** sure _____

d all right _____ **i** day _____

e today _____ **j** lesson/class _____

2 Can you remember the following ten important phrases from this unit?

a How are you doing? **f** I don't believe that!

b I'm a bit tired. **g** I'm just fine.

c How are you? **h** I don't remember.

d I forgot that. **i** Glad to see you again!

e Is it a mistake? **j** How many days have you been…?

3 These five phrases use the formal way of addressing people. Can you change them into informal Greek?

a (ti kánete)? Τι κάνετε; _____

b (pos íste)? Πώς είστε; _____

c (yásas kiría Johnson) Γεια σας, κυρία Johnson. _____

d (íste kalá)? Είστε καλά; _____

e (eΤΗό ménete)? Εδώ μένετε; _____

> **TIP**
>
> Make sure that you get at least 70% of the answers correct in this last section. Pay attention to your mistakes and find not only the correct answers but also the corresponding explanations in the unit. Although you are probably studying alone, you can also try to see if someone would like to become a study partner with you and facilitate your learning efforts. Now, see how easy this last section is for you. If you want, you can time yourself. Do not take more than five minutes to complete this section!

SELF CHECK

	I CAN. . .
○	. . . address people with names and titles.
○	. . . ask people about their health.
○	. . . say how I'm feeling today.
○	. . . say how people can call me.
○	. . . engage in 'small talk' when meeting people.
○	. . . thank someone.
○	. . . say that I'm busy or tired.
○	. . . say if I still remember or forgot something.

3 Έλα να πιούμε ένα ουζάκι!

Let's have a glass of ouzo!

In this unit you will learn how to:

▶ *order drinks.*
▶ *order breakfast.*
▶ *order Greek appetizers.*
▶ *count from 11 to 20.*

CEFR: (A1) *Can order some alcoholic or non-alcoholic drinks. Can understand a breakfast menu. Can order breakfast or small appetizer dishes. Can handle numbers, quantities and costs (0–20).*

 Ελληνικές ταβέρνες *Greek taverns*

There are many different types of taverns in Greece. Often their names show what they specialize in. **Μεζεδοπωλείο**, is an informal tavern, offering a large selection of appetizers to accompany ouzo, retsina (a kind of resinated wine) or beer. The word itself denotes **πωλείο** *selling* and **μεζέδες** *appetizers*. **Ταβέρνα** is a tavern that offers a large selection of appetizers and local specialities. Taverns are very informal places. **Χασαποταβέρνα** is a tavern which has a large selection of meat specialities and **ψαροταβέρνα** is a tavern with fish specialities.

Greek appetizers include **τζατζίκι** *tzatziki* – a yoghurt, cucumber and garlic dip; **ταραμοσαλάτα** *taramasalata* – fish-roe dip; **κεφτέδες** *keftethes* – meatballs; **τηγανιτές πατάτες** *chips or French fries*; **χωριάτικη σαλάτα** *a mixed salad*, including but not limited to tomatoes, cucumber, feta cheese, and olives; **τυροπιτάκια** *small pieces of cheese pie*; and **σπανακοπιτάκια** *small pieces of spinach pie*.

💡 **1** Can you work out what the Greek word for *pie* is?

Ⓥ Vocabulary builder

ΟΙ ΑΡΙΘΜΟΙ 11–20 *NUMBERS 11–20*

 1 03.01 **Listen to the numbers 11–20 now and repeat after the speaker.**

11	έντεκα (éndeka)	14	δεκατέσσερα (THekatésera)
			δεκατέσσερις (THekatéseris)
12	δώδεκα (THóTHeka)	15	δεκαπέντε (THekapénde)
13	δεκατρία (THekatría)	16	δεκαέξι (THekaéksi)
	δεκατρείς (THekatrís)		

17	δεκαεπτά (THekaeptá)	19	δεκαεννέα (THekaenéa)
	δεκαεφτά (THekaeftá)		δεκαεννιά (THekaeniá)
18	δεκαοκτώ (THekaoktó)	20	είκοσι (íkosi)
	δεκαοχτώ (THekaohtó)		

ΚΑΤΑΛΟΓΟΣ *MENU ITEMS AND PRICES*

 2 03.02 **Read the menu as you listen and repeat the food and drink expressions. Try to work out what the items mean in English. You can check your answers in the Key.**

ΖΕΣΤΑ ΡΟΦΗΜΑΤΑ	ΠΟΤΑ
Ελληνικός καφές............ € 2,00	*Μπίρα*....................€ 3,20
Φραπές .... € 3,20	*Ποτήρι κρασί*........€ 4,10
Τσάι................................ € 2,00	*Μπουκάλι κρασί*..........€ 12,00
Ζεστή σοκολάτα /	*Μπουκάλι ρετσίνα*.......€ 11,00
Κακάο .... € 3,00	*Ποτήρι ούζο* ....€ 4,10
Εσπρέσσο .... € 2,15	

ΑΝΑΨΥΚΤΙΚΑ	ΜΕΖΕΔΕΣ
Κόκα κόλα....................... € 2,20	*Τζατζίκι*..............................€ 5,00
Πορτοκαλάδα	*Κεφτέδες* ....€ 8,20
(μπλε/κόκκινη).............. € 2,20	*Τηγανητές πατάτες*........€ 6,00
Λεμονάδα...................... € 2,20	*Χωριάτικη σαλάτα* ....€ 7,20
Χυμοί (ανανάς,	*Σπανακοπιτάκια*.............€ 9,10
λεμόνι, πορτοκάλι) .... € 4,10	
Νερό (μικρό).................. € 1,00	

3 What are the English meanings for these food and drinks? Match the correct words.

a Χωριάτικη σαλάτα		**1**	Chips / French fries
b Κόκκινη πορτοκαλάδα		**2**	Greek coffee
c Χυμός ανανάς		**3**	Glass of wine
d Ελληνικός καφές		**4**	Mixed salad
e Τηγανητές πατάτες		**5**	Pineapple juice
f Ποτήρι κρασί		**6**	Orange drink

 4 03.03 **Now listen to the prices of some food and drinks and note the amount.**

a _____   d _____

b _____   e _____

c _____   f _____

5 03.04 **Now look at the prices for appetizers on the menu. Listen and repeat the prices.**

Conversation 1

ΕΛΑ ΝΑ ΠΙΟΥΜΕ ΕΝΑ ΟΥΖΑΚΙ! *LET'S HAVE A GLASS OF OUZO!*

 NEW EXPRESSIONS

 03.05

έλα (éla)	*come/let's*
έλα να πιούμε (éla na pyúme)	*let's have a drink* (lit. *(you) come and (we) drink*)
στης Αλεξάνδρα (stis alexánTHras)	*at Alexandra's*
το πάρκο Παναθήναια	*the Panathinean Park in Athens*
όμορφο (ómorfo)	*nice* (lit. *beautiful*)
πολλούς μεζέδες (polús mezéTHes)	*many appetizers* (m), *snacks* (cold or hot starters)
σε λίγο (se lígho)	*in a little while*
ο σερβιτόρος (o servitóros)	*waiter* (n) (lit. *the servant*)
Τι θα πάρετε; (ti tha párete;)	*What will you have?*
η ποικιλία (i pikilía)	*a plate of assorted appetizers*
αμέσως (amésos)	*straight/right away*

 03.06 *Γιώργος Παπαδόπουλος invites Mary Johnson to join him for a drink in a local ouzeri-tavern.*

1 Listen to the conversation a couple of times. What do they actually order?

Γιώργος	Μαίρη, έλα να πιούμε ένα ουζάκι στης 'Αλεξάνδρας'.
Mary	Πού είναι της 'Αλεξάνδρας';
Γιώργος	Είναι κοντά στο πάρκο Παναθήναια, ένα πολύ όμορφο μεζεδοπωλείο.
Mary	Μεζεδοπωλείο … τι είναι αυτό; Δεν καταλαβαίνω.
Γιώργος	Μεζεδοπωλείο είναι μία ταβέρνα με πολλούς μεζέδες … και πολύ ούζο. Σε λίγο στης Αλεξάνδρας…
Σερβιτόρος	Τι θα πάρετε παρακαλώ;
Γιώργος	Δύο ουζάκια και μία ποικιλία.
Σερβιτόρος	Αμέσως!
Γιώργος	(méri) (éla na pyúme) (éna uzáki stis aleksánTHras)
Mary	(pu íne tis aleksánTHras)?
Γιώργος	(íne kondá sto párko panathínea) (éna polí ómorfo mezeTHopolío)
Mary	(mezeTHopolío) (ti íne aftó)? (THen katalavéno)
Γιώργος	(mezeTHopolío íne mía tavérna) (me polús mezéTHes) (ke polí úzo) (se lígho …(stis aleksánTHras) …
Σερβιτόρος	(ti tha párete parakaló)?
Γιώργος	(THío uzákia) (ke mía pikilía)
Σερβιτόρος	(amésos)!

2 Now read the conversation and answer the questions.

    a What is μεζεδοπωλείο?

    b Is the μεζεδοπωλείο close by or far away? Which key word does Γιώργος use to say that?

    c Is the name of the μεζεδοπωλείο, Αλεξάνδρας or Παναθηναία?

 3 Listen again and pay special attention to the words that run together. Practise speaking the part of Γιώργος and pay particular attention to your pronunciation.

Language discovery 1

1 Look at Conversation 1 and complete the sentences with μία or ένα. Notice the genders (masculine, feminine, neuter) of the nouns that follow.

    a Είναι _____ ταβέρνα με πολλούς μεζέδες.

    b Έλα να πιούμε _____ ουζάκι.

    c Δύο ουζάκια και _____ ποικιλία.

    d _____ πολύ όμορφο μεζεδοπωλείο.

2 Look at the conversation once again and find the singular or plural form of the following nouns. Checking the endings of the nouns, can you come up with any rule?

Masculine nouns Singular – Plural	Feminine nouns Singular – Plural	Neuter nouns Singular – Plural
a καφές – _____	**c** _____ – ταβέρνες	**e** _____ – πάρκα
b μεζές – _____	**d** _____ – ποκιλίες	**f** _____ – ούζα

3 The words *a little*, *much*, **and** *many* **are in this conversation. Can you find them?**

Learn more

1 INDEFINITE ARTICLE

The words **ένας/έναν**, **μία/μια**, **ένα** are the Greek indefinite articles and they often stand for the English words *a* or *an*. Although there is a phonetic decision when it comes to the usage in English, one has to match the appropriate Greek indefinite article with the gender (masculine, feminine, or neuter) of the noun that it modifies. This means that it will make more sense to learn these articles in context, as part of expressions, rather than alone. As you learn to order drinks in this unit, you will learn the following phrases:

Masculine nouns:

Έναν καφέ παρακαλώ!	*A coffee please!*
Έναν μεζέ παρακαλώ!	*An appetizer please!*
Έναν φραπέ παρακαλώ!	*An iced coffee please!*

> **PHONETIC NOTE**
>
> One can hear the word **έναν** sometimes as **ένα** or the word **δεν** as **δε** depending on the first letter of the word following. We still suggest though that you use the words **έναν** or **δεν** without thinking twice about the phonetic rule. All native speakers will understand you perfectly.

Feminine nouns:

Μία ποικιλία παρακαλώ!   *A platter of assorted appetizers please!*

Μία λεμονάδα παρακαλώ!   *A lemonade please!*

Μία μπίρα παρακαλώ!   *A beer please!*

Neuter nouns:

Ένα ούζο παρακαλώ!   *An ouzo please!*

Ένα μπουκάλι κρασί παρακαλώ! *A bottle of wine please!*

Ένα ποτήρι νερό παρακαλώ!   *A glass of water please!*

2 PLURAL FORMS

Did you come up with any rules regarding the plural forms of some Greek nouns when you did Exercise 2? Now, read the singular and plural forms of these nouns and some new ones and compare them with your answers. Did you come up with the same endings as these?

Masculine nouns: (**-ες/-εδες**)

ο καφές – οι καφέδες, ο μεζές – οι μεζέδες, ο φραπές – οι φραπέδες, ο κεφτές – οι κεφτέδες

Feminine nouns: (**-α/-ες**)

η ταβέρνα – οι ταβέρνες, η ποικιλία – οι ποικιλίες, η μπίρα – οι μπίρες, η πατάτα – οι πατάτες

Neuter nouns: (**-ο/-α**)

το πάρκο – τα πάρκα, το ούζο – τα ούζα, το νερό – τα νερά, το μεζεδοπωλείο – τα μεζεδοπωλεία

Have you noticed the plural form of the Greek article (the word *the* in English)? It is **οι** (for both masculine and feminine) and **τα** (for neuter) in Greek. The examples above do not provide an exhaustive list of plural possibilities. At any rate though, it is a good start and it will help you become familiar with many Greek nouns that belong to these three groups. If you work with flash cards, you can try and see how much you can extend this list with nouns from the first three units.

Conversation 2

OYZO ME NEPO! *OUZO WITH WATER!*

 NEW EXPRESSIONS

 03.07

πώς πίνετε; (pos pínete)	*how do you drink?*
σκέτο (skéto)	*straight*
με πάγο (me págho)	*on the rocks* (lit. *with ice*)
αυτό είναι! (aftó íne)	*that's it!/this is it!*
βάλε μου (vále mu)	*pour me/give me*
ορίστε (oríste)	*here you are!*

που της αρέσει (pu tis arési)	*that she likes*
συνήθως (siníthos)	*usually*
η λεμονάδα (i lemonáTHa)	*the lemonade* (f)
ουφ! (uf)!	*phew!*
απαίσιο (apésio)	*awful* (adj.)
θαυμάσιο (thavmásio)	*marvellous* (adj.)/*wonderful*
επίσης (epísis)	*also*
Φτάνει! (ftáni)!	*That's enough!*
Δε θέλω να ακούσω άλλο πια!	*I don't want to hear any more (any longer)!*
(THe thélo n'akúso álo pya)	

 03.08 *Γιώργος and Mary are having a glass of ouzo together.*

1   What does Γιώργος want to find out in their conversation?

Mary	Πώς πίνετε το ούζο στην Ελλάδα;
Γιώργος	Σκέτο, με πάγο ή με νερό.
Mary	Ούζο με νερό! Αυτό είναι! Βάλε μου λίγο νερό.
Γιώργος	Ορίστε! Πίνετε ούζο στην Αγγλία;
Mary	Ναι, έχω μία φίλη που της αρέσει το ούζο. Πίνει συνήθως ούζο με λεμονάδα.
Γιώργος	Ουφ! Ούζο με λεμονάδα! Απαίσιο!
Mary	Όχι, είναι θαυμάσιο! Μου αρέσει πολύ. Στην Αγγλία πίνουμε επίσης Μεταξά σκέτο ή με κόκα κόλα.
Γιώργος	Μεταξά με κόκα κόλα! Φτάνει! Δε θέλω να ακούσω άλλο πια …
Mary	(pos pínete to úzo) (stin eláTHa)?
Γιώργος	(skéto) (me págho) (i me neró)
Mary	(úzo me neró) (aftó íne) (vále mu lígho neró).
Γιώργος	(oríste)! (pínete úzo stin anglía)?
Mary	(ne) (ého mía fíli) (pu tis arési to úzo) (píni siníthos) (úzo me lemonáTHa)
Γιώργος	(uf)! (úzo me lemonáTHa)! (apésio)
Mary	(óchi) (ine thavmásio) (mu arési polí) (stin anglía) (pínume epísis metaksá) (skéto i me kóka kóla)
Γιώργος	(metaksá me kóka kóla)! (ftáni)! (THe thélo n'akúso) (álo pya)

2   Now read the conversation and answer the questions.

   a How do people drink ouzo in Greece?

   b Do people drink ouzo in England?

   c Is Γιώργος fed up with the conversation?

 3   Listen again to this conversation and pay special attention to the words that run together. Practise speaking the part of Mary.

💡 Language discovery 2

1 **The Greek word for the verb** *to like* **needs some attention. The conversation has two different forms. Can you find the following?**

    a I like _____

    b she likes _____

2 **Read the conversation once again and try to find the following prepositions (words like** *on*, *in*, *with* **etc.). Do you notice anything particular in your findings?**

    a on the rocks _____

    b with water _____

    c in Greece _____

3 **Can you remember which word stands for** *without* **in Greek?**

4 **Can you figure out the Greek for the following, paying particular attention to the endings of all eight adjectives? Do you notice anything particular?**

    a awful water! _____

    b ouzo straight! _____

    c some raki! _____

    d excellent wine! _____

    e big bottle! _____

    f small glass! _____

    g white wine! _____

    h red wine! _____

Learn more

1 THE VERB *TO LIKE*

This is a particular verb in Greek. It is part of the so-called 'impersonal verbs' that are similar to some English verbs, including *it seems* or *it depends*. Contrary to most other Greek verbs with their different endings, this verb has only one form **αρέσει**! For this reason, personal pronouns precede this verb to help with the meaning.

Notice the conjugation of this particular but extremely important Greek verb. We have also included some contracted forms that are often heard in everyday Greek.

μου αρέσει/μ'αρέσει	*I like*	**μας αρέσει**	*we like*
σου αρέσει/σ'αρέσει	*you like*	**σας αρέσει**	*you like*
του αρέσει	*he likes*	**τους αρέσει**	*they like*
της αρέσει	*she likes*	**τις αρέσει**	*they like*
του αρέσει	*it likes*	**τους αρέσει**	*they like*

2 GREEK PREPOSITIONS

Prepositions, words like *on, in, at, with*, etc., are important and they will help you in many different language situations when you want to use Greek. A number of prepositions have popped up in the last three units:

από	*from*
από την Αγγλία	*from England*
σε	*in*
σε λίγο	*in a little while*
με	*with*
ούζο με νερό	*ouzo with water*
χωρίς	*without*
χωρίς ανθρακικό	*non-sparkling water*

You may have noticed something particular regarding the preposition **σε** but we want to draw your attention once again to this. First and most important is its translation. Contrary to most other prepositions, which usually have only one translation, **σε** can be easily and freely translated by the following words: *in, into, at, to, by, on* and *onto*! Second and also important is the fact that this preposition must always be used as one word when an article follows. In this case, the letter **-ε** is deleted:

Masculine:	**Ένα δώρο στον** (never **σε**+**τον**) **Κώστα.**	*A present to Kostas.*
Feminine:	**Είμαι στην** (never **σε**+**την**) **Αθήνα.**	*I am in Athens.*
Neuter:	**Πάγο στο** (never **σε**+**το**) **ούζο.**	*Ice (cubes) into ouzo.*

3 GREEK ADJECTIVES

Did you come up with the ending **-o** for all eight adjectives in Exercise 3? If yes, congratulations! Greek adjectives, words like *good, bad, small, big, excellent* or *awful*, give extra information usually to the nouns they modify. It is important to express yourself correctly when you want a small or a big bottle of water or you want to comment about good or bad ouzo, wine, or retsina! These words will pose a small challenge to your learning because they have more forms compared to English. As said before though, it is a good idea to learn them as chunks in context, e.g. **καλό ούζο** *good ouzo*, **λίγο νερό** *some water*, **άσπρο κρασί** *white wine*, instead of entries in a dictionary. By the way, these words are usually listed in dictionaries with their three main forms, including the masculine, feminine and neuter form in singular. Here's an example with the three adjectives above:

καλός, καλή, καλό	**λίγος, λίγη, λίγο**	**άσπρος, άσπρη, άσπρο**
καλ-ός/-ή/-ό	**λίγ-ος/-η/-ο**	**άσπρ-ος/-η/-ο**

Conversation 3

ΠΡΩΙΝΟ ΣΤΟ 'ΑΜΕΡΙΚΑ'! *BREAKFAST IN 'AMERICA'!*

 NEW EXPRESSIONS

 03.09

το πρωινό (to proinó)	*the breakfast (n)*
Είστε έτοιμοι; (íste étimi)	*Are you ready?*
μας φέρνετε (mas férnete) = φέρτε μας (férte mas)	*(Can/Could you) bring us*
ο κατάλογος (o katáloghos)	*menu (m) (lit. catalogue)*
κοντινένταλ (kontinéntal)	*continental*
ομελέτες (omelétes)	*omelettes*
το ζαμπόν (to zambón)	*the ham (n)*
ο χυμός (o chimós)	*the juice (m)*
το πορτοκάλι (to portokáli)	*the orange (n)*
το λεμόνι (to lemóni)	*the lemon (n)*
το γάλα (to ghála)	*the milk (n)*
το βούτυρο (to vútiro)	*the butter (n)*
η μαρμελάδα (i marmeláTHa)	*the marmalade (f)*
φρυγανιές (frighanyés)	*toast*
το ψωμί (to psomí)	*the bread (n)*
ουφ! (uf)!	*I've had it! Enough! No more! Phew!*

03.10 *Gabi, Marie-Sofie and Domenico have breakfast in 'America', the breakfast room of the Apollo Hotel.*

1 Does the waiter have problems with the order?

Σερβιτόρος	Είστε έτοιμοι;
Marie-Sofie	Όχι, μας φέρνετε τον κατάλογο παρακαλώ;
Σερβιτόρος	Ναι, βέβαια, αμέσως.
	Σε λίγο …
Σερβιτόρος	Είστε έτοιμοι τώρα;
Marie-Sofie	Θέλουμε δύο πρωινά κοντινένταλ και δύο ομελέτες με ζαμπόν. Ένα γαλλικό καφέ, ένα τσάι και δύο χυμούς πορτοκάλι.
Σερβιτόρος	Θέλετε το τσάι με λεμόνι ή γάλα;
Gabi	Τσάι με λεμόνι, ευχαριστώ.
Domenico	Φέρτε μας λίγο βούτυρο και μαρμελάδα επίσης.
Marie-Sofie	Και φρυγανιές ή ψωμί …
Σερβιτόρος	Αμέσως … αμέσως! … Ουφ!
Σερβιτόρος	(íste étimi)?
Marie-Sofie	(óchi) [mas férnete ton katálogho parakaló]

Σερβιτόρος	(ne vévea) (amésos)
	[se lígho]…
Σερβιτόρος	[íste étimi tóra)?
Marie-Sofie	(thélume THío proiná kontinéntal) (ke THío omelétes me zambón) (éna ghalikó kafé) (éna tsái) (ke THío chimús portokáli)
Σερβιτόρος	(thélete to tsái) (me lemóni i ghála)?
Gabi	(tsái me lemóni) (efharistó)
Domenico	(férte mas) (lígho vútiro ke marmeláTHa) (epísis)
Marie-Sofie	(ke frighaniés) (i psomí)
Σερβιτόρος	(amésos – amésos) (uf)!

2 **Now read the conversation and answer the questions.**

   a Do they order two or three Continental breakfasts?

   b Do they want anything in their omelettes?

   c What would Domenico also like to order?

 3 **Listen again to this conversation and pay special attention to the words that run together. Practise speaking the part of Marie-Sofie.**

Language discovery 3

1 **What are the two expressions, found in the conversation, to say** *Can you bring us …?*

   _____

2 **The conversation has three adverbs of time. Give the Greek for the following:**

   a now _____

   b right away _____

   c in a little while _____

Learn more

1 SOME USEFUL WAYS TO ORDER

This unit introduces you to different ways of ordering something in Greek. You can always order something, using what you want and the word **παρακαλώ** *please*:

Ένα μικρό μπουκάλι νερό, παρακαλώ!	*A small bottle of water, please!*
Ένα ποτήρι άσπρο κρασί, παρακαλώ!	*A glass of white wine, please!*
Έναν καφέ μέτριο, παρακαλώ!	*A Greek coffee, medium sweet, please!*
Δύο ομελέττες με ζαμπόν, παρακαλώ!	*Two omelettes with ham, please!*
Δύο χυμούς πορτοκάλι, παρακαλώ!	*Two (glasses) orange juice, please!*

Some useful verbs when you order include:

Μας φέρνετε ένα ούζο και μία ποικιλία;	*(Can/Could you) bring us an ouzo and a plate of assorted appetizers?*
Φέρτε μας μία μπίρα και δύο μέτριους καφέδες!	*(Can/Could you) bring us a beer and two Greek coffees, medium sweet?*
Θα ήθελα ένα τοστ με ζαμπόν και τυρί!	*I'd like* (more formal) *a toast with ham and cheese!*
Θέλω μία πορτοκαλάδα και δύο λεμονάδες!	*I'd like* (less formal) *one orangeade and two lemonades!*

2 ADVERBS OF TIME

Adverbs of time, words like *now*, *later*, *yesterday*, *in a little while*, etc., are important single words or phrases when you want to specify something within time limits. The last three units introduced some other adverbs, including **καλά** *well/fine*, **ωραία** *beautifully*, which are adverbs of manner, answering the question *how*, compared to the adverbs of time, which answer the question *when*. We summarize these adverbs here for you:

τώρα	*now*
ακόμα	*yet*
σήμερα	*today*
αμέσως	*immediately/right away*
άλλο πια	*any longer*
σε λίγο	*in a little while*

> **TIP**
>
> Have a short break now. It is a good idea to personalize your learning. This unit, for instance, deals with ordering a drink, food or even having breakfast in Greece. So you can start compiling a 'top 10 list' of your own preferences. What are the Greek names of the drinks and foods you like? You can look up a couple of words if the unit does not include them. Your 'top 10 lists' will grow unit by unit, you will be able to express yourself more easily, and you will become more and more confident. So, start compiling your first list now!

 ## Practice

1 See if you can deal with some more situations you are likely to encounter in Greece.

   a You are in a μεζεδοπωλείο. Order a glass of ouzo and a plate of assorted appetizers.
   b You are tasting ouzo for the first time: give your impression by saying *excellent* or *awful*.
   c You are having a drink with a friend. How would you say *I like it a lot* or *I don't like it much*?
   d You are ordering a glass of ouzo. How would you say *straight up* or *on the rocks*?
   e You are in a coffee shop. How can you ask for the menu?
   f You like tea with milk. Ask for it.

2 **Match each question with the most appropriate answer.**

   a Τι είναι μεζεδοπωλείο;   **1** Ένα ούζο και μία ποικιλία.

   b Τι θα πάρετε;   **2** Όχι, με γάλα.

   c Είστε έτοιμοι;   **3** Μία ταβέρνα με μεζέδες.

   d Θέλετε τσάι με λεμόνι;   **4** Όχι, ακόμα!

3 **Rearrange these lines to make a dialogue.**

   a Τρία Μεταξά τότε.

   b Ναι, βέβαια.

   c Ναι, βέβαια.

   d Έχετε Μεταξά επτά αστέρων (*stars*);

   e Μου φέρνετε τον κατάλογο, παρακαλώ;

   f Ναι, βέβαια.

4 **Translate the English sentences to complete the following dialogue.**

Σερβιτόρος	Τι θα πάρετε, παρακαλώ;
You	**a** *Could you bring us the menu, please?*
Σερβιτόρος	Είστε έτοιμοι;
You	**b** *Yes, an iced coffee and an instant coffee.*
Σερβιτόρος	Τίποτα άλλο;
You	**c** *Nothing else for the time being. Thanks.*
	Σε λίγο …
You	**d** *Could you bring us the bill, please?*
Σερβιτόρος	Αμέσως!

5 **Use the clues to complete the crossword. The shaded vertical word stands for 'Right away!' – often said by Greek waiters – which they actually do not mean.**

   a coffee

   b marmalade

   c coffee without sugar

   d instant coffee

   e how/what

   f cinema

6 **How many words can you recognize from Unit 3? Match the words on the left with those on the right.**

   a βούτυρο   **1** friend

   b καφέ   **2** chocolate

   c πάρκο   **3** tavern

   d μαρμελάδα   **4** catalogue/menu/list

   e σοκολατίνα   **5** omelettes

   f κατάλογος   **6** coffee

   g λεμόνι   **7** butter

h φίλος/φίλη	**8** park
i ομελέτες	**9** marmalade
j ταβέρνα	**10** lemon

 7 03.11 **Listen to the conversation and find the missing words If you want you can first find the missing words and then listen and compare your answers.**

Σερβιτόρος	Είστε **a** _____;
Marie-Sofie	Όχι, μας **b** _____ τον κατάλογο, παρακαλώ;
Σερβιτόρος	Ναι, **c** _____, αμέσως.
	Σε λίγο ...
Σερβιτόρος	Είστε έτοιμοι τώρα;
Marie-Sofie	Θέλουμε δύο **d** _____ κοντινένταλ και δύο
	e _____ με ζαμπόν.
	Ένα γαλλικό καφέ, ένα τσάι και δύο
	f _____ πορτοκάλι.
Σερβιτόρος	Θέλετε το τσάι **g** _____ λεμόνι **h** _____ γάλα;
Gabi	Τσάι με λεμόνι, ευχαριστώ.
Domenico	**i** _____ μας λίγο βούτυρο και μαρμελάδα επίσης.
Marie-Sofie	Και φρυγανιές ή **j** _____ ...
Σερβιτόρος	Αμέσως ... αμέσως! ... Ουφ!

βέβαια	έτοιμοι	φέρτε	και	με
φέρνετε	ομελέτες	χυμούς		
	πρωινά	ή	ψωμί	

? Test yourself

1 Can you remember the Greek for the following ten important words from this unit?

a water   f menu

b also   g breakfast

c bread   h butter

d milk   i awful

e usually   j beautiful

2 Can you remember the following ten important phrases from this unit?

a Here you go!   f Do you drink ouzo?

b I'd like a …   g What is 'mezeTHes'?

c That's it!   h I don't understand.

d That's enough!   i I like it a lot.

e I don't want …   j Can you please bring us…?

3 Complete the plural form of the following nouns.

a μεζές _____

b ταβέρνα _____

c ούζο _____

d καφές _____

e πορτοκαλάδα _____

f πρωινό _____

g φραπές _____

h μπίρα _____

i νερό _____

SELF CHECK

I CAN...
○ …ask for the menu.
○ …understand a menu.
○ …order breakfast or appetizer dishes.
○ …order some alcoholic drinks.
○ …order some non-alcoholic drinks.
○ …handle numbers, quantities, and costs from 0–20.
○ …use some nouns in singular or plural form.
○ …use some Greek adverbs of time.
○ …use some adjectives to describe something.

Καλή όρεξη!
Bon appétit!

In this unit you will learn how to:
▶ *order food in a restaurant.*
▶ *ask for local specialities.*
▶ *enquire about Greek eating habits.*
▶ *count from 21 to 100.*

CEFR: (A1) *Can locate specific information in text. Can read and understand many menu items. Can handle numbers, quantities and costs (especially from 21–100).* **(A2)** *Can ask for local specialities. Can understand brief food descriptions. Can express agreement or disagreement. Can ask native speakers to slow down.*

Ελληνική κουζίνα *Greek cuisine*

Greece has a long tradition and good name when it comes to its cuisine. The dishes represent different cooking methods but also local preferences of Greeks living in different corners of the country. **Μπακαλιάρος με σκορδαλιά** *codfish with garlic dip* **Κεντρική Ελλάδα** *in Central Greece;* **αρνάκι με αγκινάρες** *baby lamb with artichokes,* **Πελοπόννησος** *in Peloponnese;* **Επτάνησα** *in Ionian Islands;* **καραβίδες με λαδολέμονο** *crayfish in lemon oil sauce,* **Ήπειρος** *in Epirus;* **λαγός στιφάδο** *rabbit with small onions,* **Θεσσαλία** *in Thessaly;* **χταπόδι με δαμάσκηνα** *octopus with plums,* **Σποράδες** *in Sporades;* **ντομάτες γεμιστές** *filled tomatoes and* **μουσακάς** *moussaka (layers of aubergine, potatoes and minced meat with béchamel sauce);* **Μακεδονία** *in Macedonia,* **σπανακόριζο** *spinach-rice mix in lemon sauce,* **Νησιά Βορείου Αιγαίου** *in Northern Aegean Islands;* **γίγαντες πλακί** *Lima beans,* **Κυκλάδες** *in Cyclades;* **πατατοσαλάτα** *potato salad,* **Δωδεκάνησα** *in Dodecanese (12 island-group);* **αρνάκι με ρύζι** *baby lamb with rice.*

1 Which word in the text means *Greece*?

Vocabulary builder

ΦΑΓΗΤΑ ΚΑΙ ΤΙΜΕΣ *MENU ITEMS AND PRICES*

 **1** 04.01 **Read the menu as you listen and repeat the food expressions. Try to work out what the items mean in English. You can check your answers in the Key.**

ΣΑΛΑΤΕΣ	ΛΑΔΕΡΑ
Χωριάτικη σαλάτα	*Ντομάτες γεμιστές*
Αγγουροντομάτα	*Σεφταλιά*
Πατατοσαλάτα	*Γίγαντες πλακί*
ΣΠΕΣΙΑΛ ΠΙΑΤΑ	**ΦΡΟΥΤΑ**
Χταπόδι με δαμάσκηνα	*Φρουτοσαλάτα*
Λαγός στιφάδο	*Δαμάσκηνα*
Αρνάκι με ρύζι	*Καρπούζι*

2 What is the English for these foods? Match the correct words.

a μπακαλιάρο σκορδαλιά	**1** octopus in lemon oil sauce
b καρπούζι	**2** mixed salad
c αρνάκι με ρύζι	**3** cucumber and tomato salad
d χταπόδι με λαδολέμονο	**4** watermelon
e αγγουροντομάτα	**5** baby lamb with rice
f χωριάτικη σαλάτα	**6** codfish with garlic dip

 3 04.02 **You are going to hear two customers placing an order in a tavern. Notice what they order.**

_____

_____

 **4** 04.03 **Listen to their order once again. At this time complete the chart with the items they have ordered and add the prices. How much should the man or woman pay? Listen to the waiter who is saying the amounts and confirm your answers.**

_____

_____

_____

_____

Η τρελή γαρίδα

ΤΙΜΟΚΑΤΑΛΟΓΟΣ - PRICE LIST

ΣΑΛΑΤΕΣ / SALADS		*ΦΑΓΗΤΑ / MAIN DISHES*	
Λάχανο Cabbage	300	Καλαμαράκια Squid	800
Μαρούλι Lettuce	300	Λουκάνικο Χωριάτικο Spiced Sausage	750
Ρώσικη Russian salad	350	Μπιφτέκι Hamburger Patty	800
Τονοσαλάτα Tuna Salad	500	Γαρίδες σαγανάκι Fried Shrimps	800
Φέτα Feta cheese	400	Πατάτες Τηγανιτές French fries	500
Σαγανάκι Fried cheese	500	Ποικιλία Assorted appetizers	600

5 What is the English for these foods? Match the correct words, paying special attention to these compound words (two words in one) in Greek. Can you come up with the two different words that constitute each compound word?

a	τονοσαλάτα	**1**	price list
b	φρουτοσαλάτα	**2**	potato salad
c	πατατοσαλάτα	**3**	cucumber-tomato salad
d	λαδολέμονο	**4**	tuna salad
e	αγγουροντομάτα	**5**	lemon oil (sauce)
f	τιμοκατάλογος	**6**	fruit salad

Conversation 1

ΕΧΕΤΕ ΜΟΥΣΑΚΑ; *HAVE YOU GOT MOUSSAKA?*

 NEW EXPRESSIONS

 04.04

Δεν καταλαβαίνω τίποτα	*I don't understand anything*
(THen katalavéno típota)	
όλα (óla)	*everything, all*
Έλα τώρα! (éla tóra)!	*Come on now!*
το τζατζίκι (to tzatzíki)	*the tzatziki (yoghurt-cucumber dip) (n)*
η ταραμοσαλάτα (i taramosaláta)	*taramasalata (fish-egg dip) (f)*
η μελιτζανοσαλάτα (i melitzanosaláta)	*aubergine salad/dip (f)*
θα παραγγείλω εγώ για σένα (tha parangílo eghó ya séna)	*I will (place the) order for you*
να πάρουμε (na párume)	*let's have*
ο μουσακάς (o musakás)	*moussaka (m) (layers of aubergine, potatoes and minced meat topped with béchamel sauce)*
πιπεριές γεμιστές (piperiés ghemistés)	*bell peppers filled with rice*
ό,τι λέει ο κατάλογος (óti léi o katáloghos)	*whatever is on the menu (lit. whatever the menu says)*
σουτζουκάκια (sutzukákia)	*spicy meatballs in tomato sauce*
σαλάτα εποχής (saláta epochís)	*seasonal salad (f)*
Θα πιείτε κάτι; (tha pyíte káti)?	*Will you have anything to drink?*
το καραφάκι (to karafáki)	*the small carafe (of ouzo)*
το μπουκάλι (to bukáli)	*the bottle (n)*

 04.05 *Tim Johnson joins a colleague, Γιάννης Δημητρίου, for lunch. They go to Φίλοιστρον, a trendy tavern at the Θησείο area facing the Acropolis.*

1 Listen to the conversation a couple of times. Why is Tim at first disappointed? Did he want anything specific?

Tim	Δεν καταλαβαίνω τίποτα! Είναι όλα στα Ελληνικά!
Γιάννης	Έλα τώρα! Είναι όλα στ' Αγγλικά!
Tim	Βέβαια! Βέβαια! Τζατζίκι; Ταραμοσαλάτα; Μελιτζανοσαλάτα; Τι είναι αυτά;
Γιάννης	Εντάξει! Θα παραγγείλω εγώ για σένα. Να πάρουμε μία ποικιλία από τους ουζομεζέδες που έχουν.
Tim	Εγώ θέλω μουσακά!
Γιάννης	Δεν έχουν μουσακά εδώ. Μισό λεπτό. Έχετε μουσακά;
Σερβιτόρα	Όχι! Έχουμε μόνο ό,τι λέει ο κατάλογος.

Γιάννης	Ωραία! Τότε θέλουμε μία ταραμοσαλάτα, μία τυρόπιτα, πιπεριές γεμιστές, ντολμαδάκια και σουτζουκάκια. Α! και μία σαλάτα εποχής.
Σερβιτόρα	Μάλιστα. Θα πιείτε κάτι;
Γιάννης	Τιμ, θέλεις ρετσίνα ή ένα καραφάκι ούζο;
Tim	Μάλλον ένα καραφάκι κι ένα μπουκάλι νερό.
Tim	(THen katalavéno típota)! (íne óla sta eliniká)!
Γιάννης	(éla tóra)! (íne óla sta angliká)!
Tim	(vévea-vévea)? (tzatzíki)? (taramosaláta)? (melitzanosaláta)? (ti íne aftá)?
Γιάννης	(endáksi)! (tha parangílo eghó ya séna) (na párume mia pikilía) (apó tus uzomezéTHes pu éhun)
Tim	(eghó thélo musaká)!
Γιάννης	(THen éhun musaká eTHó) (misó leptó) (éhete musaká)?
Σερβιτόρα	(óchi)! (éhume móno) (óti léi o katáloghos)
Γιάννης	(oréa)! (tóte thélume mía taramosaláta) (mía tirópita) (piperiés ghemistés) (dolmaTHákia ke sutzukákia) (a) (ke mía saláta epochís)
Σερβιτόρα	(málista) (tha pyíte káti)?
Γιάννης	(tim) (thélis retsína) (i éna karafáki úzo)?
Tim	(málon éna karafáki) (ki éna bukáli neró)

2 Now read the conversation and answer the questions.

    a Will they have moussaka?

    b What kind of salad will they have?

    c What are they going to drink?

 3 Listen again and pay special attention to the words that run together. Practise speaking the part of Γιάννης and pay particular attention to your pronunciation.

Language discovery 1

1 The conversation includes four useful words for when you agree with somebody. Can you find them?

    a Fine! _____

    b OK! _____

    c Of course! _____

    d It goes without saying! _____

2 The conversation includes four expressions that are useful when you want to express uncertainty, disagreement, or need some extra time to think. Can you find them?

    a Oh! Just come to think of it. _____

    b I'd rather … (Perhaps …) _____

   c Just a moment! _____

   d Come on now! _____

3 The conversation includes three compound words, two words together in one. Can you find these three compound words and figure out what two words make up each one?

4 There are three words in this conversation that derive from the following words. Can you find the words and try to guess what the function of their new endings is?

   a ντολμάς _____

   b σουτζούκι _____

   c καράφα _____

Learn more

1 EXPRESSING AGREEMENT OR DISAGREEMENT

Agreeing and disagreeing is part of our daily life. This unit introduces you to some words and expressions, which can help you on these occasions. As said before, learn these words and expressions by heart. If you have done Exercises 1 and 2, you have probably come up with some of these words and phrases:

1 Expressing agreement: **Ναι!** *Yes!* (informal), **Αμέ!** *Yes!* (informal), **Πως!** *Yeah!* (informal), **Μάλιστα!** *Yes!* (formal), **Φυσικά!** *Naturally!,* **Βέβαια!** *Of course!,* **Ωραία!** *Good!,* **Κανένα πρόβλημα!** *No problem!,* **Σύμφωνοι!** *We agree (this way)!,* **Συμφωνώ!** *I agree!*

2 Expressing disagreement: **Ένα λεπτό!** *Just a moment!,* **Μισό λεπτό!** *Just a second!,* **Τι λες (τώρα);** *Is that your opinion?* or even *Are you serious (now)?,* **Έλα τώρα!** *Come on now!,* **Δε συμφωνώ!** *I don't agree!,* **Δε νομίζω!** *I don't think so!*

2 COMPOUND WORDS

Compared to some languages, such as German, Greek does not really have many compound words. However, English has considerably fewer compound words, when compared to Greek. In this unit, you have been introduced to a number of compound words. They are listed here for you:

Σπανακόριζο (**σπανάκι+ρύζι**) *spinach and rice,* **λαδολέμονο** (**λάδι+λεμόνι**) *oil and lemon,* **αγγουροντομάτα** (**αγγούρι+ντομάτα**) *cucumber and tomato,* **τιμοκατάλογος** (**τιμή+κατάλογος**) *price and menu,* **πατατοσαλάτα** (**πατάτα+σαλάτα**) *potato salad,* **ουζομεζέδες** (**ούζο+μεζέδες**) *ouzo snacks,* **φρουτοσαλάτα** (**φρούτο+σαλάτα**) *fruit salad,* **τονοσαλάτα** (**τόνος+σαλάτα**) *tuna salad.*

If you pay close attention to the last one or two letters of the first compound word in all examples above, you'll notice that when the compound word is formed, sometimes the letter **-ο** is needed in order to connect the two different words into one compound word. A letter, or letters might be deleted from the ending of the first word, before the formation of the compound word. As every other rule, this one has also some exceptions: **Δωδεκάνησα** (**δώδεκα+νησιά**) *12 islands,* **Επτάνησα** (**επτά+νησιά**) *seven islands,* **Πεντάγωνο** (**πέντε+γωνίες**) *Pentagon* (five corners).

3 DIMINUTIVE ENDINGS

You have already come across some words ending in **-άκι** such as **καραφάκι**, **ντολμαδάκι**, **σουτζουκάκι** and **σουβλάκι**. Some of these words might not be found in a dictionary because they are the diminutive form of main words. Here are some examples and the words they derive from:

η καράφα	*carafe*
το καραφάκι	*small carafe*
ο ντολμάς	*vine leaf stuffed with rice, minced meat and spices*
το ντολμαδάκι	*stuffed vine leaf as before but smaller in size*
το σουτζούκι	*sausage*
το σουτζουκάκι	*smaller sausage*
η σούβλα	*the whole or a big part of an animal on the spit*
το σουβλάκι	*some chunks of meat on the spit*

The three diminutive endings most commonly used in Greek are: **-άκι**, **-ούλα**, and **-ίτσα**. These correspond roughly to the English endings of *-let* and *-ing*: *book* → *booklet*, *drop* → *droplet*, *duck* → *duckling*.

These endings imply something 'smaller' or 'younger' especially in names. **Άννα** *Anne*, for example, becomes **Αννούλα** *little/young Anne, Annette*. They might also be used as a term of endearment, such as **Αννούλα** or **Νούλα** (for an older Anne). They are also used affectionately, without implying 'less quantity', for example **καφέ** *coffee* becomes **καφεδάκι**; **κρασί** *wine* becomes **κρασάκι**; **μπύρα** *beer* becomes **μπυρίτσα**.

Conversation 2

ΣΟΥΒΛΑΚΙ Η' ΓΥΡΟΣ; *SOUVLAKI OR GYROS?*

 NEW EXPRESSIONS

 04.06

ο/η ταμείας (o/i tamías)	*the cashier (m/f)*
το ποτήρι (to potíri)	*glass (n)*
μία πατάτες (mía patátes)	*a portion of chips (French fries)*
ορίστε! (oríste)!	*here you are! here you go!*
καλή σας όρεξη! (kalí sas óreksi)!	*bon appétit (to you)!*

 04.07 *Tim and Mary have discovered a souvlaki place in the centre of Athens and they often go there for a snack.*

1 **Listen to the conversation a couple of times. Which beer are they going to have: Heineken or Amstel?**

Tim	Γεια σας!
Ταμείας	Γεια σας! Τι θα πάρετε;
Tim	Ένα σουβλάκι Λωξάντρας, μία πατάτες και δύο μπύρες.
Ταμείας	Μπύρα σε ποτήρι ή μπουκάλι;
Tim	Μπύρα μπουκάλι. Έχετε Heineken;
Ταμείας	Μόνο Amstel.
Tim	Εντάξει, δύο Amstel. Πόσο κάνουν;
Ταμείας	Πέντε ευρώ (€5).
Tim	Ορίστε, ευχαριστώ.
Ταμείας	Καλή σας όρεξη!
Tim	(yásas)!
Ταμείας	(yásas)! (ti tha párete)?
Tim	(éna suvláki loksándras) (mía patátes) (ke THío bíres)
Ταμείας	(bíra se potíri) (i bukáli)?
Tim	(bíra bukáli) (éhete Heineken)?
Ταμείας	(móno Amstel)
Tim	(endáksi THío Amstel) (póso kánun)?
Ταμείας	(pénde evró)
Tim	(oríste, efharistó)
Ταμείας	(kalí sas óreksi)!

2 Now read the conversation and answer the questions.

  a Which words stand for glass and bottle in the conversation?

  b What are they finally going to get: draught or bottled beer?

  c Did you pick up the expression for *bon appétit* in the conversation?

 3 Listen again and pay special attention to the words that run together. Practise speaking the part of Tim and pay particular attention to your pronunciation.

Language discovery 2

  1 The conversation includes the word σας in two different expressions, one wish and one greeting. Can you find them? Do you think you can use the expressions without the word σας?

  a Bon appétit! _____

  b Hello! _____

  The word σας can be omitted in these two expressions. True or false? _____

  2 The conversation has only one of these two questions. Can you come up with the other?

  a How much is it? _____

  b How much are they? _____

Learn more

1 USING WISHES, GREETINGS, OR FAREWELLS

You have already learnt wishes like **Καλή όρεξη!** *Bon appétit!* or greetings like **Γεια!** *Hi!*, **Καλημέρα!** *Good morning!* and farewells like **Καληνύχτα!** *Good night!* For all these expressions and many others, Greek often makes use of the two pronouns, **σου** and **σας**, which signal formal or informal language and they can be used or omitted altogether in these expressions. Look at the table and try to grasp the fine nuances that distinguish the different versions.

General version (without particular emphasis)	Personal version (knowing someone well)	Formal version (showing someone respect)
Καλή όρεξη!	Καλή σου όρεξη!	Καλή σας όρεξη!
Bon appétit!	*Bon appétit (to you)!*	*Bon appétit! (to you)!*
Γεια!	Γεια σου!	Γεια σας!
Hi!/Hello!	*Hi (to you)! Hello (to you)!*	*Hi (to you)! Hello (to you)!*
Καληνύχτα!	Καληνύχτα σου!	Καληνύχτα σας!
Goodnight!	*Goodnight (to you)!*	*Goodnight (to you)!*

2 ASKING FOR THE PRICE

You will often be confronted with the task of asking for a price and of course, of understanding the answer. Make sure that you listen carefully, especially when it has to do with money, and do not hesitate to ask for the menu, price tag, or something else that can help you be on top of things. When asking for a price, you will have to distinguish whether you should use the singular form (one item) or the plural form (more than one item) of the question. The most important questions when asking for the price are:

Πόσο κάνει;	*How much is it?*
Πόσο κάνουν;	*How much are they?*
Πόσο είναι;	*How much is it? How much are they?*
Πόσο κοστίζει;	*How much does it cost?*
Πόσο κοστίζουν;	*How much do they cost?*

The words for **ευρώ** *euro* and **λεπτό – λεπτά** *cent(s)* are good to know, although you might not always hear them as they can be omitted.

3 NUMBERS 21–100

 04.08 **So far you have learnt the numbers 0–20. You can now practise the numbers 21–100. Listen carefully and repeat the numbers. You can try to say the numbers by heart after a couple of times.**

21	**είκοσι ένα** (eikosi éna)	30	**τριάντα** (triánda)
22	**είκοσι δύο** (íkosi THío)	31	**τριάντα ένα** (triánda éna)
23	**είκοσι τρία** (íkosi tría)	40	**σαράντα** (saránda)

50	**πενήντα** (penínda)	80	**ογδόντα** (oghTHónda)
60	**εξήντα** (eksínda)	90	**ενενήντα** (enenínda)
70	**εβδομήντα** (evTHomínda)	100	**εκατό** (ekató)

TIP

Have a short break now and challenge yourself with some numbers. Make a list of numbers that are significant in your life! Include your age (also the age of friends and family), your house number, your home and office telephone numbers, or even the numbers on your number plate.

4 UNDERSTANDING THE WAITER

In all different kinds of eateries, waiters often use similar questions and answers when waiting on customers. It will be helpful for you to practise and learn some of these expressions to assist you when placing an order. Notice the following examples.

Είστε έτοιμοι; / Είστε έτοιμες;	*Are you ready (to order)?*
Τι θέλετε παρακαλώ;	*What would you like (lit. do you want) please?*
Τι θα πάρετε παρακαλώ;	*What will you have please?*
Τι θα παραγγείλετε παρακαλώ;	*What would you like to order (lit. will you order) please?*
Τι θα πιείτε παρακαλώ;	*What would you like to drink (lit. will you drink) please?*
Τι θα φάτε;	*What would you like to drink (lit. will you drink)?*
Κάτι άλλο;/Τι άλλο;/Τίποτα άλλο;	*Anything else?*

Here are some additional useful expressions you may need when eating out:

Τον κατάλογο παρακαλώ!	*The menu please!*
Το λογαριασμό παρακαλώ!	*Can I pay please? (lit. The bill please!)*

Typical answers you might hear are:

Αμέσως!	*Right away!*
Έφτασε!	*I'll be right there! (lit. it's coming!)*

Conversation 3

ΣΤΟΝ ΠΑΓΚΟ *AT THE COUNTER*

 NEW EXPRESSIONS

 04.09

ο πάγκος (o pángos)	*the counter (m)*
απ' όλα (ap'óla)?	*everything on it?*
Τι είπατε; (ti ípate)?	*What did you say?*
μέσα στην πίτα (mésa stin pita)	*on (the pitta) (lit. in the pitta bread)*
απορρημένος/-η/-ο (aporiménos/-i/-o)	*confused*
το κρεμμύδι (to kremíTHi)	*the onion (n)*
και στα δύο; (ke sta THío)?	*in both?*
και … και … (ke … ke …)	*both … and …*

04.10 *Tim is trying to place the order but he can't quite understand one question.*

1 Which question baffles Tim?

Υπάλληλος	Απ'ό λα;
Tim	Τι; Τι είπατε;
Υπάλληλος	Θέλετε απ' όλα μέσα στην πίτα;
Tim	Δεν καταλαβαίνω.
Υπάλληλος	Θέλετε τζατζίκι, κρεμμύδι, ντομάτα;
Tim	Α! ναι, ναι!
Υπάλληλος	Και στα δύο; Και στο καλαμάκι και στον γύρο;
Tim	Ναι, ναι(;!).
Υπάλληλος	(ap'óla)?
Tim	(ti)? (ti ípate)?
Υπάλληλος	(thélete ap'óla) (mésa stin píta)?
Tim	(THen katalavéno)
Υπάλληλος	(thélete tzatzíki, kremíTHi, domáta)?
Tim	(a) (ne-ne)!
Υπάλληλος	(ke sta THío)? (ke sto kalamáki) (ke ston híro)?
Tim	(ne-ne)!?

2 Now read the conversation and answer the questions.

a When you order a γύρο with everything on it, what does it usually have on it?

b What's the difference between καλαμάκι and γύρο?

c Did you pick up the expression for *everything on it* in the conversation?

 3 Listen again and pay special attention to the words that run together. Practise speaking the part of Tim and pay particular attention to your pronunciation.

Language discovery 3

1 The conversation includes three expressions that can help you slow down people who speak too fast, or that you simply cannot follow. Can you find these expressions?

a I can't understand! _____

b What did you say? _____

c What? _____

2 What belongs together? Match up the expressions. You have already come across one expression in the conversation.

a …neither…nor…   **1** …ή…ή…

b …either…or…   **2** …και…και…

c …both…and…   **3** …ούτε…ούτε…

Learn more

1 USEFUL EXPRESSIONS TO SLOW DOWN NATIVE SPEAKERS

It is imperative for you to develop an active vocabulary which can slow down native speakers whenever you are confronted with speed, accent, or unknown vocabulary. These expressions will help in many different situations and will relieve you from confusing or frustrating moments in your early attempts to grasp and use Greek. Do not hesitate to repeat yourself using one of these expressions:

Πιο σιγά!	*Slower!*
Πιο αργά!	*Slower!*
Ξανά παρακαλώ!	*Again please!*
Πάλι παρακαλώ!	*Again please!*
Άλλη μια φορά παρακαλώ!	*One more time, please! Once again please!*
Δεν καταλαβαίνω!	*I don't understand!*
Δεν κατάλαβα!	*I didn't understand!*
Δεν (το) άκουσα!	*I didn't hear (that)!*
Τι είπες;/Τι'πες;	*What did you say?* (informal language)
Τι είπατε;/Τι'πατε;	*What did you say?* (formal language)
Τι;	*What?*

2 GIVING AN ANSWER WHEN YOU HAVE AN OPTION

Exercise 2 introduced you to three useful expressions that you can use when you have an option in your reply:

Ποιος θέλει 100 ευρώ; – Δε θυμάμαι. Ή ο Κώστας ή η Νίκη.

Who wants 100 euros? – I can't remember. Either Kostas or Niki.

Αυτός είναι ο Γιώργος ή ο Γιάννης; – Αυτός δεν είναι ούτε ο Γιώργος ούτε ο Γιάννης!

Is this George or John? – This is neither George nor John!

Σ'αρέσει η Μαρία ή η Ελένη; – Μ'αρέσει και η Μαρία και η Ελένη!

Do you like Maria or Helen? – I like both Maria and Helen!

Practice

1 Can you respond to the following situations?

  a Say *Bon appétit!* to someone at the beginning of a meal.

  b You are not sure whether a restaurant has a specific dish or not. How could you ask for an aubergine salad and a platter of assorted appetizers to accompany your ouzo order?

  c Ask for the menu and the bill.

  d How would you ask *What would you like to drink?*

e How would you ask for a small bottle of ouzo 'Mitilinis'?

f How do you say *Come on now!*?

g Ask the following questions: *How much is it?* and *How much are they?*

2 Match each question with the most appropriate answer.

a Τι είναι αυτά;

b Έχετε γύρο;

c Τι θα παραγγείλετε;

d Τι θέλετε παρακαλώ;

1 Δύο μπύρες και μία κόκα κόλα.

2 Δεν καταλαβαίνω! Ξανά σας παρακαλώ!

3 Βεβαίως! Απ' όλα;

4 Ποικιλία και ουζομεζέδες.

 3 04.11 **Rearrange these lines to make up a dialogue. Then listen and check your answers. At the end listen once again and repeat what you hear.**

a Τίποτα! Μόνο νερό! Ευχαριστούμε.

b Τι θα πιείτε;

c Τι θα πάρετε;

d Μία σαλάτα εποχής.

e Είστε έτοιμοι;

f Βέβαια!

4 Complete the following dialogue.

Σερβιτόρος	Τι θα πάρετε παρακαλώ;
You	**a** *The menu, please.*
Σερβιτόρος	Είστε έτοιμοι τώρα;
You	**b** *Yes. Have you got any potato salad?*
Σερβιτόρος	Δυστυχώς όχι. Μόνο σπανακόρυζο και αγγουροντομάτα σήμερα.
You	**c** *OK! A spinach-rice, a moussaka, and a seasonal salad.*
Σερβιτόρος	Θα πιείτε τίποτα;
You	**d** *A small bottle of ouzo. What kinds of ouzo do you have?*
Σερβιτόρος	12, Τσάνταλη ή Μυτιλήνης.
You	**e** *A small bottle of Mitilinis.*
Σερβιτόρος	Τίποτα άλλο;
You	**f** *Nothing else for the time being.*

5 You are in a pizza restaurant in Greece. Look at the menu. Can you recognize and match up the ingredients, before you place your order?

a πράσινες πιπεριές

b τόνος

c μπέικον

d πεπερόνι

e φρέσκια τομάτα

f μοτσαρέλλα

g τσένταρ

1 pepperoni

2 fresh tomato

3 green peppers

4 tuna

5 bacon

6 Monterrey Jack

7 mozzarella

h	μοντερέυ τζακ	8	green salad
i	πράσινη σαλάτα	9	chef's salad
j	σαλάτα σεφ	10	cheddar

You have decided on a Greek Lover's pizza. Do you understand most of the ingredients? Compare your answers to the Answer Key.

PIZZA SPECIALITIES

	ΜΙΚΡΟ	ΜΕΣΑΙΟ	ΟΙΚΟΓΕΝΕΙΑΚΟ
SUPREME: Μοτσαρέλλα, πεπερόνι, μοσχάρι, πράσινη πιπεριά, κρεμμύδι και μανιτάρια	4€	6.50€	7.00€
SUPER SUPREME: Μοτσαρέλλα, χοιρινό με μπαχαρικά, πιπερόνι, μοσχάρι, ζαμπόν, πράσινη πιπεριά, κρεμμύδι, μαύρες ελιές και μανιτάρια	4€	6.50€	7.00€
CHICKEN SUPREME: Μοτσαρέλλα, κοτό πουλο, κρεμμύδι, πράσινη πίπεριά και μανιτάρια	4€	6.50€	7.00€
CHEESE LOVER'S: Η πίτσα με το σπέσιαλ μείγμα μας από 3 τυριά, μοτσαρέλλα, τσένταρ, μοντερέυ τζακ, συν δύο από τα υλικά που προτιμάτε	4€	6.50€	7.00€
GREEK LOVER'S: Μοτσαρέλλα, φρέσκια ντομάτα, φέτα, μαύρες ελιές, πράσινη πιπεριά, κρεμμύδι, ρίγανη, πεπερόνι, μανιτάρια και το σπέσιαλ μείγμα μας από 3 τυριά	4€	6.50€	7.00€

6 04.12 **Χωριάτικη σαλάτα** is probably the most popular salad in Greece. It is a tossed salad consisting of the following ingredients. Listen carefully and complete the crossword puzzle.

a olives
b feta cheese
c tomatoes
d onions
e peppers
f cucumbers
g vinegar
h oil

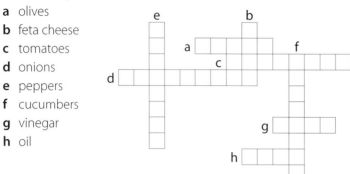

 7 04.13 Listen to the conversation and find the missing words. If you want, find the missing words first and then listen and compare your answers.

Υπάλληλος	Απ' όλα;
Tim	Τι; Τι **a** _____;
Υπάλληλος	**b** _____ απ' όλα **c** _____ στην πίτα;
Tim	Δεν **d** _____
Υπάλληλος	**b** _____, τζατζίκι, κρεμμύδι,
	e _____;
Tim	Α, ναι, ναι!
Υπάλληλος	Και στα δύο; **f** _____ στο καλαμάκι **f** _____ στο γύρο;
Tim	Ναι, ναι (;!).

ντομάτα	μέσα	είπατε
καταλαβαίνω	και	θέλετε

1 Can you remember the Greek for the following ten important words from this unit?

a	menu	**f**	tomato
b	bottle	**g**	chicken
c	glass	**h**	ten
d	chips/French fries	**i**	twenty
e	bill	**j**	thirty

2 Can you remember the Greek for the following ten important phrases from this unit?

a	Bon appétit!	**f**	A bottle of water.
b	It's all in Greek!	**g**	Do you want retsina?
c	It's all in English!	**h**	(Can I have) the bill please?
d	I'll order for you!	**i**	How much are they?
e	I want stuffed peppers.	**j**	How much is it?

3 Can you give a possible answer to these five questions?

a Να πάρουμε μία ποικιλία;

b Θέλεις ρετσίνα ή ένα καραφάκι ούζο;

c Τι είπατε;

d Θέλετε απ' όλα στο γύρο;

e Θα πιείτε κάτι;

SELF CHECK

	I CAN...
⚪	. . . name some Greek appetizers, salads, and main dishes.
⚪	. . . name some ingredients.
⚪	. . . read and understand many things on a menu.
⚪	. . . ask for or understand the price of certain items.
⚪	. . . ask for the menu and place an order.
⚪	. . . express agreement or disagreement with somebody or about something.
⚪	. . . use compound or diminutive words.
⚪	. . . understand and use the numbers 21–100.
⚪	. . . use useful expressions to slow down native speakers.

Revision test 1

In this unit you will review:

▶ *Greek greetings.*
▶ *introductions.*
▶ *common daily activities.*
▶ *food and drink.*
▶ *numbers.*
▶ *cities, countries and languages.*

> **TIP**
>
> Check your progress so far. Once you have completed the following exercises, compare your answers with the correct ones in the Answer Key. Identify any areas that still need some work and go over them again before you start the next unit.

 1 Respond to the following situations in Greek.

   a You are tasting Greek coffee for the first time. Give your opinion by saying *It's excellent!* or *It's awful!*.

   b Ask for the menu or the bill.

   c Ask for a medium, sweet or black Greek coffee.

   d Ask for a tea with milk or tea with lemon.

   e A friend tells you Έλα να πιούμε ένα ουζάκι. What will you do?

   f A friend asks you Πάμε σε μια ψαροταβέρνα; Where does he or she want you to go?

   g You would like a light breakfast. Ask for some toast with butter and marmalade.

   h You look tired. Say to a friend that you are tired because you didn't sleep at all.

   i You have been asked: Θα πάμε σινεμά ή όχι; What does it mean and how could you answer?

   j Someone asks you: Πού μένετε τώρα;. What does he or she want to know? How will you answer?

 2 04.14 **Rearrange these lines to make a dialogue. First, try ... without listening to the audio.**

   a Και πού μένεις;

   b Δεν είμαι πολύ καλά σήμερα.

   c Γιατί; Τι έχεις;

   d Εγώ μένω με τη Μονίκ από το Παρίσι. Πάμε για ένα ουζάκι;

   e Δεν το πιστεύω. Έχεις μόνο δύο μέρες στην Αθήνα και . . .

   f Πώς πας; Είσαι καλά;

   g Το ξέρω . . . αλλά χαίρομαι που είμαι εδώ.

   h Ναι. Νομίζω είναι καλό για τον πόνο.

i Έχω εδώ ένα πόνο.

j Τώρα μένω με μία άλλη Γερμανίδα στο κέντρο. Εσύ;

3 Read the conversation in Exercise 2 once again and find the following expressions.

    a it is good for the pain _____

    b in the centre _____

    c I'm not very well _____

    d How are you doing? _____

    e Are you doing alright? _____

    f I've been two days _____

    g I've got a pain here _____

    h I'm glad to be here _____

4 04.15 **Listen to the conversation again and pay special attention to the words that run together. Practise speaking the part of the first speaker and pay particular attention to your pronunciation. Make a list of the words you find most challenging to pronounce. Then, compare your list with the following.**

σήμερα

ουζάκι

πιστεύω

χαίρομαι

Γερμανίδα

5 Singular or plural? You have learned a lot of words in the singular and plural forms in the first four units. Can you find the missing singular or plural forms?

Singular	Plural
a _____	μπουκάλια
b γλώσσα	_____
c χυμός	_____
d φρυγανιά	_____
e _____	κατάλογοι
f δωμάτιο	_____
g _____	μέρες
h ουζάκι	_____
i μεζές	_____
j _____	ποικιλίες
k ομελέτα	_____
l ούζο	_____
m _____	μαθήματα
n _____	συνάδελφοι

6 Masculine, feminine or neuter? You have probably realized how important it is to know the articles of Greek nouns. Test your memory; which of the words in the box are masculine, feminine and neuter. To help you, there are five of each gender.

> πρόγραμμα μέρα μουσείο
> χυμός λάθος νύχτα καφές
> τυρόπιτα ξενοδοχείο ταξίδι
> ταβέρνα μεζές πόλη
> πόνος κατάλογος

7 Here is a list of 26 countries. Can you make out the names for *Great Britain*, *Ireland*, *Australia*, *France* and *Spain*? How many more can you recognize before looking at the answers?

a ΑΥΣΤΡΑΛΙΑ
b ΙΡΛΑΝΔΙΑ
c ΟΛΛΑΝΔΙΑ
d ΑΥΣΤΡΙΑ
e ΙΣΠΑΝΙΑ
f ΟΥΓΓΑΡΙΑ
g ΒΕΛΓΙΟ
h ΙΤΑΛΙΑ
i ΠΟΡΤΟΓΑΛΙΑ

j ΓΑΛΛΙΑ
k ΚΥΠΡΟΣ
l ΕΛΛΑΔΑ
m ΓΕΡΜΑΝΙΑ
n ΛΟΥΞΕΜΒΟΥΡΓΟ
o ΣΟΥΗΔΙΑ
p ΓΙΒΡΑΛΤΑΡ
q ΜΑΡΟΚΟ
r ΤΑΫΛΑΝΔΗ

s ΔΑΝΙΑ
t ΜΕΓΑΛΗ ΒΡΕΤΑΝΙΑ
u ΤΟΥΡΚΙΑ
v ΕΛΒΕΤΙΑ
w ΝΟΡΒΗΓΙΑ
x ΦΙΝΛΑΝΔΙΑ
y ΕΣΘΟΝΙΑ
z ΝΟΤΙΑ ΑΦΡΙΚΗ

8 Ordering a souvlaki. You are with some friends at the ΠΙΤΤΑ ΠΑΝ (*Pitta Pan*) a souvlaki place somewhere in Greece. You order the following:

one item under ΠΙΤΤΑ ΠΑΡΑΔΟΣΙΑΚΗ (Traditional pitta) _____

two items under ΠΙΤΤΑ ΧΩΡΙΑΤΙΚΗ (Villager's pitta) _____

three items under ΕΛΛΗΝΙΚΕΣ ΝΟΣΤΙΜΙΕΣ (Greek specialities) _____

one small and two large bottles of beer _____

9 Look at the menu once again. Can you find the Greek for the following words?

a draught beer _____
b village _____
c portion _____
d price list _____
e small _____
f big _____
g non-alcoholic beverages _____
h since _____

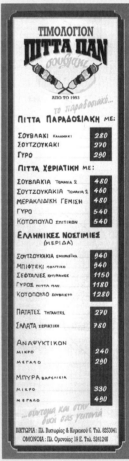

10 Reading Greek. Here is a label from everyday Athenian life. Can you make out its message?

11 Here is a list of the ten largest cities in the world in 1995 and a projection of the ten largest cities in 2015. The numbers represent millions of inhabitants. Can you make out the names of the cities and the countries?

ΟΙ 10 ΠΟΛΥΠΛΗΘΕΣΤΕΡΕΣ ΠΟΛΕΙΣ

Σε εκατομμύρια κατοίκους

1995		2015	
Τόκιο (Ιαπωνία)	26,8	Τόκιο (Ιαπωνία)	28,7
Σάο Πάολο (Βραζιλία)	16,4	Βομβάη (Ινδία)	27,4
Νέα Υόρκη (ΗΠΑ)	16,3	Λάγος (Νιγηρία)	24,4
Πόλη του Μεξικού	15,6	Σαγκάη (Κίνα)	23,4
Βομβάη (Ινδία)	15,1	Τζακάρτα (Ινδονησία)	21,2
Σαγκάη (Κίνα)	15,1	Σάο Πάολο (Βραζιλία)	20,8
Λος Αντζελες (ΗΠΑ)	12,4	Καράτσι (Πακιστάν)	20,6
Πεκίνο (Κίνα)	12,4	Πεκίνο (Κίνα)	19,4
Καλκούτα (Ινδία)	11,7	Ντάκα (Μπαγκλαντές)	19,0
Σεούλ (Νότιος Κορέα)	11,6	Πόλη του Μεξικού	18,8

Πηγή: Ηνωμένα Εθνη

(*Source:* United Nations)

12 Foreign languages. Greeks often ask what languages you speak. Here is an advertisement for language-learning courses. What languages can you recognize?

ΓΛΩΣΣΕΣ ΠΟΥ ΜΠΟΡΕΙΤΕ ΝΑ ΜΑΘΕΤΕ . . .		
❏ Αγγλικά για business	❏ Ελληνικά για ξένους	❏ Κορεάτικα
❏ Αγγλικά για αρχαρίους	❏ Εβραϊκά	❏ Μαλαισιακά
❏ Αγγλικά για προχωρημένους	❏ Ιαπωνικά	❏ Νορβηγικά
❏ Αραβικά	❏ Ινδονησιακά	❏ Ολλανδικά
❏ Αφρικάνικα	❏ Ινδικά	❏ Πολωνικά
❏ Γαλλικά για αρχαρίους	❏ Ιρλανδικά	❏ Πορτογαλικά
❏ Γαλλλικά για προχωρημένους	❏ Ισλανδικά	❏ Ρωσικά
❏ Γερμανικά για αρχαρίους	❏ Ισπανικά	❏ Σερβοκροάτικα
❏ Γερμανικά για ημιπροχωρημένους	❏ Ισπανικά Λατινικής Αμερικής	❏ Σουηδικά
❏ Γερμανικά για προχωρημένους	❏ Ιταλικά	❏ Ταϋλανδικά
❏ Δανέζικα	❏ Κινέζικα	❏ Φινλανδικά

13 Now, match the two columns. The words come from the previous question.

a for beginners   **1** Λατινική Αμερική

b for intermediate learners   **2** για ξένους

c for advanced learners   **3** για ημιπροχωρημένους

d for foreigners   **4** για προχωρημένους

e Latin America   **5** για αρχαρίους

 14 04.16 Two friends place an order at a hamburger place. Listen to the conversation a couple of times and find the missing words that are provided in the box.

Υπάλληλος	Έχετε **a** _____ ;
Νίκος	Όχι. Θα ήθελα ένα χάμπουργκερ με τυρί, τηγανιτές **b** _____ και μία κόκα κόλα μικρό **c** _____ .
Γιάννης	Εγώ θέλω να **d** _____ κάτι. Τι έχει το Greenburger μέσα;
Υπάλληλος	Έχει αγγουράκι πίκλα, **e** _____ , ντομάτα, πράσινη **f** _____ και dressing.
Γιάννης	Εντάξει, ένα Greenburger γεύμα για **g** _____ με 7up και ένα club σάντουϊτς για την Τόνια.
Υπάλληλος	Δεν **h** _____ 7up μόνο Sprite.
Γιάννης	Εντάξει, Sprite τότε …

> έχουμε   πατάτες   μένα
> σαλάτα   ρωτήσω   μέγεθος
> εξυπηρετηθεί   κρεμμύδι

15 Go over the conversation in the previous activity once again and find the following expressions and phrases.

   a What does the Greenburger come with?

   b I'd like a cheese burger with chips.

   c Have you been waited on?

   d OK, Sprite then …

   e … and a small coke.

   f I want to ask something.

16 Listen to this last conversation once again and practise speaking the part of Γιάννης. Pay particular attention to your pronunciation of the following words. Then translate them into English.

   a Εγώ _____

   b θέλω _____

   c ρωτήσω _____

   d κάτι _____

   e μέσα _____

   f Εντάξει _____

   g γεύμα _____

   h σάντουϊτς _____

17 Read the following conversation between two people who meet at a party and decide whether the statements are true or false.

Άρης	Συγνώμη, είσαι Ιταλίδα;
Σούζαν	Όχι. Είμαι Αγγλίδα. Εσύ από πού είσαι;
Άρης	Από την Αθήνα αλλά τώρα μένω στη Ρόδο. Εσύ;
Σούζαν	Εγώ είμαι από το Μπούξτον κοντά στο Μάντσεστερ.
Άρης	Μιλάς ωραία Ελληνικά. Μπράβο!
Σούζαν	Σε ευχαριστώ. Εσύ ξέρεις Αγγλικά;
Άρης	Ναι, βέβαια! Θέλεις να πιούμε ένα ουζάκι;
Σούζαν	Καλή ιδέα! Πίνεις ούζο με λεμονάδα;
Άρης	Τι; Τι λες τώρα; Ούζο με λεμονάδα; Απαίσιο!

                                                                  True   False

   a Η Σούζαν είναι Ιταλίδα.   _____ _____

   b Ο Άρης είναι Έλληνας.   _____ _____

   c Η Σούζαν μένει στο Μάντσεστερ.   _____ _____

   d Ο Άρης μιλάει Αγγλικά.   _____ _____

   e Ο Άρης πίνει ούζο με λεμονάδα.   _____ _____

   f Η Σούζαν δεν πίνει ούζο με λεμονάδα. _____ _____

18 Read the conversation once again and find the following phrases or expressions.

   a You speak good Greek.

   b That's a good idea!

   c I'm from Buxton, close to Manchester.

   d What are you talking about now?

   e Excuse me, are you Italian?

   f Do you want us to have a glass of ouzo?

19 Complete the following dialogue.

Σερβιτόρος	Τι θα πάρετε παρακαλώ;
You	**a** *The menu, please.*
Σερβιτόρος	Είστε έτοιμοι τώρα;
You	**b** *Yes. Have you got a tzatziki and an aubergine salad?*
Σερβιτόρος	Δυστυχώς όχι. Μόνο σπανακόριζο και αγγουροντομάτα σήμερα.
You	**c** *Don't you have a seasonal salad?*
Σερβιτόρος	Όχι, μόνο σπανακόριζο και αγγουροντομάτα! θα πιείτε τίποτα;
You	**d** *A small bottle of ouzo. What kinds of ouzo do you have?*
Σερβιτόρος	12, Τσάνταλη ή Μυτιλήνης.
You	**e** *A small bottle of Mitilinis.*
Σερβιτόρος	Τίποτα άλλο;
You	**f** *Nothing else for the time being.*

Πού είναι η Ακρόπολη;

Where is the Acropolis?

In this unit you will learn how to:

▶ *ask for directions.*
▶ *understand simple instructions.*
▶ *find your way around.*
▶ *count from 101 to 1,000.*

CEFR: (A1) *Can ask for/or give directions. Can understand simple instructions. Can find my way around. Can talk about means of transport. Can count from 101 to 1,000.* **(A2)** *Can use synonyms and opposites to say something. Can use time adverbials to express myself in time frames. Can understand or use the names of places or shops around town.*

Μέσα μεταφοράς *Greek public transport*

The busiest **αεροδρόμιο** or **αερολιμένας** *airport* is **Ελευθέριος Βενιζέλος** in Athens. The Athens Underground (**το Μετρό της Αθήνας** or **Υπόγειος** or **Ηλεκτρικός**) is being extended. The original line connects **το Λιμάνι Πειραιά** *Piraeus harbour* with **Κηφισιά** the northern suburbs of the city. The two new lines reach many Athenian suburbs.

The **εκδοτήρια εισιτηρίων** *ticket booths* are small, one-manned, self-standing booths centrally located throughout the city where single tickets, packs of ten tickets or **μηνιαία κάρτα** *monthly cards* are for sale. Neither taxi nor bus journeys are expensive, compared to many other cities in Europe and you are guaranteed a memorable experience that you might, or might not, want to repeat!

---

1 Without looking at the text, can you remember the different ways to say *airport* and *underground*?

Vocabulary builder

ΜΕΣΑ ΜΕΤΑΦΟΡΑΣ *MEANS OF TRANSPORT*

1 05.01 **These means of transport are all useful in and around Athens. Listen carefully and repeat.**

με τα πόδια	*on foot*
με το λεωφορείο	*by bus*
με το τρόλεϊ	*by tram*
με το πούλμαν	*by coach*
με το τρένο	*by train*

με τη βάρκα	*by boat*
με το πλοίο	*by ship*
με το καράβι	*by ship*
με το αεροπλάνο	*by plane*
με το ποδήλατο	*by bicycle*
με το μηχανάκι	*by motorcycle*

Years ago you would have gone:

με το γαϊδούρι	*by donkey*
με το άλογο	*by horse*

CULTURE TIP

Travelling **με το ταξί** *by taxi* is another popular way of travelling in Greece, but in Athens particularly this can be a memorable experience because:

▶ a taxi won't always stop when you hail. Shout your destination point as the taxi slows down!

▶ you'll often have to share a taxi with other passengers!

▶ a taxi might not take you exactly to where you want to go, but drop you off at the closest point en route!

Although nowadays things have much improved, it does not hurt to keep an eye out. Most taxi drivers speak English and are helpful.

In other cities and in smaller towns the taxi situation is much better, with taxi ranks at designated and central points, but usually there are not enough taxis to cope with the high-season influx of tourists.

ΧΡΟΝΙΚΑ ΕΠΙΡΡΗΜΑΤΑ *ADVERBS OF TIME*

 2 05.02 **You are going to hear some people telling you how they get to work. Listen carefully and number the sentences from 1 to 6 as you hear the descriptions. Then listen again and repeat.**

a ___ Εγώ πάω πάντα με το λεωφορείο στη δουλειά.

b ___ Εγώ παίρνω το τρένο για τη δουλειά.

c ___ Εγώ πάω συχνά με τα πόδια.

d ___ Εγώ παίρνω ταξί πολλές φορές στη δουλειά.

e ___ Σπάνια πάω με το ποδήλατο αλλά σχεδόν πάντα με το μηχανάκι.

f ___ Κάθε μέρα πάω στη δουλειά με το αυτοκίνητο.

3 **Read the sentences once again and try to find the following adverbs of time.**

a always _____

b almost always _____

c often _____

d many times _____

e rarely _____

f every day _____

Conversation 1

ΠΟΥ ΕΙΝΑΙ Η ΑΚΡΟΠΟΛΗ; *WHERE IS THE ACROPOLIS?*

 NEW EXPRESSIONS

 05.03

ο Αθηναίος	*the Athenian*
συγγνώμη	*excuse me*
πάτε με τα πόδια;	*are you going on foot?*
με λεωφορείο	*by bus*
μακριά	*far*
τουλάχιστον	*at least*
δε μας πειράζει να περπατάμε	*we don't mind walking*
μας αρέσει να κάνουμε βόλτες	*we like to take a stroll* (lit. *strolls*)
η γυμναστική	*the exercise* (lit. *gymnastics*)
μείνετε	*stay*
μέχρι	*until*
Στήλες του Ολυμπίου Διός	*Temple of Zeus* (lit. *Olympus Zeus's Columns*)
στο φανάρι	*at the traffic lights*
στρίψτε δεξιά	*turn right*
στο τέλος της ανηφόρας	*at the end of the uphill*
θα δείτε	*you will see*
αριστερά	*left*
στα δεξιά σας	*on your right*

 05.04 *Tim and Mary are having some difficulties finding the way to the Acropolis.*

1 Listen to the conversation a couple of times. How do they want to get there?

Tim	Συγγνώμη, πού είναι η Ακρόπολη;
Αθηναίος	Πάτε με τα πόδια ή με λεωφορείο;
Tim	Με τα πόδια. Είναι μακριά;
Αθηναίος	Όχι, δεν είναι μακριά. Είναι όμως τουλάχιστον δέκα (10) λεπτά με τα πόδια.
Mary	Εντάξει δε μας πειράζει να περπατάμε! Μας αρέσει να κάνουμε βόλτες με τα πόδια. Είναι καλή γυμναστική.
Αθηναίος	Τότε, μείνετε σ' αυτόν το δρόμο μέχρι τις Στήλες του Ολυμπίου Διός. Στο φανάρι στρίψτε δεξιά και στο τέλος της ανηφόρας θα δείτε την Ακρόπολη.
Mary	Δεξιά ή αριστερά;
Αθηναίος	Στα δεξιά σας.
Tim	Ευχαριστούμε πολύ.
Mary	Γεια σας!

2 Now read the conversation and answer the questions.

   a How far is the Acropolis from the place where they are?

   b Mary says 'It's good exercise.' What is she referring to?

   c Are they going to find the Acropolis on their left?

 3 Listen again to the conversation and pay special attention to the words that run together. Practise speaking the part of Tim or Mary and pay particular attention to your pronunciation.

Language discovery 1

1 The conversation has two impersonal verbs (verbs that do not have a person/object as a subject) with a particular conjugation. Can you find these verbs and guess whether the verb endings change when the verb is conjugated or not.

   a We mind … / We don't mind … _____

   b We like to … / We don't like to … _____

2 The conversation has two expressions in the genitive case. (This case indicates some kind of possession or ownership, for example, *John's car* **or** *the days of the week.*) **Can you find the following expressions and guess which word is masculine and which word is feminine genitive?**

   a Olympus Zeus's Columns (Columns of Olympus Zeus) _____

   b at the end of the uphill road _____

3 There are two imperative (command) forms in this conversation. Can you find these forms and guess whether the verbs have a new verb form or remain unchanged, as is the case in English.

   a Stay! (main verb form: μένω) _____

   b Turn! (main verb form: στρίβω) _____

Learn more

1 IMPERSONAL VERBS AND PERSONAL PRONOUNS

What is particular with these verbs, as already stated in Unit 3, is that the personal pronouns are needed because the verb form remains unchanged. If you compare the conjugation of the verb *to like* from Unit 3 with the verb *to mind* from this unit, you will quickly notice some differences in the use of the personal pronouns. In order not to make things more complicated, we can simply say that most Greek verbs are conjugated with the personal pronouns in nominative case, i.e. **εγώ κάνω** *I do/make*, not too many with personal pronouns in genitive case, i.e. **μου αρέσει** *I like*, and not too many with personal pronouns in accusative case, i.e. **με πειράζει** *I mind*. These three different cases do not officially exist in English, with the exception of *who, whose* and *whom*, and the best translation remains often the same for all three pronouns. Note the changes:

Personal Pronouns in Nominative	Personal Pronouns in Genitive	Personal Pronouns in Accusative
εγώ κάνω	μου αρέσει	με πειράζει
εσύ κάνεις	σου αρέσει	σε πειράζει
αυτός/-ή/-ό κάνει	του/της/του αρέσει	τον/την/το πειράζει
εμείς κάνουμε	μας αρέσει	μας πειράζει
εσείς κάνετε	σας αρέσει	σας πειράζει
αυτοί/-ές/-ά κάνουν	τους αρέσει	τους πειράζει

Read these examples and notice how these verbs are used in context.

Εγώ κάνω μπάνιο κάθε μέρα.   *I take a shower (lit. I make a bath) every day.*

Μου αρέσει πάρα πολύ ο   *I like frappé coffee a lot in the morning.*
φραπές το πρωί.

Δε με πειράζει καθόλου να   *I don't mind at all walking every day.*
περπατάω κάθε μέρα.

2 GENITIVE CASE IN NOUNS

The three Greek articles in genitive case are: **του** for masculine and neuter and **της** for feminine. What comes as a challenge, when using the genitive case of Greek nouns, is that the main noun form (what you find in a dictionary) changes. There are two different ways in English, either with the Saxon genitive's, e.g. *John's car*, or with a genitive using the preposition *of*, e.g. *the days of the week*. Greek has only one way to do this by using the article in the genitive case, **το αυτοκίνητο του Γιάννη** *John's car* (lit. *the car of John*) or **οι ημέρες της εβδομάδας** *the days of the week*. Useful information for this unit is that street, avenue, and square names are found in the genitive case in Greek, e.g. **Οδός Πανόρμου** *Panormou Street* (lit. *Street of Panormou*), **Λεωφόρος Βασιλίσης Σοφίας** *Queen Sofia Avenue* (lit. *Avenue of Queen Sofia*), **Πλατεία Καραϊσκάκη** *Karaiskaki Square* (*Square of Karaiskaki*). As mentioned before, learn these expressions as chunks, especially in your early steps to learn Greek.

3 IMPERATIVE FORMS

The imperative forms of Greek verbs are a bit more challenging compared to the English ones. There are usually two forms one has to learn: one when you give an order to a friend of yours, e.g. **έλα** *come*, **κάθισε** *sit down*, **φύγε** *go*, **μείνε** *stay*, **στρίψε** *turn* and one when you give an order to a group of people or one person but you want to show respect because of age, status, hierarchy, etc., for example **ελάτε** *come*, **καθίστε** *sit down*, **φύγετε** *go*, **μείνετε** *stay*, **στρίψτε** *turn*. These last two imperatives were found in the conversation above. Unfortunately, the translation remains the same for both Greek forms in English! We'll expand this list with useful imperatives when giving directions later on in this unit.

Conversation 2

ΜΕ ΣΥΓΧΩΡΕΙΤΕ ... *EXCUSE ME...*

 NEW EXPRESSIONS

 05.05

η Αθηναία	*the Athenian*
ο περαστικός	*the passer-by*
με συγχωρείτε	*I'm sorry/excuse me*
στην πρώτη γωνία	*on the first corner*
μπροστά σας!	*(directly) in front of you*
πιο σιγά	*slower*
στη γωνία	*on the corner*
να!	*there!* (showing something)
Δε βλέπετε;	*Can't you see?*

 05.06 *Tim and Mary are wondering if they have taken a wrong turning so they ask for directions again.*

1 **Listen to the conversation a couple of times. Are they still too far from the Acropolis?**

Tim	Με συγχωρείτε, ξέρετε πού είναι οι Στήλες του Ολυμπίου Διός;
Αθηναία	Ναι βέβαια, είστε πολύ κοντά. Στρίψτε στην πρώτη γωνία δεξιά και θα δείτε τις Στήλες του Ολυμπίου Διός μπροστά σας.
Tim	Δεν καταλαβαίνω καλά Ελληνικά. Μιλάτε λίγο πιο σιγά;
Αθηναία	Ναι βέβαια. Στη γωνία, δεξιά. Δεξιά, καταλαβαίνετε; Μετά οι Στήλες είναι κοντά, πολύ κοντά, καταλαβαίνετε;
Tim	Ναι, ναι, καταλαβαίνω. Ευχαριστώ.
	Σε λίγο ...
Mary	Συγγνώμη, πού είναι οι Στήλες του Ολυμπίου Διός;
Περαστικός	Να! Δε βλέπετε; Εδώ μπροστά σας!

2 **Now read the conversation and answer the questions.**
   a What are they looking for in this specific conversation: the Acropolis or the Zeus Temple?
   b What phrases does Tim use to slow down the passer-by?
   c Both people have used the phrase μπροστά σας . What does it mean?

 3 **Listen to the conversation again now and pay special attention to the words that run together. Practise speaking the part of Tim and pay particular attention to your pronunciation.**

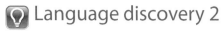 Language discovery 2

1 You have already learnt the antonyms or synonyms of expressions that were presented in this conversation. Can you find the previously studied synonyms or antonyms?

   a Με συγχωρείτε… _____

   b Παρακαλώ! _____

   c Πιο αργά … _____

   d μακριά _____

   e πίσω σας _____

2 The conversation has five verbs in the second person plural simple tense. Can you find them and decide which two verbs have a different verb ending compared to the other three?

   a …you see… _____

   b …you know… _____

   c …you understand… _____

   d …you excuse… _____

   e …you speak… _____

Learn more

1 DIFFERENT VERB CATEGORIES

You have already learnt some different verb categories. To remind you of these categories:

▸ Verb group 1: verbs like **μένω** and **ξέρω** (see Unit 1).

▸ Verb group 2: verbs like **είμαι, θυμάμαι** or **χαίρομαι** (see Unit 2).

▸ Verb group 3: verbs like **μου αρέσει** and **με πειράζει** (see this unit).

Now we'd like to bring your attention to a new verb group, with two verbs found in this last conversation: **συγχωρώ** *to excuse* and **μιλάω/μιλώ** *to speak*. The endings in this particular group resemble the endings from Group 1, apart from minor changes, so this should not be a problem for you. Here is a full conjugation of these two verbs. The second verb has some alternative, possible forms.

συγχωρώ, συγχωρείς, συγχωρεί, συγχωρούμε, συγχωρείτε, συγχωρούν

μιλάω/μιλώ, μιλάς, μιλάει/μιλά, μιλάμε, μιλάτε, μιλάν(ε)/μιλούν(ε)

What is important for you to remember is that most Greek verbs end in **-ω**. This means that Verb group 1 above includes more than 60% of all Greek verbs, Verb groups 2 and 3 no more than 15%, which leaves us with 25% for group 4 (verbs like **συγχωρώ** *to excuse* and **μιλάω/μιλώ** *to speak*) and for group 5 (any irregular verbs). We have deliberately decided to simplify the Greek verbs into only five major groups instead of presenting you with several sub-categories that extend this number to more than 65!

2 USING SYNONYMS AND ANTONYMS

Do not forget the value of synonyms and antonyms (opposites) while learning Greek. This unit, but also past units, has introduced you to a number of word sets. Take this opportunity and make some flash cards where you can practise these sets. When you learn some synonyms you might be able to express yourself even if certain words have slipped your mind. So go ahead and make some flash cards! What are you waiting for?

Conversation 3

ΜΠΡΟΣΤΑ ΣΤΗΝ ΑΚΡΟΠΟΛΗ *IN FRONT OF THE ACROPOLIS*

 NEW EXPRESSIONS

 05.07

η είσοδος	the entrance
εκεί πάνω!	over there!
ανεβείτε	go up
το σκαλοπάτι	the step
κουρασμένος	tired
απλά (aplá)	simply
από εδώ	from here
πίσω από	behind
αυτά τα δέντρα	these trees
πενήντα (50) μέτρα	50 metres
επιτέλους!	at last!
φτάσαμε	we arrived
αντέχω	I stand
δεν αντέχω την πολλή ζέστη	I can't stand too much heat
αλήθεια!	really!/that's true!
κάνει πολύ ζέστη	it is very hot

 05.08 *Tim and Mary are next to the Acropolis entrance.*

1 Why can't they see it? Listen to the conversation carefully a couple of times before you give your answer.

Mary	Συγγνώμη, πού είναι η είσοδος για την Ακρόπολη;
Αθηναίος	Εκεί πάνω! Ανεβείτε αυτά τα σκαλοπάτια. Στο τέλος θα δείτε την είσοδο.
Mary	Είναι μακριά; Είμαστε ήδη πολύ κουρασμένοι …
Αθηναίος	Όχι. Είστε πολύ κοντά. Είστε μπροστά στην Ακρόπολη. Απλά δεν μπορείτε να δείτε την είσοδο από εδώ.
Tim	Τι είπατε;
Αθηναίος	Η είσοδος για την Ακρόπολη είναι πίσω από αυτά τα δέντρα. Είστε μόνο πενήντα (50) μέτρα από την είσοδο.
Mary	Ωραία! Επιτέλους φτάσαμε! Δεν αντέχω την πολύ ζέστη στην Αθήνα.
Αθηναίος	Αλήθεια! Κάνει πολύ ζέστη …

2 Now read the conversation and answer the questions.

    a Are they actually far from the Acropolis entrance?

    b Are they already tired? Who says what?

    c Is the entrance hidden behind some bushes or behind some trees?

 3 Listen again to the conversation and pay special attention to the words that run together. Practise speaking the part of Mary and pay particular attention to your pronunciation.

Language discovery 3

1 The word *entrance* **can be found four times in this conversation. Find these instances. Can you work out why the spellings are different?**

    a Where is the entrance… _____

    b You'll see the entrance… _____

    c The entrance for the … _____

    d 50 metres from the entrance _____

    e The reason for its different spelling is _____

2 The conversation makes use of useful vocabulary for giving directions. Can you find these expressions?

    a Over there! _____

    b At the end… _____

    c Is it far? _____

    d You are very close. _____

    e in front of _____

    f behind _____

    g 50 metres from _____

Learn more

1 ACCUSATIVE CASE IN NOUNS

The accusative case of Greek nouns is often used. This is because most Greek verbs and prepositions are followed by accusative. Hidden examples in this last conversation are:

Ανεβείτε αυτά τα σκαλοπάτια. (verb + accusative) **Στο τέλος θα δείτε την είσοδο.** (verb + accusative) **Είστε μπροστά στην Ακρόπολη.** (preposition + accusative) **Απλά δεν μπορείτε να δείτε την είσοδο από εδώ.** (verb + accusative) **Η είσοδος για την Ακρόπολη είναι πίσω από αυτά τα δέντρα.** (preposition + accusative) **Είστε μόνο πενήντα (50) μέτρα από την είσοδο.** (preposition + accusative) **Δεν αντέχω την πολύ ζέστη στην Αθήνα.** (verb + accusative)

The definite articles change correspondingly to:

Masculine: singular **o** → **τον**, plural **οι** → **τους**

Feminine: singular **η** → **την**, plural **οι** → **τις**

Neuter: singular **το** → **το**, plural **τα** → **τα**

2 GIVING OR UNDERSTANDING DIRECTIONS

Have a look at these verbs that are essential to giving or understanding directions.

you (informal)	you (formal)	
έλα	**ελάτε**	*come*
ανέβα	**ανεβείτε**	*go up*
κατέβα	**κατεβείτε**	*go down*
μείνε	**μείνετε**	*stay*
στρίψε	**στρίψτε**	*turn*
περπάτα	**περπατήστε**	*walk*
πήγαινε	**πηγαίνετε/πηγαίντε**	*go*
πάνε	**πάτε**	*go*
συνέχισε	**συνεχίστε**	*continue, carry on*
δείξε	**δείξτε**	*show*

The following words and phrases are important when giving or trying to understand directions.

στο φανάρι	*at the traffic lights*		
στο σταυροδρόμι	*at the crossroads/intersection*		
στο βάθος	*at the end (of a corridor)*		
στο τέλος	*at the end (of a street)*		
στο κέντρο	*at the centre (of a town/city)*		
εδώ	*here*	**εκεί**	*there*
πάνω	*over*	**κάτω**	*below*
εδώ πάνω	*over here*	**εδώ κάτω**	*down here*
εκεί πάνω	*over there*	**εκεί κάτω**	*down there*
(ε)μπρός	*in front of*	**πίσω**	*behind*
κοντά	*near/close to*	**μακριά**	*far away*
δίπλα	*next to*	**ανάμεσα**	*between*

στ'αριστερά
on the left

ευθεία, ίσια
straight ahead

στα δεξιά
on the right

The following expressions are also important:

… στρίψτε στην πρώτη γωνία (f)	*… turn at the first corner*
δεύτερη	*second*
τρίτη	*third*
τέταρτη	*fourth*
πέμπτη	*fifth*
… στρίψτε στον πρώτο δρόμο (m)	*… turn in to the first street*
δεύτερο	*second*
τρίτο	*third*
τέταρτο	*fourth*
πέμπτο	*fifth*
… στρίψτε στο πρώτο στενό (n)	*… turn in to the first side street*
δεύτερο	*second*
τρίτο	*third*
τέταρτο	*fourth*
πέμπτο	*fifth*

Notice the different articles (**ο**, **η**, **το**) before the nouns in the following questions.

Πού είναι ο Παρθενώνας; (m)	*Where is the Parthenon?*
ο σταθμός;	*the station?*
η Ακρόπολη; (f)	*the Acropolis?*
η πλατεία;	*the square?*
το κέντρο; (n)	*the centre?*
το σχολείο;	*the school?*

You will also find it useful to become familiar with the names of places and shops in town.

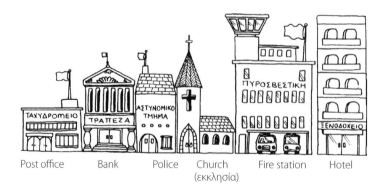

Post office   Bank   Police   Church   Fire station   Hotel
(εκκλησία)

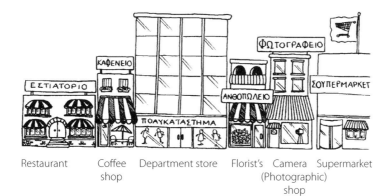

Restaurant	Coffee shop	Department store	Florist's	Camera (Photographic) shop	Supermarket

Fish shop	Greengrocer's	Butcher's	Beauty salon	Hospital	Chemist's

> **TIP**
>
> That was a long but very important presentation for this unit. One good idea is for you to draw some mind maps here. Take a small break before you do the final exercises and prepare a mind map of types of public transport, another one with places and shops around town and another one with the necessary verbs and verbal phrases for such conversations. When the mind maps are ready, check and see if you can say from memory 70% of the vocabulary listed. If not, use these vocabulary lists as reference points and come back to them as often as needed.

3 THE NUMBERS 101–1,000

 05.09 You are going to hear some numbers from 100 to 1,000. Listen carefully and repeat the numbers. Pay particular attention to your pronunciation.

100	**εκατό**
102	**εκατόν δύο**
151	**εκατόν πενήντα ένα**
200	**διακόσια/διακόσιοι/διακόσιες**
300	**τριακόσια/τριακόσιοι/τριακόσιες**
400	**τετρακόσια/τετρακόσιοι/τετρακόσιες**
500	**πεντακόσια/πεντακόσιοι/πεντακόσιες**
600	**εξακόσια/εξακόσιοι/εξακόσιες**
700	**επτακόσια/επτακόσιοι/επτακόσιες**

800	**οκτακόσια/οκτακόσιοι/οκτακόσιες**
900	**εννιακόσια/εννιακόσιοι/εννιακόσιες**
1,000	**χίλια/χίλιοι/χίλιες**

 Practice

 1 Respond to the following situations.

 a You would like to attract the attention of a passer-by. How would you say *I'm sorry* or *Excuse me*?

 b How would you ask *Where is the Apollo Hotel?*

 c You want to know if it is far or close by. How would you ask *Is it far?* or *Is it close by?*

 d Translate these directions into English: δεξιά, ευθεία, αριστερά and ίσια?

 e Which forms of transport are related to τρόλεϊ, λεωφορείο, ταξί?

 f A friendly local person has just given you instructions to get to where you want to go. How would you say goodbye and thank him for the advice?

 g You have some trouble following the directions given by another person; how would you say: *I don't understand Greek well. (Can you) speak more slowly?*

2 Match each question with the most appropriate answer.

 a Είναι μακριά ο Παρθενώνας; **1** Ναι, είναι κοντά.

 b Είναι κοντά η Ακρόπολη; **2** Όχι, δεν είναι μακριά.

 c Πού είναι το Ερέχθειο; **3** Το Ερέχθειο είναι στην Ακρόπολη.

 d Τι είναι το Ερέχθειο; **4** Δεν ξέρω.

3 05.10 Rearrange these lines to make a dialogue. Then listen to the audio and check your answers. At the end, listen once again and repeat everything, paying particular attention to your pronunciation.

 a Πάτε με τα πόδια;

 b Αυτό δεν είναι καλή γυμναστική.

 c Το ξέρουμε, αλλά δεν πειράζει!

 d Πάμε μία βόλτα στο κέντρο της Αθήνας.

 e Πού πάτε;

 f Όχι, πάμε με το αυτοκίνητο.

4 Complete the dialogue.

Αθηναίος	Συγγνώμη, πού είναι η πλατεία;
You	**a** *Stay on this street.*
Αθηναίος	Και μετά;
You	**b** *Then, turn left at/into the third back street.*
Αθηναίος	Και μετά, πού να πάω;
You	**c** *Then, continue straight on. The square is on the right.*
Αθηναίος	Ευχαριστώ πολύ.
You	**d** *You're welcome!*

5 Can you match the list on the left with the list on the right? Sometimes the associations might not be as obvious as you might expect.

a πόδια		**1**	auto(mobile)
b κέντρο		**2**	metres
c αυτο(κίνητο)		**3**	foot specialist (podiatrist)
d τρίτη γωνία		**4**	trolley
e μέτρα		**5**	gymnastics/exercise
f τρένο		**6**	trigonometry (three corners)
g τρόλεϊ		**7**	aeroplane
h ταξί		**8**	train
i αεροπλάνο		**9**	centre
j γυμναστική		**10**	taxi

6 Practise the different forms of Greek verbs that you have learnt so far. Select the correct form to complete the sentence.

a Μας αρέσει να _____ βόλτες.	κάνετε	κάνουμε	κάνουν
b _____ σ' αυτό το δρόμο!	Μείνει	Μείνετε	Μείνουν
c Πού _____ η πλατεία;	είμαι	είναι	είσαι
d Δεν _____ να δείτε την είσοδο από εδώ.	μπορείτε	μπορεί	μπορούμε
e Εγώ δεν _____ την ζέστη.	αντέχουμε	αντέχει	αντέχω
f _____ σιγά-σιγά!	Κατεβαίνει	Κατέβα	Κατεβαίνετε
g Δεν καταλαβαίνω. _____ λίγο πιο σιγά;	Μιλά	Μιλάει	Μιλάτε

7 05.11 Listen to Conversation 3 in this unit again and fill in the missing words. The box can help you further.

Mary	Συγγνώμη, πού είναι η **a** _____ για την Ακρόπολη;
Αθηναίος	Εκεί **b** _____. Ανεβείτε αυτά τα σκαλοπάτια. Στο **c** _____ θα δείτε την είσοδο.
Mary	Είναι **d** _____; Είμαστε **e** _____ πολύ **f** _____.
Αθηναίος	Όχι. **g** _____ πολύ κοντά. **g** _____ μπροστά στην Ακρόπολη. Απλά δεν **h** _____ να δείτε την είσοδο από εδώ.
Mary	Τι **i** _____;
Αθηναίος	Η είσοδος για την Ακρόπολη είναι πίσω από αυτά τα δέντρα. Είστε **j** _____ πενήντα (50) μέτρα από την είσοδο.
Mary	**k** _____. Επιτέλους φτάσαμε! Δεν **l** _____ την πολύ **m** _____ στην Αθήνα.
Αθηναίος	Αλήθεια! Κάνει πολύ **m** _____. . .

μπορείτε κουρασμένοι μόνο αντέχω
ήδη είσοδος πάνω ωραία
μακριά τέλος είστε ζέστη είπατε

8 Mary and Tim plan to see some interesting sights in Athens. Read the conversation they have with a friend of theirs and try to spot the following expressions from the text.

    a Do you want to come?

    b Where do you want to go?

    c We want to see …

    d How are we able to (can we) go?

    e You are able to (can) see …

    f Where can we start?

Tim	Θέλουμε να δούμε μερικά αξιοθέατα στην Αθήνα. Πώς μπορούμε να πάμε;
Φίλος	Πού θέλετε να πάτε;
Mary	Μας αρέσει ο Λυκαβηττός, η πλατεία Κολωνακίου και το Ζάππειο.
Φίλος	Αυτό είναι εύκολο. Μπορείτε να πάτε παντού με τα πόδια. Και είναι καλή γυμναστική, ειδικά πάνω στο Λυκαβηττό.
Mary	Από πού να ξεκινήσουμε;
Φίλος	Από το Ζάππειο. Μπορείτε να δείτε το Ζάππειο και να περπατήσετε μέσα στο πάρκο.
Mary	Έπειτα;
Φίλος	Γράφω εδώ στο χάρτη πώς να πάτε. Πρώτα στο Ζάππειο και στο πάρκο, μετά στην Πλατεία Κολωνακίου για έναν καφέ. Ίσως μέτριο, ε; Και ύστερα από εδώ (δείχνει στον χάρτη) περπατάτε προς το Λυκαβηττό.
Tim	Πολύ ωραία! Θέλεις να έρθεις;
Φίλος	Γιατί όχι;

9 Read the conversation again and answer the following questions.

    a Είναι τα αξιοθέατα στην Αθήνα;

    b Μπορούν να πάνε παντού με τα πόδια;

    c Είναι καλή γυμναστική να πάνε πάνω στο Λυκαβηττό;

    d Έχει το Ζάππειο πάρκο;

    e Θέλουν να δουν τα αξιοθέατα με τον φίλο τους;

    f Ο φίλος μπορεί να πάει;

10 Read the conversation once again and make a mind map this time. Try to include: a) places, b) expressions and c) verbs used when giving directions.

11 05.12 **Now listen to the next conversation a couple of times and pay special attention to the words which run together. Practise speaking the part of φίλος and pay particular attention to your pronunciation. At the end, listen once again and find the right sounds of the letter -υ.**

	like /i/	like /f/	like /u/
λυκαβηττός	_____	_____	_____
αυτό	_____	_____	_____
εύκολο	_____	_____	_____
γυμναστική	_____	_____	_____
πού	_____	_____	_____
ύστερα	_____	_____	_____
πολύ	_____	_____	_____

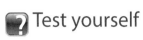 Test yourself

1 Can you remember the Greek for the following ten important words from this unit?

    a excuse me _____

    b here _____

    c far _____

    d there _____

    e left _____

    f entrance _____

    g right _____

    h square _____

    i corner _____

    j centre _____

2 Can you remember the following ten important phrases from this unit?

    a On foot. _____

    b At the traffic light _____

    c By bus. _____

    d It's good exercise! _____

    e Turn right/left. _____

    f I can't stand the heat! _____

    g I'm sorry… _____

    h We are very tired. _____

    i Where is the…? _____

    j It's very hot! _____

3 These five phrases use the formal way of addressing people. Can you change them into informal Greek?

    a Ελάτε εδώ! _____

    b Μείνετε εκεί! _____

    c Στρίψτε αριστερά! _____

    d Πηγαίντε ευθεία! _____

    e Συνεχίστε ίσια! _____

I CAN...
○ ... ask for/give directions.
○ ... understand simple instructions.
○ ... find my way around.
○ ... talk about means of transportation.
○ ... use synonyms and opposites in order to say something.
○ ... use time adverbials to express myself in time frames.
○ ... understand or use the names of places or shops around town.
○ ... count from 100–1,000.

6 Καλό ταξίδι!
Have a nice trip!

In this unit you will learn how to:
▶ *make travel arrangements.*
▶ *find out more about public transport.*
▶ *purchase tickets and make reservations.*
▶ *tell the time.*
▶ *count from 1,000 to 10,000.*

CEFR: (A1) *Can understand or say the names of the week. Can understand or tell the time. Can count from 1,000 to 10,000.* **(A2)** *Can thank or apologize to someone. Can make travel arrangements. Can find out about public transport. Can make reservations or buy tickets.*

 Εργάσιμες ημέρες *Working days*

There are five to six **εργάσιμες μέρες** *working days* in Greece. Working in an office will usually be **Δευτέρα** *Monday* to **Παρασκευή** *Friday* but working in a shop will be Monday to **Σάββατο** *Saturday*. The regular **ώρες εργασίας** *working hours* are between 9 and 10 o'clock **το πρωί** *in the morning* to about 3 o'clock **το απόγευμα** *in the afternoon* Mondays, **Τετάρτες** *Wednesdays* and **Σάββατα** *Saturdays*. On **Τρίτες** *Tuesdays*, **Πέμπτες** *Thursdays* and **Παρασκευές** *Fridays*, there is a siesta between 2 and 5 p.m. and then it's work again until 8 or 9 o'clock **το βράδυ**. The big **εμπορικά κέντρα** *shopping centres* are usually open from 10 in the morning until 10 in the evening. These centres usually have also a cinema, bowling area and restaurants, so they stay open on **Κυριακές** *Sundays* as well. The **ώρες εργασίας** *working hours* for most people varies between 38 and 42 hours **την εβδομάδα** *per week*.

 1   How do you make Tuesdays, Wednesdays, and Thursdays singular in Greek?

 Vocabulary builder

ΛΕΩ ΤΗΝ ΩΡΑ   *TELLING THE TIME*

1 06.01 **Listen for the four different ways in which you can ask for the time in Greek. Then listen again and repeat.**

Τι ώρα είναι;	*What time is it?*
Έχετε ώρα;	*Do you have the time?*
Μπορείτε να μου πείτε την ώρα;	*Can you tell me the time?*
Ξέρετε τι ώρα είναι;	*Do you know what time it is?*

2 06.02 **Listen now to how you can say the time from 1 o'clock to 2 o'clock. Then listen again and repeat.**

Telling the time in Greek is not difficult. Have a look back at Unit 4 to revise the numbers. **Πέντε** (5), **δέκα** (10), **είκοσι** (20) and **είκοσι πέντε** (25) are the most frequently used numbers when telling the time, but remember, digital watches and timetables use numbers 1–59:

1.24	**μία και είκοσι τέσσερα**
1.48	**μία και σαράντα οκτώ**

Use **και** *past* for 1–30 minutes past the hour and **παρά** *to* for 31–59 minutes past the hour; but note that **και** is the only word used when telling the time from a digital watch or clock. Look at this diagram now and listen to the times from 1 to 2 o'clock. Listen again and repeat.

Here are some other important words used in telling the time:

και τέταρτο	*quarter past*	**ώρα/ώρες**	*hour/ hours*	**η ώρα**	*o'clock*
παρά τέταρτο	*quarter to*	**νωρίς**	*early*	**στη μία**	*at 1:00*
και μισή	*half past*	**αργά**	*late*	**στις πέντε**	*at 5:00*
λεπτό/λεπτά	*minute/minutes*	**ακριβώς**	*exactly*	**σε 6 ώρες**	*in 6 hours*

3 06.03 **Listen now to the four different ways one can ask about the time and match each question with the appropriate time that you hear. Then listen again and repeat.**

a Τι ώρα είναι;
b Έχετε ώρα;
c Μπορείτε να μου πείτε την ώρα;
d Ξέρετε τι ώρα είναι;

1 Μισό λεπτό! Μία και είκοσι πέντε.
2 Η ώρα είναι οχτώμιση ακριβώς.
3 Ναι, έχω. Τώρα είναι τρεις και τέταρτο.
4 Ναι, βέβαια. Είναι δέκα παρά τέταρτο.

Greek, as in English, does not use the 24-hour system except for in train stations and airports. This means that when you want to specify between a.m. and p.m. in Greek, you can use the following expressions:

7 η ώρα το πρωί	*7 o'clock in the morning*
12 το μεσημέρι	*12 o'clock noon*
7 η ώρα το απόγευμα	*7 o'clock in the afternoon*
10 η ώρα το βράδυ	*10 o'clock at night*
12 τα μεσάνυχτα	*12 o'clock midnight*

 4 06.04 Try to say the following times in Greek. Then listen and check your answers.

  a 6.00 a.m.

  b 1.20 p.m.

  c 5.15 p.m.

  d 10.50 p.m.

  e 12.00 midnight

  f 3.40 in the morning

THE NOTION OF TIME IN GREECE

You have just learnt several important words and phrases about telling the time in Greek. Here is a quiz for you:

a Is the notion of time different in Greece?

b Is it OK when you arrive late at a café and a Greek friend has been waiting for you?

c Is supper served later and does it last longer than what you are probably used to?

If you have answered 'yes' to all these questions, you are on the right track! If not, discuss them with a Greek next time you have the chance.

Conversation 1

ΣΕ ΕΝΑ ΤΑΞΙΔΙΩΤΙΚΟ ΓΡΑΦΕΙΟ *AT A TRAVEL AGENCY*

 NEW EXPRESSIONS

 06.05

καθίστε	*take a seat, sit down*
Τι θα θέλατε;	*What would you like?*
Σκεπτόμαστε να πάμε	*We are thinking (planning) of going*
κατά την διάρκεια	(idiom) *during*
βοηθάω/βοηθώ	*I help*
ας δούμε πρώτα	*let's see first*
πετάω/πετώ	*I fly*
υπάρχει	*there is*
η πτήση	*the flight*
υπάρχουν	*there are*
Πόση ώρα είναι η πτήση;	*How long is the flight?* (lit. *how much time is the flight?*)

περίπου	around, about, approximately
πενήντα λεπτά	50 minutes
πόσο κάνει το εισιτήριο;	how much is the ticket?
με όλες τις εταιρίες	with every airline (lit. with all the companies)
η αεροπορική εταιρία	the airline company
απλός/-ή/-ό	simple (adj.)
απλή μετάβαση	one way, single
μετ' επιστροφής	return (lit. with return)
διακοπές	holiday

 06.06 Tim and Mary are planning to go on a trip outside of Athens. They ask a **ταξιδιωτικός πράκτορας**, *travel agent or simply* **πράκτορας**, *about visiting Thessaloniki.*

1 Listen to the conversation a couple of times. How do they want to travel: by bus, by train or by plane?

Πράκτορας	Καλημέρα σας! Παρακαλώ καθίστε. Τι θα θέλατε;
Tim	Σκεπτόμαστε να πάμε στη Θεσσαλονίκη κατά τη διάρκεια των διακοπών.
Πράκτορας	Πώς θέλετε να πάτε, με αεροπλάνο, τρένο ή λεωφορείο;
Mary	Αυτό είναι το πρόβλημα! Δεν ξέρουμε. Μπορείτε να μας βοηθήσετε;
Πράκτορας	Ναι, ας δούμε πρώτα το αεροπλάνο. Στη Θεσσαλονίκη πετάει η Ολυμπιακή, η Απόλλων και η Sky Bus. Υπάρχει πτήση κάθε μέρα. Υπάρχουν πτήσεις το πρωί, το μεσημέρι και το βράδυ.
Tim	Πόση ώρα είναι η πτήση;
Πράκτορας	Περίπου πενήντα (50) λεπτά.
Mary	Και πόσο κάνει το εισιτήριο;
Πράκτορας	Τώρα περίπου ενενήντα (90) ευρώ με όλες τις εταιρίες.
Mary	Απλή μετάβαση μόνο;
Πράκτορας	Όχι, μετ' επιστροφής.

2 Now read the conversation and answer the questions.
   a Is there only one flight available per day?
   b Is there more than one airline flying to Thessaloniki?
   c Does the ticket cost 90 euros for a single or return trip?

 3 Listen again and pay special attention to the words which run together. Practise speaking the part of the travel agent or Mary and pay particular attention to your pronunciation.

💡 Language discovery 1

1 The conversation includes these two important expressions. Can you find them?

    a there is _____

    b there are _____

2 The conversation includes the three most important Greek particles (the words θα, να, ας). Particles always accompany verbs. Can you figure out which particle is needed in each case, according to their usage?

    a The particle _____ is needed to connect two verbs in a phrase.

    b The particle _____ is needed when *let's* is used.

    c The particle _____ is needed when the verb is in the future tense.

Learn more

1 GREEK PARTICLES

There are three two-letter words found in this conversation, **θα, να, ας**, which are the most important particles in Greek along with a fourth one, **αν**. Particles are function words that always accompany verbs and help them form certain modes, for example:

    ▶ showing the future with **θα**

Αύριο <u>θα</u> πάω στην Αθήνα.   *Tomorrow I'm going (<u>I'll</u> go) to Athens.*

    ▶ connecting two verbs with **να**

Μπορώ <u>να</u> φάω ψάρι.   *I'm able <u>to</u> eat fish.*

    ▶ using the expression *let's* **ας**

<u>Ας</u> δούμε πρώτα το αεροπλάνο.   <u>*Let's* first see the aeroplane.</u>

    ▶ using conditionals with **αν**

<u>Αν</u> θέλεις να φας, έλα μαζί μου.   <u>*If* you want to eat, come with me.</u>

The particles always precede the verb they accompany. The verb form that follows is often a new verb form that you have to learn. For example, the verb form, after the particle in the first three examples was new, i.e. **πηγαίνω-πάω** *to go*; **τρώω-φάω** *to eat*; **βλέπω-δω** *to see*. There are verbs though, which do not have a new verb form after the particles, e.g. **είμαι** *to be*, **κάνω** *to do*, **έχω** *to have* and there are also verbs that have a new form, but when compared to the main form are not totally different, e.g. **τηλεφωνώ-τηλεφωνήσω** *to telephone*, **αρχίζω-αρχίσω** *to start*, **συνεχίζω-συνεχίσω** *to continue*. It's best then to learn the particles with their corresponding verbs as chunks.

Here is an overview of the three different verb groups when a particle is needed:

Verbs without a new form	Verbs with a slightly new form	Verbs with a totally new form
κάνω-κάνω	αρχίζω-αρχίσω	βλέπω-δω
θέλω-θέλω	συνεχίζω-συνεχίζω	τρώω-φάω

2 PARTICLES, PRONOUNS, AND WORD ORDER

Pay attention to the position of words like *us*, *me*, *them* – they come after the particle but before the verb in Greek but after the verb in English. These words are another form of personal pronouns. Actually, they are personal pronouns in nominative and accusative form. Compare the two forms:

εγώ	*I*	**με**	*me*	**εμείς**	*we*	**μας**	*us*
εσύ	*you*	**σε**	*you*	**εσείς**	*you*	**σας**	*you*
αυτός	*he*	**τον**	*him* (m)	**αυτούς**	*they*	**τους**	*them* (m+f)
αυτή	*she*	**την**	*her* (f)	**αυτές**	*they*	**τις**	*them* (f)
αυτό	*it*	**το**	*it* (m)	**αυτά**	*they*	**τα**	*them* (n)

Look now at the following examples:

Μπορώ να σε βοηθήσω.	*I can help you.*
Εγώ θα σε βοηθήσω.	*I will help you.*
Μπορεί να μας βοηθήσει.	*He can help us.*
Μπορούμε να τους βοηθήσουμε.	*We can help them.*
Μπορώ να σας βοηθήσω;	*Can I help you?*
Θα το κάνω για σένα.	*I'll do it for you.*
Ας το φάμε τώρα.	*Let's eat it now.*
Αν θέλεις να με δεις, έλα!	*If you want to see me, come here!*
Δεν μπορείτε να με βοηθήσετε.	*You cannot help me.*

Conversation 2

ΜΕ ΤΟ ΤΡΕΝΟ; *BY TRAIN?*

 NEW EXPRESSIONS

 06.07

ακριβά	*expensive*
το δρομολόγιο	*the timetable* (n)
πρέπει να πάτε	*you have to go*
το γραφείο	*the office* (n)
κάνει	*costs* (here)
δεύτερη θέση	*second class* (f)
θέλετε να κάνετε κράτηση	*would you like to make a reservation*
Μου δίνετε …	*(Could) you give me …*
πάρτε ένα από απέναντι	*get one from across (the room)*

06.08 *Ninety euros sounds expensive if they want to fly so they look into taking the train.*

1 **Listen to the conversation a couple of times. Can Tim and Mary get the information direct from the travel agency or do they need to go somewhere else?**

Tim	Ενενήντα (90) ευρώ είναι λίγο ακριβά. Ξέρετε τα δρομολόγια του ΟΣΕ;
Πράκτορας	Όχι. Για τα δρομολόγια του ΟΣΕ πρέπει να πάτε στα γραφεία του ΟΣΕ, πολύ κοντά από εδώ.
Mary	Πού είναι τα γραφεία του ΟΣΕ;
Πράκτορας	Πάρτε την Πανεπιστημίου ευθεία κάτω. Το δεύτερο στενό είναι η Σίνα. Στρίψτε δεξιά και είναι στα πενήντα (50) μέτρα δεξιά σας. *Σε λίγο …*
Tim	Συγγνώμη, πότε έχει τρένο για τη Θεσσαλονίκη, παρακαλώ;
Πράκτορας	Μισό λεπτό να δω. Έχει στις δύο και είκοσι (2:20) και κάνει τριάντα (30) ευρώ απλή μετάβαση δεύτερη θέση. Θέλετε να κάνετε κράτηση;
Tim	Δεν ξέρουμε ακόμα. Μου δίνετε ένα πρόγραμμα με τα δρομολόγια για Θεσσαλονίκη;
Πράκτορας	Πάρτε ένα από απέναντι.
Tim	Ευχαριστούμε.

2 **Now read the conversation and answer the questions.**
   a What is actually τα γραφεία του ΟΣΕ?
   b Which one costs 30 euros, the single or return ticket?
   c Are they going to make a reservation or not?

 3 **Listen again and pay special attention to the words which run together. Practise speaking the part of the travel agent or Tim and pay particular attention to your pronunciation.**

Language discovery 2

1 **The conversation includes three important expressions, which have the particle να. Can you find them?**
   a Would you like to make a reservation?
   b Just a moment so I can check (lit. in order to see)
   c You have to go to the OSE offices.

2 **Listen again to the previous conversation, which words are useful for giving directions? Can you find some in the conversations?**

Learn more

USEFUL VOCABULARY WHEN TRAVELLING

Here are the different classes available when travelling by boat or aeroplane.

πρώτη θέση	*first class*
δεύτερη θέση	*second class*
τρίτη θέση	*third class*
τουριστική θέση	*tourist class*
οικονομική θέση	*economy class*
τρίτη θέση/κατάστρωμα	*deck class*
μπίζνες κλας	*business class*

When you buy a **εισιτήριο** *ticket* you will have to specify **απλό** *single* or **με επιστροφή** *return*. You might also hear:

μόνο πήγαινε	lit. *just going*
απλή μετάβαση	lit. *single transfer*
μετά επιστροφής/μετ' επιστροφής/με επιστροφή/μ' επιστροφή	lit. *with return*
αλέ ρετούρ	lit. *with return*

You'll often hear the question: **Θέλετε (Θα θέλατε) να κάνετε κράτηση;** *Do you want (Would you like) to make a reservation?*

One answer could be: **Ναι, θέλω (θα ήθελα) να κάνω μία κράτηση.** *Yes, I want (I'd like) to make a reservation.*

Conversation 3

ΜΕ ΤΟ ΛΕΩΦΟΡΕΙΟ ΙΣΩΣ; *BY BUS PERHAPS?*

 NEW EXPRESSIONS

 06.09

η πληροφορία	*the information*
γραφείο πληροφοριών	*information desk*
το κτίριο	*the building*
κάθε πότε;	*how often* (lit. *every when*)?
φεύγω	*I leave*
σε μισή ώρα	*in half an hour*
η θέση	*the seat*
πόση ώρα κάνει;	*how long does it take* (lit. *does*)?
πριν	*in advance* (lit. *before*)
τίποτα	*not at all, don't mention it!* (lit. *nothing*)

06.10 *Tim and Mary are still checking their options, so they go to the bus port authority. Travelling by bus is still the most inexpensive way around and the place is full of people, noises and hubbub.*

1 Listen to the conversation a couple of times. Do they actually get a bus ticket or not?

Tim	Πού είναι το γραφείο πληροφοριών παρακαλώ;
Περαστικός	Μέσα σ'αυτό το κτήριο.
Tim	Ευχαριστώ.
	Σε λίγο …
Tim	Γεια σας. Κάθε πότε υπάρχει λεωφορείο για τη Θεσσαλονίκη;
Υπάλληλος	Μισό λεπτό να δω. Υπάρχει ένα που φεύγει σε μισή ώρα (1/2). Υπάρχουν θέσεις ακόμα. Πόσα εισιτήρια θέλετε;
Tim	Συγγνώμη, αλλά δε φεύγουμε σήμερα. Πόση ώρα κάνει το ταξείδι;
Υπάλληλος	Κάνει πεντέμιση (5 1/2) με έξι (6) ώρες. Θέλετε να κρατήσετε θέσεις;
Tim	Πόσο κάνει το εισιτήριο με επιστροφή;
Υπάλληλος	Το απλό είναι είκοσι (20) ευρώ και με επιστροφή τριάντα (30) ευρώ.
Mary	Πότε πρέπει να κλείσουμε θέσεις;
Υπάλληλος	Μια μέρα πριν.
Tim	Ευχαριστούμε πολύ.
Mary	Ευχαριστούμε.
Υπάλληλος	Τίποτα.

2 Now read the conversation and answer the questions.

   a What is actually το γραφείο πληροφοριών?

   b How long does the trip take by bus?

   c How far in advance do they need to make a reservation?

 3 Listen again and pay special attention to the words that run together. Practise speaking the part of the ticket agent or Tim and pay particular attention to your pronunciation.

Language discovery 3

1 The conversation includes three different ways of thanking someone. Can you find the expressions?

   a (We) thank you _____

   b (I) thank you _____

   c (We) thank you a lot _____

2 Look up three words from this conversation, κτήριο – συγγνώμη – ταξείδι, in a Greek dictionary. Would you expect to find a different spelling? Why's that? Can you guess any reasons behind that?

Possible alternatives?

κτήριο – κτίριο   συγγνώμη – συγνώμη   ταξείδι – ταξίδι

3 There are two prepositions (words like *on*, *in*, *to*, etc.) in this conversation. Can you find them?

a _____   **b** _____

Learn more

1 THANKING OR APOLOGIZING TO SOMEONE

You have already learnt the words and phrases to thank or apologize to someone in Unit 2. This conversation introduces you to a new expression: **ευχαριστούμε** *thanks* (lit. *we thank you*). Here's a reminder in case you've forgotten some of the other expressions:

ευχαριστώ	*(I) thank you*
ευχαριστώ πολύ	*thanks a lot*
χίλια ευχαριστώ	*many thanks* (lit. *a thousand thanks*)

Four possible replies you might hear are:

Παρακαλώ!	*You're welcome!*
Να είσαι (Να'σαι) καλά!	*You're welcome* (lit. *Be well*)!
Να είστε (Να'στε) καλά!	*You're welcome* (lit. *Be well*)!
Τίποτα!	*Not at all! Don't mention it!*

Χίλια συγγνώμη, literally meaning *one thousand apologies*, is used when somebody has made a serious mistake – along the lines of *I am terribly sorry* or *I am so sorry*. Simply **συγγνώμη** or **με συγχωρείτε** can be used for *sorry* or *excuse me*.

2 GREEK SPELLING

As the Greek language has undergone major shifts in the last 30 years, there is confusion about some spellings and sometimes more than one spelling is used. Don't worry about this; native speakers also have trouble with spelling sometimes.

In this unit, words like **κτήριο** *building*, **συγγνώμη** *excuse me*, or **ταξείδι** *trip* could also be spelt **κτίριο** (ι instead of η), **συγνώμη** (only one γ), or **ταξίδι** (only ι instead of ει). These are also correct spellings after the last language reform in 1982. Other examples are **εταιρεία** or **εταιρία** *company*, **πίτα** or **πίττα** *pitta bread*, **μακριά** or **μακρυά** *far*, **Μανώλης** or **Μανόλης** *Emmanuel* and **τρένο** or **τραίνο** *train*.

3 GREEK PREPOSITIONS

Words such as *on*, *to*, *at*, *in* and so on are called prepositions. Greek prepositions can be characterized as 'simple' (one word) or 'compound' (two words). There are four 'simple' prepositions:

από	*from, by*
για	*for*
με	*with, by*
σε	*at, in, on, to*

Compound prepositions include:

απέναντι (από)	*across from, opposite*
μπροστά από	*in front of*
δίπλα σε	*next to*
(ε)πάνω από/σε	*over/on to*
κάτω σε	*down by, down to, under*
μέσα σε	*inside*
έξω από	*outside*

When **σε** is followed by the definite article (words like **το**, **τα**, **την**) it is reduced to **σ-** and the two are written as one word. This is the case only with this preposition. The rest do not need to form one word. Some examples include:

Είμαι στη (σε + τη) Θεσσαλονίκη.	*I am in Thessaloniki.*
Πάω στη Θεσσαλονίκη.	*I am going to Thessaloniki.*
Ένα εισιτήριο για τη Θεσσαλονίκη.	*A ticket for Thessaloniki.*
Μένω μέσα στη Θεσσαλονίκη.	*I live in Thessaloniki.*
Η Ακρόπολη είναι απέναντι από εδώ.	*The Acropolis is across from here.*
Δίπλα στο (σε + το) σχολείο.	*Next to school.*

4 NUMBERS 1,001–10,000

 06.11 **Listen now a couple of times to numbers 1,001–10,000. Listen again and repeat.**

1,001	**χίλια ένα** (chília éna)	5,000	**πέντε χιλιάδες**
1,002	**χίλια δύο** (chília THío)	6,000	**έξι χιλιάδες**
2,000	**δύο χιλιάδες** (THío chiliádes)	7,000	**επτά χιλιάδες**
2,001	**δύο χιλιάδες ένα**	8,000	**οκτώ χιλιάδες**
3,000	**τρεις χιλιάδες**	9,000	**εννέα χιλιάδες**
4,000	**τέσσερις χιλιάδες**	10,000	**δέκα χιλιάδες**

Practice

1 You are at a travel agency and would like some details about a journey you plan to make. Ask the following questions.

   a Is there a flight every day?
   b How long is the flight?
   c How much is the flight?
   d Is it one way or a round trip?
   e Can I make a reservation now?
   f Can I have a timetable?
   g How often? How long? How much?

2 Match each question with the most appropriate answer.

   a Κάθε πότε υπάρχει τρένο;   **1** Εκεί πέρα! Δε βλέπεις;
   b Πότε πρέπει να κλείσουμε θέσεις;   **2** Δύο ώρες ακριβώς.
   c Πού είναι το Γραφείο Πληροφοριών;   **3** Κάθε μέρα νομίζω.
   d Πόση ώρα είναι η πτήση;   **4** Έξι μέρες πριν.

3 Rearrange these lines to make a dialogue.

   a Ξέρετε πόση ώρα κάνει το τρένο;
   b Από πού είστε;
   c Είμαστε από το Λονδίνο, αλλά τώρα μένουμε στην Αθήνα.
   d Συνήθως επτά ώρες.
   e Είμαι από τη Θεσσαλονίκη, αλλά πάω στην Αθήνα. Εσείς από πού είστε;
   f Α! Ωραία! Είμαι πολύ κουρασμένος. Μπορώ να κοιμηθώ (*sleep*);
   g Ναι μπορείτε! Καλό ταξείδι!

4 Complete the dialogue using the English prompts.

Πράκτορας	Καλημέρα σας! Τι θέλετε παρακαλώ;
You	**a** *I'd like two tickets for Rhodes.* (για τη Ρόδο)
Πράκτορας	Με το καράβι ή το αεροπλάνο;
You	**b** *How much is it by boat?*
Πράκτορας	Τι θέση θέλετε;
You	**c** *Second class.*
Πράκτορας	40€ μόνο πήγαινε.
You	**d** *And return?*
Πράκτορας	70€ δεύτερη θέση και 60€ κατάστρωμα.
You	**e** *How long does it take?*
Πράκτορας	Δεκαοκτώ ώρες.
You	**f** *What! 18 hours! I can't stand four hours on a boat!*

5 Match the list on the left with the list on the right.

   a ώρα   **1** problem
   b πρόγραμμα   **2** seat
   c κέντρο   **3** tourist

d ντομάτα		**4** with
e θέση		**5** polyglot
f πρόβλημα		**6** centre
g τουριστική		**7** hour
h με		**8** programme
i πολύγλωττο		**9** tomato

6 Using the central letter O and at least one other, how many words can you find? Check that you know what all the words mean! Here's an example to start you off: ΠΟΤΕ.

YOUR TARGET:

5 words – average

10 words – good

15 words – very good

and more than 20 words – excellent!

7 06.12 Listen to the conversation and find the missing words. If you want, find the words first and then listen and compare your answers.

Tim	Πού είναι το γραφείο **a** _____, παρακαλώ.
Περαστικός	**b** _____ σ' αυτό το κτίριο.
Tim	Ευχαριστώ.
	Σε λίγο …
Tim	Γεια σας. Κάθε πότε **c** _____ λεωφορείο για τη Θεσσαλονίκη;
Υπάλληλος	Μισό λεπτό να **d** _____. Υπάρχει ένα που **e** _____ σε μισή ώρα (1/2). Υπάρχουν θέσεις ακόμα. Πόσα εισιτήρια θέλετε;
Tim	Συγγνώμη αλλά δεν **f** _____ σήμερα. Πόση ώρα κάνει το **g** _____;
Υπάλληλος	Κάνει πεντέμιση (5 1/2) με έξι (6) ώρες. Θέλετε να κρατήσετε **h** _____;
Tim	Πόσο κάνει το εισιτήριο με **i** _____;
Υπάλληλος	Το απλό είναι 20 ευρώ και με **i** _____ 30 ευρώ.
Mary	**j** _____ πρέπει να κλείσουμε θέσεις;
Υπάλληλος	Μία μέρα **k** _____.
Tim	Ευχαριστούμε πολύ.
Mary	Ευχαριστούμε.
Υπάλληλος	**l** _____!

τίποτα φεύγει φεύγουμε πριν		
θέσεις πότε υπάρχει μέσα		
δω πληροφοριών επιστροφή ταξίδι		

8 06.13 **Listen to the following times a couple of times and say the English counterpart. If you want, say first the times in Greek. Then listen and compare your answers.**

a 8.15		**f** 1.00		**k** 4.23	
b 9.25		**g** 7.30		**l** 9.49	
c 6.50		**h** 2.35		**m** 7.12	
d 3.30		**i** 4.00		**n** 1.30	
e 5.45		**j** 7.52		**o** 1.43	

9 **Here is a train timetable between Athens and Thessaloniki. Read the questions and reply accordingly.**

a Πόση ώρα κάνει το ταξείδι από Αθήνα για Θεσσαλονίκη;

b Πόση ώρα κάνει το ταξείδι από Θεσσαλονίκη για Αθήνα;

c Πότε φεύγει το πρώτο τραίνο για Θεσσαλονίκη;

d Πόσα δρομολόγια υπάρχουν κάθε μέρα;

ΑΘΗΝΑ				ΘΕΣΣΑΛΟΝΙΚΗ					
–	09.30	12.30	–	ΠΕΙΡΑΙΑΣ ↑	13.46	16.48	–	–	–
07.00	10.03	13.01	17.00	ΑΘΗΝΑ	13.16	16.18	19.17	21.19	23.16
07.51	–	–	–	ΟΙΝΟΗ	–	–	18.27	20.29	–
08.32	–	–	–	ΛΕΒΑΔΕΙΑ	–	–	17.46	–	21.47
09.31	12.32	15.29	19.31	ΛΙΑΝΟΚΛΑΔΙ	10.46	13.47	16.45	18.47	20.46
11.12	14.11	17.09	21.07	ΛΑΡΙΣΑ	09.08	12.09	15.10	17.08	19.09
12.12	15.12	18.11	22.10	ΚΑΤΕΡΙΝΗ	08.08	11.06	14.05	16.04	18.05
12.48	–	18.48	22.45 ↓	ΠΛΑΤΥ	07.30	10.29	13.29	–	–
13.16	16.19	19.17	23.14	ΘΕΣΣΑΛΟΝΙΚΗ	07.02	10.01	13.00	15.00	17.01

10 06.14 **A επιβάτης** *passenger* **travelling to the airport is having a conversation with a ταξιτζής** *taxi driver*. **Listen to the conversation a couple of times without the text. Then listen again and repeat.**

Ταξιτζής	Πού πάτε, κύριε;
Επιβάτης	Στο αεροδρόμιο, παρακαλώ.
Ταξιτζής	Πού πάτε;
Επιβάτης	Πάντα τα μπερδεύω! Πάω στη Ρόδο, πιστεύω!
Ταξιτζής	Τι ώρα είναι η πτήση σας;
Επιβάτης	Στις οκτώ και δέκα (8.10).
Ταξιτζής	Α! έχουμε ώρα! Δεν έχει κίνηση σήμερα.
	Σε λίγο …
Ταξιτζής	Φτάσαμε! Μισό λεπτό να σας δώσω τις αποσκευές σας.
Επιβάτης	Ευχαριστώ. Τι οφείλω;

Ταξιτζής	Έντεκα ευρώ ακριβώς.
Επιβάτης	Ορίστε δώδεκα ευρώ. Κρατήστε τα ρέστα.
Ταξιτζής	Ευχαριστώ και καλό ταξείδι.
Επιβάτης	Ευχαριστώ, γεια σας.

Find the following expressions:

a Keep the change. _____

b I always get it mixed up! _____

c Where are you going sir? _____

d There's no traffic today. _____

e Have a nice trip. _____

f How much do I owe? _____

11 True or false? Read the conversation again and decide which statements are true and which are false.

		true	false
e	Έχουν πολύ ώρα να πάνε στο αεροδρόμιο.	_____	_____
f	Ο επιβάτης δεν έχει αποσκευές.	_____	_____
g	Η πτήση είναι στις οκτώ και τέταρτο.	_____	_____
h	Ο επιβάτης οφείλει 13€.	_____	_____
i	Ο επιβάτης πετάει στη Ρόδο.	_____	_____

❓ Test yourself

1 Can you remember the Greek for the following ten important words from this unit?

   a about _____
   b seat _____
   c flight _____
   d airport _____
   e office _____
   f traffic _____
   g information _____
   h luggage _____
   i building _____
   j change _____

2 Can you remember the following ten important phrases from this unit?

   a There's time! _____
   b It's one o'clock. _____
   c Keep the change! _____
   d It's half past one. _____
   e I always get it mixed up. _____
   f It's quarter to two. _____
   g Where are you going? _____
   h Many thanks! _____
   i What time is it? _____
   j You're welcome! _____

SELF CHECK

	I CAN...
○	. . . understand or say the names of the week.
○	. . . make travel arrangements.
○	. . . find out about public transport.
○	. . . make reservations or buy tickets.
○	. . . understand or tell the time.
○	. . . count from 1,000 to 10,000.
○	. . . thank or apologize to someone.

Έχετε δωμάτια;

Do you have any rooms?

In this unit you will learn how to:

▶ *enquire about rooms.*

▶ *make hotel reservations.*

▶ *check in and check out.*

▶ *explain a problem with your room.*

CEFR: (A1) *Can enquire about room availability. Can make positive or negative comments about a room. Can understand and use hotel vocabulary.* **(A2)** *Can ask about alternative destinations. Can complain about a room. Can compare things and situations. Can use negative phrases and understand better double negatives.*

Πληροφορίες για τουρίστες *Tourist Information*

Tourism is one of the most important sectors of the Greek economy as it often represents 8–10% of Greece's national yearly revenue. **EOT Ελληνικός Οργανισμός Τουρισμού** *Greek Tourism Organization* supervises all activities nationwide and many of its services are now available online. They have several offices around Greece and a visit is always worthwhile because you can get, apart from expert advice, maps, hotel lists and reliable regional information. Greece, although very famous for its summer vacation spots with **κολύμπι** *swimming* and **ηλιοθεραπεία** *sun tanning*, it can offer many alternative destinations for **πεζοπορίες** *hiking*, **αναρριχήσεις** *mountain climbing*, **θαλάσσια σπορ** *water sports* or **αγροτουρισμό** *farming tourism* throughout the year. All kinds of accommodation are available in Greece but early **κράτηση** *reservation* and **επιβεβαίωση** *confirmation* are essential, especially in summer.

 1 What's the name of the National Tourism Organization?

Vocabulary builder

ΧΡΗΣΙΜΟ ΛΕΞΙΛΟΓΙΟ ΞΕΝΟΔΟΧΕΙΟΥ *USEFUL HOTEL VOCABULARY*

1 07.01 **Make yourself familiar with the Greek words for this hotel vocabulary. Listen and number the words in the order you hear them. Then listen and repeat.**

a ___ η καμαριέρα *maid*

b ___ η μπανιέρα *bathtub*

c ___ δίκλινο *two beds*

d ___ το κλειδί *key*

e ___ ο/η σερβιτόρος/-α *waiter/waitress*

f ___ το/τα δωμάτιο/-α *room/s*

g ___ τρίκλινο *three beds*

h ___ το πρωινό *breakfast*

2 07.02 **One will be surprised to discover how many international words are used as hotel vocabulary in Greek. Match first the Greek words with the corresponding English ones and then listen to check your answers. Listen once again and repeat after the speaker.**

a	ο/η μάνατζερ	**1**	bar
b	το ασανσέρ	**2**	balcony
c	το φουαγιέ	**3**	toilet
d	το μπαρ	**4**	buffet
e	το λόμπυ	**5**	room service
f	το μπαλκόνι	**6**	foyer
g	η σουίτα	**7**	manager
h	η τουαλέτα	**8**	telephone
i	το σέρβις δωματίου	**9**	minibar
j	το τηλέφωνο	**10**	lift / elevator
k	το μίνι-μπαρ	**11**	suite
l	ο μπουφές	**12**	lobby

3 07.03 **Listen to some important phrases when you talk about accommodation a couple of times without looking at the list. Then listen again and repeat after the speakers.**

1 ASKING FOR A ROOM:

Θα ήθελα …	I'd like …
Έχετε … ;	Do you have … ?
ένα μονό δωμάτιο	a single room
ένα διπλό δωμάτιο	a double room
δύο διπλά δωμάτια	two double rooms
ένα δωμάτιο με δύο κρεβάτια	a room with two beds
ένα μονόκλινο	a single bed
ένα δίκλινο	twin beds

2 FINDING OUT IF THE ROOM IS:

με μπάνιο	with a bath
με ντους	with a shower
με μπαλκόνι	with a balcony
με θέα	with a view
με τουαλέτα	en suite (toilet)

3 HAVING A CHOICE OF LOCATION:

μπροστά / στην πρόσοψη	at the front
πίσω / στο πίσω μέρος	at the back
προς τη θάλασσα	facing (towards) the sea
προς την αυλή	facing (towards) the courtyard

Conversation 1

ΕΧΕΤΕ ΔΩΜΑΤΙΑ; *DO YOU HAVE ANY ROOMS?*

 NEW EXPRESSIONS

 07.04

ψάχνω για ενοικίαση	*I'm looking for for rent*
απ' εδώ!	*this way! (lit. from here)*
το αυτοκίνητο	*the car*
η βαλίτσα	*the suitcase*
να το!	*here it is!*
δε μου αρέσει!	*I don't like (it)!*
καλύτερος/-η/-ο	*better*
μεγαλύτερος/-η/-ο	*larger*
πιο	*more*
ήσυχος/-η/-ο	*quiet*
παίρνω	*I take*
θα το πάρω	*I will take it*
ο ντόπιος	*the local person*
ο τουρίστας	*the tourist*

 07.05 *A tourist has just arrived on a Greek island and talks about a room accommodation with a local.*

1 Listen to their exchange a couple of times. Did he see one or two rooms at the end?

Ντόπιος	Ψάχνετε για δωμάτια;
Τουρίστας	Ναι. Έχετε δωμάτια;
Ντόπιος	Έχω ένα δωμάτιο για ενοικίαση. Για πόσες μέρες το θέλετε;
Τουρίστας	Για τρεις μέρες. Μπορώ να δω το δωμάτιο;
Ντόπιος	Βέβαια. Ελάτε απ'ε δώ! Δεν είναι μακρυά. Έχω αυτοκίνητο. Αυτή είναι η βαλίτσα σας;
Τουρίστας	Ναι.
	Σε λίγο …
Ντόπιος	Ορίστε! Να το!
Τουρίστας	Όχι, δε μου αρέσει! Έχετε κάτι καλύτερο και μεγαλύτερο;
Ντόπιος	Έχω άλλο ένα. Είναι πιο ήσυχο αλλά πιο ακριβό.
Τουρίστας	Να το δω; Α! Μάλιστα! Αυτό είναι εντάξει. Θα το πάρω.

2 Now read the conversation and answer the questions.

   a How long does he want the room for?

   b How do they get to where the room is: on foot or by car?

   c What's wrong with the first room?

3 Listen again and pay special attention to the words that run together. Practise speaking the part of Τουρίστας and pay particular attention to your pronunciation.

💡 Language discovery 1

1 Read the conversation again and find the following words. Can you figure out what endings the adjectives take in Greek (compared to -er in English) and which word is used for *more* when making comparisons?

a bigger _____
b better _____
c more expensive _____
d more quiet _____

Learn more

MAKING COMPARISONS

Adjectives are words that usually give extra information about nouns. Greek adjectives have two different ways to build their comparative form: one can either add the word **πιο** before any adjective or add the ending **-τερος/-τερη/-τερο** at the end of most adjectives. For most adjectives, both of the options can be used, as it does not change their meaning. Adding the word **πιο** to an adjective is quite simple and does not require much thought. However when adding the ending **-τερος/-τερη/-τερο** you have to be mindful of new letters or, in case of irregular adjectives, of new words. Notice some examples:

Adjective	1st comparative	2nd comparative
καλ-ός/-ή/-ό *good*	πιο καλ-ός/-ή/-ό *better*	καλύ-τερος/-τερη/-τερο *better*
κακ-ός/-ή/-ό *bad*	πιο κακ-ός/-ή/-ό *worse*	χειρό-τερος/-τερη/-τερο *worse*
λίγ-ος/-η/-ο *little*	πιο λίγ-ος/-η/-ο *less*	λιγό-τερος/-τερη/-τερο *less*
πολύς/πολλή/πολύ *much*	πιο πολύς/πολλή/πολύ *more*	περισσό-τερος/-τερη/-τερο *more*
ακριβ-ός/-ή/-ό *expensive*	πιο ακριβ-ός/-ή/-ό *more expensive*	ακριβό-τερος/-τερη/-τερο *more expensive*

When making comparisons, the word **από** *than* is often used. Notice the following examples:

Ο Κώστας είναι πιο καλός μαθητής από τον Αντώνη.	*Kostas is a better student than Anthony.*
Η Μαρία έχει πιο ακριβό αυτοκίνητο από την Ελένη.	*Maria has a more expensive car than Helen.*
Το παιδί έχει λιγότερη όρεξη από εμένα.	*The child has less appetite than me.*
Θέλω περισσότερη ζάχαρη από τον Νίκο.	*I want more sugar than Nikos.*

Have you noticed that the word *more* has two Greek counterparts in the examples above: once as **πιο** when it modifies adjectives and once as **πιο πολύς/πολλή/πολύ** or **περισσό-τερος/-τερη/-τερο** when it modifies nouns?

Conversation 2

ΣΤΗ ΡΕΣΕΨΙΟΝ ΤΟΥ ΞΕΝΟΔΟΧΕΙΟΥ *AT THE HOTEL RECEPTION DESK*

 NEW EXPRESSIONS

 07.06

η ρεσεψιόν	the reception desk
ο/η υπάλληλος υποδοχής	the receptionist
φαρδύς/-ιά/-ύ	wide
που βλέπει	facing (lit. that faces/sees)
εσωτερικός/-ή/-ό	inner, inside
η αυλή	the courtyard
συμπληρώστε	fill out
η κάρτα παραμονής	the registration card
υπογράψτε	sign
στον έκτο όροφο	on the sixth floor
Ελάτε να σας πάω	I'll take you there (lit. I'll go you there)
ο γκρουμ	the porter
η τουρίστρια	the tourist

 07.07 *A tourist is asking about room availability at the reception desk of a local hotel.*

1 **Listen to the conversation a couple of times and try to figure out whether the tourist would like a single or a double room.**

Υπ. υπ.	Καλημέρα σας. Παρακαλώ;
Τουρίστρια	Καλημέρα σας. Έχετε δωμάτια;
Υπ. υπ.	Βεβαίως. Θέλετε μονόκλινο ή δίκλινο;
Τουρίστρια	Ένα δίκλινο για σήμερα το βράδυ μόνο. Με φαρδύ κρεβάτι αν έχετε.
Υπ. υπ.	Μάλιστα. Μισό λεπτό παρακαλώ. Έχουμε ένα που βλέπει στον κεντρικό δρόμο, έχει θέα αλλά έχει λίγη φασαρία. Επίσης έχουμε άλλο ένα που βλέπει στην εσωτερική αυλή του ξενοδοχείου, είναι πολύ πιο ωραίο και πιο ήσυχο.
Τουρίστρια	Νομίζω ότι αυτό με τη θέα θα είναι καλύτερο για μένα.
Υπ. υπ.	Συμπληρώστε αυτή την κάρτα παραμονής και υπογράψτε εδώ παρακαλώ.
Τουρίστρια	Ορίστε!
Υπ. υπ.	Το δωμάτιό σας είναι το 622 στον έκτο όροφο. Ελάτε να σας πάω. Ο γκρουμ θα σας βοηθήσει με τις βαλίτσες.

2 **Now read the conversation and answer the questions.**
   a How many days does the tourist want to stay?
   b The tourist wants φαρδύ κρεβάτι. What is that?
   c Which room will the tourist finally get: the one facing the street or the one facing the hotel courtyard?

3 Listen again and pay special attention to the words that run together. Practise speaking the part of Τουρίστρια and pay particular attention to your pronunciation.

Language discovery 2

1 Read the conversation again and find the comparative form for each adjective.

    a better   _____

    b more quiet   _____

    c nicer   _____

2 In the conversation, you will find one of the four following expressions. Find it and then see if you can figure out the remaining three expressions.

    a this morning _____

    b this afternoon _____

    c this evening _____

    d this (late) evening/tonight _____

3 Translate these four expressions into English. Do the four pronouns in bold have the same position in both languages?

    a Να **το** δω; _____

    b Θα **το** πάρω. _____

    c Ελάτε να **σας** πάω. _____

    d Ο γκρουμ θα **σας** βοηθήσει. _____

Learn more

1 USEFUL EXPRESSIONS

This conversation has a number of useful expressions for making a room reservation. Read the expressions a couple of times and come back to this section whenever necessary.

σήμερα το πρωί	*this morning*
με φαρδύ κρεβάτι	*with a wide bed*
σήμερα το μεσημέρι	*this afternoon*
έχει θέα αλλά	*it has a view but*
σήμερα το απόγευμα	*this evening*
έχει λίγη φασαρία	*it has some noise*
σήμερα το βράδυ	*this (late) evening*
αύριο το πρωί	*tomorrow morning*

2 NUMBER OF WORDS AND WORD ORDER

As you may have noticed, most foreign languages, including Greek, cannot be translated word for word, since the number of words used and their placement will not necessarily match up from one language to another.

Conversation 3

ΕΧΩ ΚΑΝΕΙ ΚΡΑΤΗΣΗ *I HAVE MADE A RESERVATION*

 NEW EXPRESSIONS

 07.08

ονομάζομαι	*my name is* (lit. *I am called/named*)
έχω κάνει κράτηση	*I have made a reservation*
καλώς ορίσατε!	*welcome!*
γράψτε	*write down*
η διεύθυνση	*the address*
ο αριθμός	*the number*
το διαβατήριο	*the passport*
ο στυλός/το στυλό	*the pen* (m/n)
ευχαρίστως	*gladly*
θα προτιμούσαμε	*we would like/prefer*
μόλις βγείτε από το ασανσέρ	*just as you come out/step out of the lift*
καλή διαμονή!	*(have) a good/nice stay!*
στο τέλος του διαδρόμου	*at the end of the corridor*

 07.09 *Tim and Mary have just arrived in the hotel where they made a reservation in the centre of Thessaloniki.*

1 Listen a couple of times to their exchange with the receptionist without looking at the text. For how many days is their reservation?

Tim	Καλημέρα σας. Ονομάζομαι Tim Johnson και έχω κάνει κράτηση για τέσσερις ημέρες.
Ρεσεψιονίστας	Καλώς ορίσατε κύριε Johnson. Παρακαλώ μπορείτε να συμπληρώσετε την κάρτα παραμονής; Γράψτε τ'όνομά σας, τη διεύθυνσή σας και τον αριθμό διαβατηρίου.
Tim	Ευχαρίστως. Μπορώ να έχω ένα στυλό;
Ρεσεψιονίστας	Ορίστε.
	Σε λίγο …
Ρεσεψιονίστας	Έχετε κάνει κράτηση για ένα δίκλινο. Θέλετε να έχει θέα ή ησυχία;
Mary	Είμαστε πολύ κουρασμένοι. Θα προτιμούσαμε ένα δωμάτιο με ησυχία.
Ρεσεψιονίστας	OK! Το δωμάτιό σας είναι το 325 στον 3ο (τρίτο) όροφο. Μόλις βγείτε από το ασανσέρ δεξιά. Ορίστε το κλειδί σας και καλή διαμονή!
Mary	Ευχαριστούμε, αλλά πού είναι το ασανσέρ;
Ρεσεψιονίστας	Α, συγγνώμη, στο τέλος του διαδρόμου.

2 Now read the conversation and answer the questions.

    a The receptionist says: Παρακαλώ μπορείτε να συμπληρώσετε την κάρτα παραμονής; What does he want?

    b Tim says: Μπορώ να έχω ένα στυλό; What does he want?

    c What room will Mary and Tim finally get: a room with a view or a quiet one?

 3 Listen again and pay special attention to the words that run together. Practise speaking the part of Ρεσεψιονίστας and pay particular attention to your pronunciation.

Language discovery 3

1 Read the conversation again and find three words which have two stress marks instead of one. Then listen to the conversation once again, focusing this time on these words. Which stressed syllable do you think is the main one in these three words: the first or the second?

    a _____   **b** _____   **c** _____

2 Now answer the questions about these three words.

    a Are all three words nouns? _____

    b Is there an article before these three words? _____

    c Is there a possessive pronoun after these three words? _____

    d If you look them up in a dictionary, do all three have only one stress mark? _____

    e Is this single stress mark always two syllables before the last one? _____

Learn more

WORDS WITH TWO STRESS MARKS

You have learnt that most one-syllable words carry no stress marks. There are a few exceptions with interrogative pronouns (question words), like **πού** _where_ or **πώς** _how_, or when the meaning is different, like **η** _the_ or **ή** _or_. You have also learnt that the stress mark appears only on the last three syllables of a word, no matter how many syllables the word might have, like **στυλό** _pen_, stressed on the last syllable; **κάρτα** _card_, stressed on the syllable before the last one; **δίκλινο** _two beds_, stressed two syllables before the last one; **συμπληρώσετε** _fill out_, stressed two syllables before the last one, although this word has five syllables. This last conversation brought your attention to three words with two stress marks. This only happens if you answer 'Yes' to all five of the questions from Exercise 2 above! Additionally, the noun must carry a stress on two syllables before the last one as its main stress mark. And although you see two stress marks on some nouns, the stressed syllable is exactly the same one as when these words appear in other contexts, with only one stress mark. In other words, this grammatical point does not change anything by pronouncing the word with one or two stress marks. Perhaps you remember other examples with words with two stress marks from past units.

Conversation 4

ΩΧ! ΤΟ ΜΠΑΝΙΟ ΔΕΝ ΕΧΕΙ ΚΟΥΡΤΙΝΑ! *OOPS! THE SHOWER CURTAIN IS MISSING!*

 NEW EXPRESSIONS

 07.10

ναι;	*hello? (on the phone)*
το μπάνιο	*the bathroom/bath tub*
η κουρτίνα	*the curtain*
το ντους	*the shower*
μα … κανένα μπάνιο δεν έχει κουρτίνα	*but … none of the bathrooms (lit.no bathroom) has a curtain*
κάνω ντους	*take a shower*
μα τα νερά;	*but the water? How about the water? (lit. the waters)*
το νερό	*the water*
μη στεναχωριέστε καθόλου!	*don't worry at all!*
στεγνώνω	*I dry up*
γρήγορα	*fast*
γρήγορα-γρήγορα	*extremely fast*
απορρημένος/-η/-ο	*confused*
κλείνει το τηλέφωνο	*she hangs up (the phone) (lit. she closes the phone)*

 07.11 *Mary has called reception to complain about there being no shower curtain in the bathroom.*

1 **Listen to the conversation a couple of times without looking at the text. Why is Mary confused by the receptionist's replies?**

Ρεσεψιονίστας	Ναι!
Mary	Ναι, είμαι η Mary Johnson από το δωμάτιο 325. Το μπάνιο δεν έχει κουρτίνα …
Ρεσεψιονίστας	Μα … κανένα μπάνιο δεν έχει κουρτίνα …
Mary	Και πώς θα κάνω ντους;
Ρεσεψιονίστας	Χωρίς κουρτίνα, κα Johnson;
Mary	Χωρίς κουρτίνα; Μα τα νερά;
Ρεσεψιονίστας	Μην στεναχωριέστε καθόλου! Τα νερά φεύγουν σ' ένα λεπτό. Το μπάνιο στεγνώνει γρήγορα-γρήγορα!
Mary	Ε? (Απορρημένη κλείνει το τηλέφωνο.)

2 **Now read the conversation and answer the questions.**
   a How does Mary identify herself on the phone?
   b What's wrong with the shower curtain?
   c Can you translate the receptionist's last three statements?

3 Listen again and pay special attention to the words that run together. Practise speaking the part of Ρεσεψιονίστας and pay particular attention to your pronunciation.

Language discovery 4

1 Read the conversation again and find five words necessary when you use negative phrases.

    a <u>no (none)</u> bathroom _____
    b <u>don't</u> worry _____
    c (do) not… <u>at all</u> _____
    d <u>doesn't</u> have _____
    e <u>without</u> curtain _____

2 The conversation makes use of one of the following two phrases. Can you figure out the difference between the two negative particles in bold and then translate these two phrases?

    a **Μη(ν)** στεναχωριέστε καθόλου! _____
    b **Δε(ν)** στεναχωριέστε καθόλου! _____

Learn more

USING NEGATIVE PHRASES AND UNDERSTANDING DOUBLE NEGATIVES

There are a number of words necessary when you want to make negative phrases. The short conversation above has five of these words in it. If you have answered the first exercise correctly, you have come up with the following words: **κανένα**, **μην**, **καθόλου**, **δεν**, **χωρίς**. Only the first word is declined, e.g. **κανένας**, **κανενός**, **κανέναν/καμία**, **καμίας/κανένα**, **κανενός** but the rest of these words remain unchanged with the exception of **μην** and **δεν** which sometimes for phonetic reasons drop their last letter, e.g. **μη**, **δε**. These last two words are necessary negative particles when used with verbs. The first is necessary, only if you have an imperative (request, command, order) form:

Μη(ν) στεναχωριέστε καθόλου!   *Don't worry at all!*

The latter is necessary at all other times:

Δε(ν) στεναχωριέστε καθόλου!   *You don't worry at all!*

If you don't have a verb, then the word **όχι** is necessary:

Όχι τώρα!   *Not now!*
Όχι στην Αθήνα!   *Not in Athens!*
Όχι με την Ελένη!   *Not with Helen!*

What is interesting, and perhaps challenging, when using negatives in Greek is the double negative. Contrary to English, double negative is necessary in certain cases in Greek:

Δεν ξέρω **κανέναν!**	*I don't know anybody* (lit. *nobody*)!
Δεν πάω **πουθενά!**	*I'm not going anywhere* (lit. *nowhere*)!
Δε μιλάω Γαλλικά **καθόλου!**	*I don't speak French at all* (lit. *not at all*)!
Δε μ' αρέσει **τίποτα!**	*I don't like anything* (lit. *nothing*)!

That means that a number of words have two meanings in Greek, either positive or negative, always depending on the context:

Τι θέλεις να φας; Τίποτα!	*What do you want to eat? Nothing!*
Αύριο δε θα φάω τίποτα!	*I'm not going to eat anything tomorrow!*

Other examples include the following words:

κανένας/καμία/κανένα	*someone/nobody*
ποτέ	*ever/never*
τίποτα	*anything/nothing*
πουθενά	*anywhere/nowhere*

Practice

1 Respond to the following situations:
  a Find out if a room is available.
  b Specify what kind of bed you want: single/double?
  c Ask if the hotel has a single room for four nights.
  d Say you want a double room with a shower/bath. It should be quiet and have an ocean view.
  e Ask for the price of the room.
  f Tell the receptionist that you have made a reservation.
  g You don't like the room they have given you. How would you say: *I don't like the room. It is not quiet and it does not have a view*?

2 Match each question to the most appropriate answer.

a	Ψάχνετε για δωμάτια;	**1**	Θα προτιμούσαμε να έχει ησυχία.
b	Έχετε κάνει κράτηση;	**2**	Ναι. Ορίστε η επιβεβαίωση.
c	Θέλετε να έχει θέα ή ησυχία;	**3**	Ναι. Έχετε δωμάτια;
d	Αυτή είναι η βαλίτσα σας;	**4**	Ναι, αυτή είναι.

3 Rearrange these lines to make a dialogue.
  a Θέλω ένα μεγάλο δωμάτιο με ωραία θέα. Έχετε;
  b Για πόσες μέρες το θέλετε;
  c Δεν ξέρω. Σας πειράζει;
  d Έχετε δωμάτια για ενοικίαση;
  e Όχι! Θέλετε μικρό ή μεγάλο;
  f Νομίζω ναι! Ελάτε απ'εδώ!

4 Complete the dialogue using the English prompts.

You	**a** *Hello! My name is Joanna Wilke. I have booked a room for two nights.*
Ρεσεψιόν	Καλώς ορίσατε, κυρία Wilke. Συμπληρώστε την κάρτα παραμονής σας, παρακαλώ. Μπορώ να έχω το διαβατήριό σας;
You	**b** *Here you are! Can I have a pen, please?*
Ρεσεψιόν	Ευχαρίστως ... Θέλετε το δωμάτιο να βλέπει προς το δρόμο ή στο πίσω μέρος;
You	**c** *I don't mind. I am very tired and I would like to sleep right away.*
Ρεσεψιόν	Το δωμάτιό σας είναι το 805. Στον όγδοο όροφο.
You	**d** *Where's the lift?*

5 Match the word on the left with the words on the right.

a μικρό		**1**	card
b ρεσεψιόν		**2**	esoteric (inner – inside)
c τουρίστρια		**3**	curtain
d κάρτα		**4**	suite
e κεντρικό		**5**	micro (-economy, -waves)
f εσωτερική		**6**	telephone
g κουρτίνα		**7**	tourist
h τηλέφωνο		**8**	service
i σουίτα		**9**	reception
j σέρβις		**10**	central

6 Can you recognize some of the words you have already learnt? You can find the words by reading the letter-squares horizontally or vertically. There are at least nine words horizontally and nine words vertically that will be familiar to you.

Α	Θ	Ε	Σ	Η	Τ	Ε	Χ	Ε	Ι
Ξ	Ε	Ν	Ο	Δ	Ο	Χ	Ε	Ι	Ο
Α	Α	Τ	Υ	Ω	Μ	Ε	Ρ	Ε	Σ
Ρ	Θ	Α	Π	Ρ	Ο	Τ	Ι	Μ	Ω
Ε	Α	Ξ	Α	Α	Ν	Ε	Ρ	Ο	Υ
Σ	Κ	Ε	Π	Τ	Ο	Ν	Τ	Α	Ι
Ω	Χ	Ι	Δ	Ι	Α	Μ	Ο	Ν	Η

7 07.12 Listen to the following list of words and write each one below its corresponding sound. If you want, you can first complete the chart and then listen to check your answers.

[af]	[ef]	[ev]
_____	_____	_____
_____	_____	_____
_____	_____	_____

> αποσκευή   γεύμα   γράφω
> εύκολο   ευχαριστώ   αυτός
> καφές   φεύγω   ευθεία

8 07.13 Listen to the conversation and find the missing words. If you want, you can first find the missing words and then listen to check your answers.

Ρεσεψιονίστας	Ναι!
Mary	Ναι, είμαι η Mary Johnson από το **a** _____ 325. Το **b** _____ δεν έχει **c** _____.
Ρεσεψιονίστας	Μα ... **d** _____ μπάνιο δεν έχει **c** _____.
Mary	Και πώς θα **e** _____ ντους;
Ρεσεψιονίστας	Χωρίς **c** _____, κυρία Johnson!
Mary	Χωρίς **c** _____ Μα τα **f** _____;
Ρεσεψιονίστας	**g** _____ στεναχωριέστε καθόλου! Τα **f** _____ φεύγουν σ' ένα λεπτό. Το μπάνιο **h** _____ γρήγορα-γρήγορα!
Mary	Ε? (Απορρημένη κλείνει το τηλέφωνο.)

> κάνω   δωμάτιο   κουρτίνα
> μπάνιο   κανένα   στεγνώνει
> νερά   μη

9 07.14 Listen to a receptionist assigning different rooms. Number them 1–10 in the order you hear them.

Το δωμάτιο σας είναι το ...

a	_____ 325	**f**	_____ 821
b	_____ 747	**g**	_____ 554
c	_____ 421	**h**	_____ 825
d	_____ 780	**i**	_____ 557
e	_____ 480	**j**	_____ 954

10 While searching on the Internet, you came across some ocean view rooms that you now wish to enquire about. You decide to send an email or make a phone call to find out more. Think about key words and expressions you will need to make such an enquiry and make a list as the person you are about to contact only speaks Greek!

Test yourself

1 Can you remember the Greek for the following ten important words from this unit?

- **a** room/s
- **b** car/s
- **c** tourist/s
- **d** suitcase/s
- **e** reservation/s
- **f** address
- **g** number
- **h** passport
- **i** pen
- **j** shower

2 Can you remember the following ten important phrases from this unit?

- **a** Don't worry!
- **b** First/second/third … floor
- **c** No, I don't like it!
- **d** My name's … /I'm called …
- **e** I've made a reservation.
- **f** A room for tonight.
- **g** Have you got rooms to let?
- **h** Have a nice stay!
- **i** I'll take it.
- **j** Just a moment please!

SELF CHECK

	I CAN...
○	… enquire about room availability.
○	… make positive or negative comments about a room.
○	… ask about alternative destinations.
○	… understand and use hotel vocabulary.
○	… complain about a room.
○	… compare things and situations.
○	… use negative phrases and understand better double negatives.

Θέλετε τίποτα;
How can I help you?

In this unit you will learn how to:
▶ *buy things.*
▶ *enquire about prices.*
▶ *state preferences.*
▶ *name fruit and vegetables.*
▶ *name colours.*

CEFR: (A1) *Can talk about the days of the week.* **(A2)** *Can ask for Greek products, state-certified for their quality. Can buy fruit and vegetables in an open market. Can make commitments and set meetings on certain days. Can talk about colours and associate products and colours. Can buy toiletries in a department store. Can buy clothes and discuss sizes, designs and prices.*

Ένα κομμάτι Ελλάδας *A piece of Greece*

One of the nicest experiences coming back home from a trip abroad is actually the small treasures you have discovered and brought back with you. Greece has many things to offer but unfortunately, some are either too local, without any widespread distribution, or unknown, for people to ask for them. Here is our top-ten list for you: **1. τυρί γραβιέρα Νάξου** *graviera cheese from Naxos;* **2. λαδοτύρι Μυτιλήνης** *ladotiri cheese from Mytiline;* **3. θρούμπα Χίου** *thrumba olives from Chios;* **4. κονσερβολιά Πηλίου** *konservolia olives from Pelion;* **5. σταφίδα Κορίνθου** *raisins from Corinth;* **6. φιστίκια Αίγινας** *pistachios from Aegina;* **7. αυγοτάραχο Μεσολογγίου** *fish-roe from Mesolonghi;* **8. Κρητικό παξιμάδι** *rusk from Crete;* **9. μέλι Ελάτης** *honey from Elatis;* and **10. Αποκορώνας λάδι Χανίων** *Apokoronas olive oil from Chania.*

 1   From the above can you guess the Greek word for *cheese?*

Vocabulary builder

ΦΡΟΥΤΑ ΚΑΙ ΛΑΧΑΝΙΚΑ *FRUIT AND VEGETABLES*

1 08.01 Listen a couple of times to some fruit and vegetables. Listen again and number the fruit from 1 to 10 and then number the vegetables from 11 to 20. At the end, listen once again and repeat after the speakers.

ΦΡΟΥΤΑ *FRUIT*

a _____ το μήλο *apple*
b _____ το πορτοκάλι *orange*
c _____ το σταφύλι *grape*
d _____ το καρπούζι *watermelon*
e _____ το πεπόνι *melon*
f _____ το ροδάκινο *peach*
g _____ το κεράσι *cherry*
h _____ η μπανάνα *banana*
i _____ η φράουλα *strawberry*
j _____ ο ανανάς *pineapple*

ΛΑΧΑΝΙΚΑ *VEGETABLES*

k _____ το καρότο *carrot*
l _____ το σέλινο *celery*
m _____ το μαρούλι *lettuce*
n _____ το κουνουπίδι *cauliflower*
o _____ το καλαμπόκι *corn*
p _____ το κολοκυθάκι *courgette*
q _____ η πατάτα *potato*
r _____ η ντομάτα *tomato*
s _____ η μελιτζάνα *aubergine*
t _____ ο άνιθος *dill*

ΧΡΩΜΑΤΑ *COLOURS*

2 08.02 Listen a couple of times to some colours in Greek. Then listen again and repeat.

άσπρο	*white*
μπορντώ	*burgundy*
μαύρο	*black*
καφέ	*brown*
γκρι	*grey*
μπλε	*blue*
πράσινο	*green*
κίτρινο	*yellow*
σιέλ	*sky blue*
κόκκινο	*red*
ροζ	*pink*

3 Can you separate the colours now into the following two groups?

Greek words for colours: _____

French words for colours: _____

4 Colours can be distinguished as ανοικτά χρώματα *light colours* **or σκούρα χρώματα** *dark colours.* **Many objects, including clothes, flags, or walls, can be:**

μονόχρωμος/-η/-ο	*one/single colour(ed)*
δίχρωμος/-η/-ο	*two colour(ed)*
τρίχρωμος/-η/-ο	*three colour(ed)*
τετράχρωμος/-η/-ο	*four colour(ed)*
πολύχρωμος/-η/-ο	*multi-colour(ed)*

Printed patterns include:

ριγέ	striped
καρό	checked
πουά	spotted/dotted
εμπριμέ	multi-coloured
λουλουδάτο	flowery/floral

The words for colours or designs are adjectives. That means that one should be aware of the noun following and use the correct form of the adjective:

άσπρος τοίχος	white wall
άσπρη τσάντα	white (hand)bag
άσπρο τραπέζι	white table

The fact that so many words are used for colours and designs makes things easier, as these words are not declined:

μπεζ ριγέ τοίχος	striped beige wall
μπεζ ριγέ τσάντα	striped beige (hand)bag
μπεζ ριγέ τραπέζι	striped beige table

Conversation 1

ΕΝΑ ΩΡΑΙΟ ΠΟΛΥΚΑΤΑΣΤΗΜΑ A NICE DEPARTMENT STORE

 NEW EXPRESSIONS

 08.03

χρειάζομαι	I need
τα ψώνια	shopping
θα ήθελα	I would like
το φόρεμα	the dress
τα καλλυντικά	the cosmetics
το πουκάμισο	the shirt
θέλεις παρέα;	do you want company?

μαζί μου	with me
ίσως	perhaps
καινούργιος/-α/-ο	new
η κρέμα προσώπου	the face cream
η κολώνια	the cologne/perfume
η κρέμα μου θα τελειώσει	my cream will be running out
σύντομα	shortly/soon
Πού λες να πάμε;	Where do you think (lit. say) we should go?
το πολυκατάστημα	the department store
άντε, πάμε!	OK, let's get going! (lit. we go)

 08.04 Mary is planning to visit a department store and a colleague of hers decides to join her.

1 Listen to the conversation a couple of times. What is Mary planning to buy?

Mary	Χρειάζομαι να κάνω μερικά ψώνια. Θα ήθελα να αγοράσω ένα φόρεμα και μερικά καλλυντικά για μένα κι ένα πουκάμισο για τον Τιμ.
Ιωάννα	Θέλεις παρέα;
Mary	Θα είναι καλύτερα για μένα αν είσαι μαζί μου. Χρειάζεσαι να αγοράσεις τίποτα;
Ιωάννα	Πάντα θέλω! Ίσως δω καμιά καινούργια κρέμα προσώπου και καμιά κολώνια. Η κρέμα μου θα τελειώσει σύντομα.
Mary	Πού λες να πάμε;
Ιωάννα	Θα πάμε στο Αθηναία. Είναι ένα ωραίο πολυκατάστημα και είναι πολύ κοντά από' δώ.
Mary	Ωραία, πάμε!
Ιωάννα	Άντε, πάμε!

2 Now read the conversation and answer the questions.
  a Would Mary like to buy anything for Tim?
  b Mary says: Θα είναι καλύτερα για μένα αν είσαι μαζί μου. Why?
  c What is Joanna planning to get?

 3 Listen again and pay special attention to the words that run together. Practise speaking the part of Mary and pay particular attention to your pronunciation.

💡 Language discovery 1

1 Translate the four words in bold into English. Which phrases are singular and which ones are plural?
  a μερικά ψώνια _____
  b μερικά καλλυντικά _____
  c καμιά κρέμα _____
  d καμιά κολώνια _____

Learn more

INDEFINITE PRONOUNS

Here is a list of indefinite pronouns in Greek (necessary words when you need to quantify something, e.g. *some, someone, something, several,* etc., without giving specific information or quantity). These pronouns can be grouped into declined or non-declined words.

Declined words	Non-declined words
κανένας, καμία, κανένα *no one* or *nobody/ any(one)* (in questions)	**κάτι** or **κατιτί** *something / anything* (in questions)
κάμποσος, κάμποση, κάμποσο *several/ enough* (in questions)	**τίποτα** or **τίποτε** *nothing / anything* (in questions)
καθένας, καθεμιά, καθένα *everyone*	**καθετί** *everything*
μερικοί, μερικές, μερικά *some*	**κάθε** *every*

What is interesting, but also challenging, is that some indefinite pronouns have two different translations, depending on whether they are in statements or questions:

Ξέρει <u>κανένας</u> εδώ Αγγλικά; Όχι, <u>κανένας</u>!	*Does <u>anyone</u> know English here? No, <u>nobody</u>!*
Θέλεις <u>κάτι</u>; Ναι, θέλω <u>κάτι</u>.	*Do you want <u>anything</u>? Yes, I want <u>something</u>.*
Χρειάζεσαι <u>καμιά</u> κρέμα προσώπου; Όχι, <u>καμία</u>!	*Do you need <u>any</u> face cream? No, <u>none</u>!*
Είπες <u>τίποτα</u>; Όχι, <u>τίποτα</u>!	*Did you say <u>anything</u>? No, <u>nothing</u>!*

Conversation 2

ΣΕ ΠΟΙΟΝ ΟΡΟΦΟ ΕΙΝΑΙ ΤΑ ΑΝΔΡΙΚΑ ΠΟΥΚΑΜΙΣΑ; *ON WHAT FLOOR ARE THE MEN'S SHIRTS?*

 NEW EXPRESSIONS

 08.05

στο τμήμα ανδρικών	*at the men's section*
ανεβαίνω	*I go up*
η σκάλα	*the staircase*
η κλειστοφοβία	*claustrophobia*
κυλιόμενες σκάλες	*escalators*
τι λες;	*how about it?*
βρίσκω	*I find*
η ποικιλία	*the selection*
σίγουρος/-η/-ο	*sure*
είμαι σίγουρη	*I'm sure*

κοίτα!	*look!*
κοιτάζω	*I look*
φοράω(-ώ)	*I wear*
το μέγεθος	*the size*
μεσαίο	*medium*
το νούμερο	*the number / size*

 08.06 *Mary wants to get a shirt for Tim and is asking her way around in a big department store.*

1 **Listen to the conversation a couple of times without looking at the text. On what floor are the men's shirts?**

Ιωάννα	Συγγνώμη, σε ποιον όροφο είναι τα ανδρικά πουκάμισα;
Πωλητής	Στον τέταρτο, στο τμήμα ανδρικών.
Ιωάννα	Mary, έλα να πάρουμε το ασανσέρ.
Mary	Εγώ θα ανέβω από τις σκάλες. Τα ασανσέρ είναι πολύ μικρά και έχω κλειστοφοβία!
Ιωάννα	Εντάξει, πάμε από τις σκάλες. Το Αθηναία έχει κυλιόμενες σκάλες. Τι λες;
Mary	Εντάξει.
	Σε λίγο …
Mary	Εδώ είμαστε, φτάσαμε!
Ιωάννα	Ναι. Θα ρωτήσω τον πωλητή για ανδρικά πουκάμισα. Συγγνώμη, πού είναι τα ανδρικά πουκάμισα;
Πωλητής	Στο βάθος.
Ιωάννα	Θα βρούμε μεγάλη ποικιλία εδώ. Είμαι σίγουρη. Κοίτα!
Mary	Α, είναι ωραίο αλλά σκούρο. Λίγο πιο ανοικτό.
Ιωάννα	Τι χρώματα φοράει ο Τιμ;
Mary	Συνήθως ανοιχτά και μονόχρωμα, άσπρο, σιέλ, κίτρινο και καμιά φορά καφέ. Εμένα μου αρέσουν τα ριγέ πουκάμισα αλλά δεν του αρέσουν καθόλου.
Ιωάννα	Τι μέγεθος φοράει;
Mary	Μεσαίο ή το 36 νούμερο.
Ιωάννα	Να ένα ωραίο. Σ' αρέσει;

2 **Now read the conversation and answer the questions.**
   a Would Mary take the lift?
   b One sales person says: Στο βάθος. What does it mean?
   c What is Tim's size?

 3 **Listen again and pay special attention to the words that run together. Practise speaking the part of Mary and pay particular attention to your pronunciation.**

Language discovery 2

1 **Read the conversation once again and find synonyms or opposites (antonyms) of the words in bold.**

    a **ανοικτό** χρώμα _____

    b Τι **μέγεθος** φοράει; _____

    c **Να** ένα ωραίο! _____

    d **μεγάλη** ποικιλία _____

2 **There are three different forms of one Greek verb in this conversation. Can you translate them into English and guess when is αρέσει and when is αρέσουν used?**

    a Εμένα μου αρέσουν … _____

    b … αλλά δεν του αρέσουν καθόλου. _____

    c Σ'αρέσει; _____

Learn more

THE VERB *TO LIKE*

Did you easily come up with the correct translations to Exercise 2? The verb *to like* poses some challenges when compared to many other Greek verbs. It certainly has some unique features! First of all, it only comes with these two different forms of **αρέσει** and **αρέσουν**; the first form is used with a singular noun and the latter form with a plural noun:

Μου αρέσει ο καφές.	*I like coffee.*
Μου αρέσουν τα γλυκά.	*I like sweets.*

Second of all, contrary to most other Greek verbs, personal pronouns must be used with this verb and are not optional. The verb *to like* must take one of the two personal pronouns. The personal pronoun in parenthesis is often omitted. It is only used for purposes of emphasis and does not affect the English translation:

Μου αρέσει ο καφές.	*I like coffee.*
(Εμένα) μου αρέσει ο καφές.	*I like coffee.*

Now, note the conjugation of this verb:

(εμένα) μου αρέσει/μου αρέσουν (μ' αρέσει/μ' αρέσουν)	*I like*
(εσένα) σου αρέσει/σου αρέσουν (σ' αρέσει/σ' αρέσουν)	*you like*
(αυτού) του αρέσει/του αρέσουν	*he likes*
(αυτής) της αρέσει/της αρέσουν	*she likes*
(αυτού) του αρέσει/του αρέσουν	*it likes*
(εμάς) μας αρέσει/μας αρέσουν	*we like*
(εσάς) σας αρέσει/σας αρέσουν	*you like*
(αυτών) τους αρέσει/τους αρέσουν	*they like*

Conversation 3

ΦΡΟΥΤΑ ΚΑΙ ΛΑΧΑΝΙΚΑ *FRUIT AND VEGETABLES*

 NEW EXPRESSIONS

 08.07

λαϊκή αγορά	*fruit, vegetable and flower market* (lit. *popular market*)
η Τρίτη	*Tuesday*
θα πάμε	*we will go*
θα φάμε	*we will eat*
η νοικοκυρά	*the housewife*
παρόμοιος/-α/-ο	*similar*
τέλος πάντων	*at last, anyhow*
κόβω	*I cut*
μαχαιρώνω	*I cut/slice something with a knife*
όλα τα κόβω, όλα τα μαχαιρώνω	*I can cut a piece for you to taste*
λέω	*I say*
μη σε νοιάζει	*never mind*
το μήλο	*the apple*
πιο κάτω	*further down*
το πορτοκάλι	*the orange*
κυρ	*Mr*
ο ξένος	*foreigner*
η Τρίπολη	*Tripolis* (Greek town)
νόστιμος/-η/-ο	*delicious*
μέρλι(ν)	*extremely sweet*
που λένε	*as they say, as the rumour goes*
το κιλό	*the kilo*
το μαρούλι	*the lettuce* (n)
χόρτα	*greens*
δίπλα μου	*next to me*

08.08 *Tim and Mary buy their fruit and vegetables and flowers in the* **λαϊκή αγορά** *market that takes place close to their hotel on Tuesdays.*

1 What do they get from Κυρ Κώστας?

Tim	Θα πάμε στη λαϊκή σήμερα;
Mary	Και βέβαια θα πάμε. Είναι Τρίτη σήμερα! Τι θα φάμε αν δεν πάμε;
Ιωάννα	Πω, πω! Μιλάς σαν Ελληνίδα νοικοκυρά! Έχετε λαϊκή αγορά στην Αγγλία;
Mary	Όχι ακριβώς το ίδιο, αλλά κάτι παρόμοιο. Θα φύγουμε τέλος πάντων; *Σε λίγο …*
Πωλητής	Όλα τα κόβω, όλα τα μαχαιρώνω!
Tim	Τι λέει αυτός;
Ιωάννα	Μη σε νοιάζει. Θα πάρετε μήλα;
Mary	Όχι από εδώ. Πιο κάτω είναι πιο φτηνά και πιο καλά. Θα πάρουμε μήλα και πορτοκάλια από τον κυρ Κώστα.
Κυρ Κώστας	Καλημέρα στους ξένους μας!
Tim	Καλημέρα, κυρ Κώστα. Δεν έχετε μεγαλύτερα μήλα σήμερα;
Κυρ Κώστας	Δεν έχω μεγαλύτερα, αλλά είναι Τριπόλεως και είναι νοστιμότατα. Και τα πορτοκάλια, μέλι που λένε, μέλι!
Mary	Εντάξει. Δώστε μας ένα κιλό μήλα και δύο κιλά πορτοκάλια. Πόσο είναι;
Κυρ Κώστας	Τρία ευρώ και δέκα λεπτά.
Mary	Ποιος έχει καλά μαρούλια και χόρτα, κυρ Κώστα;
Κυρ Κώστας	Εδώ δίπλα μου.

2 Now read the conversation and answer the questions.

    a What does Mary's question Τι θα φάμε αν δεν πάμε; mean?

    b What's the real meaning of this expression: Όλα τα κόβω, όλα τα μαχαιρώνω?

    c Does Κυρ Κώστας have καλά μαρούλια και χόρτα?

3 Listen again and pay special attention to the words that run together. Practise speaking the part of Mary and pay particular attention to your pronunciation.

Language discovery 3

Read the conversation once again. Find these four verbs in the future.

    a we'll leave _____

    b we'll eat _____

    c we'll get _____

    d we'll go _____

Learn more

1 TALKING ABOUT FUTURE ACTIONS

You have encountered **θα** *will* in the previous units. **Θα** is the marker introducing you to a future action, such as *will eat*, *will go*, *will drive*. This marker is needed when you need to talk about future actions, including the English expression *going to* which is often used as well. The verb form needed to form the future, but also for the particle **να** *to* or the particle **αν** *if*, can be listed in three possible categories as follows:

Verbs without any changes

κάνω	*I do*	θα κάνω	*I'll do*
ξέρω	*I know*	θα ξέρω	*I'll know*
έχω	*I have*	θα έχω	*I'll have*

Verbs with a small change

τελειώνω	*I finish*	θα τελειώσω	*I'll finish*
ρωτάω	*I ask*	θα ρωτήσω	*I'll ask*
φεύγω	*I leave*	θα φύγω	*I'll leave*

Verbs with a big change

βλέπω	*I see*	θα δω	*I'll see*
τρώω	*I eat*	θα φάω	*I'll eat*
λέω	*I say*	θα πω	*I'll say*

Here is the future tense of three important verbs:

θα κάνω	*I will do*	θα φύγω	*I will leave*	θα δω	*I will see*
θα κάνεις	*you will do*	θα φύγεις	*you will leave*	θα δεις	*you will see*
θα κάνει	*he/she/it will do*	θα φύγει	*he/she/it will leave*	θα δει	*he/she/It will see*
θα κάνουμε	*we will do*	θα φύγουμε	*we will leave*	θα δούμε	*we will see*
θα κάνετε	*you will do*	θα φύγετε	*you will leave*	θα δείτε	*you will see*
θα κάνουν	*they will do*	θα φύγουν	*they will leave*	θα δουν	*they will see*

2 DAYS OF THE WEEK

 08.09 **Listen now, a couple of times, to the days of the week. Then listen again and repeat.**

η Κυριακή	*Sunday*
η Δευτέρα	*Monday*
η Τρίτη	*Tuesday*
η Τετάρτη	*Wednesday*

η Πέμπτη	Thursday
η Παρασκευή	Friday
το Σάββατο	Saturday

These words are all feminine nouns except Saturday, which is neuter. You have probably noticed the association between **δεύτερος/-η/-ο** *second* and **Δευτέρα** *Monday* – the second day of the week and likewise, **Τρίτη** *third day of the week*, **Τετάρτη** *fourth day of the week*, **Πέμπτη** *fifth day of the week*. **Παρασκευή** comes from **παρασκευάζω** *to prepare*, in a religious context, **Σάββατο** from *Sabbath* and **Κυριακή** *day of the Lord*, day of rest. **Σαββατοκύριακο** stands for *weekend*.

The expressions *on Sunday*, *on Monday* and so on, and the plurals *on Sundays*, *on Mondays*, etc. are:

την Κυριακή	τις Κυριακές
την Δευτέρα	τις Δευτέρες
την Τρίτη	τις Τρίτες
την Τετάρτη	τις Τετάρτες
την Πέμπτη	τις Πέμπτες
την Παρασκευή	τις Παρασκευές
το Σάββατο	τα Σάββατα

3 LOAN WORDS

Loan words from foreign languages don't normally have different forms for genders (m/f/n) or cases (nominative, genitive or accusative), or for singular and plural. More than 80% of loan words are neuter, including the ones you have already seen in this unit, including colours and designs.

το μπαρ	*bar* (English)	το ασανσέρ	*lift* (French)
το σάντουϊτς	*sandwich* (English)	το σινεμά	*cinema* (French)
το χάμπουργκερ	*hamburger* (German)	το ζαμπόν	*ham* (French)
το πουλόβερ	*sweater* (English)	το γκαράζ	*garage* (French)
κοντινένταλ	*continental* (English)	μινιόν	*mignon* (French)

Here's a reminder of the declension of these words in singular and plural form:

the gentleman		*the seaside/beach*		*the lift*	
ο	τζέντλεμαν	η	πλαζ	το	ασανσέρ
του	τζέντλεμαν	της	πλαζ	του	ασανσέρ
τον	τζέντλεμαν	την	πλαζ	το	ασανσέρ
οι	τζέντλεμαν	οι	πλαζ	τα	ασανσέρ
των	τζέντλεμαν	των	πλαζ	των	ασανσέρ
τους	τζέντλεμαν	τις	πλαζ	τα	ασανσέρ

Practice

1 Respond to the following situations in Greek.

    a A friend of yours is going shopping. Ask him if he wants your company.

    b How would you say: *I need to do some shopping, I must do some shopping* and *I want to do some shopping*?

    c How would you ask: *Which floor is the men's/women's/children's* (ανδρικών/γυναικείων/ παιδικών) *section/department?*

    d You need to buy a skirt or shirt. How would you refer to *one, two, three* or *a multi-coloured skirt/shirt*? How would you also specify the design if you want *striped, checked* or *spotted*?

    e You are talking to a sales person. Say that you need something *smaller, better* and *cheaper!*

2 Here are five colour tests. Fill in the blanks. Each colour counts for five points to a total of one hundred points (20 × 5 points). Study the colours again if you score less than 75 points!

TEST 1	TEST 2
Traffic lights	Wine colours
red = _____	white = _____
orange = _____	red = _____
green = _____	rosé = _____

TEST 3

Psychological test: what's the colour of … ?

happiness = _____

health = _____

calmness = _____

energy = _____

TEST 4

The rainbow colours: list five colours. _____

TEST 5

Your extra points!

black = _____

white = _____

Your three favourite colours … _____

3 **Complete the dialogue using the English prompts.**

Ιωάννα	Τι θέλετε παρακαλώ;
You	**a** *Ask for one kilo of oranges and two kilos of apples.*
Ιωάννα	Τίποτα άλλο;
You	**b** *Ask if the watermelons are delicious.*
Ιωάννα	Νοστιμότατα! Μέλι που λένε, μέλι!
You	**c** *Ask for a small one, not more than five kilos.*
Ιωάννα	Ορίστε. Αυτά;
You	**d** *That's it for the time being. How much are they?*
Ιωάννα	Πέντε ευρώ. Όλα μαζί.
You	**e** *Here you go! Ten euros.*
Ιωάννα	Ορίστε τα ρέστα σας.
You	**f** *Thanks. Goodbye!*

4 **A friend has given you a list of groceries. Match the list on the left with the one on the right.**

a μουστάρδα		**1**	cherry
b μπανάνα		**2**	carrot
c ανανάς		**3**	tomato
d καρότο		**4**	celery
e πατάτα		**5**	banana
f σέλινο		**6**	chocolate
g κεράσι		**7**	coffee
h σοκολάτα		**8**	mustard
i καφές		**9**	potato
j ντομάτα		**10**	pineapple

5 **Solve the clues from a–f. All are seven-letter words that end in letter -o in the centre circle. You are trying to find: one fruit, two house floors and three colours. If you take one letter from each word you will reveal the colour 'green', which is another seven-letter word.**

Your clues:

  a floor
  b colour
  c colour
  d fruit
  e floor
  f colour

6 **08.10 Listen to the conversation and find the missing words. If you want, you can first find the missing words and then listen and check your answers.**

Tim	Θα πάμε στη λαϊκή σήμερα;
Mary	Και βέβαια θα πάμε. Είναι Τρίτη σήμερα! Τι θα **a** _____ αν δεν πάμε;
Ιωάννα	Πω, πω! Μιλάς σαν **b** _____ νοικοκυρά! Έχετε λαϊκή αγορά στην Αγγλία;
Mary	Όχι ακριβώς το **c** _____, αλλά κάτι **d** _____. Θα φύγουμε τέλος **e** _____; _Σε λίγο ..._
Πωλητής	Όλα τα κόβω, όλα τα μαχαιρώνω!
Tim	Τι λέει αυτός;
Ιωάννα	Μη σε **f** _____. Θα **g** _____ μήλα;
Mary	Όχι από εδώ. Πιο κάτω είναι πιο **h** _____ και πιο καλά. Θα **i** _____ μήλα και πορτοκάλια από τον κυρ Κώστα.
Κυρ Κώστας	Καλημέρα στους **j** _____ μας!
Tim	Καλημέρα, κυρ Κώστα. Δεν έχετε **k** _____ μήλα σήμερα;
Κυρ Κώστας	Δεν έχω **k** _____, αλλά είναι Τριπόλεως και είναι **l** _____. Και τα πορτοκάλια, μέρλι που λένε, μέρλι!
Mary	Εντάξει. **m** _____ μας ένα κιλό μήλα και δύο κιλά πορτοκάλια. **n** _____ είναι;
Κυρ Κώστας	Τρία ευρώ και δέκα λεπτά.
Mary	Ποιος έχει καλά **o** _____ και **p** _____, κυρ Κώστα;
Κυρ Κώστας	Εδώ **q** _____ μου.

> πάντων   φάμε   Δώστε   νοιάζει
> πάρουμε   ξένους   πάρεις   Πόσο
> Ελληνίδα   μεγαλύτερα   ίδιο
> νοστιμότατα   φτηνά   παρόμοιο
> μαρούλια   δίπλα   χόρτα   πάρετε

7 Look at the circles. Think of as many fruits and vegetables as you can for each
particular colour.

8 Study the three adverts. Can you be a good detective and find the following words:

opening hours, telephone, open, square, a.m., p.m. Music Hall and *information*?

ΚΟΤΟΠΟΥΛΑ
ΣΟΥΒΛΑΚΙ
ΓΥΡΟΣ

grillo

για ποιότητα
και καλή γεύση

ΑΝΟΙΧΤΑ ΚΑΘΕ ΜΕΡΑ ΑΠΟ ΤΟ ΠΡΩΙ

ΚΥΡΙΑΚΕΣ ΑΝΟΙΧΤΑ
ΠΛ. ΚΥΨΕΛΗΣ 5
ΠΛΑΤΕΙΑ ΚΥΨΕΛΗΣ

ΤΗΛ. 8624843

ΣΥΚΑΡΗΣ

ΗΡΑΚΛΕΙΤΟΥ 70, ΑΙΓΑΛΕΩ, ΤΗΛ.: 53.12.990, (9 ΓΡΑΜΜΕΣ), FAX: 5312989

- 6 ή 12 δόσεις με όλες τις πιστωτικές κάρτες.
- Ετήσιο επιτόκιο 1,99 %.
- Στις αναγραφόμενες τιμές δε συμπεριλαμβάνεται το κόστος τοποθέτησης.
- Οι τιμές είναι με τον Φ.Π.Α.

ΩΡΕΣ ΛΕΙΤΟΥΡΓΙΑΣ

ΔΕΥΤΕΡΑ-ΤΕΤΑΡΤΗ-ΣΑΒΒΑΤΟ
8.30 π.μ.-15.00 μ.μ.

ΤΡΙΤΗ-ΠΕΜΠΤΗ-ΠΑΡΑΣΚΕΥΗ
8.30 π.μ.-14.00 μ.μ.
& 17.00 μ.μ.-21.00 μ.μ.

Η ΛΕΣΧΗ ΤΟΥ ΔΙΣΚΟΥ ΣΤΟ ΜΕΓΑΡΟ ΜΟΥΣΙΚΗΣ

Μία από τις αρτιότερα ενημερωμένες δισκοθήκες
κλασικής μουσικής της Ευρώπης

Ώρες λειτουργίας:
Δε-Πα 10 π.μ.-6. μ.μ., Σα 10 π.μ.-2. μ.μ.
Κατά τις ημέρες των παραστάσεων:
Δε-Πα 10 π.μ.-8:30 μ.μ., Σα 10 π.μ.-2. μ.μ. & 6-8:30 μ.μ., Κυ 6-8:30 μ.μ.
Πληροφορίες: 72.82.159

9 **Study the opening hours mentioned in these three adverts and then decide if the following statements are true or false.**

Advert 1

		True	False
a	Έχουν καλή ποιότητα και καλή γεύση.	_____	_____
b	Είναι ανοιχτά κάθε μέρα.	_____	_____
c	Έχουν δύο τηλεφωνικές γραμμές.	_____	_____
d	Δεν έχουν κοτόπουλα ή γύρο.	_____	_____

Advert 2

a	Δεν είναι ανοικτά την Κυριακή.	_____	_____
b	Την Πέμπτη κλείνουν στις 3.00 μ.μ.	_____	_____
c	Ανοίγουν στις 8.30 π.μ. κάθε μέρα.	_____	_____
d	Δεν ανοίγουν τις Κυριακές.	_____	_____

Advert 3

a	Το Μέγαρο Μουσικής έχει Λέσχη Δίσκου.	_____	_____
b	Κατά τις παραστάσεις είναι ανοικτά και τις Κυριακές.	_____	_____
c	Για πληροφορίες στο τηλέφωνο 7282159.	_____	_____
d	Δεν ανοίγει τις Κυριακές χωρίς παράσταση.	_____	_____

Test yourself

1 Can you remember the Greek for the following ten important words from this unit?

    a shopping _____

    b dress/es _____

    c cream _____

    d soon _____

    e market/s _____

    f foreigner/s _____

    g apple/s _____

    h orange/s _____

    i white _____

    j black _____

2 Can you remember the following ten important phrases from this unit?

    a Do you want company? _____

    b I don't have it with me. _____

    c Let's take the lift. _____

    d It's on the fourth floor. _____

    e I'll ask the sales person. _____

    f What's your size? _____

    g Never mind! _____

    h Do you have bigger/better … ? _____

    i Come here, next to me! _____

    j Remember the days of the week? _____

3 These five phrases are given in the present tense. Can you change them into the future tense?

    a Τελειώνω σήμερα. _____

    b Βλέπω τηλεόραση. _____

    c Ξέρω Ελληνικά. _____

    d Κάνω γυμναστική. _____

    e Τρώω μουσακά. _____

SELF CHECK

	I CAN...
⬤	…ask for Greek products state-certified for their quality.
⬤	…buy fruit and vegetables in an open market.
⬤	…talk about the days of the week.
⬤	…make commitments and set meetings on certain days.
⬤	…talk about colours and associate products and colours.
⬤	…buy toiletries in a department store.
⬤	…buy clothes and discuss sizes, designs and prices.

Revision test 2

In this unit you will review:

▶ *simple directions.*
▶ *purchasing tickets and making reservations.*
▶ *telling the time.*
▶ *enquiring about travelling.*
▶ *asking about rooms and making hotel reservations.*
▶ *prices and buying things.*
▶ *colours.*
▶ *the numbers 101–10,000.*

> **TIP**
>
> Check your progress so far. Once you have completed the following exercises, compare your answers with the correct ones, which can be found in the Answer Key. Identify any areas that still need some work and go over them again before you start the next unit.

 1 Respond to the following situations in Greek.

a How would you ask: *Where's the station?*, *Where's the square?* and *Where's the centre?*

b Someone speaks too fast for you, tell him: *I don't understand Greek well. Can you speak a little bit slower?*

c You hear Στον πρώτο δρόμο δεξιά, Στη δεύτερη γωνία δεξιά and Στο τρίτο στενό δεξιά. Did you understand everything?

d You're looking at apples. Ask for their price. The answer was Ένα ευρώ το κιλό. How expensive are they? Ask for three kilos anyway.

e You ask a friend to go to the park with you. Her reply is Με τα πόδια ή το αυτοκίνητο; What did she ask?

f Ask for a map at a περίπτερο. As soon as you get it ask for the price.

g You are in a travel agency. Ask if there is a daily flight to Thessaloniki. The answer is positive. Now ask how many flights they have today.

h Ask for the bus timetable from Athens to Thessaloniki and when you have to book the bus seats.

i The price is είκοσι πέντε ευρώ. First, how much is it? Second, ask if this is the price for one way or a return trip.

j You are at a department store looking for shirts. The sales person asks: Σας αρέσουν τ'ανοικτά ή τα σκούρα χρώματα; Τα μονόχρωμα πουκάμισα ή πολύχρωμα; What did s/he ask and what is a possible answer from you?

2 Here is a list of many colours you already know, and some new ones. Can you match the list on the left with the list on the right?

a	μπεζ	**1**	mauve
b	μπεζ σκούρο	**2**	silver
c	κρεμ	**3**	gold
d	μωβ	**4**	fawn
e	καφέ ανοικτό	**5**	grey
f	ασημένιο	**6**	beige
g	γκρίζο	**7**	orange
h	χρυσό	**8**	green
i	πράσινο	**9**	cream
j	πορτοκαλί	**10**	tan

 3 08.11 **You are in Amerikis Square with your car. Listen to a passer-by telling you the way to the tavern Αρχοντόσπιτο. What did the speaker say? Repeat and write down the directions to this tavern.**

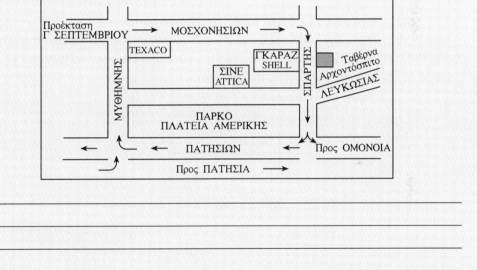

_____

_____

_____

_____

4 08.12 You want to get to ΑΝΘΙΔΩΝ 21 Anthidon Street. Luckily you've got a map. You were on the corner of Λ. ΣΥΓΓΡΟΥ Syngrou Avenue and ΧΑΡΟΚΟΠΟΥ Charokopou street. Listen and repeat what you hear. At the end, listen again and draw the directions on the map.

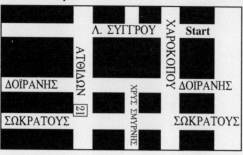

_____

_____

_____

_____

 5 08.13 Imagine you are in a Greek town, standing where the X is marked on the map in your book. You will hear three people asking about the square, the school and the station. Which letter on the plan in your book correspond to these places? Listen to the speakers and write them down.

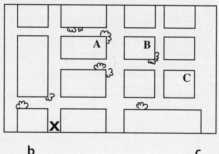

a _____   b _____   c _____

6 08.14 Listen to this conversation and find the missing words.

Η πλατεία

Πού είναι η πλατεία, παρακαλώ;

Πηγαίνετε **a** _____. Μετά από τρία **b** _____, στρίψτε **c** _____. Η πλατεία είναι στη μέση του τετραγώνου δεξιά σας.

Το σχολείο

Πού είναι το σχολείο, παρακαλώ;

Στρίψτε δεξιά στον πρώτο δρόμο. Προχωρείστε ευθεία για δύο **d** _____ και στρίψτε **e** _____. Μετά το πρώτο στενό, το σχολείο είναι στ' αριστερά σας πριν το **f** _____ του τετραγώνου.

Ο σταθμός

Πού είναι ο σταθμός, παρακαλώ;

Είναι πολύ **g** _____. Δεξιά **h** _____ στο πρώτο στενό. Μετά από τρία τετράγωνα, στρίψτε αριστερά και είναι **i** _____ στην επόμενη γωνία στ' αριστερά σας.

7 **Read the three short exchanges in Exercise 6 once again and give the Greek for the following expressions.**

   a after the first block _____

   b on the next corner _____

   c on your left _____

   d that's very easy _____

   e go straight on _____

   f before the end _____

8 **Name the following means of transport. (Here's some help: for d use με τα πόδια, and for k τρέχοντας.)**

a

b

c

d

e

f

g

h

i

j

k

l

9 Now write some sentences using some of these means of transport. Include how you get to school, work or a friend's house. You can also write which means of transport you do not like to use. The beginning of each sentence has been provided.

a Στο σχολείο συνήθως πάω ... _____

b Στον φίλο μου / Στην φίλη μου. _____

c Όταν δουλεύω συνήθως παίρνω ... _____

d Το ... δε μ'αρέσει καθόλου! _____

e Ποτέ δεν πάω στο ... με ... _____

10 08.15 Γιώργος George is planning to go to Σπέτσες Spetses for a short visit and he needs to book a hotel room. Listen to him making enquiries on the phone and decide whether the statements in your book are true or false.

Γιώργος	Καλημέρα σας. Θα ήθελα να κάνω μία κράτηση για 3 βράδια, σας παρακαλώ.
Κρατήσεις	Για πότε;
Γιώργος	Για αύριο. Έχετε δωμάτια;
Κρατήσεις	Τι δωμάτιο θέλετε, παρακαλώ;
Γιώργος	Ένα δίκλινο, με ένα διπλό κρεβάτι αλλά όχι με δύο μονά κρεβάτια!
Κρατήσεις	Μισό λεπτό, παρακαλώ, να δω το κομπιούτερ. Α μάλιστα, έχουμε δύο δωμάτια δίκλινα με διπλά κρεβάτια. Ένα βλέπει το σταθμό και το δεύτερο βλέπει τη θάλασσα.
Γιώργος	Προτιμώ τη θάλασσα. Ευχαριστώ.
Κρατήσεις	Τ' όνομά σας παρακαλώ και τη διεύθυνσή σας. Κι ένα τηλέφωνο.
Γιώργος	Ναι, λέγομαι . . .

	True	False
a Μία κράτηση για πέντε βράδια.	_____	_____
b Μία κράτηση για ένα δίκλινο.	_____	_____
c Μία κράτηση για ένα μονόκλινο.	_____	_____
d Ένα δίκλινο με δύο μονά κρεβάτια.	_____	_____
e Ένα δωμάτιο με θέα το σταθμό.	_____	_____
f Ένα δωμάτιο με θέα τη θάλασσα.	_____	_____
g Το δωμάτιο έχει τηλέφωνο.	_____	_____
h Οι κρατήσεις θέλουν όνομα, διεύθυνση και τηλέφωνο.	_____	_____

11 Read these times out loud, then write them down.

a   b

c   d

e   f

g   h

i   j

a _____   f _____
b _____   g _____
c _____   h _____
d _____   i _____
e _____   j _____

12 The following sentences are jumbled up. Put them in the right order adding the correct time at the beginning of each phrase. The times are: 10.00, 10.15, 11.30, 13.00, 14.30, 15.30.

a _____ διαβάζει εφημερίδα και βλέπει τηλεόραση.
b _____ πηγαίνει για ψώνια.
c _____ σηκώνεται από το κρεβάτι.
d _____ τρώει μεσημεριανό.
e _____ πίνει ένα νες καφέ.
f _____ πηγαίνει στο μπαρ για μία μπύρα.

13 08.16 **Listen again to the conversation and find the missing words. If you want, you can first find the missing words and then listen and compare your answers.**

Ιωάννα	Συγγνώμη, σε ποιον όροφο είναι τα ανδρικά **a** _____;
Πωλητής	Στον τέταρτο, στο **b** _____ ανδρικών.
Ιωάννα	Mary, έλα να πάρουμε το **c** _____.
Mary	Εγώ θα ανέβω από τις σκάλες. Τα **c** _____ είναι πολύ μικρά και έχω κλειστοφοβία!
Ιωάννα	Εντάξει, πάμε από τις **d** _____. Το Αθηναία έχει κυλιόμενες **d** _____. Τι λες;
Mary	Εντάξει.
	Σε λίγο...
Mary	Εδώ είμαστε, **e** _____!
Ιωάννα	Ναι. Θα ρωτήσω τον πωλητή για ανδρικά πουκάμισα. Συγγνώμη, πού είναι τα ανδρικά πουκάμισα;
Πωλητής	Στο **f** _____.
Ιωάννα	Θα βρούμε μεγάλη **g** _____ εδώ. Είμαι σίγουρη. Κοίτα!
Mary	Α, είναι ωραίο αλλά σκούρο. Λίγο πιο **h** _____.
Ιωάννα	Τι χρώματα φοράει ο Tim;
Mary	Συνήθως ανοιχτά και **i** _____ άσπρο, σιέλ, κίτρινο και καμιά φορά καφέ. Εμένα μου αρέσουν τα **j** _____ πουκάμισα αλλά δεν του αρέσουν καθόλου.
Ιωάννα	Τι **k** _____ φοράει;
Mary	Μεσαίο ή το 36 **l** _____.
Ιωάννα	Να ένα ωραίο. **m** _____;

μέγεθος	ριγέ	ασανσέρ
νούμερο	σκάλες	πουκάμισα
ανοικτό	τμήμα	μονόχρωμα
βάθος	σ' αρέσει	φτάσαμε
ποικιλία		

14 **Read the conversation once again and find the following expressions.**

a men's department _____

b sometimes _____

c escalators _____

d men's shirts _____

e in a little while _____

f he doesn't like _____

Έλα! ποιος είναι;
Hello! who is it?

In this unit you will learn how to:
▶ *make telephone calls.*
▶ *make arrangements to meet someone.*
▶ *suggest what to do and where to meet.*

CEFR: (A2) *Can have a short conversation at a kiosk before buying certain items. Can ask for someone on the phone. Can identify yourself on the phone. Can make telephone enquiries or appointments.* **(B1)** *Can describe future activities. Can participate in some business conversations.*

 ## Το ελληνικό περίπτερο! *The Greek kiosk!*

Το περίπτερο plays a very important role in everyday Greek life and it does not only sell sweets, magazines and newspapers.

The kiosks in Greece serve a similar purpose to convenience stores around the globe.

Ο περιπτεράς *the kiosk owner* will sell anything from stationery to children's toys, and from ice cream to worry beads! Kiosks used to have a public payphone, which was very useful in remote villages, but nowadays mobile phones have rendered this obsolete. Here is a list of what is readily available at a Greek **περίπτερο**:

η εφημερίδα/-ες newspaper/-s, **το περιοδικό/-κά** magazine/-s, **η σοκολάτα/-τες** chocolate/-s, **η γκοφρέτα/-τες** choco-wafer/-s, **η μαστίχα/-ες/η, τσίχλα/-ες** chewing gum, **το τσιγάρο/-α** cigarette/-s.

---

1 If you stretch your imagination, you'll find certain phonetic similarities in both languages regarding items you can get at the kiosk. How many words can you remember from the following list without looking at the text above?
a *cigarette,* **b** *newspaper,* **c** *chocolate*

 ## Vocabulary builder

ΣΤΟ ΠΕΡΙΠΤΕΡΟ *AT THE KIOSK*

 1 09.01 **Listen to a person who is buying some things at a kiosk. Note the items he wants to get.**
    a η εφημερίδα/-ες
    b το περιοδικό/-κά
    c η σοκολάτα/-τες
    d η γκοφρέτα/-τες

e η μαστίχα/-ες / η τσίχλα/-ες

f το παγωτό/-ά

g η καραμέλα/-ες

h ο στυλός/-οί / το στυλό/τα στυλό

i το μολύβι/-α

j το ξυράφι/-α

k το γραμματόσημο/-α

l ο φάκελος/-οι

m το τσιγάρο/-α

2 09.02 **Listen to the previous conversation. Note the correct price for each item.**

    a η εφημερίδα/-ες _____

    b το περιοδικό/-κά _____

    c η σοκολάτα/-τες _____

    d η γκοφρέτα/-τες _____

    e η μαστίχα/-ες / η τσίχλα/-ες _____

    f το παγωτό/-ά _____

    g η καραμέλα/-ες _____

    h ο στυλός/-οί / το στυλό/τα στυλό _____

    i το μολύβι/-α_____

    j το ξυράφι/-α_____

    k το γραμματόσημο/-α _____

    l ο φάκελος/-οι _____

    m το τσιγάρο/-α _____

ΣΤΟ ΤΗΛΕΦΩΝΟ *ON THE PHONE*

3 09.03 **Listen to some short telephone conversations and find the missing expressions. If you want, you can first find the missing expressions and then listen and check your answers. At the end, listen once again and repeat what you hear.**

    a Εγώ είμαι, η Δανάη.   **d** Ποιος τη ζητάει;

    b Ποιος τον ζητάει;   **e** Εγώ είμαι, ο Γιάννης.

    c Ο ίδιος.   **f** Η ίδια.

Διάλογος 1	**Διάλογος 2**	**Διάλογος 3**
Γεια σου, Κώστα!	Καλημέρα, Αντώνη!	Εμπρός! Ναι;
Έλα ποιος είναι;	Έλα ποια είναι;	Καλησπέρα! Είναι η Νίκη εκεί;
_____	_____	_____
Διάλογος 4	**Διάλογος 5**	**Διάλογος 6**
Παρακαλώ!	Λέγετε;	Ορίστε!
Ναι, μπορώ να μιλήσω στη Μαρία;	Τον κύριο Κοσμά, παρακαλώ.	Χαίρεται! Είναι ο Χαρίλαος εκεί;
_____	_____	_____

4 Now, read the telephone conversations again and match the English expressions to their Greek counterparts.

a Who is calling? (When you hear a male voice) _____

b Who is calling? (When you hear a female voice) _____

c Speaking! (If you are a man) _____

d Speaking! (If you are a woman) _____

e Hello! (On the phone) _____

f This is … (On the phone) _____

Conversation 1

ΜΠΟΡΩ ΝΑ ΚΑΝΩ ΕΝΑ ΤΗΛΕΦΩΝΗΜΑ; *CAN I MAKE A TELEPHONE CALL?*

 NEW EXPRESSIONS

 09.04

Έχετε τηλέφωνο;	*Do you have a phone?*
χαλασμένος/-η/-ο	*out of order*
το περίπτερο	*kiosk/news-stand*
τοπικός/-ή/-ό	*local*
υπεραστικός/-ή/-ό	*long distance*
παίρνει τον αριθμό	*he dials* (lit. *takes*) *the number*
λέγομαι	*my name is* (lit. *I am called*)
θα ήθελα	*I would like*
να κλείσω ένα ραντεβού	*(I'd like) to make* (lit. *'close'*) *an appointment*
θα μπορούσε	*he/she/it would be able to, could*
αν είναι δυνατόν	*if it is possible*
ο περιπτεράς	*news-stand salesperson/owner*

 09.05 *Tim is organizing a meeting with a colleague who works for a bank.*

1 Listen to the conversation a couple of times without looking at the text. When will Tim have the meeting: today or tomorrow?

Tim	Έχετε τηλέφωνο;
Περιπτεράς 1	Συγγνώμη αλλά είναι χαλασμένο. Πηγαίνετε απέναντι στο άλλο περίπτερο.
Tim	Ευχαριστώ. … Μπορώ να κάνω ένα τηλέφωνο;
Περιπτεράς 2	Τοπικό ή υπεραστικό;
Tim	Τοπικό, εδώ στην Αθήνα.
Περιπτεράς 2	Αν είναι τοπικό, τι ρωτάς; Κάνε!
Tim	Ευχαριστώ … Ναι, γεια σας. Λέγομαι Tim Johnson. Θα ήθελα να κλείσω ένα ραντεβού με τον κ. Στέλιο Αμανατίδη. Πότε θα μπορούσε να με δει;

Γραμματέας	Θα θέλατε αργότερα σήμερα ή αύριο;
Tim	Αύριο θα ήταν καλύτερα για μένα, αν είναι δυνατόν.
Γραμματέας	Ένα λεπτό να δω το πρόγραμμα του … Μπορεί να σας δει αύριο στις 2.00 το μεσημέρι. Μπορείτε;
Tim	Ναι μπορώ, ευχαριστώ πολύ. Θα σας δω αύριο στις 2.00.

2 Now read the conversation and answer the questions.

a How is Tim identifying himself on the phone?

b What's the difference between τοπικό and υπεραστικό telephone call?

c Can Tim come to the appointment at 2 o'clock?

 3 Listen again and pay special attention to the words that run together. Practise speaking the part of Tim and pay particular attention to your pronunciation.

Language discovery 1

1 Look at Conversation 1 and complete the *would* **phrases in Greek.**

a … it would be … _____

b … would you like … _____

c … I would like … _____

d … would he be able to … _____

2 Look at Conversation 1 once again and find four phrases that use the verb *can* **or** *could* **in Greek. Then translate the phrases into English.**

a _____   **c** _____

b _____   **d** _____

Learn more

THE PARTICLE ΘΑ IS USED AS *WILL* OR *WOULD*

In the last unit you were introduced to **θα** *will* in the future tense. To recap, the verb form that follows this particle could be exactly the same, e.g. **κάνω** – **θα κάνω**; it could have a small difference, e.g. **τελειώνω** – **θα τελειώσω**; it could also be irregular, e.g. **τρώω** – **θα φάω**. In this unit, **θα** has been used with three verbs, which are in a past tense form. Now, notice how Greek changes the verb form that follows the particle **θα**, contrasted with English which changes *will* to *would* but keeps the form of the main verb unchanged:

Θα κάνω/θα έκανα	*I will do/I would do*
Θα τελειώσω/θα τελείωνα	*I will finish/I would finish*
Θα φάω/θα έτρωγα	*I will eat/I would eat*
Θα θέλω/θα ήθελα	*I will want/I would like*
Θα μπορώ/θα μπορούσα	*I will be able/I would be able*
Θα είμαι/θα ήμουν	*I will be/I would be*

Four examples are fully conjugated for you here:

θα ήθελα	I would like	θα μπορούσα	I would be able
θα ήθελες	you would like	θα μπορούσες	you would be able
θα ήθελε	he/she/it would like	θα μπορούσε	he/she would be able
θα θέλαμε	we would like	θα μπορούσαμε	we would be able
θα θέλατε	you would like	θα μπορούσατε	you would be able
θα ήθελαν	they would like	θα μπορούσαν	they would be able
θα ήμουν	I would be	θα προτιμούσα	I would prefer
θα ήσουν	you would be	θα προτιμούσες	you would prefer
θα ήταν	he/she/it would be	θα προτιμούσε	he/she/it would prefer
θα ήμασταν	we would be	θα προτιμούσαμε	we would prefer
θα ήσασταν	you would be	θα προτιμούσατε	you would prefer
θα ήταν	they would be	θα προτιμούσαν	they would prefer

Conversation 2

Τ'ΟΝΟΜΑ ΣΑΣ; *YOUR NAME?*

 NEW EXPRESSIONS

 09.06

Παρακαλώ;	*What can I do for you? How can I help you?*
καθίστε	*sit down*
τ' όνομά σας;	*your name?*
ονομάζομαι	*my name is* (lit. *I'm named*)
ο/η συνάδελφος	*the colleague*
δουλεύω	*I work*
θα τον πάρω στο εσωτερικό …	*I'll call his extension (line)*
κατεβάζει το ακουστικό	*she is hanging up the receiver*
φωνάζω	*I call*
ακολουθείστε με	*follow me*
πάρτε μια καρέκλα	*take a seat*
τα χαιρετίσματα	*greetings/regards*
εκ μέρους σας	*on your behalf*
τις θερμότερες ευχές μου	*my warmest wishes*
τα φιλικότερα χαιρετίσματά μου	*my best* (lit. *friendlier*) *regards*
να μην το ξεχάσετε!	*don't forget that!*

 09.07 *Tim is already at Mr Amanatides office speaking to his secretary.*

1 Listen to the conversation a couple of times without looking at the text. Should Tim wait a little before he sees Mr Amanatides?

Γραμματέας	Καλημέρα σας. Παρακαλώ;
Tim	Καλημέρα σας. Έχω ραντεβού με τον κ. Αμανατίδη.
Γραμματέας	Μάλιστα, καθίστε παρακαλώ. Τ' όνομά σας;
Tim	Ονομάζομαι Tim Johnson, είμαι συνάδελφος του κ. Αμανατίδη. Δουλεύω στην Westminster Bank.
Γραμματέας	Α! Μάλιστα. Μισό λεπτό θα τον πάρω στο εσωτερικό … Ο κ. Αμανατίδης θα σας δει σε δύο λεπτά. Θα σας φωνάξω εγώ.
Tim	Ευχαριστώ …
Γραμματέας	Παρακαλώ, ακολουθήστε με.
Tim	Χαίρετε, κύριε Αμανατίδη. Χαίρομαι πολύ που σας ξαναβλέπω.
Αμανατίδης	Γεια σας κ. Johnson, τι κάνετε; Ελάτε, πάρτε μια καρέκλα.
Tim	Έχετε χαιρετίσματα από τη σύζυγό μου. Κι αυτό είναι ένα μπουκάλι ουίσκι για σας.
Αμανατίδης	Α! Πολύ ευγενικό εκ μέρους σας. Να της δώσετε τις θερμότερες ευχές μου και τα φιλικότερα χαιρετίσματά μου. Να μην το ξεχάσετε!
Tim	Όχι, όχι. Δε θα το ξεχάσω.

2 Now read the conversation and answer the questions.

   a How is Tim identifying himself to Mr Amanatides' secretary?

   b Can you find the following phrases: *Just a moment!* and *In two minutes*?

   c What does the phrase Χαίρομαι πολύ που σας ξαναβλέπω! mean?

 3 Listen again and pay special attention to the words that run together. Practise speaking the part of Tim and pay particular attention to your pronunciation.

Language discovery 2

1 Look at these phrases from Conversation 2 and select the personal pronouns. Notice their position and compare it to English. Is it a perfect match?

   a … θα τον πάρω …   **d** … που σας ξαναβλέπω …

   b … θα σας δει …   **e** … να της δώσετε …

   c … θα σας φωνάξω …   **f** … να μην το ξεχάσετε …

2 There are five phrases in this conversation using the word σας. Does it mean the same thing when it accompanies nouns, prepositions, or verbs, or not? Translate the phrases into English.

   a Τ' όνομά σας; _____

   b … θα σας δει … _____

   c … θα σας φωνάξω … _____

   d … για σας … _____

   e … εκ μέρους σας … _____

Learn more

1 PERSONAL PRONOUNS

Personal pronouns can be quite challenging, especially when compared to English. The exercises above intended to point out two major differences about Greek personal pronouns. First, Greek personal pronouns come before the verb as opposed to after the verb as in English. Second, Greek personal pronouns are categorized into three subgroups: nominative, genitive, and accusative, a feature that does not exist in English. The following table will give you a better overview and clarify this challenging grammatical concept. Of course, you can come back to this reference table as often as needed.

Personal pronouns in nominative	Personal pronouns in genitive	Personal pronouns in accusative
εγώ, εσύ, αυτός, αυτή, αυτό	μου, σου, του, της, του	με, σε, τον, την, το
εμείς, εσείς, αυτοί, αυτές, αυτά	μας, σας, τους	μας, σας, τους, τις, τα

2 SAYING YOUR NAME

You have already learnt the question **Πώς σε λένε;** *What's your name?* and its corresponding answer **Με λένε...** *My name's...* In this conversation two new phrases popped up: **Τ'όνομά σας;** *(What's) your name?* and **Ονομάζομαι...** *My name's...* (lit. *I'm called...*) As you probably guessed, there are many different ways of asking this question or replying to it: **ονομάζομαι, λέγομαι, το όνομά μου είναι**, but remember also **με λένε**. These all mean *my name is*. When referring to your first name you can use **μικρό όνομα** (lit. *small name*) and for your last name or surname **επίθετο** or **επώνυμο**.

 09.08 **Listen to some examples which show you how to ask for a name or say your name with alternative ways. Listen to the examples a couple of times and then listen again and repeat after each one.**

Ποιο είναι το επίθετό σας;	*What's your last name?*
Γράψτε το επώνυμό σας.	*Write your surname.*
Ποιο είναι το μικρό σου όνομα;	*What's your first name?*
Με λένε Κωνσταντίνο.	*My name is Konstantine.*
Πώς λέγεσαι;	*What's your name?*
Ονομάζομαι Κώστας Αμανατίδης.	*My name is Kostas Amanatides.*
Πώς σε λένε;	*What's your name?*
Πώς ονομάζεσαι;	*What's your name?*

Conversation 3

ΚΑΛΩΣΟΡΙΣΑΤΕ ΣΤΗΝ ΕΛΛΑΔΑ! *WELCOME TO GREECE!*

 NEW EXPRESSIONS

 09.09

να σας γνωρίσω …	*let me introduce … to you*
χαίρω πολύ	*glad to meet you*
προσπαθώ	*I try*
η κάρτα	*the card*
υπέροχα	*excellent*
μακάρι	*I wish/would that/if only/may*
προσφέρω	*I offer*
το αναψυκτικό	*the refreshment*
αν δεν σας κάνει κόπο	*if it's no trouble to you*
η τράπεζα	*bank*
ελπίζω	*I hope*
ξεκινώ	*I start*
η συνεργασία	*the co-operation*
εύχομαι	*I wish/I hope*
τραπεζικό σύστημα	*bank system*

 09.10 *The president of a UK-based company is visiting Mr Amanatides and exploring the possibility of setting up a branch of her company in Greece. Tim introduces her to Mr Amanatides.*

1 Listen to this conversation a couple of times without looking at the text. Does Ms Smith speak Greek?

Tim	Να σας γνωρίσω την κυρία Smith.
Αμανατίδης	Χαίρω πολύ, κυρία Smith (Σμιθ). Καλώς ορίσατε στην Ελλάδα. Καθίστε.
Smith	Κι εγώ χαίρω πολύ. Δεν μιλάω καλά Ελληνικά αλλά προσπαθώ. Αυτή είναι η κάρτα μου.
Αμανατίδης	Μιλάτε υπέροχα! Μακάρι να μιλούσαν όλοι έτσι! Μα καθίστε, καθίστε! Να σας προσφέρω κάτι; Θα πιείτε κάτι; Έναν καφέ, ένα αναψυκτικό ίσως;
Smith	Ένα νες, αν δεν σας κάνει κόπο.
Tim	Κι ένα μέτριο για μένα.
Αμανατίδης	Η τράπεζά μας ελπίζει να ξεκινήσουμε μία καλή συνεργασία.
Smith	Κι εγώ αυτό εύχομαι …
Tim	Να φύγω; Εσείς μιλάτε καλύτερα ελληνικά από μένα.
Smith	Να μη φύγεις! Σε χρειάζομαι γιατί ξέρεις πολλά από το ελληνικό τραπεζικό σύστημα.

2 Now read the conversation and answer the questions.

  a How does Tim introduce Ms Smith to Mr Amanatides?

  b What expressions are used for *Nice to meet you!* or *Nice to meet you, too!* in the conversation?

  c What does the phrase *Να σας προσφέρω κάτι;* mean?

 3 Listen again and pay special attention to the words that run together. Practise speaking the part of Ms Smith and pay particular attention to your pronunciation.

Language discovery 3

1 Look at the nouns from the conversation in the following table. Can you classify them by the correct gender (masculine, feminine or neuter)? Does the ending help you make an educated guess?

a κυρία	**d** καφέ	**g** τράπεζα
b Ελλάδα	**e** αναψυχτικό	**h** συνεργασία
c κάρτα	**f** κόπο	**i** σύστημα

Masculine nouns	Feminine nouns	Neuter nouns
_____	_____	_____
_____	_____	_____
_____	_____	_____
_____	_____	_____
_____	_____	_____

2 Look at the following idiomatic expressions from the conversation. Can you match them to their English counterparts? Remember, idioms cannot be translated word for word!

  a Take a seat please …   **1** Να σας γνωρίσω …

  b Should I go now?   **2** Θα πιείτε κάτι;

  c Let me introduce you to …   **3** Μα καθίστε, καθίστε …

  d Will you have anything?   **4** Να φύγω;

Learn more

1 THIS IS MY CARD!

Κάρτα in this conversation means *business card*; it can also mean *postcard* and can be used in with various other words:

πιστωτική κάρτα	*credit card*
τραπεζική κάρτα	*bank card*
τηλεφωνική κάρτα	*phone card*
εκπτωτική κάρτα	*discount card*

| επαγγελματική κάρτα | business card |
| ασφαλιστική κάρτα | insurance card |

2 IF IT'S NO TROUBLE TO YOU!

Here are some useful Greek phrases to learn by heart:

Αν (δε) σου/σας κάνει κόπο.	If it is (no) trouble to/for you.
Αν (δεν) είναι δυνατό.	If it is (not) possible.
Αν (δεν) επιτρέπεται.	If it is (not) allowed.

The word **κόπο** *toil* has many useful meanings in different contexts. This book should have been **Ελληνικά χωρίς κόπο!** *Greek without toil!/Greek without hard work!* If you look back at the earlier units, you will see how far you have come. Congratulations!

Study these examples and see how important **κόπος** is. Don't forget: **Τα αγαθά κόποις κτώνται!** *No pain, no gain!*

Μην κάνεις τον κόπο να'ρθεις.	Don't bother to come.
Δεν είναι καθόλου κόπος.	It's no bother at all.
Ευχαριστώ για τον κόπο σου.	Thanks for your trouble.
Μαθαίνω Ελληνικά χωρίς κόπο.	I learn Greek without any difficulty.
Αξίζει τον κόπο.	It's worthwhile.
Είναι χαμένος κόπος.	It's a waste of energy/effort.

3 THE SUBJUNCTIVE

You will have noticed the extensive use of **να** to connect two verbs. Examples from this unit include:

Μπορώ να κάνω.	I am able to do.
Θα ήθελα να κλείσω.	I would like to make.
Μπορεί να σας δει.	He is able to see you.

It is essential for you to remember here that the verb form of the second verb (the subjunctive – see the **Glossary of grammatical terms** at the back of the book) takes the same verb forms in the future tense preceded by **θα**. Notice that in the following examples, the same changes occur in the future and the subjunctive.

Main verb form		Future verb form	Subjunctive verb form
τελειώνω	to end	θα τελειώσω	θέλω να τελειώσω
πηγαίνω	to go	θα πάω	θέλω να πάω
βλέπω	to see	θα δω	θέλω να δω
ανεβαίνω	to go up	θα ανέβω/ανεβώ	θέλω να ανέβω
ρωτάω/ρωτώ	to ask	θα ρωτήσω	θέλω να ρωτήσω
τρώω	to eat	θα φάω	θέλω να φάω
φεύγω	to leave	θα φύγω	θέλω να φύγω
παίρνω	to take	θα πάρω	θέλω να πάρω

The verb form is the same in the future and subjunctive. You also use this verb form in situations where two verbs in the same sentence have different personal pronouns, as in *I want him to go.*

θέλω να πά<u>ω</u>	*I want (<u>me</u>) to go*
θέλω να πα<u>ς</u>	*I want <u>you</u> to go*
θέλω να πά<u>ει</u>	*I want <u>him</u>/<u>her</u>/<u>it</u> to go*
θέλω να πά<u>με</u>	*I want <u>us</u> to go*
θέλω να πά<u>τε</u>	*I want <u>you</u> to go*
θέλω να πάν<u>(ε)</u>	*I want <u>them</u> to go*

The subjunctive has two main functions in Greek. The first one was mentioned in the previous paragraph – as the second verb in a sentence preceded by **να**: **Θέλω να πάω**. *want to go.*

The second main function is more idiomatic. The simplest way of grasping this function of the subjunctive is to learn examples in phrases, as you come across them. You have encountered many examples in this unit's conversations:

Ένα λεπτό να δω το πρόγραμμά του.	*Just a minute, let me see* (lit. *(let me) to see*) *his schedule.*
Να της δώσετε τις θερμότερες ευχές μου.	*Give her my best regards.*
Να μην το ξεχάσετε!	*Don't forget that!*
Να σας γνωρίσω τον κύριο Smith.	*Let me introduce Mr Smith to you.* (lit. *(I would like) to introduce to you Mr Smith.*)
Μακάρι να μιλούσαν όλοι έτσι!	*If only everybody could speak like this!* (lit. *(I wish that) everybody speaks so!*)
Να σας προσφέρω κάτι;	*Can I offer you anything?* (lit. *(Can) I (to) offer you anything?*)
Να φύγω;	*Shall I go?* (lit. *(May) I to go?*)
Έλα να με δεις.	*Come and see me.* (lit. *Come to see me.*)

 TIP

The previous conversations might be a bit 'business oriented' for you if you do not have any business meetings on your next trip to Greece. If this is the case, we suggest that you still learn this new vocabulary, especially words and expressions that can also be used on different social occasions. Can you continue your list and come up with a 'top 10 list' before you tackle the next section? Our suggestions include:

1 Let me introduce … to you.

2 I wish …

3 If it's no trouble to you …

Practice

1 **Respond to the following situations you are likely to encounter in Greek.**

a You are at a περίπτερο. Ask the περιπτεράς for one local and one long-distance telephone call.

b Introduce yourself and say where you work.

c Someone is saying: Παρακαλώ, ακολουθείστε με. What will you do?

d Someone is visiting you. How could you say *Sit down* or *Have a seat*?

e You are talking to a colleague. How could you say: *My regards to your wife*?

f Use the phrase *Don't forget that!*

g Introduce Mr Smith to your friend.

h Introduce Γιώργος to Γιάννης.

i Welcome someone to your home. Write out both phrases.

2 **Match each question with the most appropriate answer.**

a Έχετε τηλέφωνο;

b Θέλετε για τοπικό ή υπεραστικό τηλέφωνο;

c Πότε θα θέλατε να κλείσετε ραντεβού;

d Χαίρεσαι που με ξαναβλέπεις;

e Να σου προσφέρω κάτι;

1 Μισό λεπτό να δω το πρόγραμμά μου.

2 Ναι, ένα αναψυκτικό αν δε σου κάνει κόπο.

3 Ναι, πάρα πολύ.

4 Για υπεραστικό. Έχετε μετρητή (unit metre);

5 Ναι, γιατί το θέλετε;

3 **Rearrange these lines to make up a dialogue.**

a Ναι από τις 8.30 π.μ.–2.00 μ.μ.

b Είναι δύο παρά τέταρτο.

c Σε ποια τράπεζα θα πας;

d Εύχομαι να πάω πριν (να) κλείσουν.

e Πότε ανοίγουν οι τράπεζες; Ξέρεις;

f Τι ώρα είναι τώρα;

g Στην Τράπεζα Πίστεως.

 4 09.11 **Take part in a dialogue with Mr Amamatides. Say your lines first before listening to the dialogue and then listen again and compare your answers.**

Αμανατίδης	Ποιον χρειάζεσαι γι' αυτό το ραντεβού;
You	**a** *I need Nicholas because his Greek is very good.*
Αμανατίδης	Ο Γιώργος ξέρει καλύτερα και είναι φτηνότερος.
You	**b** *I don't care who is cheaper. I care who is better!*
Αμανατίδης	Νομίζω ο Γιώργος. Εσύ τι λες;
You	**c** *Let's start with Nicholas and if there is a problem with* (προβληματική) *co-operation, then we will see.*
Αμανατίδης	Μπορεί να είναι πολύ αργά τότε.
You	**d** *It's never too late!*
Αμανατίδης	Ελπίζω να έχεις δίκιο! (*I hope you are right* (lit. *you have right*).)

5 **Match the words on the left with those on the right.**

a τοπικό		**1** internal
b αριθμός		**2** system
c τηλέφωνο		**3** schedule/programme
d εσωτερικό		**4** all
e κάρτα		**5** number
f σύστημα		**6** telephone
g πρόγραμμα		**7** magazine/periodical
h ραντεβού		**8** local
i όλοι		**9** appointment/rendezvous
j περιοδικό		**10** card

 6 **Write out the future or subjunctive forms of the following verbs.**

    a ανεβαίνω   θα/να _____

    b βλέπω   θα/να _____

    c παίρνω   θα/να _____

    d πηγαίνω   θα/να _____

    e ρωτάω(ώ)   θα/να _____

    f τελειώνω   θα/να _____

    g τρώω   θα/να _____

    h φεύγω   θα/να _____

7 **Use your translation skills to say the following in Greek.**

    a I want to go to the square.

    b Hello! I have an appointment with Mr Petrou.

    c He wants us to go to Thessaloniki tomorrow.

    d I would like a single room with a bath and a TV.

    e Where's the restaurant?

    f That would have been (lit. would be) better for me.

    g I would prefer a room with a view.

    h A refreshment (a soft drink) if it's no trouble for you.

8 **Can you recognize some of the words you have learnt in this unit? Remember you can find the words horizontally and vertically.**

Η	Σ	Α	Σ	Τ	Α	Ν	Π
Θ	Κ	Α	Ι	Ρ	Ο	Σ	Α
Ε	Λ	Α	Τ	Ω	Ρ	Α	Ι
Λ	Ε	Ο	Μ	Ω	Σ	Τ	Ρ
Α	Ν	Ε	Β	Ω	Τ	Η	Ν
Ξ	Ε	Κ	Ι	Ν	Η	Σ	Ω

9 09.12 Listen to Conversation 3 again and find the missing words. If you want, you can first find the missing words and then listen and compare your answers.

Tim	Να σας **a** _____ την κυρία Smith.
Αμανατίδης	**b** _____ πολύ, κυρία Smith (Σμιθ). Καλώς ορίσατε στην Ελλάδα. **c** _____.
Smith	Κι εγώ **b** _____ πολύ. Δεν μιλάω καλά ελληνικά αλλά **d** _____. Αυτή είναι η κάρτα μου.
Αμανατίδης	Μιλάτε **e** _____! Μακάρι να μιλούσαν όλοι έτσι! Μα **c** _____, **c** _____! Να σας **f** _____ κάτι; Θα πιείτε κάτι; Έναν καφέ, ένα αναψυκτικό ίσως;
Smith	Ένα νες, αν δεν σας κάνει **g** _____.
Tim	Κι ένα μέτριο για μένα.
Αμανατίδης	Η τράπεζά μας **h** _____ να ξεκινήσουμε μια καλή **i** _____.
Smith	Κι εγώ αυτό **j** _____.
Tim	Να φύγω; Εσείς μιλάτε καλύτερα ελληνικά από μένα.
Smith	Να μη **k** _____! Σε **l** _____ γιατί ξέρεις πολλά από το ελληνικό τραπεζικό σύστημα.

> χρειάζομαι   φύγεις   ελπίζει
> καθίστε   γνωρίζω   προσφέρω
> συνεργασία   κόπο   εύχομαι
> χαίρω   προσπαθώ   υπέροχα

 Test yourself

1 Can you remember the Greek for the following ten important words from this unit?

  a telephone/s _____

  b later _____

  c kiosk/s _____

  d tomorrow _____

  e card/s _____

  f today _____

  g bank/s _____

  h regards _____

  i appointment/s _____

  j refreshments _____

2 Can you remember the following ten important phrases from this unit?

  a Can I make a telephone call? _____

  b Sit down please! _____

  c I'd like to make an appointment. _____

  d Don't forget that. _____

  e If it is possible. _____

  f My regards to your wife. _____

  g I'm glad to see you again. _____

  h Let me introduce Mr X to you. _____

  i Take a seat! _____

  j How do you do? _____

3 The following five phrases are given in the present tense. Can you change them into the future tense?

  a Πηγαίνω αύριο. _____

  b Ρωτάω αύριο. _____

  c Φεύγω νωρίς. _____

  d Παίρνω τηλέφωνο. _____

  e Ανεβαίνω τώρα. _____

SELF CHECK

I CAN...
○ ...understand the cultural activities that take place in a kiosk.
○ ...ask for someone on the phone.
○ ...identify yourself on the phone.
○ ...make telephone enquiries or appointments.
○ ...describe future or subjunctive activities in Greek.
○ ...participate in some business conversations.

10 Είχα ένα τρομερό πονοκέφαλο!

I had a terrible headache!

In this unit you will learn how to:

▶ *express feelings.*
▶ *talk to a doctor.*
▶ *ask for remedies.*
▶ *name different professions.*
▶ *name different sports.*

CEFR: (B1) *Can ask for a doctor or medical assistance in case of emergency. Can explain to a doctor where or what hurts. Can ask for remedies. Can tell a story that took place in the past. Can understand some frequent wishes.* **(A2)** *Can name different professions including your own. Can tell what sports you like or dislike. Can explain how often you do things in general or daily routines.*

Ο πληθυσμός της Ελλάδας και οι Έλληνες του εξωτερικού *The population of Greece and Greeks abroad*

The **πληθυσμός** *population* of Greece reached a peak of 10.2 million in 1991. Since then, it declined with slightly fewer than 10 million at the start of 2000 and then rose to slightly over 10 million in 2013. There are approximately 4 million Greeks living abroad, particularly in **Ευρώπη** *Europe*, **Καναδάς** *Canada*, **Αμερική** *the USA*, **Νότια Αφρική** *South Africa* and **Αυστραλία** *Australia*. The number of migrants and refugees in Greece has dramatically increased, reaching over 1 million by the turn of the century and over 2 million by 2013. Most of these people come from **Ανατολική Ευρώπη** *Eastern Europe* and **Βόρεια Αφρική** *North Africa*.

 1 How do you say *Europe* and *Africa* in Greek?

Vocabulary builder

ΣΕ ΠΕΡΙΠΤΩΣΗ ΑΝΑΓΚΗΣ *IN CASE OF EMERGENCY*

 1 **10.01 Listen to some useful phrases when feelings, talking to doctors, asking for remedies and understanding basic medical jargon. Here are a few basic phrases. Listen carefully and repeat out loud.**

Χρειάζομαι ένα γιατρό γρήγορα/αμέσως.	*I need a doctor quickly/at once.*
Ένα γιατρό που να μιλά Αγγλικά.	*A doctor who can speak English.*
Πού είναι το ιατρείο;	*Where's the doctor's office?*
Πού είναι η κλινική;	*Where's the clinic?*
Πού είναι το νοσοκομείο;	*Where's the hospital?*

Δεν αισθάνομαι καλά.	I don't feel well.
Έχω πυρετό.	I have got a fever/temperature.
Έχω πονοκέφαλο.	I have got a headache.
Έχω κοιλόπονο.	I have got a stomach ache.
Έχω πονόλαιμο.	I have got a sore throat.
Αισθάνομαι άρρωστος.	I feel ill.
Αισθάνομαι αδιάθετος.	I feel sick.
Αισθάνομαι ναυτία.	I feel seasick.
Αισθάνομαι ζάλη.	I feel dizzy.

You might hear from a doctor:

Τι έχετε;	What's the trouble?
Πού πονάτε;	Where does it hurt?
Πόσο καιρό έχετε αυτόν τον πόνο;	How long have you had this pain?
Σηκώστε το μανίκι σας.	Roll up your sleeve.
Παρακαλώ, γδυθείτε/ξαπλώστε.	Please, undress/lie down.

2 Here is some useful vocabulary including some health problems and some remedies. Take a close look, some of these words are similar in Greek and English.

το κρύωμα	the cold	το άσθμα	the asthma
το άγχος	the stress	η διάρροια	the diarrhoea
η γρίππη	the flu	η πνευμονία	the pneumonia
ο/η ειδικός	the specialist	η εξέταση	the examination
ο/η αλλεργικός	the allergyic	η κορτιζόνη	the cortisone
το φάρμακο	the medicine	το αντιβιοτικό	the antibiotic
το αντισηπτικό	the antiseptic	η θεραπεία	the therapy/treatment
		η συνταγή	the prescription

 3 10.02 You will now hear the basic body parts. Listen to them a couple of times before you repeat them out loud.

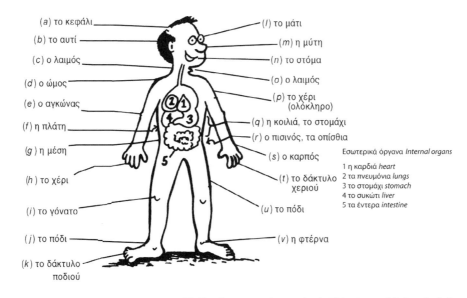

(a) το κεφάλι
(b) το αυτί
(c) ο λαιμός
(d) ο ώμος
(e) ο αγκώνας
(f) η πλάτη
(g) η μέση
(h) το χέρι
(i) το γόνατο
(j) το πόδι
(k) το δάκτυλο ποδιού
(l) το μάτι
(m) η μύτη
(n) το στόμα
(o) ο λαιμός
(p) το χέρι (ολόκληρο)
(q) η κοιλιά, το στομάχι
(r) ο πισινός, τα οπίσθια
(s) ο καρπός
(t) το δάκτυλο χεριού
(u) το πόδι
(v) η φτέρνα

Εσωτερικά όργανα *Internal organs*

1 η καρδιά *heart*
2 τα πνευμόνια *lungs*
3 το στομάχι *stomach*
4 το συκώτι *liver*
5 τα έντερα *intestine*

4 **Tell the doctor what's wrong with you using these expressions. Match the pictures to the phrases.**

a Το κεφάλι μου βουίζει.

b Νομίζω ότι θα κάνω εμετό. (*vomit*)

c Έχω κρυάδες (*chill*).

d Έχω τρομερό πονοκέφαλο.

e Δεν έχω καθόλου όρεξη.

f Έχω τρομερό κοιλόπονο.

g Με πονάει ο δεξιός μου ώμος.

Conversation 1

ΠΟΥ ΗΣΟΥΝ ΕΧΘΕΣ; *WHERE WERE YOU YESTERDAY?*

 NEW EXPRESSIONS

 10.03

ήσουν	*you were*
(ε)χθές/(ε)χτές	*yesterday*
σε χάσαμε	*we missed you*
αδιάθετος/-η/-ο	*sick, ill*
είχα	*I had*
τρομερός/-ή/-ό	*awful, terrible*
κι έτσι	*so, because of that*

έμεινα σπίτι	*I stayed home (lit. house)*
όλα βούιζαν στο κεφάλι μου	*my head was spinning*
πήγες;	*did you go?*
ο/η γιατρός	*the doctor (m + f)*
το φαρμακείο	*the chemist's/pharmacy*
ο/η φαρμακοποιός	*the chemist (m + f)*
έδωσε	*she gave*
ισχυρός/-ή/-ό	*strong*
το χάπι	*the pill*
η ημικρανία	*the migraine*
το παιδί	*the child*
κάθισες	*you stayed (lit. you sat down)*
καθόμουν	*I had been sitting*
συνέχεια	*continually*
βαρέθηκα	*I was bored*
ήρθα στην δουλειά να	*I came to work to get some*
πάρω λίγο καθαρό αέρα!	*fresh air!*
νόμιζα σκληρά	*I thought hard*

 10.04 *Mary didn't go to her office yesterday and one of her colleagues is quizzing her.*

1 Listen to the conversation a couple of times without looking at the text. Was Mary sick or did she have the day off?

Τασία	Καλημέρα Μαίρη. Σε χάσαμε χθες! Πού ήσουν;
Mary	Ήμουν αδιάθετη. Είχα ένα τρομερό πονοκέφαλο κι έτσι έμεινα σπίτι.
Τασία	Είσαι καλύτερα σήμερα;
Mary	Ναι, αλλά εχτές όλα βούιζαν στο κεφάλι μου.
Τασία	Πήγες σε κανένα γιατρό;
Mary	Δεν πήγα σε γιατρό. Εχτές το μεσημέρι πήγα σ' ένα φαρμακείο. Ο φαρμακοποιός μου έδωσε ένα ισχυρό χάπι για πονοκεφάλους και ημικρανίες.
Τασία	Γιατί είχες ημικρανίες;
Mary	Δυστυχώς, έχω ημικρανίες από τότε που ήμουν μικρό παιδί.
Τασία	Αν είναι έτσι, γιατί δεν κάθισες σπίτι;
Mary	Καθόμουν σπίτι συνέχεια εχθές. Βαρέθηκα! Ήρθα στη δουλειά να πάρω λίγο καθαρό αέρα! Δεν θα δουλέψω όμως!
Τασία	Α! Ωραία! Εγώ νόμιζα πως μόνο οι Έλληνες δε δουλεύουν σκληρά.
Mary	Και οι Άγγλοι όταν έχουν πονοκέφαλο …

2 **Now read the conversation and answer the questions below.**

    a What was wrong with Mary yesterday?

    b What does Ναι, αλλά εχτές όλα βούιζαν στο κεφάλι μου. mean?

    c Why did she go to work today?

 3 **Listen again and pay special attention to the words that run together. Practise speaking the part of Mary and pay particular attention to your pronunciation.**

Language discovery 1

The conversation includes eight verbs in the past tense. Can you find them? Do you notice anything different in the endings of the past tense?

    a I was _____

    b I thought _____

    c I went _____

    d he gave me _____

    e I came _____

    f did you have _____

    g didn't you stay _____

    h I was bored _____

Learn more

TALKING ABOUT THE PAST

So far you have encountered the present and the future tenses in Greek. In the next few units we are going to look at the past tense. Here are two important verbs **είμαι** *to be* and **έχω** *to have* in the past tense.

ήμουν(α)	*I was*	**είχα**	*I had*
ήσουν(α)	*you were*	**είχες**	*you had*
ήταν(ε)	*he/she/it was*	**είχε**	*he/she/it had*
ήμασταν	*we were*	**είχαμε**	*we had*
ήσασταν	*you were*	**είχατε**	*you had*
ήταν(ε)	*they were*	**είχαν**	*they had*

Note that the usual endings **-ω** or **-μαι** for the first person singular become **-α**, and there is an additional letter at the beginning of some verbs. Here is a long list of all verbs you have already seen in the past tense. You can copy them on to your flash cards and try to learn them by heart.

Main verb form		**Past verb form**	
ξεχνώ	*I forget* (Unit 2)	**ξέχασα**	*I forgot*
λέ(γ)ω	*I say* (Unit 5)	**είπα**	*I said*
φτάνω	*I arrive* (Unit 5)	**έφτασα**	*I arrived*

164

είμαι	*I am*	ήμουν(α)	*I was*
χάνω	*I miss*	έχασα	*I missed*
μένω	*I stay*	έμεινα	*I stayed*
πηγαίνω	*I go*	πήγα	*I went*
δίνω	*I give*	έδωσα	*I gave*
κάθομαι	*I sit/stay*	κάθισα	*I sat/stayed*
βαριέμαι	*I am bored*	βαρέθηκα	*I was bored*
έρχομαι	*I come*	ήρθα	*I came*
νομίζω	*I think*	νόμισα	*I thought*
παθαίνω	*I suffer*	έπαθα	*I suffered*
κάνω	*I do/make*	έκανα	*I did/made*
περνώ	*I spend*	πέρασα	*I spent*
κολυμπώ	*I swim*	κολύμπησα	*I swam*
περπατώ	*I walk*	περπάτησα	*I walked*
τρέχω	*I run*	έτρεξα	*I ran*
συνηθίζω	*I get used to*	συνήθισα	*I got used to*
αγαπάω	*I love*	αγάπησα	*I loved*
ξέρω	*I know*	ήξερα	*I knew*

If you look at the list closely, you might notice that many verbs with two syllables form the past tense by adding one or two letters before the stem of the verb. Some examples include: **χάνω – έχασα, μένω – έμεινα,δίνω – έδωσα, κάνω – έκανα, τρέχω – έτρεξα, ξέρω – ήξερα**. Of course, you have also noticed that some are completely irregular, e.g. **λέ(γ)ω – είπα, έρχομαι – ήρθα**.

What you have learnt for the future or subjunctive form will come in handy when forming the past tense of Greek verbs. The second stem needed for future or subjunctive is also needed for the past tense. Notice the changes that take place in the present, future and past tenses of the verb **μένω**.

Stem/Ending	Stem/Ending	Prefix/Stem/Ending
μέν – ω	θα μείν – ω	έ – μειν – α
μέν – εις	θα μείν – εις	έ – μειν – ες
μέν – ει	θα μείν – ει	έ – μειν – ε
μέν – ουμε	θα μείν – ουμε	– μείν – αμε
μέν – ετε	θα μείν – ετε	– μείν – ατε
μέν – ουν	θα μείν – ουν	έ – μειν – αν

I stay, you stay, etc.   *I will stay, you will stay*, etc.   *I stayed, you stayed*, etc.

The additional letter **ε-** is missing from the first and second person plural. The following verbs have a similar conjugation in the past tense: **έφτασα** *I arrived*, **έπαθα** *I underwent/I suffered*, **έχασα** *I lost*, **έκανα** *I did/made*, **έμεινα** *I stayed*, **έτρεξα** *I ran*, **έδωσα** *I gave*, **ήξερα** *I knew*.

Conversation 2

ΠΩΣ ΠΕΡΑΣΑΤΕ ΤΟ ΣΑΒΒΑΤΟΚΥΡΙΑΚΟ; *HOW WAS YOUR WEEKEND?*

 NEW EXPRESSIONS

 10.05

καλή βδομάδα!	*have a good nice week!*
περάσατε	*you spent*
το Σαββατοκύριακο	*weekend* (lit. *Saturday–Sunday*)
πουθενά	*nowhere/anywhere*
τι να σου πω;	*what can I tell you?*
ο εφιάλτης	*the nightmare*
θέλω να μάθω	*I want to know*
έπαθα	*I had* (lit. *I suffered/I went through*)
τροφικός/-ή/-ό	*food*
η δηλητηρίαση	*the poisoning*
έμεινα	*I stayed*
το φάρμακο	*the medicine*
σοβαρός/-ή/-ό	*serious*
το νοσοκομείο	*the hospital*
το κολύμπι	*the swimming*
το βάδην	*the walking/jogging*
κολύμπησε	*he swam*
αρκετά	*enough*
περπάτησε	*he walked*
έτρεξε	*he run*
ο/η νοσοκόμος/-α	*the nurse* (m + f)
μπα!	*wow!* (surprise)
η υπερκόπωση	*the overexhaustion*
η κόπωση	*the fatigue, exhaustion*
χρειάζομαι	*I need*
η ανάπαυση	*the rest*
αναπαύομαι	*I rest*
δηλαδή	*in other words, that is to say*
μην το λες!	*I wouldn't say that!*

10.06 *Tim and Mary visited the island of Spetses last weekend. Mary explains their adventures there.*

1 Listen to the conversation a couple of times without looking at the text. Did they have a good time?

Στέλιος	Γεια σου, Mary. Καλή βδομάδα!
Mary	Καλημέρα, Στέλιο. Τι κάνεις;
Στέλιος	Καλά. Πώς περάσατε το Σαββατοκύριακο; Πήγατε πουθενά;
Mary	Τι να σου πω; Ήταν ένας εφιάλτης! Πήγαμε στις Σπέτσες και εκεί …
Στέλιος	Πες μου, πες μου! Θέλω να μάθω …
Mary	Εκεί που λες έπαθα τροφική δηλητηρίαση. Έμεινα στο κρεβάτι και τις δύο ημέρες. Έπρεπε να πάρω κάτι φάρμακα … πάλι καλά που δεν ήταν σοβαρό να μείνω μέσα σε νοσοκομείο.
Στέλιος	Λυπάμαι που έγινε έτσι. Ο Tim τι έκανε;
Mary	Ο Tim πέρασε ωραία! Ξέρεις ότι του αρέσει το κολύμπι και το βάδην. Έτσι κολύμπησε αρκετά, περπάτησε αρκετά και έτρεξε αρκετά. Τις άλλες ώρες ήταν νοσοκόμος σ' εμένα!
Στέλιος	Μπα, έτσι ο Tim. Ωραία πέρασε.
Mary	Ωραία πέρασε αλλά όχι τώρα. Έπαθε υπερκόπωση και τώρα είναι σπίτι, χρειάζεται ανάπαυση.
Στέλιος	Αναπαύεται δηλαδή πάλι ωραία περνάει.
Mary	Μην το λες. Δε νομίζω …

2 Now read the conversation and answer the questions.
  a What was wrong with Mary on the island of Spetses?
  b Did she have to go to the hospital?
  c What did Tim do on the island?

 3 Listen again and pay special attention to the words that run together. Practise speaking the part of Mary or Stelios and pay particular attention to your pronunciation.

Language discovery 2

1 The conversation includes eight verbs in the past tense. Can you find them?
  a I had (suffered) _____
  b I should (had to) _____
  c we went _____
  d it happened _____
  e I stayed _____

f did you spend _____

g he walked _____

h he swam _____

2 **The conversation has four expressions with the verb** *say/tell*. **Can you find them?**

    a Don't say that. _____

    b What can I tell you? _____

    c Tell me. _____

    d you're saying _____

3 **Make a list of words from this conversation that have to do with health.**

4 **This conversation has some idiomatic time registers. Can you find them?**

    a at the time being … (Now …) _____

    b the rest of the time _____

    c both days _____

Learn more

1 SPORT

Do you like sport? Do you like to participate in sport or do you prefer to watch it on TV? Many **σπορ** *sports* have the same name as in English, but are spoken with a slight Greek accent, such as **τένις** *tennis*. *Jogging* is **τζόγκιν** or **γρήγορο βάδην** *brisk walking*. Study these sports and learn the ones you like to watch or participate in.

το τρέξιμο	*running*	**το τζούντο**	*judo*
το σκι	*skiing*	**το κολύμπι**	*swimming*
το ποδόσφαιρο	*football*	**η ποδηλασία**	*cycling*
το βόλεϋ	*volleyball*	**η ιππασία**	*horse riding*
η κωπηλασία	*rowing*	**το χάντμπολ**	*handball*
η ξιφασκία	*fencing*	**το μπάσκετ**	*basketball*

Though in English articles are not necessarily used with sports, they are required in Greek:

Μου αρέσει το ποδόσφαιρο.	*I like football.*
Η ιππασία δεν είναι σπορ για μένα!	*Horse riding is not a sport for me!*

2 IN TERMS OF FREQUENCY

Here is some useful vocabulary (adverbs and adverbial phrases) for talking about how often you do something:

Indefinite frequency

πάντα/συνέχεια	*always/continually*
σχεδόν πάντα	*almost always*
συνήθως/νορμάλ/σχεδόν πάντα	*usually/normally*

συχνά	often/frequently
μερικές φορές/περιοδικά	sometimes/periodically
σπάνια	rarely/seldom
σχεδόν ποτέ	hardly ever
ποτέ	never

Definite frequency

κάθε λεπτό	every minute
κάθε ώρα/ωριαίως/-α	every hour/hourly
κάθε μέρα/ημερησίως/-α	every day/daily
κάθε εβδομάδα/εβδομαδιαίως/-α	every week/weekly
κάθε μήνα/μηνιαίως/-α	every month/monthly
κάθε χρόνο/ετησίως	every year/yearly

Conversation 3

ΑΙΣΘΑΝΟΜΑΙ ΑΚΟΜΑ ΑΔΙΑΘΕΤΟΣ *I STILL FEEL SICK*

 NEW EXPRESSIONS

 10.07

άρρωστος/-η/-ο	ill
χλωμός/-ή/-ό	pale
φαίνομαι	I look
έπαθα ναυτία	I was seasick
τι άλλο θα γίνει;	what else is going to happen?
πολύ μαύρα τα βλέπεις	you are very pessimistic (lit. *you see everything black*)
απαισιόδοξος/-η/-ο	pessimist
μέρα με την ημέρα	day by day
συνήθισες	you became used to
αγάπησες	you loved, you fell in love
ο/η υπάλληλος	the officer, clerk, employee (m + f)
να ήμουν γιατρός!	I wish I were a doctor!
να ήξερα …	(so I could) know …
τι έχω πάθει	what I am suffering from
ο μάγειρας	the cook
να μαγείρευα	(so I could) cook
ο/η πιλότος	the pilot (m + f)
υψηλός/-ή/-ό	high
γκρινιάζω	I complain/moan
έτσι να μην μπορεί να σε	so, it is not possible for
ακούει κανένας!	anyone to hear you!
η συμβουλή	advice

10.08 *Tim goes back to work, but he looks really pale. His boss tries to find out what's wrong with him.*

1 Listen to the conversation a couple of times without looking at the text. What is Tim complaining about?

κ. Παύλου	Καλημέρα, Tim. Είσαι άρρωστος; Λίγο χλωμός φαίνεσαι.
Tim	Δεν είμαι άρρωστος αλλά αισθάνομαι ακόμα αδιάθετος. Δεν ξαναπάω στις Σπέτσες!
κ. Παύλου	Γιατί; Είναι ένα ωραίο νησί …
Tim	Στο ταξίδι έπαθα ναυτία. Στο νησί η Mary έμεινε στο κρεβάτι με τροφική δηλητηρίαση. Και τώρα εγώ έπαθα υπερκόπωση. Και είμαι χλωμός. Τι άλλο θα γίνει;
κ. Παύλου	Πολύ μαύρα τα βλέπεις. Μην είσαι τόσο απαισιόδοξος. Τα Ελληνικά σου γίνονται καλύτερα μέρα με την ημέρα. Συνήθισες την Αθήνα. Αγάπησες την ελληνική κουζίνα. Και είσαι ένας πολύ καλός τραπεζικός υπάλληλος. Τι άλλο θέλεις;
Tim	Να ήμουν γιατρός! Να ήξερα τι έχω πάθει … ή μάγειρας … να μαγείρευα στη Mary για να μην πάθει τροφική δηλητηρίαση.
κ. Παύλου	Εγώ λέω να ήσουν πιλότος! Για να είσαι πολύ ψηλά όταν γκρινιάζεις έτσι να μη μπορεί να σε ακούει κανένας!
Tim	Καλή συμβουλή! Σας ευχαριστώ, κύριε Παύλου.

2 Now read the conversation and answer the questions.
   a Who had food poisoning: Tim or Mary?
   b Who is now exhausted after the trip to Spetses: Tim or Mary?
   c The boss tries to boost Tim's ego. What arguments did he use?

3 **Listen again and pay special attention to the words that run together. Practise speaking the part of Tim or Mr Pavlou and pay particular attention to your pronunciation.**

Language discovery 3

1 The conversation includes six adjectives modifying nouns. Can you find them?
   a good advice _____
   b food poisoning _____
   c bank employee _____
   d Greek cuisine _____
   e nice island _____
   f good employee _____

2 **Make a list of words from this conversation related to professions and jobs. Add another two, including your own.**

Learn more

1 PROFESSIONS AND JOBS

The following professions can be found in this unit:

ο/η γιατρός	*the doctor*	**ο/η υπάλληλος**	*the clerk*
ο/η φαρμακοποιός	*the chemist*	**ο μάγειρας**	*the cook*
ο/η νοσοκόμος/-α	*the nurse*	**ο πιλότος**	*the pilot*

Now test your memory on some professions from previous units by covering up the Greek:

ο/η σερβιτόρος/-α	*the waiter/waitress*
ο ταξιτζής	*the taxi driver*
ο περιπτεράς	*the kiosk owner*
ο/η γραμματέας	*the secretary*
ο πωλητής	*the salesman*
η πωλήτρια	*the saleswoman*

The cartoons depict some other popular professions. Look out for those that are similar in both languages.

ο μαθητής	*student*
ο δάσκαλος	*teacher*
ο εργάτης	*worker*
ο κτίστης	*builder*
ο κτηνίατρος	*vet*
ο λογιστής	*book keeper*
ο αρχιτέκτονας	*architect*
ο ζωγράφος	*painter*
ο αστυνομικός	*policeman*
ο οδηγός	*driver*
ο πιανίστας	*pianist*

Have we listed your job or profession here? If not, look it up in a dictionary! Do not move on until you have personalized all pieces of information and vocabulary focus. For instance, we have listed some sports for you but perhaps your favorite sport was not included in that list. If it was not, look it up!

2 A LIST OF WISHES

In Greek there are many expressions of 'good wishes' that have no direct English equivalents. Greeks use most of them frequently and it will be helpful for you to understand when you hear them in daily exchanges.

Καλή (ε)βδομάδα!	*Have a good week!* (lit. *Have a nice, productive week!*) (a wish heard on Mondays when people go back to work).
Καλό μήνα!	*Have a good month!* (lit. *Have a nice, productive, healthy month!*) (a wish heard on the 1st of each month).
Καλό χρόνο (έτος) or **Καλή χρονιά!**	*Happy New Year!* (lit. *Have a nice, productive and healthy year!*) (a wish heard on the first days of each year).
Καλό Σαββατοκύριακο!	*Have a nice weekend!* (a wish heard on Fridays/ Saturdays).
Καλή ξεκούραση! or **Καλή ανάπαυση!**	*Have a nice rest!* (a wish heard when people leave work at the end of the day).
Καλό δρόμο!	*Be careful!* (a wish heard when you go somewhere).
Καλό διάβασμα!	*Study well!* (a wish heard when somebody must study, especially for a test or exam).
Καλό μεσημέρι!	*Have a nice siesta!*
Καλό απόγευμα!	*Have a nice afternoon!*
Καλό βράδυ!	*Have a nice evening!*
Καλά να περάσετε!	*Have a good time!*
Καλό ταξίδι!	*Have a nice trip!*

Can you remember these expressions from previous units?

Καλή όρεξη!	*Bon appétit!*
Καλή χώνεψη!	*Have a good digestion!*
Καλή διαμονή!/Καλή παραμονή!	*Have a nice stay! (at hotels)*

 Practice

 **1 Respond to the following situations in Greek.**

   a It's Monday. You meet someone who wishes you καλή (ε)βδομάδα. What will you answer?

   b It's the first day of the month. You want to wish a Greek friend a good month! What do you say?

c You have just finished eating. A friend of yours says, Καλή χώνεψη! What will you say?

d You haven't seen someone for some time. How would you say *We missed you. Where have you been?*

e It's Monday. Ask a friend how his weekend was and where he spent it.

f There is an emergency. Ask for a doctor right away.

g A friend of yours does not look well. Ask *Are you sick? You look kind of* (lit. *a little bit*) *pale!*

2 Match each question with the most appropriate answer.

a Πώς πέρασες το Σαββατοκύριακο;   **1** Ναι βέβαια. Έχετε και ημικρανίες;

b Πήγες πουθενά;   **2** Έτσι κι έτσι. Λίγο καλύτερα από εχθές.

c Έχετε χάπια για πονοκεφάλους;   **3** Αρκετά καλά αν και δεν έκανα τίποτα!

d Τι πρέπει να κάνω, γιατρέ;   **4** Πρέπει να μείνετε σπίτι συνέχεια.

e Πώς αισθάνεστε σήμερα;   **5** Ναι, πήγα στις Σπέτσες.

3 Tell the doctor what's wrong with you using these expressions. Match the pictures to the phrases.

a ___ Το κεφάλι μου βουίζει.

b ___ Νομίζω ότι θα κάνω εμετό.

c ___ Έχω κρυάδες.

d ___ Έχω τρομερό πονοκέφαλο.

e ___ Δεν έχω καθόλου όρεξη.

f ___ Έχω τρομερό κοιλόπονο.

g ___ Με πονάει ο δεξιός μου ώμος.

4 10.09 **Take part in the next dialogue. Try your lines first, then listen and compare your answers. Listen again and repeat after the speakers.**

Στέλιος	Καλημέρα, σε χάσαμε! Πού ήσουν;
You	**a** *I was on a trip in Crete (Κρήτη).*
Στέλιος	Για δουλειές ή ταξίδι αναψυχής (pleasure);
You	**b** *It was a business trip (lit. trip for business).*
Στέλιος	Πόσο καιρό έμεινες;
You	**c** *I stayed for three days.*
Στέλιος	Πήγες μόνος σου (alone) ή με τη γυναίκα σου;
You	**d** *I went alone and my wife came the next (επόμενος/-η/-ο) day.*
Στέλιος	Περάσατε ωραία;
You	**e** *We had a good time. Especially (ειδικά) my wife because she went shopping every day!*
Στέλιος	Τυχεροί! (*Lucky you!*) Εμείς μείναμε σπίτι γιατί η Στέλλα ήταν άρρωστη.
You	**f** *Ill? What was wrong with her?*
Στέλιος	Είχε συνέχεια διάρροια.
You	**g** *That's not nice. How is she now?*
Στέλιος	Καλύτερα, καλύτερα.
You	**h** *I hope she gets (να γίνει) better soon!*

5 **You are looking for two words about sport, two words from your list of definite and indefinite frequency vocabulary, two words about health, and two professions. The vertical, shaded word means *continually*.**

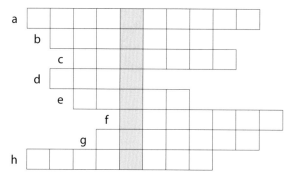

6 **Match the words on the left with the words on the right.**

a πόνος		**1** nausea
b τζούντο		**2** antibiotic
c χάντμπολ		**3** pilot
d φαρμακείο		**4** pneumonia
e ημικρανία		**5** allergic
f ναυτία		**6** judo
g πιλότος		**7** handball

h πνευμονία	**8** migraine
i αλλεργικός	**9** chemist/pharmacy
j αντιβιοτικό	**10** pain

 7 **10.10 Listen to the conversation and find the missing words. If you want you can try to find the missing words first and then listen and compare your answers.**

κ. Παύλου	Καλημέρα, Tim. Είσαι **a** _____; Λίγο χλωμός **b** _____.
Tim	Δεν είμαι **a** _____ αλλά αισθάνομαι ακόμα αδιάθετος. Δεν ξαναπάω στις Σπέτσες!
κ. Παύλου	Γιατί; Είναι ένα ωραίο **c** _____.
Tim	Στο ταξίδι έπαθα ναυτία. Στο **c** _____ η Mary έμεινε στο κρεβάτι με τροφική δηλητηρίαση. Και τώρα εγώ έπαθα **d** _____. Και είμαι χλωμός. Τι άλλο θα γίνει;
κ. Παύλου	Πολύ μαύρα τα βλέπεις. Μην είσαι τόσο **e** _____. Τα Ελληνικά σου γίνονται καλύτερα μέρα με την ημέρα. **f** _____ την Αθήνα. Αγάπησες την ελληνική κουζίνα. Και είσαι ένας πολύ καλός τραπεζικός **g** _____. Τι άλλο θέλεις;
Tim	Να ήμουν γιατρός! Να ήξερα τι έχω πάθει … ή **h** _____ … να μαγείρευα στη Mary για να μην πάθει τροφική δηλητηρίαση.
κ. Παύλου	Εγώ λέω να ήσουν πιλότος! Για να είσαι πολύ **i** _____ όταν γκρινιάζεις έτσι να μη μπορεί να σε ακούει κανένας!
Tim	Καλή **j** _____! Σας ευχαριστώ, κύριε Παύλου.

> **νησί   υπάλληλος   άρρωστος   φαίνεσαι**
> **απαισιόδοξος   συνήθισες   ψηλά**
> **συμβουλή   υπερκόπωση   μάγειρας**

 Test yourself

1 **Can you remember the Greek for the following ten important words from this unit?**

   a yesterday _____
   b weekend _____
   c sick _____
   d enough _____
   e doctor/s _____
   f serious _____
   g pharmacy _____
   h swimming _____
   i medicine _____
   j jogging _____

2 **Can you remember the following ten important phrases from this unit?**

   a I need some fresh air! _____
   b How was your weekend? _____
   c It was a nightmare! _____
   d It was wonderful! _____
   e I like swimming a lot. _____
   f I need some rest. _____
   g Don't say that! _____
   h It's good advice! _____
   i I feel ill/sick/dizzy/seasick! _____
   j I've got a fever/headache/sore throat. _____

3 **These five phrases are given in the present tense. Can you change them into the past tense?**

   a Αγαπάω την Ελλάδα. _____
   b Κολυμπώ πολύ. _____
   c Ξέρω ελληνικά. _____
   d Κάνω γυμναστική. _____
   e Τρώω μουσακά. _____

I CAN. . .
. . . ask for a doctor or medical assistance in case of emergency.
. . . explain to a doctor where or what hurts.
. . . ask for remedies.
. . . tell a story that took place in the past.
. . . name different professions including my own.
. . . tell what sports I like or dislike.
. . . explain how often I do things in general or daily routines.
. . . understand some frequent wishes.

11 Τι καιρό έκανε;

What was the weather like?

In this unit you will learn how to:

▶ *talk about the weather.*
▶ *use expressions of time.*
▶ *get the gist of a weather forecast.*
▶ *name the months and seasons.*

CEFR: (A1) *Can understand weather conditions. Can report on weather conditions. Can talk about the weather with friends. Can understand and talk about months and seasons. Can talk about past holidays. Can understand and use some verbs talking about past events both in past tense or present perfect tense. Can complain and disagree with other people.* **(A2)** *Can use Greek articles appropriately.*

Ο καιρός στην Ελλάδα *The weather in Greece*

Greece is famous for its mild winter weather and its warm summers. Many tourists are not aware though of the harsh **χειμώνας** *winters* in some northern parts of the country, where small villages are cut off from civilization sometimes for 30 to 40 days! Tourists are also not aware that some heat waves reach over 40 degrees Centigrade (or 104 degrees Fahrenheit) in the summer months. Although Greece is known as a **καλοκαίρι** *summer* holiday destination, it is worth mentioning that there are 17 winter resorts in Greece, available to locals and travellers alike who are keen on winter sports. The EOT Greek National Tourist Organization has flyers and maps promoting these winter resorts and of course many other promotional materials for all other regions around the country. In **Αύγουστος** *August* temperatures often reach 36 degrees Centigrade (or 96 degrees Fahrenheit) and in **Δεκέμβριος** *December* they can drop to 4 degrees Centigrade (or 40 degrees Fahrenheit).

1 What would you guess is the gender of the 2 months as they end in **-ος**?

Vocabulary builder

ΜΗΝΕΣ ΚΑΙ ΕΠΟΧΕΣ *MONTHS AND SEASONS*

 1 11.01 Listen to the seasons and months a couple of times without looking at the list. Then listen again and repeat out loud. Pay particular attention to your pronunciation.

The four seasons are:

ο χειμώνας	*winter*
η άνοιξη	*spring*
το καλοκαίρι	*summer*
το φθινόπωρο	*autumn*

The 12 months of the year are:

ο Ιανουάριος/ο Γενάρης	*January*
ο Φεβρουάριος/ο Φλεβάρης	*February*
ο Μάρτιος/ο Μάρτης	*March*
ο Απρίλιος/ο Απρίλης	*April*
ο Μάιος/ο Μάης	*May*
ο Ιούνιος/ο Ιούνης	*June*
ο Ιούλιος/ο Ιούλης	*July*
ο Αύγουστος	*August*
ο Σεπτέμβριος/ο Σεπτέμβρης	*September*
ο Οκτώβριος/ο Οκτώβρης	*October*
ο Νοέμβριος/ο Νοέμβρης	*November*
ο Δεκέμβριος/ο Δεκέμβρης	*December*

ΤΙ ΚΑΙΡΟ ΚΑΝΕΙ; *WHAT'S THE WEATHER LIKE?*

2 11.02 Read some typical questions and answers about weather conditions as you listen and repeat the phrases.

Typical questions about the weather are:

Τι καιρό <u>κάνει</u> σήμερα;	*What's the weather like today?*
Τι καιρό <u>έχει</u> στην Αθήνα;	*What's the weather like in Athens?*
Πώς <u>είναι</u> ο καιρός στο Λονδίνο;	*What's the weather like in London?*
Τι θερμοκρασία <u>υπάρχει</u> στη Βέροια σήμερα;	*What's the temperature in Veria today?*

Some typical answers to these questions:

Είναι υπέροχος, εξαίσιος, θαυμάσιος.	*It's marvellous, brilliant, wonderful.*
Είναι άσχημος, απαίσιος, κακός.	*It's awful, terrible, bad.*
Είναι αίθριος, είναι άστατος.	*It's fair, it's unsettled.*
Έχει συννεφιά, λιακάδα.	*It's cloudy, sunny.*
Έχει ψιχάλα, βροχή, χαλάζι.	*There's drizzle, rain, hail.*
Κάνει ζέστη, κρύο, ψύχρα, παγωνιά.	*It's hot, cold, chilly, freezing.*
Κάνει παγωνιά έξω.	*There's frost out.*

Ψιχαλίζει, βρέχει, χιονίζει.	It's drizzling, it's raining, it's snowing.
Ρίχνει χαλάζι, βροντές, αστραπές.	It's hailing, it's thundering, it's lightening.
Υπάρχει υγρασία σήμερα.	It's humid today.
Έχει 25 βαθμούς σήμερα.	It's 25 degrees today.

3 Check the questions and answers above once again and focus on the verbs used. Can you find four alternatives for the following question and four possible answers?

What's … ?	It's …
a _____	e _____
b _____	f _____
c _____	g _____
d _____	h _____

4 11.03 Listen to a conversation about weather conditions in different cities around Greece. Which verb does the second speaker use to answer the questions? Choose the verb you hear.

> υπάρχει έχει είναι
> ρίχνει κάνει

a Τι καιρό έχει στη Θεσσαλονίκη; _____ αίθριο καιρό.

b Πώς είναι ο καιρός στην Καβάλα; Σήμερα _____ υπέροχος καιρός.

c Κάνει ζέστη στα Χανιά σήμερα; Όχι, _____ χαλάζι!

d Τι καιρό κάνει στη Ρόδο; Σήμερα ο καιρός _____ άσχημος.

e Βρέχει στα Γιάννενα σήμερα; Όχι, _____ λίγη συννεφιά.

Conversation 1

ΤΙ ΚΑΙΡΟ ΕΚΑΝΕ; *WHAT WAS THE WEATHER LIKE?*

 NEW EXPRESSIONS

 11.04

πες μας	*tell us*
είχαμε προγραμματίσει	*we had planned*
τόσα πολλά πράγματα	*so many things*
ακούγεσαι	*you sound*
φαίνεσαι	*you look*
στεναχωρημένος/-η/-ο	*worried, troubled, concerned*
έχουμε πάει	*we have been to* (lit. *we have gone*)
το γεγονός	*the event, fact* (n)
δεν έχει ξανασυμβεί	*it has never happened (occurred) before*
πω, πω! Θεέ μου!	*oh, my goodness!*
μας έχεις βγάλει την πίστη!	(lit.) *you've sweated our guts out!*

τι συνέβη	*what happened*
δεν έχω στεναχωρηθεί	*I have not been troubled, worried*
ποτέ άλλοτε	*never before*
έτσι	*like that*
έχουμε τηλεφωνήσει	*we have called*
το τριήμερο	*the long weekend* (lit. *three-day event*)
έχουν σχεδιάσει	*they have planned*
τελικά	*at the end, finally*
ο καιρός μας τα χαλάει όλα	*the weather messes up everything*
τέλος πάντων	*after all*
τέτοιο παλιόκαιρο!	*such awful weather!*
εκείνος/-η/-ο	*that*
ο Θεός	*God* (m)
μη λες τέτοια λόγια!	*don't say this kind of thing* (lit. *such words*)

 11.05 *Tim and Mary have just come back from a long weekend in Lamia. The weather messed up all their plans so now they are complaining about it to a couple of friends.*

1 **Listen to their conversation a couple of times without looking at the text. Did they have a good time?**

Ηλέκτρα	Έλα Tim πες μας. Πώς ήταν το ταξείδι σας στη Λαμία; Πού πήγατε; Τι καιρό έκανε; Όλα!
Tim	Δεν κάναμε τίποτα! Είχαμε προγραμματίσει να κάνουμε τόσα πολλά πράγματα και δεν κάναμε τίποτα.
Αριστείδης	Έλα τι έγινε; Ακούγεσαι και φαίνεσαι πολύ στεναχωρημένος.
Tim	Έχουμε πάει κι άλλες φορές στη Λαμία. Αυτό το γεγονός δεν έχει ξανασυμβεί. Πω, πω, Θεέ μου!
Αριστείδης	Μας έχεις βγάλει την πίστη! Mary, γιατί δε μας λες εσύ τι συνέβη;
Mary	Τι να σας πω; Δεν έχω στεναχωρηθεί ποτέ άλλοτε έτσι. Έχουμε τηλεφωνήσει στους φίλους μας για το τριήμερο. Αυτοί έχουν σχεδιάσει να κάνουμε τόσα πράγματα και τελικά ο καιρός μας τα χαλάει όλα.
Ηλέκτρα	Μα τι καιρό έκανε τέλος πάντων; Η Λαμία δεν είναι τόσο μακριά από την Αθήνα.
Mary	Τέτοιο παλιόκαιρο! Εκείνο το τριήμερο είχαν άλλο Θεό εκεί.
Ηλέκτρα	Έλα τώρα, μη λες τέτοια λόγια!

2 **Now read the conversation and answer the questions.**
   a How long did they go to Lamia for?
   b How far is Lamia from Athens?
   c What was the weather like there?

3 Listen again and pay special attention to the words that run together. Practise speaking the part of Tim or Mary.

Language discovery 1

1 **The conversation has four phrases with the verb** *to tell/to say*. **Can you find them?**

  a Don't say these kind of things! _____

  b What can I tell you? _____

  c Why don't you tell us? _____

  d Come on, tell us! _____

2 **The conversation makes use of some verbs in the present perfect tense. Can you find them?**

  a you've sweated _____

  b I have worried _____

  c we've called/telephoned _____

  d we have gone _____

  e they have planned _____

  f it has not happened before _____

Learn more

1 VERBS IN THE PERFECT TENSE

This unit introduces you to another important verb tense in the past called 'present perfect'. It is similar to English, in examples like *have gone, has taken* or *has said*. It is formed with the verb **έχω** + the present perfect form (always ending in **-ει**). Here are some examples from this unit:

Έχουμε πάει.	*We have been (gone).*
Μας έχεις βγάλει την πίστη.	*You have sweated our guts out.*
Έχω στεναχωρηθεί.	*I have worried.*
Έχουμε τηλεφωνήσει.	*We have called/telephoned.*
Έχουν σχεδιάσει.	*They have planned.*
Αυτό δεν έχει ξανασυμβεί.	*This has not happened before.*

An important point, which is not always initially obvious, is that the verb form used in the present perfect is a familiar form already learnt as part of the future tense.

Main verb	Future form	3rd person	Present perfect
πηγαίνω	θα πάω	θα πάει	(έχω) πάει
βγάζω	θα βγάλω	θα βγάλει	(έχω) βγάλει
στεναχωριέμαι	θα στεναχωρηθώ	θα στεναχωρηθεί	(έχω) στεναχωρηθεί

τηλεφωνώ	θα τηλεφωνήσω	θα τηλεφωνήσει	(έχω) τηλεφωνήσει
σχεδιάζω	θα σχεδιάσω	θα σχεδιάσει	(έχω) σχεδιάσει

Here is the simple conjugation of this tense:

έχω	**τηλεφωνήσει**	*I have called*
έχεις	**τηλεφωνήσει**	*you have called*
έχει	**τηλεφωνήσει**	*he/she/it has called*
έχουμε	**τηλεφωνήσει**	*we have called*
έχετε	**τηλεφωνήσει**	*you have called*
έχουν	**τηλεφωνήσει**	*they have called*

Conversation 2

ΕΒΡΕΧΕ ΣΥΝΕΧΕΙΑ ΚΑΡΕΚΛΟΠΟΔΑΡΑ! *IT HAD CONSTANTLY BEEN RAINING CATS AND DOGS!*

 NEW EXPRESSIONS

 11.06

όλα ακούγονται μαύρα κι άραχνα!	*everything sounds (is) gloom and doom!*
έβρεχε καρεκλοπόδαρα	*it was raining (it had been raining) cats and dogs* (lit. *chair legs*)
δε σταμάτησε ποτέ	*it never stopped*
φτάσαμε	*we arrived*
επιστρέψαμε	*we returned*
η ιστορία	*the story* (lit. *history*)
δεν είδατε;	*didn't you watch?* (lit. *see*)
δε φάγατε;	*didn't you eat?*
δε μιλήσατε;	*didn't you talk?*
να ακούσουμε το ράδιο	*to listen to radio*
του σκασμού!	*(eating) to bursting point!*
το κάστρο	*the castle*
θα μας οδηγούσαν	*they would drive us*
οι Θερμοπύλες	*an archaeological site*
το θέρετρο	*the resort*
το μπάνιο	*the swim*
για μπάνιο	*for swimming*
πού τέτοια τύχη όμως!	*out of luck! no such luck!*
αντί	*instead*
έχει γυρίσματα ο τροχός!	*the tables turn!* (Greek expression)
ο τροχός	*the wheel*
η ευκαιρία	*the chance*
του χρόνου!	*next year!*

11.07 *Ηλέκτρα and Αριστείδης finally hear the end of the story. Mary tells them everything.*

1 Why was Mary so upset with the rain?

Ηλέκτρα	Όλα ακούγονται μαύρα κι άραχνα! Θα μας πείτε τελικά τι έγινε;
Mary	Ναι! Έβρεχε συνέχεια καρεκλοπόδαρα! Έβρεξε καρεκλοπόδαρα για εβδομήντα δύο ώρες. Δε σταμάτησε ποτέ. Φτάσαμε στο σπίτι των φίλων μας με βροχή, πολλή βροχή. Μείναμε τρεις μέρες μέσα στο σπίτι συνέχεια και μετά επιστρέψαμε στην Αθήνα. Αυτή είναι η ιστορία μας.
Αριστείδης	Οι φίλοι σας τι έκαναν; Δεν είδατε καθόλου τηλεόραση; Δε φάγατε; Δε μιλήσατε;
Mary	Όχι! Δε θέλαμε να δούμε τηλεόραση ή να ακούσουμε ράδιο. Δε θέλαμε να φάμε του σκασμού! Θέλαμε να πάμε στο κάστρο στην Ακρολαμία και σε δύο μουσεία μέσα στη Λαμία. Έπειτα οι φίλοι μας θα μας οδηγούσαν στις Θερμοπύλες και ύστερα στα Καμένα Βούρλα που μας έλεγαν ότι είναι ωραίο θέρετρο για κανένα μπάνιο …
Tim	Πού τέτοια τύχη όμως; Αντί για όλα αυτά εμείς μείναμε σπίτι.
Ηλέκτρα	Έχει γυρίσματα ο τροχός! Θα έχετε την ευκαιρία να πάτε πίσω ξανά. Έτσι δεν είναι;
Mary	Έτσι είναι. Βέβαια! Του χρόνου!

2 Now read the conversation and answer the questions.
  a Did they watch TV when they were at their friends' home?
  b Which place did they want to visit in the town of Lamia?
  c Did they actually go swimming in Καμένα Βούρλα?

 3 Listen again and pay special attention to the words that run together. Practise speaking the part of Mary.

Language discovery 2

1 The conversation has some idiomatic phrases. Can you find the following?
  a There should be a second chance! _____
  b We didn't want to eat to bursting point! _____
  c Everything sounds gloom and doom! _____
  d It had been raining cats and dogs non-stop! _____

2 The conversation makes use of some verbs in the past tense. Can you find them?

   a Didn't you see? _____

   b We came back ... _____

   c Didn't you speak? _____

   d We stayed ... _____

   e Didn't you eat? _____

   f It rained ... _____

   g It didn't stop _____

   h What did they do? _____

Learn more

1 SOME GREEK IDIOMS

Greek is rich in idioms. It is best to learn them by heart because word-for-word translation does not often work. Idioms add a new linguistic dimension to the language, which would otherwise be very sterile. Look at the difference between *it is raining heavily* and *it is raining cats and dogs*. The latter brings extra 'weight' and 'importance' to the meaning. Likewise in Greek: **Βρέχει πάρα πολύ** contrasted to **Ρίχνει καρεκλοπόδαρα**, or **Ρίχνει παπάδες**, or **Βρέχει με το τουλούμι**. Here is a list of all the idioms from this unit.

Μας έχεις βγάλει την πίστη!	*We have no more patience left! (because of you)*
Έβρεξε καρεκλοπόδαρα!	*It rained cats and dogs!*
Όλα ακούγονται μαύρα κι άραχνα!	*It is all gloom and doom!*
Τρώω του σκασμού!	*I eat until I am ready to burst!*
Έχει γυρίσματα ο τροχός!	*The tables turn!*
Του χρόνου, του παραχρόνου!	*Next year, the year after next!*
Περίμενα πώς και πώς!	*I was very eager/excited; I was dying to...*
Αυτό να λέγεται!	*That goes without saying!*

2 'TAG' QUESTIONS

The following examples show you the different forms of 'tag' questions in English that have only one equivalent in Greek! It's very easy for you to remember "**Έτσι δεν είναι;** *Isn't it?*

Ο Γιώργος διαβάζει πολύ, <u>έτσι δεν είναι;</u>	*George studies hard, <u>doesn't he</u>?*
Η Μαίρη δε δουλεύει, <u>έτσι</u> δεν είναι;	*Mary does not work, <u>does she</u>?*
Ο Τιμ δεν μπορεί να κολυμπήσει, <u>έτσι δεν είναι;</u>	*Tim cannot swim, <u>can he</u>?*
Η Τζόαν δεν μπορεί να διαβάσει, <u>έτσι δεν είναι;</u>	*Joan can read, <u>can't she</u>?*
Αυτό είναι εύκολο, <u>έτσι</u> <u>δεν είναι;</u>	*It's easy, <u>isn't it</u>?*
Αυτό δεν είναι δύσκολο, <u>έτσι δεν είναι;</u>	*It's not hard, <u>is it</u>?*

So Greek is quite easy, isn't it? What answer would you give to:

Τα Ελληνικά δεν είναι πολύ δύσκολα, έτσι δεν είναι;

If you say: **Ναι, έτσι είναι!** then you are on the right track! Keep up the good work!

3 EXPRESSIONS OF TIME

The cartoon illustrates the Greek notion of time, especially in a business context and particularly in the public sector where assignments move slowly, or stand still, before or after, coffee! The cartoon's question probably refers to a supervisor or boss and a certain deadline. It reads: *(for) when did he/she say that he/she wants it?*

για μεθαύριο	*for the day after tomorrow*
για αύριο	*for tomorrow*
για σήμερα	*for today*
για τώρα	*for (right) now*

Other useful phrases include:

του χρόνου	*next year*
του παραχρόνου	*the year after next*
αύριο	*tomorrow*
μεθαύριο	*the day after tomorrow*
πέρσι	*last year*
πρόπερσι	*the year before last*
(ε)χθές	*yesterday*
προχθές	*the day before yesterday*

4 SIMPLE PAST AND PAST PROGRESSIVE

The last conversation had some verbs in the past tense, simple or progressive. Study the following list and compare the two verb forms in the past:

πήγα	I went	**πήγαινα**	I was going
τηλεφώνησα	I called	**τηλεφωνούσα**	I was calling
σχεδίασα	I planned	**σχεδίαζα**	I was planning
είπα	I said	**έλεγα**	I was saying
έβρεξε	it rained	**έβρεχε**	it was raining
έφυγα	I left	**έφευγα**	I was leaving
έφαγα	I ate	**έτρωγα**	I was eating

These two past tenses have exactly the same ending:

έφαγα	I ate	**έτρωγα**	I was eating/I had been eating
έφαγες	you ate	**έτρωγες**	you were eating
έφαγε	he/she/it ate	**έτρωγε**	he/she/it was eating
φάγαμε	we ate	**τρώγαμε**	we were eating
φάγατε	you ate	**τρώγατε**	you were eating
έφαγαν	they ate	**έτρωγαν**	they were eating

Conversation 3

ΗΘΕΛΑ ΗΛΙΟ, ΘΑΛΑΣΣΑ ΚΑΙ ΑΜΜΟΥΔΙΑ! *I WANTED SUN, SEA, AND SAND!*

 NEW EXPRESSIONS

 11.08

έχουμε αποφασίσει	we have decided
ούτε … ούτε …	neither … nor …
του παραχρόνου	the year after next
βρε	adds emphasis to a statement
δροσερός/-ή/-ό	cool
το αεράκι	(little) wind, the breeze
ο αέρας	the wind
λένε ότι	rumour has it that (lit. *it is said that*)
μπορεί να βρέξει	it might rain
δεν έχεις δίκιο όμως	you are not right though
έριξε χαλάζι	it hailed (lit. *hail was dropped*)
βρεγμένος/-η/-ο	wet
επικίνδυνος/-η/-ο	dangerous
έχω έλθει	I have come
βροχές και χιόνια	rain and snow (lit. *rains and snows*)
το κρύο	the cold
η παγωνιά	the frost
ο ήλιος	the sun
η θάλασσα	the sea

η αμμουδιά	the sand
δεν σε έστειλε	you were not sent
η Καβάλα/η Ξάνθη	towns in northern Greece
εκεί να δεις χειμώνες!	there you (could) realize (lit. see) winters!
περίμενα πώς και πώς	I looked forward to (idiom), I was very eager/excited
η εποχή	season (f)
αυτό να λέγεται!	that goes without saying!
πράγματι	indeed

 11.09 *Tim and Mary now explain what actually went wrong on their excursion.*

1 Listen to this conversation a couple of times without looking at the text. Who was finally to blame? Was it the weather, the season, Lamia or London itself?

Tim	Έχουμε αποφασίσει να μην πάμε στη Λαμία ξανά! Ούτε του χρόνου, ούτε του παραχρόνου, ούτε ποτέ!
Αριστείδης	Γιατί, βρε Tim; Κοίτα τον καιρό σήμερα. Έχει μία υπέροχη λιακάδα κι ένα δροσερό αεράκι. Λένε ότι μπορεί να βρέξει το βράδυ, αλλά δε νομίζω. Κι ο καιρός είναι παρόμοιος στη Λαμία σήμερα.
Mary	Μην του μιλάτε για τη Λαμία!
Ηλέκτρα	Δεν έχεις δίκιο όμως Tim. Στο Λονδίνο βρέχει κάθε μέρα. Προχτές έριξε χαλάζι. Όλοι οι δρόμοι είναι βρεγμένοι κι επικίνδυνοι. Εδώ όμως, δε βλέπεις;
Tim	Μη μου μιλάτε για το Λονδίνο! Γι 'αυτό έχω έλθει στην Ελλάδα. Δεν ήθελα άλλες βροχές και χιόνια. Άλλο κρύο και παγωνιά. Ήθελα ήλιο, θάλασσα και αμμουδιά!
Αριστείδης	Χαίρομαι που η Westminster Bank δε σ' έστειλε στην Καβάλα ή την Ξάνθη. Εκεί να δεις χειμώνες ...
Mary	Δεν είναι όμως χειμώνας τώρα. Είναι άνοιξη και περίμενα πώς και πώς αυτή την εποχή. Όλοι μας έλεγαν ότι είναι η καλύτερη εποχή στην Αθήνα.
Ηλέκτρα	Αυτό να λέγεται! Είναι πράγματι η καλύτερη εποχή ...

2 Now read the conversation and answer the questions.
   a Will Tim and Mary go back to Lamia?
   b What's the weather like today?
   c What exactly did Tim want to leave behind him in London?

 3 Listen again and pay special attention to the words that run together. Practise speaking the part of all four speakers!

Language discovery 3

1 The conversation has some idiomatic phrases. Can you find the following?

    a That goes without saying! _____

    b There you can actually experience winters! _____

    c Don't talk to me about London! _____

    d I have come to Greece for that reason! _____

2 The conversation makes use of some verbs in the past progressive. Can you find them?

    a I was expecting… _____

    b Everybody was saying to us… _____

    c I wanted… (lit. I was wanting…) _____

3 Read the following list of words. As you see, they are all in plural. Can you translate them into English?

    a βροχές _____

    b χιόνια _____

    c χειμώνες _____

Learn more

1 SOME NOTES ON GREEK NOUNS

Singular and plural forms

The purpose of the last exercise was to point out that most Greek nouns have a singular and plural form even if they are uncountable nouns. The examples of **βροχή/βροχές, χιόνι/ χιόνια, χειμώνας/χειμώνες** are best translated by the singular in English. Other examples in Greek include:

λάδι/λάδια	*oil*
ζάχαρη/ζάχαρες	*sugar*
έπιπλο/έπιπλα	*furniture*

Either singular or plural form

There are also some nouns that have either a singular or a plural form. Some examples in the singular include:

ξενιτιά	*abroad*
πίστη	*faith*
οξυγόνο	*oxygen*
Λαμπρή	*Easter*
Πεντηκοστή	*Whit Sunday*

Some examples of plural only:

γενέθλια	*birthday*
διακοπές	*holidays*
Χριστούγεννα	*Christmas*
Χανιά	*Chania* (Greek town)
μεσάνυχτα	*midnight*
ελληνικά	*Greek*

Greek nouns with articles

There are also some cases where an article is needed in Greek but not in English. Consider these examples.

With proper names

Είμαι ο Νίκος.	*I am Nick.*
Η Ελλάδα είναι ωραία.	*Greece is nice.*
Η Αθήνα είναι μεγάλη.	*Athens is big.*

With weekdays or months

Δε μ'αρέσει ο Ιούλιος.	*I don't like July.*
Η Κυριακή είναι η αγαπημένη μου μέρα.	*Sunday is my favourite day.*

With holidays

Τα Χριστούγεννα δεν είναι για μένα.	*Christmas is not for me.*
Το Πάσχα είναι η αγαπημένη μου γιορτή.	*Easter is my favourite holiday.*

Idiomatic use (Greek articles instead of English prepositions)

Την Κυριακή.	*On Sunday.*
Το Σάββατο.	*On Saturday.*
Τον Απρίλιο.	*In April.*
Το Σεπτέμβριο.	*In September.*

2 EXPRESSIONS WITH SEASONS AND MONTHS

Here are some useful expressions related to seasons:

την άνοιξη	*in spring*
το καλοκαίρι	*in summer*
το φθινόπωρο	*in autumn*
το χειμώνα	*in winter*

Expressions with months take **τον** or **το**:

τον Ιανουάριο	*in January*	**τον Ιούλιο**	*in July*
τον Απρίλιο	*in April*	**τον Αύγουστο**	*in August*
τον Ιούνιο	*in June*	**τον Οκτώβριο**	*in October*

...but

το Φεβρουάριο	*in February*	**το Σεπτέμβριο**	*in September*
το Μάρτιο	*in March*	**το Νοέμβριο**	*in November*
το Μάϊο	*in May*	**το Δεκέμβριο**	*in December*

3 *THIS* **AND** *THAT*

You have encountered lots of words like **αυτός**, **αυτό** and **αυτά** in previous units, and **τόσα**, **αυτό**, **τόσο**, **τέτοιο**, **εκείνο**, **τέτοια** and **αυτή** in this unit. These are all pronouns; like the other pronouns you have already learnt they have different forms for gender (m/f/n), singular or plural. These are 'demonstrative' pronouns rather than personal, or possessive, pronouns, which were explained in previous units.

The most important demonstrative pronouns are:

αυτός, αυτή, αυτό	*this*
εκείνος, εκείνη, εκείνο	*that*
τόσος, τόση, τόσο	*so, so much, so big, so many*
τέτοιος, τέτοια, τέτοιο	*such (a), of such a kind*

Here are some other examples you have already seen:

αυτά τα δέντρα	*these trees*
αυτός ο δρόμος	*this street*
αυτό το κτίριο	*this building*
τόσα πολλά πράγματα	*so many things*
αυτό το γεγονός	*this fact*
τόσο μακριά	*so far*
τέτοιο παλιόκαιρο!	*such terrible weather!*
εκείνο το τριήμερο!	*that three-day (weekend!)*
τέτοια λόγια!	*such words!*

Don't confuse the use of **αυτός**, **αυτή** and **αυτό** as demonstrative pronouns with **αυτός**, **αυτή**, **αυτό** as personal pronouns! The first always come before nouns and the latter before verbs. Some examples:

... (before nouns)

αυτός ο δρόμος	_this_ street (m)
αυτή η γυναίκα	_this_ woman (f)
αυτό το κτίριο	_this_ building (n)

But ... (before verbs)

Αυτός έχει δύο σπίτια.	_He_ has two houses.
Αυτή είναι νοσοκόμα.	_She_ is a nurse.
Αυτό είναι ακριβό.	_It_ is expensive.

4 NEGATIVE SENTENCES

Can you remember how to make negative sentences in Greek? If you are still not sure, this section will review the most important uses in daily speech.

Δε(ν)

This is used with a verb for negative meaning.

Θέλω	_I want_	**Δε θέλω**	_I don't want_
Είμαι	_I am_	**Δεν είμαι**	_I am not_
Μπορώ	_I can_	**Δεν μπορώ**	_I cannot_
Θέλει	_He wants_	**Δε θέλει**	_He doesn't want_
Ήθελε	_He wanted_	**Δεν ήθελε**	_He didn't want_
Θα πάω	_I will go_	**Δε θα πάω**	_I won't go_
Σε έστειλε	_He sent you_	**Δε σε έστειλε**	_He didn't send you_

Notice that it is always not only before the verb but also before other particles or pronouns:

Δε(ν) + verb	**Δε θέλω**	_I don't want_
Δε(ν) + θα + verb	**Δε θα πάω**	_I won't go_
Δε(ν) + (personal pronoun) + verb	**Δε σε έστειλε**	_He didn't send you_
Δε(ν) + (pronouns) + verb	**Δε μου το είπε**	_He didn't say that to me_

Μη(ν)

There are two basic uses:

With imperatives

Μην τρως!	_Don't eat!_
Μην πας!	_Don't go!_
Μην το κάνεις!	_Don't do it!_
Μη μου μιλάς!	_Don't talk to me!_
Μην του μιλάτε!	_Don't talk to him!_

With the second verb in a subjunctive form

Αποφασίσαμε να μην πάμε.   *We decided not to go.*

Μπορεί να μη φύγω.   *I might not leave.*

Μπορώ να μη φάω.   *I am able not to eat.*

Δεν μπορώ να μη φάω.   *I am not able not to eat.*

Όχι

This is used like the English *no*.

Όχι, δε θέλω να φάω.   *No, I don't want to eat.*

Όχι, δε με λένε Γιώργο.   *No, my name is not George.*

Όχι, δεν μπορώ.   *No, I can't.*

Όχι, δεν μπορούμε.   *No, we cannot.*

Όχι, δε θα φύγουμε.   *No, we won't leave.*

Practice

 1 Can you talk about the weather in Greek?

   a How would you ask: *What's the weather like in Greece?*

   b If they ask you the same question about the weather back home, how would you say: *It's often cloudy?*

   c How would you say: *It's often rainy?*

   d How would you say: *It snows in the winter, and it is very cold?*

   e How would you say: *I like it when it is sunny and chilly?*

   f How would you say: *Does it snow or hail in Greece?*

   g Someone told you: Το καλοκαίρι κάνει πολύ ζέστη στην Ελλάδα αλλά δεν έχει υγρασία! What did he say?

2 Match each question with the most appropriate answer.

   a Τι σου αρέσει στην Ελλάδα;   **1** Ήταν μαύρο κι άραχνο. Μη ρωτάς!

   b Τι καιρό έκανε;   **2** Ο ήλιος, η θάλασσα, η αμμουδιά!

   c Είσαι στεναχωρημένη;   **3** Ναι προχθές. Γιατί ρωτάς;

   d Πώς ήταν το ταξίδι σου;   **4** Ήταν αίθριος συνέχεια.

   e Έχει τηλεφωνήσει στη Μαρία;   **5** Πάρα πολύ, γιατί ψιχαλίζει έξω!

3 11.10 Listen to the dialogue and compare your answers. At the end, listen once again and repeat out loud.

   a Μα καλά (*OK*, but idiom atic)! Τι καιρό είχε;

   b Ναι, αλλά δεν κάναμε τίποτα λόγω (*due to*) του καιρού.

   c Δηλαδή, δεν πήγατε πουθενά;

   d Λυπάμαι που το ακούω.

   e Είχατε προγραμματίσει να κάνετε πολλά πράγματα;

f Απαίσιο και άστατο κάθε μέρα.

g Ακριβώς! Δεν πήγαμε πουθενά!

h Κι εγώ. Πάρα πολύ …

 4 11.11 **Complete the dialogue. Then listen to the dialogue and compare your answers. At the end, listen once again and repeat out loud.**

Ηλέκτρα	Μας έχεις βγάλει την πίστη! Γιατί δε μας λες τι συμβαίνει;
You	**a** *What can I tell you?*
Ηλέκτρα	Γιατί δε μας τα λες όλα; Είναι πιο εύκολο.
You	**b** *I don't know. I have never been so concerned before.*
Ηλέκτρα	Μα καλά! Τι συνέβη;
You	**c** *The weather was awful and very unsettled.*
Ηλέκτρα	Ναι, αλλά δεν το ήξερες;
You	**d** *No. Everybody was telling me that the weather would be fair and wonderful. Instead (here αντίθετα) …*
Ηλέκτρα	Έλα μην κάνεις έτσι τώρα.
You	*f What would you like me to do?*

5 Match the words on the left with the words on the right.

a κάστρο		**1** letter
b ιστορία		**2** June
c χαλάζι		**3** story
d γράμμα		**4** March
e Ιούλιος		**5** I telephone
f Ιούνιος		**6** castle
g τηλεφωνώ		**7** May
h Μάιος		**8** July
i Μάρτιος		**9** hail

6 What are the past tense (simple and continuous) forms of the following verbs?

		simple	continuous
a	ανεβαίνω	ανέβηκα	ανέβαινα
b	βλέπω	_____	_____
c	παίρνω	_____	_____
d	πηγαίνω	_____	_____
e	ρωτάω(ώ)	_____	_____
f	τελειώνω	_____	_____
g	τρώω	_____	_____
h	φεύγω	_____	_____

7 Can you remember the names of the four seasons and months of the year? This quiz will test your memory and knowledge!

a Which season?

1 _____ 2 _____ 3 _____ 4 _____

b Which months belong to each season?

Winter:	**1** _____	**2** _____	**3** _____
Spring:	**4** _____	**5** _____	**6** _____
Summer:	**7** _____	**8** _____	**9** _____
Autumn:	**10** _____	**11** _____	**12** _____

8 Test your translation skills

a You look very concerned. What happened? _____

b You have often been to Corfu, haven't you? _____

c The weather messed up our plans. _____

d What awful weather! I don't like it at all. _____

e Did you watch TV? Did you eat? Did you talk? _____

f You'll have the chance to go back again. _____

g Yes, indeed. Next year, at the earliest! _____

9 Can you recognize some of the words you have already learnt? Remember to look horizontally and vertically.

Λ	Ι	Α	Κ	Α	Δ	Α
Α	Π	Ο	Ρ	Ω	Υ	Σ
θ	Ο	Ρ	Υ	Β	Ο	Σ
Ο	Β	Ρ	Ο	Χ	Η	Ο
Σ	Ι	Ν	Ε	Μ	Α	Σ
Π	Α	Γ	Ω	Ν	Ι	Α

Tim	Έχουμε **a** _____ να μην πάμε στη Λαμία ξανά! Ούτε του χρόνου ούτε του **b** _____, ούτε ποτέ!
Αριστείδης	Γιατί, βρε Tim; **c** _____ τον καιρό σήμερα. Έχει μια υπέροχη λιακάδα κι ένα δροσερό αεράκι. Λένε ότι μπορεί να **d** _____ το βράδυ αλλά δε νομίζω. Κι ο καιρός είναι **e** _____ στη Λαμία σήμερα.
Mary	Μην του μιλάτε για τη Λαμία!
Ηλέκτρα	Δεν έχεις **f** _____ όμως Tim. Στο Λονδίνο βρέχει κάθε μέρα. **g** _____ έριξε χαλάζι. Όλοι οι δρόμοι είναι βρεγμένοι κι **h** _____. Εδώ όμως, δε βλέπεις;
Tim	Μη μου μιλάτε για το Λονδίνο! Γι' αυτό έχω **i** _____ στην Ελλάδα. Δεν ήθελα άλλες βροχές και χιόνια. Άλλο **j** _____ και παγωνιά. Ήθελα **k** _____, θάλασσα και αμμουδιά!
Αριστείδης	Χαίρομαι που η Westminster Bank δε **l** _____ στην Καβάλα ή την Ξάνθη. Εκεί να δεις χειμώνες …
Mary	Δεν είναι όμως **m** _____ τώρα. Είναι άνοιξη και **n** _____ πώς και πώς αυτή την **o** _____. Όλοι μας **p** _____ ότι είναι η καλύτερη **o** _____ στην Αθήνα.
Αριστείδης	Αυτό να λέγεται! Είναι πράγματι η καλύτερη **o** _____ …

> δίκιο   επικίνδυνοι   εποχή
> παραχρόνου   έλθει   περίμενα
> χειμώνας   παρόμοιος   προχτές
> έλεγαν   αποφασίσει   κοίτα
> κρύο   σ' έστειλε   ήλιο   βρέξει

11 Look at the following weather information on the map and match the Greek words with their English counterparts.

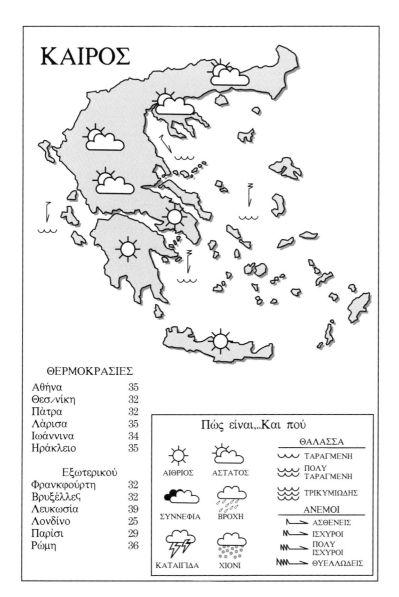

ΚΑΙΡΟΣ

ΘΕΡΜΟΚΡΑΣΙΕΣ

Αθήνα	35
Θεσ/νίκη	32
Πάτρα	32
Λάρισα	35
Ιωάννινα	34
Ηράκλειο	35

Εξωτερικού

Φρανκφούρτη	32
Βρυξέλλες	32
Λευκωσία	39
Λονδίνο	25
Παρίσι	29
Ρώμη	36

Πώς είναι,...Και πού

ΑΙΘΡΙΟΣ   ΑΣΤΑΤΟΣ

ΣΥΝΝΕΦΙΑ   ΒΡΟΧΗ

ΚΑΤΑΙΓΙΔΑ   ΧΙΟΝΙ

ΘΑΛΑΣΣΑ

～～	ΤΑΡΑΓΜΕΝΗ
～～～	ΠΟΛΥ ΤΑΡΑΓΜΕΝΗ
～～～～	ΤΡΙΚΥΜΙΩΔΗΣ

ΑΝΕΜΟΙ

⊾→	ΑΣΘΕΝΕΙΣ
⋏→	ΙΣΧΥΡΟΙ
⋀→	ΠΟΛΥ ΙΣΧΥΡΟΙ
⋀⋀→	ΘΥΕΛΛΩΔΕΙΣ

a	θερμοκρασίες ___	**1**	winds
b	αίθριος ___	**2**	strong
c	συννεφιά ___	**3**	temperatures
d	ταραγμένη ___	**4**	sunny
e	άνεμοι ___	**5**	rough
f	ισχυροί ___	**6**	cloudy

12 Look at the map again and decide which statements are true and which are false.

		True	False
a	Η θερμοκρασία στη Φρανκφούρτη είναι παρόμοια με την θερμοκρασία στις Βρυξέλλες.	_____	_____
b	Η Ρώμη έχει την υψηλότερη θερμοκρασία.	_____	_____
c	Το Λονδίνο έχει τη χαμηλότερη (lowest) θερμοκρασία.	_____	_____
d	Υπάρχουν τρεις ελληνικές πόλεις με την ίδια θερμοκρασία.	_____	_____
e	Μερικοί άνεμοι είναι ισχυροί στη θάλασσα.	_____	_____
f	Σε μερικά μέρη της Ελλάδας ο καιρός είναι άστατος.	_____	_____
g	Σε μερικά σημεία η θάλασσα είναι πολύ ταραγμένη.	_____	_____
h	Στην Κρήτη ο καιρός είναι άστατος.	_____	_____
i	Στη Θεσσαλονίκη ο καιρός είναι αίθριος.	_____	_____

ΕΠΙΣΗΜΕΣ ΑΡΓΙΕΣ *PUBLIC HOLIDAYS*

Here is a list of most of the Greek public holidays.

Πρωτοχρονιά	**Ιαν.** 1 *Jan.*	*New Year's Day*
Θεοφάνεια	**Ιαν.** 6 *Jan.*	*Epiphany*
Καθαρά Δευτέρα	**Μαρ.** 6 *Mar.*	*Ash Monday*
Ευαγγ. Θεοτόκου	**Μαρ.** 25 *Mar.*	*National Holiday*
Έθνική Επέτειος		
Μεγάλη Παρασκευή	**Απρ.** 21 *Apr.*	*Good Friday*
Άγιον πάσχα	**Απρ.** 23 *Apr.*	*Easter Day*
Δευτέρα του Πάσχα	**Απρ.** 24 *Apr.*	*Easter Monday*
Πρωτομαγιά	**Μάι.** 1 *May*	*Labour Day*
Αγίου Πνεύματος	**Ιουν.** 12 *Jun.*	*Whit Monday*
Κοίμηση Θεοτόκου	**Αυγ.** 15 *Aug.*	*Assumption*
Εθνική Επέτειος	**Οκτ.** 28 *Oct.*	*National Holiday*
Χριστούγεννα	**Δεκ.** 25 *Dec.*	*Christmas Day*
Σύναξις της Θεοτόκου	**Δεκ.** 26 *Dec.*	*Assembly Day*

 Test yourself

1 Can you remember the Greek for the following ten important words from this unit?

a water _____

b July _____

c trip/s _____

d sunshine _____

e weather _____

f breeze _____

g worried _____

h rain _____

i May _____

j snow _____

2 Can you remember the following ten important phrases from this unit?

a I've planned/called. _____

b You are (not) right. _____

c You sound/look … _____

d This is the best time in Athens. _____

e The rain never stopped. _____

f It's not winter now, it's spring! _____

g It rained cats and dogs! _____

h What's the weather like? _____

i You'll have the chance to go back again. _____

j It's fair/unsettled/awful/marvellous. _____

3 The following phrases are given in the present tense. Can you change them into the past tense, both simple and progressive?

a Πηγαίνω ταξίδι. _____

b Ρωτάω στ' Αγγλικά. _____

c Φεύγω νωρίς. _____

d Παίρνω τηλέφωνο. _____

e Κάνει ζέστη. _____

SELF CHECK

	I CAN...
○	. . . understand weather conditions.
○	. . . report on weather conditions.
○	. . . talk about the weather with friends.
○	. . . understand and talk about months and seasons.
○	. . . talk about past holidays.
○	. . . use Greek articles appropriately.
○	. . . understand and use some verbs talking about past events both in past tense or present perfect tense.
○	. . . complain and disagree with other people.

12 *Πού πήγατε για Πάσχα;*
Where did you go for Easter?

In this unit you will learn how to:
▶ *use appropriate language at a social function.*
▶ *express wishes or congratulations.*
▶ *express opinions and state preferences.*
▶ *describe past events.*

CEFR: (B1) *Can understand some Easter customs and traditions. Can understand and express wishes or congratulations. Can express opinions and state preferences. Can describe past events. Can use adverbs of sequence to describe the order of events. Can use Greek adverbs when necessary. Can use the past perfect tense with several verbs. Can be more aware of Greek cultural heritage.*

Πάσχα στην Ελλάδα *Easter in Greece*

Greek Orthodox Easter is probably the most important religious holiday in Greece; it usually falls one or two weeks after Western Easter. The week before **Κυριακή του Πάσχα** *Easter Sunday*, you'll notice Athens getting emptier and emptier, and by **Μεγάλη Παρασκευή** *Good Friday* approximately four million people have left the city for the **χωριά** *villages* they come from. Around this time the Greeks use lots of expressions of good wishes:

Καλό Πάσχα! *Happy Easter!* This is a wish used usually before Easter Sunday, particularly when people are leaving for the break and they probably won't see each other again until after Easter.

1 What is the Greek word for Easter?

Vocabulary builder

ΣΥΓΧΑΡΗΤΗΡΙΑ ΚΙ ΑΛΛΕΣ ΕΛΛΗΝΙΚΕΣ ΕΥΧΕΣ *CONGRATULATIONS AND OTHER GREEK WISHES*

1 12.01 **You are going to hear some expressions used when congratulating someone or when expressing wishes. Which two expressions do you hear on each different occasion?**
   a On a birthday:
      1 Να τα εκατοστήσεις!   **2** Καλές γιορτές!   **3** Πολύχρονος!/-η!/-ο!
   b On a name day:
      1 Καλή Ανάσταση!   **2** Να χαίρεσαι τη γιορτή σου! **3** Και του χρόνου!
   c *Cheers!* when having a drink:
      1 Στην υγειά μας!   **2** Εις υγείαν!   **3** Καλή όρεξη!
   d *Have a nice trip!* when going on a trip:
      1 Καλή πρόοδο!   **2** Καλό ταξίδι!   **3** Στο καλό!

e On New Year's Day:

    1 Καλή χρονιά!   **2** Καλό Πάσχα!   **3** Ευτυχισμένος ο καινούριος χρόνος!

f On Easter Sunday:

    1 Χριστός ανέστη!   **2** Αληθώς ανέστη!   **3** Στην υγειά σου!

g On Christmas Day:

    1 Καλά Χριστούγεννα!   **2** Καλή σταδιοδρομία!   **3** Χρόνια πολλά!

h When buying something new:

    1 Η Παναγιά μαζί σου!   **2** Καλορίζικο!   **3** Με γεια!

i When going to bed to sleep:

    1 Καλό ξημέρωμα!   **2** Όνειρα γλυκά!   **3** Καλό απόγευμα!

j Finishing school or graduating from college:

    1 Συγχαρητήρια!   **2** Να' σαι καλά!   **3** Καλή πρόοδο!

2 **Listen now to these expressions once again and repeat them out loud. Pay special attention to your pronunciation.**

3 **There were ten expressions in Exercise 1 that you have not heard. Can you find the best possible occasion for each of these ten expressions? Do not look for word-for-word translations!**

    a Have a nice evening! _____

    b Cheers! _____

    c You're welcome! _____

    d God be with you! _____

    e Happy holidays! _____

    f Bon appétit! _____

    g Happy Easter! _____

    h Happy Easter! _____

    i Next year again! _____

    j Have a successful professional life! _____

Conversation 1

ΠΟΥ ΠΗΓΑΤΕ ΓΙΑ ΠΑΣΧΑ ΦΕΤΟΣ; *WHERE DID YOU GO AT EASTER TIME THIS YEAR?*

 NEW EXPRESSIONS

 12.02

είχαμε πάει	*we had gone*
Πού κάνατε Ανάσταση;	*Where did you celebrate Easter? (lit. did you do Resurrection?)*
μας είχε καλέσει	*he had invited us*
ακουστά το έχω	*I've heard about it*
το είχαμε ξανακούσει	*we had heard it before*
γνωρίσαμε	*we met*
παραδοσιακός/-ή/-ό	*traditional*
ο οικισμός	*the settlement*

που άντεξε	*that withstood, survived*
ο σεισμός	*the earthquake*
ήρεμη/-η/-ο	*tranquil*
η ζωή	*the life*
το γιωτ/η θαλαμηγός	*the yacht*
το κόт(τ)ερο	*the cutter*
το ιστιοφόρο	*the sailing boat*
φημισμένος/-η/-ο	*famous*
οπωσδήποτε	*definitely*
η ψαροταβέρνα	*the fish taverna*
φάγατε;	*did you eat?*
δηλαδή	*in other words*
είχαν ήδη βάλει	*they had already prepared* (lit. *put*)
ήδη	already
αρνάκι στο φούρνο	*baby lamb in the stove (oven)*
κατσικάκι στη σούβλα	*kid (young goat) on the spit*
τι λες, βρε παιδί μου;	*what are you telling me, my dear?* (lit. *my child*)
τόσο καλό;	*so good?*
πού να σας λέμε	*where (how) can we start? What can we tell you?*

 12.03 *Tim and Mary are talking about their Easter holiday.*

1 Listen to the conversation a couple of times without looking at the text. Did they have a good time?

Δημήτρης	Πού πήγατε για Πάσχα φέτος;
Tim	Και πού δεν πήγαμε; Είχαμε πάει στο Φισκάρδο, μετά στην Ιθάκη, μετά στη Δωδώνη, και τέλος στα Γιάννενα.
Δημήτρης	Καλά, μα πού κάνατε Ανάσταση;
Tim	Ανάσταση κάναμε στο Φισκάρδο. Έχουμε έναν καλό φίλο τον Παναγή που μας είχε καλέσει στο Φισκάρδο όλη τη Μεγάλη Βδομάδα.
Δημήτρης	Πού είναι το Φισκάρδο; Ακουστά το έχω αλλά δε θυμάμαι.
Mary	Ούτε κι εμείς το είχαμε ξανακούσει. Αλλά όταν γνωρίσαμε τον Παναγή όλο γι' αυτό μας μιλούσε. Μας έλεγε ότι είναι ένας παραδοσιακός οικισμός που άντεξε τους σεισμούς το 1953. Μας έλεγε για την ήσυχη, ήρεμη βραδινή ζωή, για τα μεγάλα γιωτ, κότερα και ιστιοφόρα φημισμένων ελλήνων και ξένων που πάνε εκεί και οπωσδήποτε για την ψαροταβέρνα της Τασίας, της αδελφής του.
Δημήτρης	Φάγατε καλό ψάρι δηλαδή;
Mary	Όλη τη Μεγάλη Βδομάδα. Και την Κυριακή ενώ είχαν ήδη βάλει αρνάκι στο φούρνο και κατσικάκι στη σούβλα, εμείς φάγαμε πάλι ψάρι!
Αναστασία	Τι λες, βρε παιδί μου; Τόσο καλό;
Tim	Πού να σας λέμε …

2 **Now read the conversation and answer the questions.**

    a How many places did they visit? Which ones? List them.

    b Where did they celebrate Easter: στο Φισκάρδο or στην Ιθάκη;

    c What did they eat all week long: αρνάκι στο φούρνο or ψάρι;

 3 **Listen again and pay special attention to the words that run together. Practise speaking the part of Tim or Mary and pay particular attention to your pronunciation.**

Language discovery 1

1 **Some words help you tell a story in parts, focusing on time segments. Can you find the rest of this working vocabulary in the conversation?**

    a At first… _____

    b Then… _____

    c Afterwards… _____

    d At the end… _____

2 **The conversation has several verbs in the past tense. Can you find them?**

    a We ate… _____

    b Where did you go? _____

    c we celebrated… _____

    d we met… _____

    e which withstood… _____

    f Where did you celebrate…? _____

3 **Look at the last two lines of this conversation in which the verb λέ(γ)ω is used idiomatically. Can you translate these two lines?**

    Αναστασία   Τι λες βρε παιδί μου; Τόσο καλό; _____

    Tim   Πού να σας λέμε … _____

Learn more

1 TALKING ABOUT PAST EVENTS

This unit contains more verbs in the past tense. The following list has the main and the past form of the most important ones.

πάω	I go	→	πήγα	I went
κάνω	I do	→	έκανα	I did
γνωρίζω	I meet	→	γνώρισα	I met
αντέχω	I stand	→	άντεξα	I stood, I endured
τρώω	I eat	→	έφαγα	I ate
ξεχνώ	I forget	→	ξέχασα	I forgot
πιάνω	I hold	→	έπιασα	I held
φτάνω	I arrive	→	έφτασα	I arrived

σταματάω	I stop	→	σταμάτησα	I stopped
είμαι	I am	→	ήμουν	I was
βλέπω	I see	→	είδα	I saw
καταλαβαίνω	I understand	→	κατάλαβα	I understood

As a reminder, here's the full conjugation of two of these important verbs in the past tense.

I went …	I ate …
πήγ – α	έ – φαγ – α
πήγ – ες	έ – φαγ – ες
πήγ – ε	έ – φαγ – ε
πήγ – αμε	φάγ – αμε
πήγ – ατε	φάγ – ατε
πήγ – αν(ε)	έ – φαγ – αν

2 IDIOMATIC USES OF THE VERB *TO SAY/TO TELL*

The verb **λέω** or **λέγω** *to say/to tell* has many idiomatic uses.

<u>Πες</u> μου κάτι.	*<u>Tell</u> me something.*
<u>Πες</u> κάτι.	*<u>Say</u> something.*
<u>Λέω</u> μία ιστορία/ένα μυστικό.	*I <u>tell</u> a story/secret.*
Πώς το <u>λέτε</u> στα ελληνικά;	*How do you <u>say</u> that in Greek?*
Δεν ξέρει τι <u>λέει</u>.	*He doesn't know what he is <u>talking</u> about.*
Ασ'τους να <u>λένε</u>!	*Let them <u>talk</u>! Never mind what they <u>say</u>!*
Τι ώρα <u>λες</u> να είναι;	*What time do you <u>think</u> it is?*
Έλα, ας <u>πούμε</u> στις πέντε.	*Come, <u>say</u> around five.*
Δεν ξέρω τι να <u>πω</u>.	*I am at a loss for <u>words.</u>*
<u>Λέω</u> ότι έχω να <u>πω</u>!	*Let me say what I think!*
Κάτι μου <u>λέει</u> ότι …	*I <u>have a hunch</u>/feeling that …*
<u>Λες</u> να βρέξει;	*Do you <u>think</u> it's going to rain?*
Μη μου <u>πεις</u>!	*Really! Is that so? You don't <u>say</u> so!*
<u>Πες</u> το λοιπόν!	*<u>Come</u> out with it!*
Τι <u>είπατε</u>;	*What did you <u>say</u>? I beg your pardon?*
Τι <u>λες</u> για μια πίτσα;	*What <u>about</u> a pizza?*

Λέω has some irregular forms in certain tenses. The main ones are:

λέω	*I say/tell*
θα πω	*I will say/will tell*
είπα	*I said/told*
έχω/είχα πει	*I have/had said/told*
πες – πείτε – (πέστε)	*say/tell*

Conversation 2

 NEW EXPRESSIONS

 12.04

γιόρταζες;	*have you had your name day* (also birthday)?
να ζήσεις!	*may you live long!/enjoy your life!*
εκπλήσσω	*I surprise*
η ευχή	*the wish*
είχαμε υποσχεθεί	*we had promised*
ο καθηγητής	*the teacher, tutor*
μαθαίνω	*I learn*
χρησιμοποιώ	*I use*
ιδού λοιπόν!	*here you go!/here's the proof!*
μπράβο σας!	*well done (to you), Bravo!*
τώρα θυμήθηκα	*I've just remembered* (lit. *now I remembered*)
να χαίρεσαι τη γυναίκα σου!	*congratulations to your wife!* (lit. *enjoy your wife!*)
κι εσείς ό,τι επιθυμείτε!	*may your wish come true!* (lit. *and whatever you like/wish!*)
σ'έπιασα	*I got you* (idiom) (lit. *I caught you*)

12.05 *Tim and Mary have just realized that it was their friend Anastasia's name day a few days earlier.*

 1 Listen to the conversation a couple of times without looking at the text. Why is Anastasia impressed?

Mary	Πω, πω θεέ μου! Το ξέχασα! Αναστασία, γιόρταζες;
Αναστασία	Ναι. Γιορτάζω την ημέρα του Πάσχα.
Tim	Συγνώμη και χρόνια πολλά τότε.
Mary	Ναι, ναι χρόνια σου πολλά! Να ζήσεις!
Αναστασία	Ευχαριστώ, ευχαριστώ. Μ' εκπλήσσετε όμως. Ξέρετε όλες τις ελληνικές ευχές …
Mary	Είχαμε υποσχεθεί στον καθηγητή μας των ελληνικών να τις μάθουμε και να τις χρησιμοποιούμε. Ιδού λοιπόν! Ωραία;
Δημήτρης	Και βέβαια ωραία. Μπράβο σας!
Tim	Α! Τώρα θυμήθηκα. Κι εσύ Δημήτρη να χαίρεσαι την γυναίκα σου! Σωστά;
Δημήτρης	Σωστά, σωστά, ευχαριστώ. Κι εσείς ό,τι επιθυμείτε!
Mary	Ό,τι επιθυμούμε; Ε; Αα! Αυτό δεν το καταλαβαίνω …
Δημήτρης	Τελικά σ' έπιασα Mary …

2 Now read the conversation and answer the questions.

  a What did Mary forget?

  b When is Anastasia's name day?

  c What did Mary promise her language teacher?

3 Listen again and pay special attention to the words that run together. Practise speaking the part of Tim or Mary and pay particular attention to your pronunciation.

💡 Language discovery 2

1 There are four congratulations and/or wishes in the conversation. Translate them into English. Do they all have a verb?

    a Χρόνια (σου) πολλά! _____

    b Να ζήσεις! _____

    c Να χαίρεσαι τη γυναίκα σου! _____

    d Κι εσείς ό,τι επιθυμείτε! _____

2 The conversation has three verbs in the past tense. Can you find them?

    a I forgot it. _____

    b Now I remembered. _____

    c I got you finally! _____

Learn more

CONGRATULATIONS AND OTHER GREEK WISHES

This conversation extends the list of congratulations and wishes you encountered in the beginning of this unit, with the expressions such as **Να χαίρεσαι τη γυναίκα σου/τον άντρα σου/το παιδί σου!** *Congratulations to your wife/husband/child!* These expressions are used when you address the husband or wife upon the birthday or name day of his wife/her husband/their child. A frequent reply is **Κι εσύ ό,τι επιθυμείς!** or **Κι εσείς ό,τι επιθυμείτε!** *May your wish(es) come true!* **Να ζήσεις!** *May you live long!* (you singular) or **Να ζήσετε!** *May you live long!* (you plural) are two expressions addressed to the person who celebrates a name day or birthday. **Να σας ζήσει!** *May he/she live long!* is an expression addressed to the parents of a newly-born baby. **Ευχαριστώ** or **ευχαριστούμε** are possible answers to the last three expressions.

Conversation 3

ΔΕΝ ΕΙΧΑΜΕ ΚΟΙΜΗΘΕΙ ΚΑΘΟΛΟΥ ... *WE HADN'T SLEPT AT ALL ...*

 NEW EXPRESSIONS

 12.06

είχε κιόλας μιλήσει σε	*(he) had already talked to*
το σκάφος	*motorboat* (n)
δε μας έχετε πει ακόμα	*you haven't told us yet*
βόρειος/-α/-ο	*northern*
πες το	*say it, come out with it*
κρατάω(-ώ) μυστικό	*keep a secret*
και που λέτε	*to continue my story*

είχαμε περάσει	*we had sailed*
το νησί	*the island*
ο Ωνάσης	*Onasis* (a Greek tycoon)
σταματήσαμε	*we stopped*
πριν να φτάσουμε	*before arriving/getting*
δεν είχαμε κοιμηθεί καθόλου	*we hadn't slept at all*
φυσικά	*of course, naturally*
έπρεπε να	*(we) had to*
την άλλη μέρα	*the next* (lit. *other*) *day*
γνωστός/-ή/-ό	*the acquaintance* (lit. *the known person or thing*)

 12.07 *Tim and Mary are still telling their friends about their Easter holiday and what it was like leaving Fiscardo.*

1 **Listen to the conversation a couple of times without looking at the text. What time did they finally get to Yannena?**

Αναστασία	Και μετά πώς πήγατε στην Ιθάκη;
Mary	Ο Παναγής είχε κιόλας μιλήσει σε κάποιους φίλους του που είχαν ένα μικρό σκάφος. Αυτοί μας πήγαν απέναντι στο νησί του Οδυσσέα. Είναι πολύ κοντά. Ξέρεις, έτσι δεν είναι;
Δημήτρης	Όχι, δεν ξέρουμε. Δε μας έχετε πει ακόμα πού είναι το Φισκάρδο!
Tim	Ωχ! Συγνώμη! Το Φισκάρδο είναι στο πιο βόρειο μέρος της Κεφαλλονιάς.
Δημήτρης	Α, στην Κεφαλλονιά πήγατε! Πες το, βρε Tim! Τι το κρατάς μυστικό; *Σε λίγο …*
Tim	… Και που λέτε με το σκάφος είχαμε περάσει κοντά από το Σκορπιό, το νησί του Ωνάση, έπειτα πήγαμε στην Λευκάδα, απ' εκεί στην Πρέβεζα και σταματήσαμε στο Μαντείο της Δωδώνης πριν να φτάσουμε στα Γιάννενα.
Αναστασία	Και τι ώρα φτάσατε στα Γιάννενα;
Tim	Μετά από δέκα ώρες ταξείδι φτάσαμε στα Γιάννενα γύρω στις πέντε το πρωί. Δεν είχαμε κοιμηθεί καθόλου και ήμασταν πολύ κουρασμένοι.
Αναστασία	Πέντε η ώρα το πρωί; Το Μαντείο ήταν ανοικτό εκείνη την ώρα;
Mary	Φυσικά και όχι. Έπρεπε να ξαναπάμε την άλλη μέρα με τους γνωστούς μας από τα Γιάννενα …

2 **Now read the conversation and answer the questions.**
   a Does Dimitris know where Fiscardo is?
   b Why did they have to go back to the Dodonis Oracle?
   c How long was their trip before reaching Yannena?

3 Listen again and pay special attention to the words that run together. Practise speaking the part of Tim and pay particular attention to your pronunciation.

Language discovery 3

1 You have learnt some transition words in the first conversation, to help you connect parts of a story together. This conversation extends that list with four new possibilities. Can you find them?

   a Talking about it _____

   b later _____

   c and from there _____

   d before reaching _____

2 The conversation has several time registers. Can you find them?

   a before _____

   b yet _____

   c already _____

   d in a little while _____

   e later _____

   f around _____

Learn more

1 ADVERBS

You have encountered several time registers in this conversation. Words such as **ακόμα**, **πια**, **κιόλας**, **πάλι**, **ξανά** and **μόλις** are adverbs. Adverbs can be divided into four groups according to their meaning:

   a place or direction

   b of time

   c of manner

   d of quantity

You have already learnt many adverbs in the previous units. Here is a list of the most important in each group. Remember that most adverbs have one form. Study the list and refer back to it whenever you need to.

Place or direction	Time	Manner	Quantity
πού *where?*	**πότε** *when?*	**πώς** *how?*	**πόσο** *how much?*
πουθενά *nowhere*	**τότε** *then*	**αλλιώς** *otherwise*	**τόσο** *so, so much*
εδώ *here*	**τώρα** *now*	**έτσι** *so, like*	**όσο** *as much as*
εκεί *there*	**ποτέ** *never*	**μαζί** *together, with*	**περίπου** *about*
επάνω *up, above*	**αμέσως** *at once*	**όπως** *as, like*	**πολύ** *much, very*
κάτω *down, under*	**πάλι** *again*	**σαν** *as, like*	**πιο** *more*
μέσα *in, inside*	**ξανά** *again*	**σιγά** *slowly*	**λίγο** *some, little*

έξω *out, outside*	**ακόμα(η)** *still, yet*	**μόνο** *only*	**αρκετά** *enough*
μεταξύ *between*	**κιόλας** *already*	**ωραία** *fine*	**σχεδόν** *almost*
γύρω *(a)round*	**ήδη** *already*	**επίσης** *too, also*	**τουλάχιστο(ν)** *at least*
κοντά *near*	**πια** *already*	**κυρίως** *mainly*	**καθόλου** *not at all*
μακριά *far*	**μόλις** *just*	**ιδίως** *especially*	

2 TRANSLATING THE WORD *AGAIN*

If you check the column with the time registers above, you'll find two words for *again* in Greek: **ξανά** and **πάλι**. **Ξανά** appears often as a prefix to many verbs, as you have seen in previous units, such as:

ξαναβλέπω	*I see again*
ξανακούω	*I listen/hear again*
ξανατρώω	*I eat again*
ξαναπηγαίνω	*I go again*

Πάλι cannot be used as a prefix although it could be used with the above verbs as a second word:

βλέπω πάλι	*I see again*
ακούω πάλι	*I listen/hear again*
τρώω πάλι	*I eat again*
πηγαίνω πάλι	*I go again*

Instead of **πάλι** you could have used the word **ξανά** in the last four examples e.g. **βλέπω ξανά** *I see again*.

Ξανά also has another meaning with certain verbs:

Δεν το είχαμε ξανακούσει.	*We hadn't heard about it before.*

Conversation 4

ΠΟΥ ΑΛΛΟΥ ΠΗΓΑΤΕ; *WHERE ELSE DID YOU GO?*

 NEW EXPRESSIONS

 12.08

θα μας πήγαιναν	*they would have taken us*
το πανηγύρι	*the (religious) fair*
έξω από	*outside*
τοπικός/-ή/-ό	*local*
ντόπιος/-α/-ο	*local/native*
χορεύω	*to dance*
ενδιαφέρον	*interesting*
πού αλλού;	*where else?*

δείχνω/δείξω	to show
κέρινος/-η/-ο	wax
το ομοίωμα	model, image, figure
συναρπαστικός/-ή/-ό	unique/exciting
αντίστοιχος/-η/-ο	corresponding
τρομερό!	awesome!
φανταστικό!	fantastic!
είχαμε κάνει έρευνα	we had done (some) research
η χώρα	the country
πριν να έρθουμε	before coming (lit. before we (to) come)
κιόλας	already
παραπάνω	more than
και δεν πέσαμε έξω!	and we didn't miscalculate!/and we guessed right! (lit. and we didn't fall outside!)
μακάρι να είχα κι εγώ	I wish I had the same
την ίδια εντύπωση	impression

 12.09 *Tim and Mary are still recounting their exciting adventures in Yannena.*

1 Listen to the conversation a couple of times without looking at the text. Why are they particularly excited about the Vrellis Wax Museum?

Αναστασία	Και στα Γιάννενα; Πού πήγατε;
Mary	Μας είχαν πει ότι θα μας πήγαιναν σ' ένα πανηγύρι έξω από τα Γιάννενα. Εκεί ακούσαμε τοπική, παραδοσιακή μουσική και είδαμε ντόπιους να χορεύουν. Ήταν πολύ ενδιαφέρον και κάτι διαφορετικό για μας.
Αναστασία	Πού αλλού πήγατε;
Mary	Μας είχαν υποσχεθεί να μας δείξουν το Μουσείο Κέρινων Ομοιωμάτων του Βρέλλη. Μόλις δέκα λεπτά έξω από τα Γιάννενα. Ήταν πολύ συναρπαστικό και ενδιαφέρον. Και είναι το μοναδικό στην Ελλάδα απ' όσο ξέρουν οι γνωστοί μας. Είναι κάτι αντίστοιχο με το Μουσείο της Madame Tussaud στο Λονδίνο.
Αναστασία	Πω, πω! Δεν είχα ξανακούσει! Τρομερό! Φανταστικό! Έχουμε τέτοιο μουσείο στην Ελλάδα;
Tim	Η Ελλάδα έχει τόσα μυστικά που μολονότι είχαμε διαβάσει και είχαμε κάνει έρευνα πριν να έρθουμε στη χώρα σας κιόλας την πρώτη μέρα εδώ καταλάβαμε ότι η διαμονή μας θα είναι παραπάνω από συναρπαστική. Και δεν πέσαμε έξω!
Δημήτρης	Χαίρομαι που τ'ακούω. Μακάρι να είχα κι εγώ την ίδια εντύπωση όταν πήγα …

2   Now read the conversation and answer the questions.

    a What did they do in the street fair?

    b What was unique about the Vrellis Wax Museum?

    c Is Tim excited about what Greece has to offer?

 3 Listen again and pay special attention to the words that run together. Practise speaking the part of Mary and pay particular attention to your pronunciation.

Language discovery 4

1   **There are four verbs in the past perfect tense in this conversation. Can you find them?**

    a we had read… _____

    b they had promised us _____

    c they had told us _____

    d we had not heard _____

1 THE PAST PERFECT TENSE

This unit introduces you to the past perfect tense. Now that you are familiar with the present perfect tense, this new tense will create no difficulties for you. It is formed with the past tense form of the verb **έχω** followed by the same verb form as in the present perfect. Some examples:

έχω πάει	I have gone	→	είχα πάει	I had gone
έχεις πάει	you have gone	→	είχες πάει	you had gone
έχει πάει	s/he/it has gone	→	είχε πάει	s/he/it had gone
έχουμε πάει	we have gone	→	είχαμε πάει	we had gone
έχετε πάει	you have gone	→	είχατε πάει	you had gone
έχουν πάει	they have gone	→	είχαν πάει	they had gone

Here is a list of verbs from this unit in the past perfect tense:

είχαμε πάει	we had gone	→	πάω	I go
είχε καλέσει	he had invited	→	καλώ	I invite
είχαμε ξανακάνει	we had done again	→	ξανακάνω	I do again
είχαν βάλει	they had prepared	→	βάζω	I prepare
είχαμε υποσχεθεί	we had promised	→	υπόσχομαι	I promise
είχε μιλήσει	he had talked	→	μιλάω(ώ)	I talk
είχαμε περάσει	we had sailed	→	περνάω(ώ)	I sail/spend
είχαμε κοιμηθεί	we had slept	→	κοιμάμαι	I sleep
είχαν πει	they had said	→	λέ(γ)ω	I say
είχα ξανακούσει	I had heard again	→	ξανακούω	I hear again
είχαμε διαβάσει	we had read	→	διαβάζω	I study/read
είχαμε κάνει	we had done	→	κάνω	I do

Important key words used with this new tense or the present perfect include:

ακόμα/ακόμη	*still, till, yet*
πια	*not longer, (no) more*
ήδη	*already*
κιόλας	*already*
μόλις	*just*

Here are some examples you have come across:

Ενώ είχαν ήδη βάλει αρνάκι στο φούρνο …	*Since they had already put a lamb in the oven …*
Ο Παναγής είχε κιόλας … μιλήσει	*Panagis had already spoken/ talked to …*
Δεν είχα φάει ακόμα, όταν ήρθε ο Γιώργος.	*I hadn't eaten yet when Giorgios came.*
Μόλις δέκα λεπτά έξω από τα Γιάννενα.	*Just ten minutes outside Yannena.*
Δε θέλω πια καφέ.	*I don't want coffee any more.*
Δε μπορώ πια!	*I can't take it any longer!*
Ακόμα μαθαίνω Ελληνικά.	*I am still learning Greek.*
Μόλις είχα φάει, ήρθε ο Γιώργος στο σπίτι.	*I had just finished eating (lit. eaten), (when) Giorgios came home.*

2 MORE IDIOMATIC EXPRESSIONS

If you look up a word in a dictionary, you'll often realise that there are several meanings for one word depending on the context. Here is a list with some examples using the verb **πέφτω** *to fall*.

Δεν <u>πέσαμε</u> έξω!	*We <u>guessed</u> right!*
<u>Έπεσε</u> έξω από το αυτοκίνητο/τρένο.	*He <u>fell</u> out of the car/train.*
Το βάζο <u>έπεσε</u> από τα χέρια μου.	*The vase <u>fell</u> from my hands.*
Το χιόνι <u>έπεφτε</u> συνέχεια.	*The snow was <u>coming down/falling</u> steadily.*
Η τιμή για τα φρούτα <u>έπεσε</u>.	*The price of fruit <u>fell</u>.*
Η θερμοκρασία <u>πέφτει</u>.	*The temperature is <u>dropping</u>.*
<u>Έπεσα</u> πάνω στη Μαρία.	*I <u>came upon</u> Maria/I bumped into Maria.*
<u>Έπεσα</u> από τα σύννεφα!	*I was completely <u>taken aback</u>! I was completely surprised.*
<u>Πέφτω</u> άρρωστος.	*I've <u>fallen</u> ill/I I've been <u>taken</u> ill.*
<u>Πέφτω</u> για ύπνο!	*I'm <u>going</u> to bed!*

The different forms of the verb **πέφτω** are:

πέφτω	*I fall*
θα πέσω	*I will fall*
έπεσα	*I fell*
έχω/είχα πέσει	*I have/had fallen*
πέσε – πέστε	*fall*

 Practice

1 **Respond to the following situations in Greek.**
   a You want to ask someone *How do you say that in Greek?*
   b You want to find out if someone has had his/her name day.
   c What are the expressions used when congratulating someone for his wife/her husband/their child's name day?
   d What will your answer be when you hear: Να ζήσεις! Να ζήσετε! Να σας ζήσει!
   e Χρόνια πολλά is a very common expression. How will you reply?
   f You want to find out two specific details: Ask *Where did you go?* and *What did you do?*
   g Ask also *Where else did you go?*

2 **Match each question with the most appropriate answer.**
   a Ποιος σας είχε καλέσει;   1 Όχι, ήταν η πρώτη φορά.
   b Το είχατε ξανακούσει;   2 Γιατί δεν είχαμε κοιμηθεί καθόλου.
   c Γιόρταζες, έτσι δεν είναι;   3 Πουθενά, γιατί δεν είχαμε αυτοκίνητο.
   d Γιατί ήσασταν τόσο   4 Ο φίλος μας ο Παναγής.
      κουρασμένοι;
   e Πού αλλού πήγατε;   5 Ναι εχθές. Ήταν τα γενέθλιά μου.

3 12.10 **Have you rearranged the lines? Now listen and compare your answers. At the end, listen once again and repeat out loud.**
   a Έλα πες μας. Τι κάνατε;
   b Κι ακόμα καλύτερα. Ήταν τόσο ενδιαφέρον.
   c Γνωρίσαμε τη βραδινή ζωή της Ρόδου.
   d Περάσατε ωραία τις διακοπές;
   e Είναι πράγματι όπως λένε;
   f Πού να σας λέω!
   g Πες μας, πες μας. Μας έσκασες!

4 Complete the dialogue using the English prompts.

Δημήτρης	Δεν μας έχετε πει ακόμα που είναι το Φισκάρδο.
You	**a** *It's in the most northern point of Cephalonia.*
Δημήτρης	Αα! Τώρα κατάλαβα. Και πώς περάσατε;
You	**b** *We had a good time. We stopped there for a whole weekend.*
Δημήτρης	Κάνατε τίποτα; Είδατε τίποτα;
You	**c** *There was a fair and we had the chance [ευκαιρία] to see local dances and hear traditional folk music.*
Δημήτρης	Θα έπρεπε να ήταν ωραία!
You	**d** *Yes, it was very exciting. Especially for a foreigner.*
Δημήτρης	Δηλαδή, θα ξαναπάτε εκεί αν έχετε άλλη ευκαιρία;
You	**e** *Definitely, yes. I like whatever is nice and I wouldn't mind seeing it again.*
Δημήτρης	Καλή τύχη τότε!

5 Match the words on the left with the words on the right.

a	κότερο	**1**	fantastic
b	γιωτ	**2**	famous
c	μουσείο	**3**	bravo
d	ύπνος	**4**	museum
e	φανταστικό	**5**	yacht
f	φημισμένος	**6**	naturally, physically
g	μπράβο	**7**	hypnotherapist
h	φυσικά	**8**	cutter

6 Practise the different forms of Greek verbs in past tenses. Choose the correct words from the boxes to complete the sentences.

a _____ στην Αθήνα εχτές.

> Έχω φτάσει   Είχα φτάσει
> Έφτασα

b Πότε _____ το Γιώργο;

> γνώρισες   γνώριζες
> είχες γνωρίσεις

c Τι _____ πριν να έλθω;

> έχεις φάεις   είχες φάει
> είχες τρώει

d Δεν ήθελα να _____ πριν να φτάσω στην Αθήνα, αλλά βλέπεις …

> σταματούσα
> είχες σταματήσει
> έχω σταματήσει

e Τι _____ στην τηλεόραση προχτές;

> έχεις δει   είδες
> είχες δει

f Αα! Αυτό το _____ που μου είπες!

> έχω ξεχάσει   είχα ξεχάσει
> ξέχασα

7 Choose the correct adverb of place, time, manner or quality to complete the sentences.

a _____ είχες πάει στην Αθήνα;

πόσο	τόσο	πότε

b _____ κάνει αυτό το πουκάμισο;

πόσο	τόσο	πώς

c Δεν πήγα _____ πέρσι.

ποτέ	πουθενά	μεταξύ

d Το σπίτι μας είναι _____ του σχολείου και του φαρμακείου.

κοντά	έξω	μεταξύ

e Η Κατερίνη είναι _____ στη Θεσσαλονίκη.

κοντά	έξω	μεταξύ

f Αυτό κάνει _____ πέντε ευρώ.

τουλάχιστον	καθόλου λίγο

g Το ταξείδι κάνει _____ στις οκτώ ώρες.

μόλις	ήδη	γύρω

h Γνώρισα το Γιώργο _____.

όπως	αμέσως	μαζί

i Δε θέλω να φάω _____.

πιο	πάλι	περίπου

j Είχε πάει _____ με την Ελένη για διακοπές.

μεταξύ	μέσα	μαζί

8 Can you find some of the words you have already learnt?

Σ	Π	Ο	Τ	Ε	Η
Τ	Ο	Τ	Ε	Φ	Π
Ο	Σ	Α	Ν	Τ	Ο
Κ	Ο	Ν	Τ	Α	Λ
Μ	Ε	Τ	Α	Ξ	Υ

9 **12.11** Listen to the conversation and find the missing words. If you want you can find the missing words first and then listen and compare your answers.

Αναστασία	Και στα Γιάννενα; Πού πήγατε;
Mary	Μας είχαν πει ότι θα μας πήγαιναν σ' ένα **a** _____ έξω από τα Γιάννενα. Εκεί ακούσαμε τοπική, **b** _____ μουσική και είδαμε ντόπιους να χορεύουν. Ήταν πολύ **c** _____ και κάτι διαφορετικό για μας.
Αναστασία	Πού αλλού πήγατε;
Mary	Μας είχαν **d** _____ να μας δείξουν το Μουσείο Κέρινων Ομοιωμάτων του Βρέλλη. Μόλις δέκα λεπτά έξω από τα Γιάννενα. Ήταν πολύ **e** _____ και **c** _____ Και είναι το μοναδικό στην Ελλάδα απ' όσο ξέρουν οι **f** _____ μας. Είναι κάτι αντίστοιχο με το Μουσείο της Madame Tussaud στο Λονδίνο.

Αναστασία	Πω, πω! Δεν είχα ξανακούσει! **g** _____ Φανταστικό! Έχουμε τέτοιο μουσείο στην Ελλάδα;
Tim	Η Ελλάδα έχει τόσα **h** _____ που μολονότι είχαμε διαβάσει και είχαμε κάνει έρευνα πριν να έρθουμε στη **i** _____ σας κιόλας την πρώτη μέρα εδώ καταλάβαμε ότι η διαμονή μας θα είναι **j** _____ από συναρπαστική. Και δεν πέσαμε έξω!
Δημήτρης	**k** _____ που τ' ακούω. Μακάρι να είχα κι εγώ την ίδια **l** _____ όταν πήγα …

μυστικά	πανηγύρι	εντύπωση	γνωστοί
υποσχεθεί	ενδιαφέρον	παραπάνω	παραδοσιακή
συναρπαστικό	τρομερό	χώρα	χαίρομαι

10 12.12 Listen to the conversation a couple of times without looking at the text. Try to pick up some highlights about the island from Kostas' explanations. Rhodes is one of the most popular destinations for tourists in Greece. It has a very cosmopolitan summer life and many things to offer young adults. Listen to this dialogue.

_____

_____

_____

11 Now read the conversation and match the Greek words with their English counterparts.

Κώστας	Στη Ρόδο πήγατε;
Tim	Όχι ακόμα. Αλλά έχουμε ακούσει τόσα πολλά γι' αυτήν. Είναι όλα πράγματι αλήθεια;
Κώστας	Ναι είναι. Έχει τόσα πολλά να προσφέρει. Έχει την παλιά πόλη, το Μαντράκι, το Ενυδρείο, το Μουσείο, αρχαιολογικούς χώρους, την Ακρόπολη στη Λίνδο …
Tim	Κι από βραδινή ζωή;
Κώστας	Εκεί δεν έχει να ζηλέψει τίποτα από τη βραδινή ζωή οποιασδήποτε άλλης κοσμοπολίτικης πόλης. Δισκοθήκες, νάιτ κλαμπ, μπουάτ, μπυραρίες, μπαρ, εστιατόρια … Παντού κόσμος, παντού κοσμοσυρροή.
Tim	Και πώς πάει κανείς εκεί;
Κώστας	Εύκολα. Με το αεροπλάνο σε 45 λεπτά και με το πλοίο σε 14 ώρες. Αλλά το βιοτικό επίπεδο είναι από τα πιο ακριβά σ' όλη την Ελλάδα. Είναι ακριβά να πας εκεί, να μείνεις εκεί, να διασκεδάσεις εκεί. Αλλά είναι ωραία.
Tim	Μήπως τελικά ένας χρόνος να μην είναι αρκετός στην Ελλάδα! Πρέπει μάλλον να ζητήσουμε άλλον ένα χρόνο παράταση από τις δουλειές μας για να τη μάθουμε καλύτερα …
Κώστας	Αυτό νομίζω κι εγώ. Καλή τύχη!

a	η αλήθεια	**1**	nightclub
b	παλιά πόλη	**2**	pub
c	το ενυδρείο	**3**	extension
d	ο χώρος	**4**	bar
e	η δισκοθήκη	**5**	standard of living
f	το νάιτ κλαμπ	**6**	truth
g	η μπουάτ	**7**	work, job, employment
h	η μπυραρία	**8**	old town, old quarters
i	το μπαρ	**9**	site, space, area
j	το βιοτικό επίπεδο	**10**	disco/discotheque
k	η δουλειά	**11**	nightclub with Greek music
l	η παράταση	**12**	aquarium

12 Now read the conversation once again and say which statements are true and which are false.

		True	False
a	Η Ρόδος μπορεί να προσφέρει πολλά στον τουρίστα.	_____	_____
b	Δεν είναι όμως πολύ κοσμοπολίτικη πόλη.	_____	_____
c	Υπάρχει και ακρόπολη στο χωριό της Λίνδου.	_____	_____
d	Η βραδινή ζωή της δεν είναι όπως άλλες κοσμοπολίτικες πόλεις.	_____	_____
e	Έχει πολλές δισκοθήκες, νάιτ κλαμπ και μπουάτ.	_____	_____
f	Έχει πολύ κόσμο αλλά όχι και κοσμοσυρροή.	_____	_____
g	Το πλοίο κάνει 14 ώρες.	_____	_____
h	Το βιοτικό επίπεδο είναι χαμηλό.	_____	_____
i	Ο Tim χρειάζεται ένα χρόνο παράταση για να δει κι άλλο την Ελλάδα.	_____	_____
j	Ο Κώστας του δίνει την ευχή 'Καλή τύχη'.	_____	_____

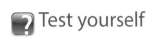 Test yourself

1 Can you remember the Greek for the following ten important words from this unit?

   a this year _____

   b teacher/s _____

   c friend/s _____

   d island/s _____

   e life _____

   f music _____

   g sailing boat/s _____

   h of course _____

   i fish _____

   j museum/s _____

2 Can you remember the following ten important phrases from this unit?

   a Where did you go for Easter last year? _____

   b We had heard it before. _____

   c We ate a lot of fish. _____

   d Did you have your name day? _____

   e Many happy returns! _____

   f May you live long! _____

   g May your wish come true! _____

   h He has already spoken to some friends. _____

   i You have not told us yet… _____

   j It was very interesting. _____

3 The following phrases are given in the present tense. Change them into the past tense.

   a Πού πάτε; _____

   b Είναι συναρπαστικό; _____

   c Έχω την εντύπωση. _____

   d Το βάζο πέφτει. _____

   e Πώς πας; _____

SELF CHECK

I CAN...
. . . understand some Easter customs and traditions.
. . . understand and express wishes or congratulations.
. . . express opinions and state preferences.
. . . describe past events.
. . . use time registers to highlight time segments.
. . . use Greek adverbs when necessary.
. . . use the past perfect tense with several verbs.
. . . be more aware of Greek cultural heritage.

Revision test 3

In this unit you will revise:

▶ *making arrangements and meeting someone.*
▶ *initiating and carrying out business talks.*
▶ *talking to a doctor and asking for remedies.*
▶ *talking about the weather.*
▶ *using appropriate language at a social function.*
▶ *expressing opinions and stating preferences.*
▶ *different professions and sports.*
▶ *naming months and seasons.*

TIP

Check your progress so far. Once you have completed the following exercises compare your answers with the correct ones, which can be found in the **Answer Key**. Identify any areas that still need some work and go over them again so that you're completely satisfied.

1 **Respond to the following situations in Greek.**

  a What are the expressions used when congratulating someone for his wife/her husband/their child's name day? _____

  b What are the expressions used on Mondays/first day of the month/first day of the year? If someone else uses those expressions what will your answer be? _____

  c When do you use Χρόνια πολλά! ? If you are addressed with this expression, what will your reply be? _____

  d Ask about the weather: *What's the weather like in Greece today?* or *What was the weather like in Greece yesterday?* or *What will the weather be like in Greece tomorrow?* _____

  e You are asked: Ρίχνει βροχές ή χαλάζι στην Αθήνα; Give an appropriate answer. _____

  f You are asked Πώς είναι συνήθως ο καιρός στην Μεγάλη Βρετανία; Give an appropriate answer. _____

  g A friend of yours does not look well. Ask *Are you sick? You don't look very well. Shall I call a doctor?* _____

  h *Long time no see! Where have you been? I've missed you George!* If George is a good but 'long-lost' friend, how will you say these phrases? _____

  i You want to find out someone's profession. Ask *What do you do for a living?* then tell him/her that you know someone who is a banker, painter, bookkeeper, nurse, builder or teacher. _____

  j Ask someone what kind of sports he or she likes. Then tell him or her that you know someone who likes swimming, cycling, horse riding, volleyball, running and soccer.

    _____

2 Someone has handed you the two business cards shown. You look at them and you want to ask some questions. How would you say the following in Greek?

   a Oh, you are a manager! _____

   b What's the name of your hotel in Greek? _____

   c Rhodes is an island, isn't it? _____

   d Do you have both rooms and apartments to let? _____

   e Where's Fiscardo? _____

   f Please give me your telephone number. _____

Nicholas Statiras
F&B Manager

ESPEROS PALACE HOTEL

faliraki p.o. box 202 – 85100 rhodes (0241) 85751-4

telex: 292601 espp GR-fax: (0241) 85744

DENDRINOS SINCE 1972

Food and Lodging

FISCARDO 28084

KEFALONIA GREECE

TEL 0674 91205

---

3 The following advertisement offers some good deals to major European cities. Look at it and answer the following questions:

   a Πόσο ακριβή είναι η πτήση για Λονδίνο; _____

   b Η πτήση για το Δουβλίνο είναι φτηνότερη ή ακριβότερη από την πτήση για το Εδινβούργο; _____

   c Ποια είναι η ακριβότερη πτήση στην Ευρώπη; _____

   d Τα εισιτήρια είναι μόνο να πας ή με επιστροφή; _____

   e Πώς είναι η Κωνσταντινούπολη στ' Αγγλικά; _____

   f Ποιες είναι οι ιταλικές πόλεις; _____

Ευρωπαϊκές εκπλήξεις σε τιμές			
TRAVEL PLAN			
• ΛΟΝΔΙΝΟ	€380	• ΑΜΣΤΕΡΝΤΑΜ	€400
• ΠΑΡΙΣΙ	€350	• ΔΟΥΒΛΙΝΟ	€500
• ΡΩΜΗ	€325	• ΜΑΔΡΙΤΗ	€350
• ΦΛΩΡΕΝΤΙΑ	€370	• ΒΑΡΚΕΛΩΝΗ	€325
• ΒΕΝΕΤΙΑ	€380	• ΕΔΙΜΒΟΥΡΓΟ	€365
• ΜΙΛΑΝΟ	€360	• ΚΩΝΣΤΑΝΤΙΝΟΥΠΟΛΗ	€200
• ΒΙΕΝΝΗ	€375	• ΒΕΡΟΛΙΝΟ	€350
Αεροπορικά εισιτήρια με επιστροφή!			

 4 12.13 **You are going to hear a special announcement from a travel agency which combines some cities in Europe from some advertisement. What the price you hear and then the amount you can save if you take this special offer instead of visiting individual cities.**

a Λονδίνο – Δουβλίνο _____

b Φλωρεντία – Βενετία _____

c Μαδρίτη – Βαρκελώνη _____

d Βιέννη – Βερολίνο _____

5 The map shows the temperatures in most major European cities. See if you can answer the following questions.

a Πώς είναι ο καιρός στο Λονδίνο;

b Πού έχει την υψηλότερη θερμοκρασία;

c Πού έχει την χαμηλότερη θερμοκρασία;

d Τι σημαίνει ΑΤΛΑΝΤΙΚΟΣ ΩΚΕΑΝΟΣ στα Αγγλικά;

e Τι σημαίνει ΜΕΣΟΓΕΙΟΣ ΘΑΛΑΣΣΑ στα Αγγλικά;

f Πώς λένε στα ελληνικά Prague, Black Sea, Lisbon, Berlin και Brussels;

g Πού έχει μόνο λιακάδα;

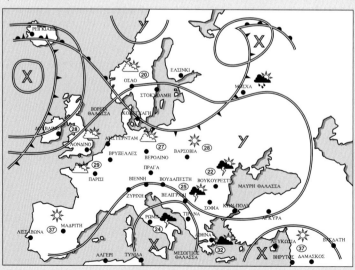

6 12.14 You are going to hear some questions regarding temperatures in some European cities. Check the map and find the name of the city and its corresponding temperature.

a _____

b _____

c _____

d _____

e _____

f _____

7 Here is a list of many emergency telephone numbers in Greece. Study the list, and answer the questions:

What are the telephone numbers for the following?

a Police _____

b Fire _____

c Port Authority _____

d Ambulance _____

e Tourist police _____

f Nowadays there is a Cyber Crime Division. Do you know it? _____

ΧΡΗΣΙΜΑ ΤΗΛΕΦΩΝΑ

ΠΡΩΤΕΣ ΑΝΑΓΚΕΣ

Άμεση Δράση Αστυνομίας.............................100
Λιμεναρχείο..108
Ασθενοφόρο...166
Πυροσβεστική...199
Τουριστική Αστυνομία.................................1571
Δίωξη Ηλεκτρονικού Εγκλήματος...........11188
Δίωξη Ναρκωτικών...109
Αντιμετώπιση Πυρκαγιών.............................191
Εφημερεύοντα Διανυχτερεύοντα
  Φαρμακεία Αθηνών.....................................107
Εφημερεύοντα Διανυχτερεύοντα
  Φαρμακεία Προαστίων................................102
Πρώτες Βοήθειες...150
Εφημερεύοντες Γιατροί
  Αθηνών-Πειραιώς..105
EXPRESS SERVICE.......................................1154
ΕΛΠΑ ΟΔΙΚΗ ΒΟΗΘΕΙΑ....................10400
HELLAS SERVICE...1057
INTERAMERICAN..1158
Δελτίο Καιρού...1448

8 Being able to decipher information about cultural events from the Greek press is handy when visiting Greece. Here are advertisements for two different cultural events. Read the information and answer the following questions.

a When do they both take place? _____

b What kind of events are they? _____

c How long (how many days) is each event? _____

d Does the first event start in the morning or in the evening? _____

e How would you translate ΑΓΓΛΙΚΟ ΦΕΣΤΙΒΑΛ ΜΠΑΧ? _____

f Do you know the name ΓΙΩΡΓΟΥ ΝΤΑΛΑΡΑ? _____

g Which one of the two events is less expensive and why? _____

i

> **Στο Μέγαρο Μουσικής Αθηνών**
>
> **Παρασκευή 25, Σάββατο 26 Αυγούστου**
>
> **ώρα 9:00 μ.μ.**
>
> **Συναυλίες**
>
> **ΓΙΩΡΓΟΥ ΝΤΑΛΑΡΑ**
>
> **Συμμετέχουν:**
>
> **Αναστασία Μουτσάτσου**
>
> **Αθηνά Μόραλη**
>
> **Οπισθοδρομικοί**
>
> **Τάκης Μπουρμάς**
>
> **Τιμή εισιτηρίου: 15€**

ii

Αύγουστος

ΚΑΛΛΙΤΕΧΝΙΚΕΣ ΕΚΔΗΛΩΣΕΙΣ

ΩΔΕΙΟ ΗΡΩΔΟΥ ΑΤΤΙΚΟΥ

Κυριακή 1

Δευτέρα 2

C.W. GLUCK: ΙΦΙΓΕΝΕΙΑ Η ΕΝ ΤΑΥΡΟΙΣ

Δ/ντής Ορχήστρας: Marc Minkowski

Σκηνοθεσία: Alain Germain

Εισιτήρια: 15€, 10€

Φοιτητικά: 5€

9 🎧 **12.15 You are going to hear some Greeks telling you their favourite month and the month of their birthday. Complete the information in the table below.**

a	Φοίβος:	
b	Ορέστης:	
c	Ηρακλής:	
d	Ελπίδα:	
e	Αγάπη:	
f	Ζωή:	

10 Write out the names in Greek of the months that have 30 days. Then write out the names of the months that have 31 days. Then write the names of the days of the week. Use the definite articles (ο, η, το) if you can remember them.

    a Months with 30 days: _____

    b Months with 31 days: _____

    c Days of the week: _____

11 Can you match the pictures of the following office items with the list of items?

    a τα βιβλία _____

    b ο κατάλογος _____

    c το τηλέφωνο _____

    d η ατζέντα _____

    e η τηλεόραση _____

    f το ράδιο-κασετόφωνο _____

    g το επιστολόχαρτο _____

    h το κομπιούτερ _____

    i Nowadays, most of us have *mobile phones*, *iPods*, *iPads*, or *lap tops* and send *SMS* (texts) or *emails*. We usually *chat* or *surf the Internet*. Can you find the words in italics in Greek? Do you notice anything?

    _____

    _____

12 🎧 **12.16 Listen to the conversation and find the missing words. If you want, you can find the missing words first and then listen and check your answers. At the end, listen again and practise speaking Tim's part.**

Κώστας	Στη Ρόδο πήγατε;
Tim	Όχι ακόμα. Αλλά έχουμε **a** _____ τόσα πολλά γι'αυτήν. Είναι όλα πράγματι **b** _____;
Κώστας	Ναι, είναι. Έχει τόσα πολλά να **c** _____ Έχει την παλιά πόλη, το Μαντράκι, το Ενυδρείο, το Μουσείο, αρχαιολογικούς χώρους, την Ακρόπολη στη Λίνδο . . .
Tim	Κι από βραδινή **d** _____;
Κώστας	Εκεί δεν έχει να ζηλέψει τίποτα από την βραδινή **d** _____ οποιασδήποτε άλλης **e** _____ πόλης. **f** _____, νάιτ κλαμπ, μπουάτ, μπυραρίες, μπαρ, εστιατόρια . . . Παντού **g** _____, παντού κοσμοσυρροή.
Tim	Και πώς πάει κανείς εκεί;
Κώστας	**h** _____. Με το αεροπλάνο σε 45 λεπτά και με το **i** _____ σε 14 ώρες. Αλλά το **j** _____ επίπεδο είναι από τα πιο ακριβά σ' όλη την Ελλάδα. Είναι ακριβά να πας εκεί, να μείνεις εκεί, να **k** _____ εκεί. Αλλά είναι ωραία.
Tim	Μήπως **l** _____ ένας χρόνος να μην είναι αρκετός στην Ελλάδα! Πρέπει **m** _____ να ζητήσουμε άλλον ένα χρόνο παράταση από τις δουλειές μας για να τη μάθουμε καλύτερα . . .
Κώστας	Αυτό νομίζω κι εγώ. Καλή **n** _____!

> ζωή εύκολα κόσμος δισκοθήκες
> τελικά ακούσει βιοτικό αλήθεια
> πλοίο μάλλον τύχη προσφέρει
> διασκεδάσεις κοσμοπολίτικης

13 12.17 **Some people speak to their doctor saying what's troubling them. Listen carefully a couple of times and then match the photo that corresponds to what each speaker says.**

a Γιατρέ μου, έχω τρομερό πονοκέφαλο! _____

b Γιατρέ, δεν κοιμάμαι καλά. Με πονάει η κοιλιά μου! _____

c Γιατρέ, με πονάει ένα δόντι. Μπορείτε να το κοιτάξετε; _____

d Δεν έχω καθόλου όρεξη γιατρέ. Γιατί; _____

14 12.18 **Look at the remaining three pictures that were not mentioned in the previous exercise. Imagine that a friend of yours has these symptoms but he cannot speak a word of Greek! Can you help him?**

a _____

b _____

c _____

Congratulations on choosing *Complete Greek* in your efforts to learn this beautiful and rich language. Aristarhos Matsukas, the author of this book, will be more than happy to hear your comments. Your comments and/or suggestions will help us to improve future editions.

You can contact the author directly at the following e-mail address: aja14@web.de or by writing c/o Teach Yourself, John Murray Press, Carmelite House, 50 Victoria Embankment, London, EC4Y 0DZ.

Even though you have reached the end of the book, you should not close it, but instead continue practising to improve your Greek. Set yourself goals, and speak the language whenever you are in the company of Greeks, so that you keep on learning. *Good luck!* **Καλή τύχη!**

Answer key

INTRODUCTION

1 Γ, Δ, Θ, Λ, Ξ, Π, Σ, Φ, Ψ, Ω. **2** β, γ, δ, θ, κ, λ, μ, ξ, σ, φ, ψ, ω. **3 a** (v), **b** (i), **c** (r), **d** (h). **4 a** α, ε, η, ι, κ, ν, ο, π, σ/ς, τ, υ, ω; **b** β, δ, ζ, θ, λ; **c** γ, μ, ρ, φ, χ, ψ. **5 a** γ, **b** δ, **c** η, **d** κ, **e** λ, **f** μ, **g** ν, **h** ξ, **i** σ/ς, **j** τ **k** υ, **l** ω. **6 a** 3, **b** 4, **c** 1, **d** 2.
7 μπάσκετ (básket) – τέννις (ténis); κιθάρα (kithára) – πιάνο (piáno); Αγγλία (anglía) – Ελλάδα (eláTHa); τρένο (tréno) – αεροπλάνο (aeropláno). **8 a** 5, **b** 4, **c** 1, **d** 6, **e** 3, **f** 2. **9** h (ipiros) – ΗΠΕΙΡΟΣ was not on the recording.

UNIT 1

Greetings and farewells

1 The prefix καλο- or καλη- means good. **2** The word καλησπέρα is a greeting and means good afternoon or good evening. The expression καλό απόγευμα is a farewell and it means Have a nice afternoon.

Vocabulary builder

1 afternoon, night, Good day, evening. **2 a** Γεια σου, Πέτρο. **b** Χαίρετε, κυρία Αντωνίου. **c** Καληνύχτα, Τούλα. **d** Καλό απόγευμα, Σούλα. **4 a** 3, **b** 5, **c** 6, **d** 2, **e** 4, **f** 1.

Conversation 1

1 Mary speaks to a French person. **2 a** Mr Depardieu is from France. **b** He's from Paris. **c** Mary is from England. **d** She is from London.

Language discovery 1

1 a Είμαι από τη Γαλλία. **b** Είμαι από το Παρίσι. **c** Είμαι από την Αγγλία. **d** Είμαι από το Λονδίνο. **2 a** η, **b** το, **c** η, **d** το, **e** τη, **f** το, **g** την, **h** το. **3 a** ποια, **b** πώς, **c** πού.

Conversation 2

1 They talk about languages. **2 a** Πώς σας λένε; **b** Τι γλώσσες μιλάτε;.

Language discovery 2

1 a Πώς σας λένε; **b** Τι γλώσσες μιλάτε; **c** Μόνο Ιταλικά; **2** Full stop: ., Exclamation mark: !, Question mark: ; **3** One-syllable words without an accent: τι, σας, και, ποιο, με, το, την, One-syllable words with an accent: πώς, πού.

Conversation 3

1 They talk about their names, the cities they come from, and the languages they speak. **2 a** Antonio is from Milan. **b** He can't speak English. **c** Μαίρη/Μαρία

Language discovery 3

1a Ελληνικά, **b** Ιταλικά, **c** Αγγλικά, **2 a** Από ποιο μέρος; **b** Από ποια πόλη; **3 a** τώρα, **b** αλλά, **c** ωραία, **d** ναι, **e** όχι, **f** ή, **g** εγώ, **h** δυστυχώς, **i** μόνο, **j** και, **4** 'i' as in 'pin': είσαι, πόλη, ξέρεις, δυστυχώς, Αθήνα, Λονδίνο, Αγγλικά, Μαίρη, Αντόνιο, 'e' as in '*bed*': είμαι, μένω, εγώ, ωραία, σε. **5** Different letters for the sound 'i' as in 'pin' are: ει, η, υ, ι, Different letters for the sound 'e' as in 'bed' are: ε, αι.

The definite article

1 a ο, **b** η, **c** το, **2 a** ο, **b** η, **c** το, **3 a** ο, **b** η, **c** η, **d** το, **e** η **4 a** την, **b** το, **c** τη, **5 a** στην, **b** στο, **c** στη

Practice

1 a Πώς σας λένε; **b** Γεια σου! Τι κάνεις; **c** Γεια σας! Τι κάνετε; **d** Ξέρετε αγγλικά; **2 a** 3, **b** 4, **c** 2, **d** 1. **3** c, a, d, b. **4 a** Με λένε Ρόμπερτ, **b** Είμαι από την Αγγλία, **c** Από το Λονδίνο, **d** Αγγλικά (γαλλικά, ιταλικά, ελληνικά). **5 a** 6, **b** 7, **c** 1, **d** 2, **e** 3, **f** 4, **g** 7. **6 a** Ρόμπερτ, **b** Ελένη, **c** Ελληνίδα, **d** Αγγλία, **e** Δεν, **f** Είσαι. **7 a**: αλλά, να, από, σας. **e:** λένε, ναι, ξέρω, με. **8 a** είσαι, **b** είμαι, **c** πόλη, **d** αλλά, **e** Ξέρεις, **f** μόνο, **g** Εσένα, **h** Ωραία. **9** There are seven greetings and/or farewells: Γεια σου, καλημέρα, καλησπέρα, γεια σας, καλό απόγευμα, καληνύχτα, τα λέμε.

Test yourself

1 a γεια σας (yásas), **b** γεια (ya), **c** καλά (kalá), **d** από (apó), **e** εδώ (eTHó), **f** πού (pu), **g** ναι (ne), **h** όχι (óchi), **i** με (me), **j** κοντά (kondá)). **2 a** Πώς σε λένε; (pos se léne?), **b** Από πού είσαι; (apó puíse?), **c** Από ποια πόλη; (apó pya póli?), **d** Από το Λονδίνο, Αγγλία (apó to lonTHíno anglía), **e** Με λένε … (me léne), **f** Μιλάς Αγγλικά; (milás angliká)?, **g** Μένω στο/στην … (méno sto/stin), **h** Μένω στο/στην … (méno sto/stin), **i** Είναι κοντά. (íne kondá). **j** Δεν ξέρω. (THen kséro) **3 a** Πώς σας λένε; (pos sas léne)?, **b** Από πού είστε; (apópu íste)?, **c** Πού μένετε; (pu ménete)?, **d** Μιλάτε Αγγλικά; (miláte anglíka)?, **e** Γεια σας. (yásas).

UNIT 2

Names and titles in Greek

1 The prefix Θεο- means God and the prefix Αριστ- means perfect.

Vocabulary builder

2 a 3, **b** 4, **c** 1, **d** 5, **e** 2

Conversation 1

1 The man says: Τι κάνεις; The woman says: Τι κάνετε; **2 a** His first name is Γιώργος; **b** The man is a little bit tired. **c** Εντάξει.

Language discovery 1

1a Δεν ξέρω! **b** Δεν ξέρω καλά Ελληνικά. **c** Όχι, δεν είναι λάθος. Yes! This word always comes before the verb in Greek. **2 a** μου μιλάς (English: you speak to me), **b** με φωνάζουν (English: they call me / everybody calls me). **3** Formal language: **a** Τι κάνετε; **b** Ευχαριστώ, εσείς; Informal language: **c** … αλλά γιατί μου μιλάς στον πληθυντικό; **d** Εντάξει, Γιώργο. **4 /i/** as in pin: κύριε, πληθυντικό, συνάδελφοι, **/u/** as in put: Παπαδόπουλε, κουρασμένος, μου, **/f/** as in foot: Ευχαριστώ

Conversation 2

1 The man says: εσύ πώς είσαι σήμερα; The woman says: Τι κάνετε; **2 a** She has five classes today. **b** Mr Antoniou makes her class schedule. **c** He has forgotten that he is the one who makes her class schedule.

Language discovery 2

1 a you (singular/informal): εσύ, **b** you (formal/plural): εσείς. **2 a** Who? Ποιος; **b** What? Τι; **c** How? Πώς; **d** Why? Γιατί; **3** μένει, μένετε, μένουν / κάνεις, κάνουμε, κάνετε / φωνάζω, φωνάζουμε, φωνάζετε / έχω, έχει, έχετε.

Conversation 3

1 a Δεν το πιστεύω! **b** Δε θυμάμαι. **2 a** Yes, she does. **b** Yes, they are both fine. **c** He has been three or four days in Athens. He can't remember!

Language discovery 3

1 a νομίζω, **b** πιστεύω, **c** ξαναβλέπω. **2** χαίρομαι, είμαι, θυμάμαι. **3 a** εγώ, **b** -ω, **c** –μαι. **4** ξαναχαίρομαι, ξαναπιστεύω, ξαναβλέπω, ξανασκέφτομαι, ξαναθυμάμαι. **5** Three: τρία, τρεις, Four: τέσσερα, τέσσερις

Practice

1 a Είμαι πολύ καλά. **b** εσύ; – εσείς; **c** Τι κάνετε; **d** Είμαι λίγο κουρασμένος/κουρασμένη. **e** Α! το ξέχασα! **f** Έχω (είμαι) δύο/τρεις/τέσσερις πέντε μέρες στην Αθήνα. **2 a** 4, **b** 3, **c** 1, **d** 2. **3** c, a, b, d, e. **4 a** Με λένε William Jones, αλλά όλοι με φωνάζουν Bill. **b** Από την Αγγλία, αλλά γιατί μου μιλάς στον πληθυντικό; **c** Από το Λίβερπουλ, εσύ; **d** Νομίζω δύο ή τρεις μέρες μόνο. **5 a** 7, **b** 5, **c** 8, **d** 1, **e** 9, **f** 2, **g** 6, **h** 3, **i** 4. **6** Horizontal ΕΣΥ, ΜΗ, ΜΕ, ΠΑΣ, ΚΥΡΙΕ; Vertical ΟΜΩΣ, ΠΕΝΤΕ; Diagonal ΕΧΩ, ΝΑΙ, ΣΕ. **7** ι: κύριε, είναι, τρεις, στην. ο: κοντά, μόνο, πώς, όμως. **8 a** χαίρομαι, **b** είσαι, **c** πιστεύω, **d** είμαι, **e** πώς, **f** πόσες, **g** νομίζω, **h** θυμάμαι. **9** The cartoon means: Does anyone speak English?

Test yourself

1 a Ευχαριστώ (efharistó), **b** Ελληνικά (eliniká), **c** κουρασμένος (kurazménos), **d** εντάξει (endáksi), **e** σήμερα (símera), **f** αλλά (alá), **g** συγγνώμη (sighnómi), **h** βέβαια (vévea), **i** ημέρα (imera), **j** μάθημα (mathima). **2 a** Τι κάνεις; (ti kánis?), **b** Είμαι κουρασμένος (íme kurazménos), **c** Τι κάνετε; (ti kánete?), **d** Το ξέχασα (to kséhasa), **e** Είναι λάθος; (íne láthos), **f** Δεν το πιστεύω! (THen to pistévo), **g** Είμαι πολύ καλά (íme polí kalá), **h** Δε θυμάμαι (THe thimáme), **i** Χαίρομαι που σε ξαναβλέπω! (herome pou se ksanavlepo!), **j** Πόσες μέρες είσαι; (poses meres ise?). **3 a** Τι κάνεις; (ti kánis)?, **b** Πώς είσαι; (pos íse)?, **c** Γεια σου (yásu), **d** Είσαι καλά; (íse kalá)? **e** Εδώ μένεις; (eTHó ménis)?

UNIT 3

Greek taverns, Greek coffees, and Greek drinks

1 The Greek word for pie is πιτάκια.

Vocabulary builder

2 ΖΕΣΤΑ ΡΟΦΗΜΑΤΑ hot drinks, Ελληνικός καφές Greek coffee, Φραπές frappe (iced coffee), Τσάι tea, Ζεστή σοκολάτα / Κακάο hot chocolate / cocoa, Εσπρέσσο espresso, ΑΝΑΨΥΚΤΙΚΑ Refreshments, Κόκα κόλα coke, Πορτοκαλάδα (μπλε/κόκκινη) fanta / orange drink (blue – without fizz and red – with fizz), Λεμονάδα lemonade, Χυμοί (ανανάς, λεμόνι, πορτοκάλι), juices (pineapple, lemon, orange), Νερό (μικρό) water (small), ΠΟΤΑ alcoholic beverages, Μπίρα beer, Ποτήρι κρασί wine (glass), Μπουκάλι κρασί wine (bottle), Μπουκάλι ρετσίνα retsina (bottle), Ποτήρι ούζο ouzo (glass), ΜΕΖΕΔΕΣ appetizers, Τζατζίκι yoghurt, cucumber, garlic dip, Κεφτέδες meatballs, Τηγανητές πατάτες French fries, Χωριάτικη σαλάτα mixed salad, Σπανακοπιτάκια small spinach-cheese pies, **3 a** 4, **b** 6, **c** 5, **d** 2, **e** 1, **f** 3, **4 a** φραπές 3,20, **b** χυμοί 4,10, **c** νερό μικρό 1,00, **d** μπουκάλι κρασί 12,00, **e** κεφτέδες 8,20, **f** σπανακόπιτα 9,10.

Conversation 1

1 They order an appetizer's platter and two ouzos. **2 a** It is a tavern with a selection of appetizer platters to accompany ouzo or wine most of the times. **b** He says: Είναι κοντά στο πάρκο Παναθήναια, **c** The name of the μεζεδοπωλείο is Αλεξάνδρας.

Language discovery 1

1 a Είναι μία ταβέρνα με πολλούς μεζέδες. **b** Έλα να πιούμε ένα ουζάκι. **c** Δύο ουζάκια και μία ποικιλία. **d** Ένα πολύ όμορφο μεζεδοπωλείο. **2 a** καφές – καφέδες, **b** μεζές – μεζέδες, **c** ταβέρνα – ταβέρνες, **d** ποικιλία – ποικιλίες, **e** πάρκο – πάρκα, **f** ούζο – ούζα, **3 a** a little: λίγο, **b** much: πολύ, **c** many: πολλούς

Conversation 2

1 He wants to find out if they drink ouzo in England. **2 a** They drink ouzo either straight, on the rocks, or with water. **b** Yes. They drink ouzo with lemonade. **c** Yes, he's fed up.

Language discovery 2

1 a Μου αρέσει, **b** Της αρέσει, **2 a** με πάγο, **b** με νερό, **c** στην Ελλάδα, **3** χωρίς **4 a** απαίσιο νερό, **b** ούζο σκέτο, **c** λίγο ρακί, **d** θαυμάσιο κρασί, **e** μεγάλο μπουκάλι, **f** μικρό ποτήρι, **g** άσπρο κρασί, **h** κόκκινο κρασί.

Conversation 3

1 Yes. They order too many things and at the same time. **2 a** They order two Continental breakfasts. **b** Yes, they want ham. **c** He would like to order butter and some marmalade.

Language discovery 3

1 a Μας φέρνετε …; **b** Φέρτε μας … **2 a** now: τώρα, **b** right away: αμέσως, **c** in a little while: σε λίγο.

Practice

1 a Ένα ούζο (ουζάκι) και μία ποικιλία. **b** Θαυμάσιο! – Απαίσιο! **c** Μου αρέσει πολύ – Δε μου αρέσει. **d** σκέτο – με πάγο. **e** Τον κατάλογο, παρακαλώ! **f** Ένα τσάι με γάλα, παρακαλώ. **2 a** 3, **b** 1, **c** 4, **d** 2. **3** e, b, d, c, a, f. **4 a** Μας φέρνετε τον κατάλογο, παρακαλώ; **b** Ναι, ένα φραπέ και ένα νες (καφέ). **c** Τίποτα άλλο για την ώρα. Ευχαριστώ. **d** (Μας φέρνετε) το λογαριασμό, παρακαλώ; **5 a** ΚΑΦΕ, **b** ΜΑΡΜΕΛΑΔΑ, **c** ΣΚΕΤΟ, **d** ΝΕΣ, **e** ΠΩΣ, **f** ΣΙΝΕΜΑ. **6 a** 7, **b** 6, **c** 8, **d** 9, **e** 2, **f** 4, **g** 10, **h** 1, **i** 5, **j** 3. **7 a** έτοιμοι, **b** φέρνετε, **c** βέβαια, **d** πρωινά, **e** ομελέτες, **f** χυμούς, **g** με, **h** ή, **i** Φέρτε, **j** ψωμί.

Test yourself

1 a νερό (neró), **b** επίσης (epísis), **c** ψωμί (psomí), **d** γάλα (ghála), **e** συνήθως (siníthos), **f** κατάλογος (katáloghos), **g** πρωινό (proinó), **h** θαυμάσιο (thavmásio), **i** απαίσιο (apésio), **j** όμορφο (ómorfo) **2 a** Ορίστε (oríste), **b** Βάλε μου λίγο (vále mu lígho), **c** Αυτό είναι (aftó íne), **d** Φτάνει (ftáni), **e** Δεν θέλω (THe thélo), **f** Πίνετε ούζο; (pínete úzo)? **g** Τι είναι 'μεζέδες'; (ti ine mezéTHes)?, **h** Δεν καταλαβαίνω (THen katalavéno), **i** Μου αρέσει πολύ (mu arési polí), **j** Μπορείτε παρακαλώ να μας φέρετε … ; (mporeite parakalo na mas ferete …?). **3 a** μεζές / μεζέδες, **b** ταβέρνα / ταβέρνες, **c** ούζο / ούζα, **d** καφές / καφέδες, **e** πορτοκαλάδα / πορτοκαλάδες, **f** πρωινό / πρωινά, **g** φραπές / φραπέδες, **h** μπίρα / μπίρες, **i** νερό / νερά.

UNIT 4

Greek cuisine

1 Ελλάδα means Greece.

Vocabulary builder

1 ΣΑΛΑΤΕΣ salads, Χωριάτικη σαλάτα mixed salad, Αγγουροντομάτα cucumber-tomato salad, Πατατοσαλάτα potato salad, ΣΠΕΣΙΑΛ ΠΙΑΤΑ special dishes, Χταπόδι με δαμάσκηνα octopus with plums, Λαγός στιφάδο rabbit with small onions, Αρνάκι με ρύζι baby lamb with rice, ΛΑΔΕΡΑ ready made dishes cooked in oil, Ντομάτες γεμιστές stuffed tomatoes, Σεφταλιά special dish from Cyprus, Γίγαντες πλακί Lima beans, ΦΡΟΥΤΑ Fruit, Φρουτοσαλάτα fruit salad, Δαμάσκηνα plums, Καρπούζι watermelon.

2 a 6, **b** 4, **c** 5, **d** 1, **e** 3, **f** 2, **3** Man: Εγώ θέλω ένα λουκάνικο χωριάτικο, μία ρώσικη σαλάτα και γαρίδες σαγανάκι. Ευχαριστώ. Woman: Εγώ θα πάρω ένα σαγανάκι, μία φέτα κι ένα μπιφτέκι. Σας ευχαριστώ. **4** Man: λουκάνικο χωριάτικο 7,50, μία ρώσικη σαλάτα 3,50 και γαρίδες σαγανάκι 8,00. Total: 19,00. Woman: ένα σαγανάκι 5,00, μία φέτα 4,00 κι ένα μπιφτέκι 8,00, Total: 17,00. **5 a** 4, **b** 6, **c** 2, **d** 5, **e** 3, **f** 1.

Conversation 1

1 Yes. He wanted moussaka but they do not have it. **2 a** No. It's not on the menu. **b** They want a seasonal salad. **c** They are going to have ouzo and water.

Language discovery 1

1 a Fine! Ωραία, **b** OK! Εντάξει, **c** Of course! Μάλιστα, **d** It goes without saying! Βέβαια! Βέβαια! **2 a** Oh! Just come to think of it…. Α!, **b** I'd rather … (Perhaps …) Μάλλον, **c** Just a moment! Μισό λεπτό, **d** Come on now! Έλα τώρα. **3 a** ταραμοσαλάτα (ταραμάς + σαλάτα), **b** μελιτζανοσαλάτα (μελιτζάνα + σαλάτα), **c** ουζομεζέδες (ούζο +μεζέδες), **4 a** ντολμάς (ντολμαδάκι/-ια), **b** σουτζούκι (σουτζουκάκι/-ια), **c** καράφα (καραφάκι/-ια). This ending denotes that something is less or smaller but sometimes it is used as a term of endearment, e.g. καφεδάκι (καφές) or νεράκι (νερό) .

Conversation 2

1 They are going to have Amstel. True, the word σας can be omitted. **2 a** ποτήρι stands for glass and μπουκάλι for bottle. **b** They are going to have draught beer. **c** Καλή σας όρεξη!

Language discovery 2

1 a Bon appétit! Καλή σας όρεξη! **b** Hello! Γεια σας! True, the word σας can be omitted. **2 a** How much is it? Πόσο κάνει; **b** How much are they? Πόσο κάνουν;

Conversation 3

1 Tim cannot follow the question: Θέλετε απ 'όλα μέσα στην πίτα; **2 a** It usually has tomatoes, onions and tzatziki. **b** καλαμάκι is chunks of meat on a wooden stick and γύρο is slices of meat. **c** The expression *everything on it* was found in the following question: Θέλετε απ 'όλα μέσα στην πίτα;

Language discovery 3

1 a I can't understand! Δεν καταλαβαίνω! **b** What did you say? Τι είπατε; **c** What? Τι; **2 a** 3, **b** 1, **c** 2

Practice

1 a Καλή όρεξη! **b** Μήπως έχετε μελιτζανοσαλάτα; ποικιλία; μικρή ποικιλία για το ούζο; **c** Τον κατάλογο, παρακαλώ – το λογαριασμό, παρακαλώ; **d** Θα πιείτε κάτι; **e** Ένα μικρό μπουκάλι ούζο Μυτιλήνης; **f** Έλα τώρα! **g** Πόσο κάνουν; **2 a** 4, **b** 3, **c** 1, **d** 2, **3** e, f, c, d, b, a. **4 a** Τον κατάλογο, παρακαλώ. **b** Ναι. (Μήπως) έχετε πατατοσαλάτα; **c** Εντάξει! Ένα σπανακόρυζο, ένα μουσακά και μία σαλάτα εποχής. **d** Ένα μικρό μπουκάλι ούζο. Τι ούζο έχετε; **e** Ένα μικρό μπουκάλι Μυτιλήνης. **f** Τίποτα άλλο για την ώρα. **5 a** 3, **b** 4, **c** 5, **d** 1, **e** 2, **f** 7, **g** 10, **h** 6, **i** 8, **j** 9. **6 a** ΕΛΙΕΣ, **b** ΦΕΤΑ, **c** ΝΤΟΜΑΤΕΣ, **d** ΚΡΕΜΜΥΔΙΑ, **e** ΠΙΠΕΡΙΕΣ, **f** ΑΓΓΟΥΡΙΑ, **g** ΞΥΔΙ, **h** ΛΑΔΙ. **7 a** είπατε, **b** θέλετε, **c** μέσα, **d** καταλαβαίνω, **e** ντομάτα, **f** και. **8 a** ✓, **b** Χ, **c** Χ, **d** ✓, **e** ✓, **f** Χ.

Test yourself

1a κατάλογος, **b** μπουκάλι, **c** ποτήρι, **d** τηγανιτές πατάτες, **e** λογαριασμός, **f** ντομάτα, **g** κοτόπουλο, **h** δέκα, **i** είκοσι, **j** τριάντα, **2 a** Καλή όρεξη, **b** Είναι όλα στα Ελληνικά! **c** Είναι όλα στα Αγγλικά! **d** Θα παραγγείλω εγώ για σένα! **e** Εγώ θέλω γεμιστές πιπεριές. **f** Ένα μπουκάλι νερό. **g** Θέλεις ρετσίνα; **h** Τον λογαριασμό παρακαλώ. **i** Πόσο κάνουν; **j** Πόσο κάνει; **3 a** Ναι, καλή ιδέα! **b** Θέλω ρετσίνα. **c** Τίποτα! **d** Ναι, απ' όλα σας παρακαλώ. **e** Ναι, ένα μπουκάλι άσπρο κρασί.

REVISION TEST 1

1 a Είναι υπέροχος! Είναι απαίσιος! **b** Μου δίνετε τον κατάλογο, παρακαλώ. Φέρτε μου το λογαριασμό, παρακαλώ. **c** Φέρτε μου (θα ήθελα/θέλω) ένα μέτριο, γλυκό, σκέτο (Ελληνικό) καφέ. **d** Ένα τσάι με γάλα. Ένα τσάι με λεμόνι, παρακαλώ. **e** The invitation was *Come and have a glass of ouzo (with me)*. You could probably answer Ωραία, πάμε για ένα ουζάκι or Συγγνώμη, είμαι κουρασμένος/-η. **f** The invitation is to go to a fish taverna. **g** Μου φέρνετε λίγες φρυγανιές, βούτυρο και μαρμελάδα, **h** Είμαι κουρασμένος γιατί δεν κοιμάμαι καθόλου. **i** Shall we go to the cinema? Γιατί όχι; Πάμε! Or Όχι σήμερα! **j** He or she wants to know where you live. Μένω στην Αθήνα τώρα. Μένω στο Λονδίνο τώρα, and so on. **2** f, b, c, i, e, g, a, j, d, h. **3 a** it is good for the pain είναι καλό για τον πόνο. **b** in the centre στο κέντρο. **c** I'm not very well Δεν είμαι πολύ καλά **d** How are you doing? Πώς πας; **e** Are you doing alright? Είσαι καλά; **f** You've been two days Έχεις μόνο δύο μέρες **g** I've got a pain here Έχω εδώ ένα πόνο **h** I'm glad to be here χαίρομαι που είμαι εδώ. **5 a** μπουκάλι, **b** γλώσσες, **c** χυμοί, **d** φρυγανιές, **e** κατάλογος, **f** δωμάτια, **g** μέρα, **h** ουζάκια, **i** μεζέδες, **j** ποικιλία, **k** ομελέτες, **l** ούζα, **m** μάθημα, **n** συνάδελφος. **6** ο: πόνος, καφές, κατάλογος, χυμός, μεζές; η: πόλη, μέρα, νύχτα, ταβέρνα, τυρόπιτα; το: πρόγραμμα, λάθος, ξενοδοχείο, ταξίδι, μουσείο. **7 a** Australia, **b** Ireland, **c** Holland, **d** Austria, **e** Spain, **f** Hungary, **g** Belgium, **h** Italy, **i** Portugal, **j** France, **k** Cyprus, **l** Greece, **m** Germany, **n** Luxembourg, **o** Sweden, **p** Gibraltar, **q** Morocco, **r** Thailand, **s** Denmark, **t** Great Britain, **u** Turkey, **v** Switzerland, **w** Norway, **x** Finland, **y** Estonia, **z** South Africa. **8** Μου δίνετε ένα σουβλάκι καλαμάκι παρακαλώ, δύο πίτες χωριάτικες με γύρο, μια μερίδα μπιφτέκι πολίτικο, μία μερίδα σεφταλιές Κυπριακές και μία σαλάτα χωριάτικη. Επίσης μία μικρή μπύρα και δύο μεγάλες. (This is of course not the only possible order you could place for this exercise. It serves only as an example.) **9 a** draught beer βαρελίσια μπίρα, **b** village χωριάτικη, **c** portion μερίδα, **d** price list τιμολόγιον, **e** small μικρό, **f** big μεγάλο, **g** non-alcoholic beverages αναψυκτικών, **h** since από το **10** The Athenian, open since 1932; its speciality is ouzo with appetizers. **11** 1995: Tokyo (Japan), Sao Paolo (Brazil), New York (USA), Mexico City, Bombay (India), Shanghai (China), Los Angeles (USA), Beijing (China), Calcutta (India), Seoul (South Korea); 2015: Lagos (Nigeria), Jakarta (Indonesia), Karatchi (Pakistan), Dhaka (Bangladesh). **12 a** Business English, Beginner's English, Advanced English, Arabic, Afrikaans, Beginner's French, Advanced French, Beginner's German, Advanced German, Danish; **b** Greek for foreigners, Hebrew, Japanese, Indonesian, Hindi, Irish, Icelandic, Spanish, Spanish (Central and South America), Italian, Chinese; **c** Korean, Malay, Norwegian, Dutch, Polish, Portuguese, Russian, Serbo-Croat, Swedish, Thai, Finnish. **13 a** 5, **b** 3, **c** 4, **d** 2, **e** 1 **14 a** εξυπηρετηθεί, **b** πατάτες, **c** μέγεθος, **d** ρωτήσω, **e** κρεμμύδι, **f** σαλάτα, **g** μένα, **h** έχουμε. **15 a** αγγουράκι πίκλα, κρεμμύδι, ντομάτα, πράσινη σαλάτα, και dressing **b** Θα ήθελα ένα χάμπουργκερ με τυρί και τηγανιτές πατάτες, **c** Έχετε εξυπηρετηθεί; **d** Εντάξει Sprite τότε. **e** Και μία κόκα κόλα μικρό μέγεθος. **f** Εγώ θέλω να ρωτήσω κάτι. **16 a** Εγώ I, **b** θέλω I want, **c** ρωτήσω (want to) ask, **d** κάτι something, **e** μέσα in, inside, **f** Εντάξει OK, **g** γεύμα meal, **h** σάντουϊτς sandwich. **17 a** F, **b** T, **c** F, **d** T, **e** F, **f** F. **18 a** You speak good Greek. Μιλάς ωραία Ελληνικά. **b** That's a good idea! Καλή ιδέα! **c** I'm from Buxton close to Manchester. Εγώ είμαι από το Μπούξτον κοντά στο Μάντσεστερ. **d** What are you talking about now? Τι λες τώρα; **e** Excuse me, are you Italian? Συγγνώμη, είσαι Ιταλίδα; **f** Do you want us to have a glass of ouzo? Θέλεις να πιούμε ένα ουζάκι; **19 a** The menu, please. Τον κατάλογο παρακαλώ. **b** Yes. Have you got a tzatziki and an aubergine salad? Ναι. Έχετε τζατζίκι και μελιτζανοσαλάτα; **c** Don't you have a seasonal salad? Δεν έχετε χωριάτικη σαλάτα; **d** A small bottle of ouzo. What kinds of ouzo do you have? Ένα μικρό μπουκάλι ούζο. Τι είδος ούζο (ούζα) έχετε; **e** A small bottle of Mitilinis. Ένα μικρό μπουκάλι Μυτιλήνης. **f** Nothing else for the time being. Τίποτα άλλο για την ώρα.

UNIT 5

Greek public transport

1 The ways to say *airport* are αεροδρόμιο or αερολιμένας and the ways to say *underground* are Μετρό or Υπόγειος or Ηλεκτρικός.

Vocabulary builder

2 a 3 Εγώ πάω πάντα με το λεωφορείο στη δουλειά. **b** 6 Εγώ παίρνω το τρένο για τη δουλειά. **c** 5 Εγώ πάω συχνά με τα πόδια. **d** 1 Εγω παίρνω ταξί πολλές φορές στη δουλειά. **e** 4 Σπάνια πάω με το ποδήλατο αλλά σχεδόν πάντα με το μηχανάκι. **f** 2 Κάθε μέρα πάω στη δουλειά με το αυτοκίνητο.
3 a always πάντα, **b** almost always σχεδόν πάντα, **c** often συχνά, **d** many times πολλές φορές, **e** rarely σπάνια, **f** every day κάθε μέρα.

Conversation 1

1 They want to go on foot. **2 a** About ten minutes on foot. **b** It's good exercise when you walk. **c** Acropolis is on the right.

Language discovery 1

a We mind … / We don't mind … (δε) μας πειράζει, Verb endings do not change, **b** We like to … / We don't like to … (δε) μας αρέσει, Verb endings do not change, **2 a** Olympus Zeus's Columns (Columns of Olympus Zeus) οι Στήλες του Ολυμπίου Διός, **b** …at the end of the road uphill … στο τέλος της ανηφόρας. **3 a** Stay! (main verb form: μένω) μείνετε, **b** Turn! (main verb form: στρίβω) στρίψτε.

Conversation 2

1 No. Now they are close. **2 a** They are looking for the Zeus Temple. **b** Δεν καταλαβαίνω καλά Ελληνικά. Μιλάτε λίγο πιο σιγά; **c** In front of you.

Language discovery 2

1 a Με συγχωρείτε… Συγγνώμη, **b** Παρακαλώ! Ευχαριστώ, **c** Πιο αργά … Πιο σιγά, **d** μακριά κοντά, **e** πίσω σας μπροστά σας. **2 a** …you see… βλέπετε, **b** …you know… ξέρετε, **c** …you understand… καταλαβαίνετε, **d** …you excuse… συγχωρείτε, **e** …you speak…μιλάτε. The last two verbs (συγχωρείτε and μιλάτε) have a different ending compared to the first three verbs.

Conversation 3

1 They cannot see the entrance because it is behind the trees. **2 a** No. They are very close. **b** Mary says that they are already tired. **c** The entrance is hidden behind some trees.

Language discovery 3

1 a Where is the entrance… πού είναι η είσοδος, **b** You'll see the entrance… θα δείτε την είσοδο, **c** The entrance for the … Η είσοδος για…, **d** 50 metres from the entrance πενήντα (50) μέτρα από την είσοδο. **e** The reason for its different spelling is because the accusative case is often used in Greek when the noun is after a verb or preposition. The first example is an exemption here because the verb είμαι to be is followed by nouns in nominative case. The different noun cases in Greek are often detected by the word spelling. **2 a** Over there! Εκεί πάνω! **b** At the end… Στο τέλος, **c** Is it far? Είναι μακριά; **d** You are very close. Είστε πολύ κοντά. **e** in front of μπροστά, **f** behind πίσω από, **g** 50 metres from πενήντα (50) μέτρα από.

Practice

1 a Συγγνώμη – Με συγχωρείτε. **b** Πού είναι το Ξενοδοχείο Απόλλων; **c** Είναι μακριά; – είναι κοντά; **d** right, straight, left, straight ahead, **e** trolley, bus, taxi, **f** Γεια σας και ευχαριστώ (πολύ)! **g** Δεν καταλαβαίνω Ελληνικά καλά. Μιλάτε λίγο πιο σιγά; **2 a** 2, **b** 1, **c** 3, **d** 4. **3** e, d, a, f, b, c. **4 a** Μείνετε σ' αυτόν τον δρόμο. **b** Μετά, στρίψτε αριστερά στο τρίτο στενό. **c** Μετά, συνεχίστε ίσια (ευθεία). Η πλατεία είναι στα δεξιά. **d** Παρακαλώ. **5 a** 3, **b** 9, **c** 1, **d** 6, **e** 2, **f** 8, **g** 4, **h** 10, **i** 7, **j** 5. **6 a** κάνουμε, **b** Μείνετε, **c** είναι, **d** μπορείτε, **e** αντέχω, **f** Κατέβα, **g** Μιλάτε. **7 a** είσοδος, **b** πάνω, **c** τέλος, **d** μακριά, **e** ήδη, **f** κουρασμένοι, **g** είστε, **h** μπορείτε, **i** είπατε, **j** μόνο, **k** ωραία, **l** αντέχω, **m** ζέστη. **8 a** Do you want to come? Θέλεις να έρθεις; **b** Where do you want to go? Πού θέλετε να πάτε; **c** We want to see … Θέλουμε να δούμε… **d** How are we able to (can we) go? Πώς μπορούμε να πάμε; **e** You are able to (can) see … Μπορείτε να δείτε… **f** Where can we start? Από πού να ξεκινήσουμε; **9 a** Είναι τα αξιοθέατα στην Αθήνα; Ναι, τα αξιοθέατα είναι στην Αθήνα. **b** Μπορούν να πάνε παντού με τα πόδια; Ναι. **c** Είναι καλή γυμναστική να πάνε πάνω στο Λυκαβηττό; Ναι. **d** Έχει το Ζάππειο πάρκο; Ναι. **e** Θέλουν να δουν τα αξιοθέατα με τον φίλο τους; Ναι. **f** Ο φίλος μπορεί να πάει; Ναι. **10** ο Λυκαβηττός, η πλατεία Κολωνακίου και το Ζάππειο. **11** like /i/: Λυκαβηττός, γυμναστική, ύστερα, πολύ, like /f/: αυτό, εύκολο, like /u/: πού

Test yourself

1 a συγγνώμη (sighnómi), **b** εδώ (eTHo), **c** μακριά (makria), **d** εκεί (eki), **e** αριστερά (aristera), **f** είσοδος (isoTHos), **g** δεξιά (THeksia), **h** πλατεία (platia), **i** γωνία (ghonia), **j** κέντρο (kéndro) **2 a** Με τα πόδια (me ta póTHia), **b** Στο φανάρι (sto fanari), **c** Με (το) λεωφορείο (me to leoforio), **d** Είναι καλή γυμναστική! (íne kalí ghimnastikí!), **e** Στρίψτε δεξιά/αριστερά (strípste THeksía/aristerá), **f** Δεν αντέχω την ζέστη! (THen andeho tin zesti!), **g** Με συγχωρείτε (me sinhorite), **h** Είμαστε πολύ κουρασμένοι (imaste poli kurazmeni), **i** Πού είναι το/η/ο (pu ine o/i/to), **j** Κάνει πολύ ζέστη! (káni polí zésti!) **3 a** Έλα εδώ! (éla eTHó!), **b** Μείνε εκεί! (míne ekí!), **c** Στρίψε αριστερά! (strípse aristerá!), **d** Πήγαινε ευθεία! (píghene efthía!) **e** Συνέχισε ίσια! (sinéchise ísia!)

UNIT 6

Working days

1 To make Tuesdays, Wednesdays and Thursdays singular in Greek, drop the -η and add -ες

Vocabulary builder

3 a 2, **b** 4, **c** 1, **d** 2.

Conversation 1

1 They do not know. **2 a** No. There are at least three flights per day. **b** Yes. There are at least three airlines. **c** 90 euros is for the return.

Language discovery 1

a …there is … υπάρχει, **b** …there are… υπάρχουν, **2 a** The particle να is needed to connect two verbs in a phrase. **b** The particle ας is needed when *let's* is used. **c** The particle θα is needed when the verb is in the future tense.

Conversation 2

1 They need to go to the Railway Information Office. **2 a** ΟΣΕ stands for Greek Railway Organization and it has information/ticket offices in many cities around Greece. **b** 30 euros costs the single ticket. **c** They are not going to make a reservation yet.

Language discovery 2

1 a Would you like to make a reservation? Θέλετε να κάνετε κράτηση; **b** Just a moment so I can check (lit. in order to see) Μισό λεπτό να δω. **c** You have to go to the OSE offices. Πρέπει να πάτε στα γραφεία του ΟΣΕ … **2** Verbs: πάτε, πάρτε, στρίψτε, Not verbs: στενό, δεξιά, μέτρα

Conversation 3

1 It is not clear. **2 a** The phrase το γραφείο πληροφοριών means *information desk*. **b** 5 ½–6 hours. **c** One day earlier.

Language discovery 3

1 a (We) thank you Ευχαριστούμε. **b** (I) thank you Ευχαριστώ. **c** (We) thank you a lot Ευχαριστούμε πολύ. **2** There was a big language reform in 1982. Many words have nowadays a new spelling although one can still find the older spelling in many printed materials and texts. **3** The two prepositions are: σε and με.

Practice

1 a Υπάρχει πτήση κάθε μέρα; **b** Πόση ώρα κάνει η πτήση; **c** Πόσο κάνει η πτήση; **d** Είναι μόνο πήγαινε ή μετ 'επιστροφής; **e** Μπορώ να κάνω κράτηση τώρα; **f** Μπορώ να έχω ένα πρόγραμμα; **g** Κάθε πότε; Πόσο συχνά; (both mean 'how often?'). Πόση ώρα …; is 'how long?' and 'how much?' is Πόσο κάνει …; **2 a** 3, **b** 4, **c** 1, **d** 2. **3** b, e, c, a, d, f, g. **4 a** Θα ήθελα δύο εισιτήρια για (την) Ρόδο. **b** Πόσο κάνει με το καράβι; **c** Δεύτερη θέση. **d** Και μετ' επιστροφής; **e** Πόση ώρα κάνει; **f** Τι; Δέκα οκτώ (18) ώρες! Εγώ δεν αντέχω τέσσερις (4) ώρες στο καράβι! **5 a** 7, **b** 8, **c** 6, **d** 9, **e** 2, **f** 1, **g** 3, **h** 4, **i** 5. **6** TO the, ΠΟΥ where, ΤΟΥ of the, ΤΟΝ (in) to the, ΝΤΟ do, ΠΟΥ that, ΤΟΣΟ so much, ΠΟΤΕ when, ΠΟΤΕ never, ΠΟΣΗ how long, ΤΟΣΗ so much, ΝΕΡΟ water, ΣΟΥΤ shoot, ΣΤΟΝ (in) to the, ΡΕΝΟ Renault, ΝΕΤΟ net, ΤΡΕΝΟ train, ΣΤΕΝΟ back street, ΠΕΤΡΟ Peter, ΝΤΟΥΣ shower, ΤΟΥΠΕ wig, ΠΕΣΤΟ say it, ΠΟΥΡΕΣ mashed potatoes, ΠΟΡΤΕΣ doors, ΤΟΥΡΝΕ tour. **7 a** πληροφοριών, **b** μέσα, **c** υπάρχει, **d** δω, **e** φεύγει, **f** φεύγουμε **g** ταξίδι, **h** θέσεις, **i** επιστροφή, **j** πότε, **k** πριν, **l** τίποτα. **8 a** οκτώ και τέταρτο, **b** εννέα και είκοσι πέντε, **c** επτά παρά δέκα, **d** τρεισήμιυ, **e** έξι παρά δέκα, **f** μία, **g** επτάμιση, **h** τρεις παρά είκοσι πέντε, **i** τέσσερις, **j** επτά και πενήντα δύο, **k** τέσσερις και είκοσι τρία, **l** εννέα και σαράντα εννιά, **m** επτά και δώδεκα, **n** μιάμιση, **o** μία και σαράντα τρία. **9 a** Κάνει από τις 7.00 μέχρι τις 13.16. **b** Κάνει από τις 7.02 μέχρι τις 13.46. **c** Φεύγει στις 7.00 ακριβώς. **d** Υπάρχουν 4 από την Αθήνα και 5 από τη Θεσσαλονίκη. **10 a** Keep the change. Κρατήστε τα ρέστα. **b** I always get it mixed up! Πάντα τα μπερδεύω! **c** Where are you going sir? Πού πάτε κύριε; **d** There's no traffic today. Δεν έχει κίνηση σήμερα. **e** Have a nice trip. καλό ταξείδι **f** How much do I owe? Τι οφείλω; **11 a** T, **b** F, **c** F, **d** F, **e** T

Test yourself

1 a περίπου (perípu), **b** θέση (thesi), **c** πτήση (ptisi), **d** αεροδρόμιο (aeroTHromio), **e** γραφείο (ghrafio), **f** κίνηση (kinisi), **g** πληροφορία/ες (pliroforia/es), **h** αποσκευή/ ές (aposkevi/es), **i** κτίριο (ktirio), **j** ρέστα (résta) **2 a** Έχουμε καιρό! (éhume keró!), **b** Είναι μία (η ώρα) (ine mia i ora), **c** Κρατήστε τα ρέστα! (kratiste ta resta!), **d** Είναι μιάμιση (ine miamisi), **e** Πάντα τα μπερδεύω (panda ta berTHevo), **f** Είναι δύο παρά τέταρτο (ine THio para tetarto), **g** Πού πάτε; (pu pate)? **h** Χίλια ευχαριστώ! (chilia efharisto!), **i** Τι ώρα είναι; (ti ora ine)? **j** Παρακαλώ! (parakaló!).

UNIT 7

Tourist information

1 The way to say National Tourism Organization is EOT Ελληνικός Οργανισμός Τουρισμού.

Vocabulary builder

1 d 1 κλειδί, **f** 2 δωμάτιο, **b** 3 μπάνιο, **g** 4 τρίκλινο, **a** 5 καμαριέρα, **h** 6 πρωινό, **c** 7 δίκλινο, **e** 8 σέρβις. **2 a** ο/η μάνατζερ manager, **b** το ασανσέρ lift/elevator, **c** το φουαγιέ foyer, **d** το μπαρ bar, **e** το λόμπυ lobby, **f** το μπαλκόνι balcony, **g** η σουίτα suite, **h** η τουαλέτα toilet, **i** το σέρβις δωματίου room service, **j** το τηλέφωνο telephone, **k** το μίνι-μπαρ mini-bar, **l** ο μπουφές buffet

Conversation 1

1 He saw two different rooms at the end. **2 a** He wants it for three days. **b** They get there by car. **c** The room must be better and bigger.

Language discovery 1

a bigger μεγαλύτερο, **b** better καλύτερο, **c** more expensive πιο ακριβό, **d** more quiet πιο ήσυχο The ending that the adjectives take in Greek (compared to -er in English) in these two examples is: -τέρο and the word used for *more* is πιο when making comparisons.

Conversation 2

1 The tourist would like a double room. **2 a** She would like to stay only one night. **b** She wants a wide bed (wider than normal) or twin bed. **c** She wants to stay in the room facing the street.

Language discovery 2

1 a better καλύτερο, **b** more quiet πιο ήσυχο, **c** nicer πιο ωραίο, **2 a** this morning σήμερα το πρωί, **b** this afternoon σήμερα το μεσημέρι, **c** this evening σήμερα το απόγευμα, **d** this (late) evening / tonight σήμερα το βράδυ, **3 a** Να το δω; (Can) I see it? **b** Θα το πάρω. I'll take it. **c** Ελάτε να σας πάω. Come, I'll give you a lift. **d** Ο γκρουμ θα σας βοηθήσει. The bell boy will help you. No. The pronouns are before the verb in Greek and after the verb in English.

Conversation 3

1 They have made a reservation for four days. **2 a** Can you fill out the registration card? **b** Can I have a pen? **c** They would like to get a quiet room.

Language discovery 3

1 όνομά, διεύθυνσή, δωμάτιό. The first stressed syllable is the main one. **2 a** Yes, **b** Yes, **c** Yes, **d** Yes. **e** Yes.

Conversation 4

1 Mary is confused because she cannot understand why the receptionist does not see any problem that the bathtub does not have a curtain and the water can flow everywhere. **2 a** Ναι, είμαι η Mary Johnson από το δωμάτιο 325. **b** There is no shower curtain. **c** Μην στεναχωριέστε καθόλου! Don't worry at all! Τα νερά φεύγουν σ'ένα λεπτό. Water can go away in a minute. Το μπάνιο στεγνώνει γρήγορα-γρήγορα! The bathroom will be dry very fast.

Practice

1 a Έχετε δωμάτια; **b** Θα ήθελα ένα μονόκλινο/δίκλινο. **c** Έχετε ένα μονόκλινο για τέσσερις ημέρες; **d** Θα ήθελα ένα δίκλινο με ντους/ μπάνιο, ήσυχο με θέα τη θάλασσα. **e** Πόσο κάνει/είναι (αυτό το δωμάτιο); **f** Έχω κάνει κράτηση. **g** Δε μου αρέσει το δωμάτιο. Δεν είναι ήσυχο και δεν έχει θέα. **2 a** 3, **b** 2, **c** 1, **d** 4. **3** d, b, c, e, a, f. **4 a** Γεια σας! Με λένε Joanna Wilke. Έχω κλείσει ένα δωμάτιο για δύο μέρες. **b** Ορίστε! Μπορώ να έχω ένα στυλό παρακαλώ; **c** Δε με πειράζει. Είμαι πολύ κουρασμένη και θα προτιμούσα να κοιμηθώ αμέσως. **d** Πού είναι το ασανσέρ; **5 a** 5, **b** 9, **c** 7, **d** 1, **e** 10, **f** 2, **g** 3, **h** 6, **i** 4, **j** 8. **6** Horizontal: ΘΕΣΗ, ΕΧΕΙ, ΞΕΝΟΔΟΧΕΙΟ, ΜΕΡΕΣ, ΘΑ, ΠΡΟΤΙΜΩ, ΝΕΡΟ(Υ), ΣΚΕΠΤΟΝΤΑΙ, ΑΝΑΜΟΝΗ (waiting). Vertical: ΑΡΕΣΩ, ΘΕΑ, ΘΑ, ΕΝΤΑΞΕΙ, ΣΟΥ, ΠΑΠΑ (priest), ΔΩΡΑ (presents) Ο, ΜΟΝΟ, ΕΧΕΤΕ, ΧΕΡΙ (hand), ΤΟ, ΙΟΣ (virus) **7** /af/ γράφω, αυτός, καφές, /ef/ εύκολο, ευχαριστώ, ευθεία, /ev/ αποσκευή, γεύμα, φεύγω. **8 a** δωμάτιο, **b** μπάνιο, **c** κουρτίνα, **d** κανένα, **e** κάνω, **f** νερά, **g** μη, **h** στεγνώνει. **9 a** 10–325, **b** 6–747, **c** 7–421, **d** 9–780, **e** 8–480, **f** 1–821, **g** 3–554, **h** 2–825, **i** 5–557, **j** 4–954.

Test yourself

1 a δωμάτιο/α (THomátio/a), **b** αυτοκίνητο/α (aftokínito/a), **c** τουρίστας/ες (turístas/es), **d** βαλίτσα/ ες (valítsa/es), **e** κράτηση/ κρατήσεις (krátisi/kratísis), **f** διεύθυνση (THiéfthinsi), **g** αριθμός (arithmós), **h** διαβατήριο (THiavatírio), **i** στυλός (stilós), **j** ντους (duz) **2 a** Μη στεναχωριέστε! (mi stenahoríeste!), **b** Πρώτο(ς)/ δεύτερο(ς)/ τρίτο(ς) όροφος (prótos/THéfteros/trítos órofos), **c** Όχι, δε μου αρέσει! (óchi

THe mu arési!), **d** Τ' όνομα μου είναι … (t'ónoma mu íne …), Λέγομαι … (léghome …), Με λένε … (me l'éne …), **e** Έχω κάνει κράτηση (ého káni krátisi), **f** Ένα δωμάτιο για απόψε/σήμερα (το βράδυ), (éna THomátio ya apópse/símera to vráTHi), **g** Έχετε δωμάτια για ενοικίαση; (éhete THomátia ya enikíasi)? **h** Καλή διαμονή! (kalí THiamoní!), **i** Θα το πάρω (tha to páro), **j** Μισό λεπτό παρακαλώ! (misó leptó parakaló!)

UNIT 8

A piece of Greece

1 The Greek word for *cheese* is τυρί.

Vocabulary builder

1 a ροδάκινο, **b** καρπούζι, **c** κεράσι, **d** σταφύλι, **e** φράουλα, **f** μήλο, **g** ανανάς, **h** πεπόνι, **i** πορτοκάλι, **j** μπανάνα, **k** κουνουπίδι, **l** κολοκυθάκι, **m** σέλινο, **n** άνιθος, **o** μελιτζάνα, **p** καρότο, **q** καλαμπόκι, **r** ντομάτα, **s** πατάτα, **t** μαρούλι. **3** Greek words for colours: άσπρο white, μαύρο black, πράσινο green, κίτρινο yellow, κόκκινο red, French words for colours: μπορντώ burgundy, καφέ brown, μπεζ beige, γκρι grey, μπλε blue, σιέλ sky blue, ροζ pink

Conversation 1

1 She wants to get a dress and some cosmetics for her and a shirt for Tim. **2 a** Yes. She wants to get him a shirt. **b** She wants her company and Joanna can speak Greek. **c** She might get a perfume and a new face cream.

Language discovery 1

1 a μερικά ψώνια some shopping, **b** μερικά καλλυντικά some cosmetics, **c** καμιά κρέμα a (face) cream, **d** καμιά κολώνια a perfume. The first two are in plural form and the last two are in singular form.

Conversation 2

1 They are on the fourth floor. **2 a** No. She is afraid of small, tight spaces. **b** It means: at the end of. **c** Medium or 36.

Language discovery 2

1 a ανοικτό χρώμα σκούρο, **b** Τι μέγεθος φοράει; Νούμερο, **c** Νά ένα ωραίο! Κοίτα, **d** μεγάλη ποικιλία μικρή, **2 a** Εμένα μου αρέσουν … I personally like, **b** … αλλά δεν του αρέσουν καθόλου. … but he does not like them at all. **c** Σ'αρέσει; Do you like it? The verb form αρέσει is used with nouns in singular and the verb form αρέσουν is used with nouns in plural.

Conversation 3

1 They get one kilo apples and two kilos oranges. **2 a** It means: What shall we eat if we don't go and buy things from the street market? **b** It means that the sales person is so sure about the good quality of his watermelons that he is willing to cut any watermelon and let his customers taste it before buying it. **c** No, but they can find them on the stand next to Mr Kostas's.

Language discovery 3

1 a we'll leave θα φύγουμε, **b** we'll eat θα φάμε, **c** we'll get θα πάρουμε, **d** we'll go θα πάμε

Practice

1 a Θέλεις παρέα; **b** Χρειάζομαι να/ Πρέπει να/Θέλω να -> κάνω μερικά ψώνια. **c** Σε ποιον όροφο είναι το τμήμα ανδρικών/γυναικείων/ παιδικών; **d** Θα ήθελα μία μονόχρωμη/δίχρωμη/τρίχρωμη/

εμπριμέ φούστα. Θα ήθελα ένα μονόχρωμο/δίχρωμο/τρίχρωμο/εμπριμέ πουκάμισο. Ριγέ, καρό ή πουά. **e** Θα προτιμούσα κάτι μικρότερο, καλύτερο και φθηνότερο! **2** TEST 1: κόκκινο, πορτοκαλί, πράσινο; TEST 2: άσπρο, κόκκινο, ροζέ; TEST 3: (probably optional!) κίτρινο, καφέ, μπλε, κόκκινο; TEST 4: κόκκινο, πορτοκαλί, κίτρινο, πράσινο, γαλάζιο, μπλέ, μωβ. TEST 5: μαύρο, άσπρο **3 a** Θα ήθελα ένα κιλό πορτοκάλια και δύο κιλά μήλα. **b** Είναι νόστιμα τα καρπούζια; **c** Δώστε μου ένα μικρό, όχι πιο πολύ από πέντε κιλά. **d** Αυτά για την ώρα. Πόσο κάνουν; **e** Ορίστε!, Δέκα ευρώ **f** Ευχαριστώ, Γεια σας. **4 a** 8, **b** 5, **c** 10, **d** 2, **e** 9, **f** 4, **g** 1, **h** 6, **i** 7, **j** 3. **5 a** ΥΠΟΓΕΙΟ, **b** ΚΙΤΡΙΝΟ, **c** ΓΑΛΑΖΙΟ, **d** ΒΥΣΣΙΝΟ, **e** ΙΣΟΓΕΙΟ, **f** ΚΟΚΚΙΝΟ. **6 a** φάμε, **b** Ελληνίδα, **c** ίδιο, **d** παρόμοιο, **e** πάντως, **f** νοιάζει, **g** πάρεις **h** φτηνά, **i** πάρουμε, **j** ξένους, **k** μεγαλύτερα, **l** νοστιμότατα, **m** Δώστε, **n** Πόσο, **o** μαρούλια, **p** χόρτα, **q** δίπλα. **8** opening hours ώρες λειτουργίας, telephone τηλέφωνο (τηλ), open ανοιχτά, square πλατεία (πλ), a.m. and p.m π.μ. / μ.μ., Music Hall Μέγαρο Μουσικής, and information πληροφορίες, **9 a** ✓, **b** ✓, **c** , **d** X, **e** ✓, **f** X, **g** ✓, **h** ✓, **i** ✓, **j** ✓, **k** ✓, **l** ✓.

Test yourself

1 a i ψώνια (psónia), **b** φόρεμα/φορέματα (fórema/forémata), **c** κρέμα (kréma), **d** σύντομα (síndoma), **e** αγορά/ές (aghorá/és), **f** ξένος/η (ksénos/i), **g** μήλο/α (mílo/a), **h** πορτοκάλι/α (portokáli/a), **i** άσπρο (áspro), **j** μαύρο (mávro) **2 a** Θέλεις παρέα; (thélis paréa)?, **b** Δεν το έχω μαζί μου (THen to ého mazí mu), **c** Έλα να πάρουμε το ασανσέρ (éla na párume to asansér), **d** Είναι στον τέταρτο όροφο (íne ston tétarto órofo), **e** Θα ρωτήσω τον πωλητή (tha rotíso ton polití), **f** Τι μέγεθος φοράς; (ti méghethos forás)?, **g** Μη σε νοιάζει! (mi se niázi), **h** Έχετε μεγαλύτερα/καλύτερα; (éhete meghalítera/kalítera)?, **i** Έλα εδώ, δίπλα μου! (éla eTHó THípla mu), **j** Κυριακή (kiriakí), Δευτέρα (THeftéra), Τρίτη (tríti), Τετάρτη (tetárti), Πέμπτη (pémdi), Παρασκευή (paraskeví), Σάββατο (sávato) **3 a** Θα τελειώσω σήμερα, (tha telióso símera), **b** Θα δω τηλεόραση (tha THo tileórasi), **c** θα ξέρω Ελληνικά (σύντομα) (tha kséro eliniká (síndoma)), **d** Θα κάνω γυμναστική (tha káno ghimnastikí), **e** Θα φάω μουσακά (tha fáo musaká).

REVISION TEST 2

1 a Πού είναι ο σταθμός; – Πού είναι η πλατεία; – Πού είναι το κέντρο; **b** Δεν καταλαβαίνω Ελληνικά καλά. Μιλάτε λίγο πιο σιγά; **c** Right on the first street, Right on the second corner, Right on the third block (side street), **d** Πόσο κάνουν τα μήλα; – €1/kilo – Μου δίνετε τρία κιλά μήλα, σας παρακαλώ; **e** Πάμε στο πάρκο; On foot or by car? **f** Έχετε χάρτες; Πόσο κάνει (αυτός) ο χάρτης; **g** Υπάρχει πτήση για Θεσσαλονίκη κάθε μέρα; Πόσες πτήσεις υπάρχουν την ημέρα; Και πότε; **h** Μου δίνετε το πρόγραμμα με τα δρομολόγια από Αθήνα για Θεσσαλονίκη; Πότε πρέπει να κλείσω θέση; **i** €25 Είναι μόνο πήγαινε ή μετ'επιστροφής; **j** Do you like light or dark colours? Single-coloured shirts or multiple colours? Μου αρέσουν τ' ανοιχτά χρώματα και συνήθως τα μονόχρωμα. This is not the only possible answer. **2 a** 6, **b** 4, **c** 9, **d** 1, **e** 10, **f** 2, **g** 5, **h** 3, **i** 8, **j** 7. **3** Στρίψτε δεξιά στη Μυθήμνης. Πηγαίνετε δύο στενά. Κάντε δεξιά στη γωνία που είναι το TEXACO. Πηγαίνετε μόνο ένα τετράγωνο και στη Σπάρτης στρίβετε πάλι δεξιά. Η ταβέρνα το Αρχοντόσπιτο είναι στ'αριστερά σας απέναντι από το γκαράζ της SHELL. **4** Πηγαίνω ευθεία για δύο τετράγωνα. Στρίβω δεξιά στη Σωκράτους και η Αθίδων είναι το δεύτερο στενό. Ο αριθμός 27 είναι στη γωνία Αθίδων και Σωκράτους. **5** Η πλατεία – Πού είναι η πλατεία παρακαλώ; – Πηγαίνετε ευθεία. Μετά από τρία στενά, στρίψτε δεξιά. Η πλατεία είναι στη μέση του τετραγώνου δεξιά σας = Letter A. Το σχολείο – Πού είναι το σχολείο παρακαλώ; – Στρίψτε δεξιά στον πρώτο δρόμο. Προχωρείστε ευθεία για δύο τετράγωνα και στρίψτε αριστερά. Μετά το πρώτο στενό το σχολείο είναι στ'αριστερά σας πριν το τέλος του τετραγώνου. = Letter B. Ο σταθμός – Πού είναι ο σταθμός παρακαλώ; – Είναι πολύ εύκολο. Δεξιά εδώ στο πρώτο στενό. Μετά από τρία τετράγωνα στρίψτε αριστερά και είναι ακριβώς στην επόμενη γωνία στ'αριστερά σας. = Letter C. **6 a** ευθεία, **b** στενά, **c** δεξιά, **d** τετράγωνα, **e** αριστερά, **f** τέλος, **g** εύκολο, **h** εδώ, **i** ακριβώς **7 a** after the first block Μετά το πρώτο στενό, **b** on the next corner στην επόμενη γωνία, **c** on your left στ'αριστερά σας, **d** That's very easy Είναι πολύ εύκολο, **e** go straight on Προχωρείστε ευθεία, **f** before the end πριν το τέλος **8 a** με το αεροπλάνο, **b** με το ποδήλατο, **c** με τον ηλεκτρικό/υπόγειο, με το μετρό, **d** με τα πόδια, **e** με το τρένο, **f** με το λεωφορείο, **g** με το καράβι/ πλοίο, **h** με το αυτοκίνητο,

i με το ταξί, **j** με το τρόλεϊ, **k** τρέχοντας, **l** με το πούλμαν. **9** Here are just sample answers. Please, check your answers with a native speaker **a** Στο σχολείο συνήθως πάω με το ποδήλατο. **b** Στον φίλο μου / Στην φίλη μου πάω μόνο με το αυτοκίνητό μου. **c** Όταν δουλεύω συνήθως παίρνω το μετρό. **d** Το λεωφορείο δε μ' αρέσει καθόλου! **e** Ποτέ δεν πάω στο γραφείο με ταξί. **10 a** Χ, **b** ✓, **c** Χ, **d** ✓, **e** Χ, **f** Χ. **g** We don't know. It is not mentioned in the dialogue! **h** ✓. **11 a** οκτώ, **b** έξι, **c** έντεκα, **d** επτά, **e** δώδεκα, **f** τρεις, **g** δύο, **h** μία, **i** πέντε, **j** τέσσερις. **12 a** Στις τρεισήμισυ … **b** Στις εντεκάμισυ … **c** Στις δέκα … **d** Στη μία … **e** Στις δέκα και τέταρτο … **f** Στις δύομισυ … ; c, e, b, d, f, a. **13 a** πουκάμισα, **b** τμήμα, **c** ασανσέρ, **d** σκάλες, **e** φτάσαμε, **f** βάθος, **g** ποικιλία, **h** ανοικτό, **i** μονόχρωμα, **j** ριγέ, **k** νούμερο, **l** μέγεθος, **m** Σ' αρέσει.
14 a Men's department τμήμα ανδρικών , **b** sometimes καμιά φορά, **c** escalators κυλιόμενες σκάλες **d** men's shirts ανδρικά πουκάμισα, **e** in a little while σε λίγο, **f** he doesn't like δεν του αρέσουν

UNIT 9

The Greek kiosk!

1 a cigarette το τσιγάρο/-α, **b** newspaper/-s η εφημερίδα/-ες **c** chocolate η σοκολάτα/-τες

Vocabulary builder

1 εφημερίδα/-ες, σοκολάτα/-τες, παγωτό/-ά, τσιγάρο/-α, **2** η εφημερίδα: 2,25, η σοκολάτα: 1,15, το παγωτό: 2,00, το τσιγάρο: 4,50. Total: 9,90, **3 a** 2, **b** 5, **c** 6, **d** 4, **e** 1, **f** 3. **4 a** Who is calling? (When you hear a male voice) Έλα ποιος είναι; **b** Who is calling? (When you hear a female voice) Έλα ποια είναι; **c** Speaking! (If you are a man.) Ο ίδιος, **d** Speaking! (If you are a woman.) Η ίδια. **e** Hello! (On the phone) Εμπρός! Ναι; Ορίστε! Λέγετε; Παρακαλώ! **f** This is … (On the phone) Εγώ είμαι ο…(Γιάννης.) / Εγώ είμαι η…(Δανάη.)

Conversation 1

1 Tim will have the meeting tomorrow. **2 a** Ναι, γεια σας. Λέγομαι Tim Johnson. **b** Τοπικό means local telephone call and υπεραστικό out of city/state telephone call. **c** Yes he can.

Language discovery 1

1 a …it would be… θα ήταν , **b** …would you like… Θα θέλατε, **c** …I would like … Θα ήθελα να, **d** … would he be able to … θα μπορούσε, **2** Μπορώ να κάνω ένα τηλέφωνο; Can I make a telephone call? Πότε θα μπορούσε να με δει; When could he (is he able to) see me? Μπορεί να σας δει αύριο στις 2.00 το μεσημέρι. He can see you at 2 o'clock in the afternoon. Ναι μπορώ, ευχαριστώ πολύ. Yes I can, thanks a lot.

Conversation 2

1 He should wait a couple of minutes. **2 a** Ονομάζομαι Tim Johnson, είμαι συνάδελφος του κ. Αμανατίδη. **b** Μισό λεπτό, σε δύο λεπτά, **c** I'm glad to see you again.

Language discovery 2

1 a …θα τον πάρω… I'll call him…, **b** …θα σας δει … he'll see you…, **c** … θα σας φωνάξω … I'll call you, **d** … που σας ξαναβλέπω … that I see you again, **e** …να της δώσετε …give her…, **f** … να μην το ξεχάσετε … do not forget it. No it is not a perfect match. The personal pronouns come before the verb in Greek and after the verb in English. **2 a** Τ' όνομά σας; Your name? **b** …θα σας δει … he'll see you…, **c** … θα σας φωνάξω …I'll call you, **d** … για σας …for you …**e** … εκ μέρους σας …on your behalf. It means you when it is with verbs or prepositions and it means 'your' with nouns.

Conversation 3

1 She speaks Greek well. **2 a** Να σας γνωρίσω την κυρία Smith. **b** Nice to meet you! Χαίρω πολύ κυρία Smith (Σμιθ). Nice to meet you, too! Κι εγώ χαίρω πολύ. **c** Can I offer you something?

Language discovery 3

1 Masculine nouns: **d** καφέ, **f** κόπο, Feminine nouns: **a** κυρία, **b** Ελλάδα, **c** κάρτα, **g** τράπεζα, **h** συνεργασία, Neuter nouns: **e** αναψυχτικό, **i** σύστημα, **2 a** 3, **b** 4, **c** 1, **d** 2

Practice

1 a Μπορώ να κάνω ένα τοπικό και ένα υπεραστικό τηλέφωνο; **b** Με λένε … και δουλεύω/εργάζομαι στην … **c** You have to follow him/her! **d** Καθίστε! Πάρτε μια καρέκλα! **e** Τα χαιρετίσματα μου στη σύζυγο σου/σας. **f** Μην το ξεχάσεις! **g** (Γιάννη) Να σου γνωρίσω/συστήσω τον κ. Smith. **h** Γιάννη, να σου γνωρίσω/συστήσω το Γιώργο. **i** Καλώς όρισες! Καλώς ήρθατε! **2 a** 5, **b** 4, **c** 1, **d** 3, **e** 2. **3 a** e, a, f, b, d, c, g. **4 a** Χρειάζομαι το Νικόλα γιατί ξέρει πολύ καλά Ελληνικά. **b** Δεν με νοιάζει ποιος είναι φτηνότερος. Με νοιάζει ποιος είναι ο καλύτερος. **c** Ας ξεκινήσουμε με το Νικόλα και αν υπάρχει πρόβλημα με την συνεργασία τότε βλέπουμε. **d** Ποτέ δεν είναι πολύ αργά. **5 a** 8, **b** 5, **c** 6, **d** 1, **e** 10, **f** 2, **g** 3, **h** 9, **i** 4, **j** 7. **6 a** ανέβω, **b** δω, **c** πάρω, **d** πάω, **e** ρωτήσω, **f** τελειώσω, **g** φάω, **h** φύγω. **7 a** Θέλω να πάω στην πλατεία. **b** Ναι! Έχω ραντεβού με τον κ. Πέτρου. **c** Θέλει να πάμε στη Θεσσαλονίκη αύριο. **d** Θα ήθελα ένα μονόκλινο με μπάνιο και τηλεόραση. **e** Πού είναι το εστιατόριο; **f** (Αυτό) θα ήταν καλύτερα για μένα. **g** Θα προτιμούσα ένα δωμάτιο με θέα. **h** Ένα αναψυκτικό, αν δεν σας κάνει κόπο. **8** Horizontal: ΣΑΣ, ΑΝ, ΚΑΙΡΟΣ, ΕΛΑ, ΤΩΡΑ, ΟΜΩΣ, ΑΝΕΒΩ, ΤΗΝ ΞΕΚΙΝΗΣΩ; Vertical: ΗΘΕΛΑ, ΤΡΩΩ, ΣΤΗ, ΤΗΣ, ΠΑΙΡΝΩ. **9 a** γνωρίσω, **b** χαίρω, **c** Καθίστε, **d** προσπαθώ, **e** υπέροχα, **f** προσφέρω, **g** κόπο, **h** ελπίζει, **i** συνεργασία, **j** εύχομαι, **k** φύγεις, **l** χρειάζομαι.

Test yourself

1 a τηλέφωνο/α, **b** αργότερα, **c** b περίπτερο/α, **d** αύριο, **e** κάρτα/ες, **f** σήμερα, **g** τράπεζα/ες, **h** χαιρετίσματα, **i** ραντεβού, **j** αναψυκτικό/ά. **2 a** Μπορώ να κάνω/πάρω ένα τηλέφωνο/τηλεφώνημα; **b** Καθίστε παρακαλώ, **c** Θα ήθελα να κλείσω ένα ραντεβού, **d** Να μην το ξεχάσετε, **e** Αν είναι δυνατόν, **f** Τα χαιρετίσματα μου στη σύζυγο σας, **g** Χαίρομαι που σε ξαναβλέπω, **h** Να σας γνωρίσω τον κύριο 'χ', **i** Πάρτε μια καρέκλα! **j** Χαίρω πολύ; **3 a** Θα πάω αύριο (tha páo ávrio), **b** Θα ρωτήσω αύριο (tha rotíso ávrio), **c** Θα φύγω νωρίς (tha fígho norís), **d** Θα πάρω τηλέφωνο (tha páro tiléfono), **e** Θα ανέβω τώρα (tha anévo tóra)

UNIT 10

Population in Greece and Greeks abroad

1 The word for Europe is Ευρώπη and the word for Africa is Αφρική.

Vocabulary builder

4 a 7, **b** 5, **c** 6, **d** 4, **e** 3, **f** 1, **g** 2

Conversation 1

1 She was sick yesterday. **2 a** She had migraines. **b** Yes, but everything was buzzing in my head yesterday. **c** She was bored yesterday so she decided to go to work today.

Language discovery 1

1 a …I was … Ήμουν, **b** …I thought… νόμιζα, **c** …I went … πήγα, **d** …he gave me … μου έδωσε, **e** …I came … Ήρθα, **f** … did you have… είχες, **g** …didn't you stay … δεν κάθισες, **h** …I was bored … Βαρέθηκα. The ending of the first person singular is not –ω any more but –α.

Conversation 2

1 No, they didn't have a good time. **2 a** Mary had food poisoning. **b** No, she stayed home. **c** Tim was taking care of her and at the end he exhausted himself.

Language discovery 2

1 a …I had (suffered) … έπαθα, **b** …I should (had to)… Έπρεπε, **c** …we went … Πήγαμε , **d** … it happened… συνέβη **e** …I stayed … Έμεινα, **f** … did you spend… περάσατε, **g** …he walked … περπάτησε, **h** …he swam… κολύμπησε, **2 a** Don't say that. Μην το λες. **b** What can I tell you? Τι να σου πω; **c** Tell me. Πες μου. **d** …you're saying… Εκεί που λες … **3** τροφική δηλητηρίαση, φάρμακα, νοσοκομείο, νοσοκόμος, υπερκόπωση, ανάπαυση. **4 a** At the time being … (Now …) τώρα, **b** The rest of the time … Τις άλλες ώρες, **c** … both days … και τις δύο ημέρες.

Conversation 3

1 He is complaining about his trip to Spetses. **2 a** Mary had food poisoning. **b** Tim is now exhausted. **c** He said that he can speak good Greek, he is used to Athens now, he loves Greek cuisine, and he is a good bank clerk.

Language discovery 3

1 a …good advice… Καλή συμβουλή, **b** …food poisoning… τροφική δηλητηρίαση, **c** …bank employee… τραπεζικός υπάλληλος, **d** …Greek cuisine … ελληνική κουζίνα, **e** …nice island … ωραίο νησί, **f** …good employee… καλός υπάλληλος, **2** τραπεζικός υπάλληλος, γιατρός, μάγειρας, πιλότος. Some other examples are: δικηγόρος, δάσκαλος, καθηγητής, συγγραφέας, κτίστης, εργάτης.

Practice

1 a Καλή βδομάδα! or Επίσης! **b** Καλό μήνα! **c** Ευχαριστώ, επίσης! **d** Σε χάσαμε! Πού ήσουν; **e** Πώς πέρασες το Σαββατοκύριακο; Πού πήγες; **f** Ένα γιατρό αμέσως! (γρήγορα!) **g** Είσαι άρρωστος; Φαίνεσαι λίγο χλωμός! **2 a** 3, **b** 5, **c** 1, **d** 4, **e** 2. **3 a** 7, **b** 5, **c** 6, **d** 4, **e** 3, **f** 1, **g** 2 **4 a** Ήμουν ταξίδι στην Κρήτη. **b** Ήταν ταξίδι για δουλειές. **c** Έμεινα τρεις μέρες. **d** Πήγα μόνος και η σύζυγος μου ήλθε την επόμενη ημέρα. **e** Περάσαμε ωραία. Ειδικά η σύζυγος μου διότι πήγαινε για ψώνια κάθε μέρα. **f** Άρρωστη; Τι της συναίβει; (Τι είχε;) **g** Αυτό δεν είναι ωραίο. Πώς είναι τώρα; (Πώς πάει τώρα;) **h** Ελπίζω να γίνει καλύτερα σύντομα! **5 a** ΠΟΔΟΣΦΑΙΡΟ, **b** ΚΟΛΥΜΠΙ, **c** ΣΥΝΗΘΩΣ, **d** ΠΟΤΕ, **e** ΑΓΧΟΣ, **f** ΕΞΕΤΑΣΗ, **g** ΠΙΛΟΤΟΣ, **h** ΖΩΓΡΑΦΟΣ Shaded word: ΣΥΝΕΧΕΙΑ. **6 a** 10, **b** 6, **c** 7, **d** 9, **e** 8, **f** 1, **g** 3, **h** 4, **i** 5, **j** 2. **7 a** άρρωστος, **b** φαίνεσαι, **c** νησί, **d** υπερκόπωση, **e** απαισιόδοξος, **f** συνήθισες, **g** υπάλληλος, **h** μάγειρας, **i** ψηλά, **j** συμβουλή.

Test yourself

1 a εχθές/χθες, **b** Σαββατοκύριακο, **c** άρρωστος/η/ο, **d** αρκετά, **e** γιατρός, **f** σοβαρός/ή/ό, **g** φαρμακείο, **h** μπάνιο/κολύμπι, **i** φάρμακο/χάπι, **j** βάδην. **2 a** Χρειάζομαι λίγο καθαρό αέρα!, **b** Πώς ήταν το Σαββατοκύριακο σου; **c** Ήταν ένας εφιάλτης!, **d** Ήταν θαύμα!, **e** Μου αρέσει πολύ το κολύμπι, **f** Χρειάζομαι λίγη ανάπαυση, **g** Μην το λες!, **h** Είναι καλή συμβουλή!, **i** Αισθάνομαι άρρωστος/αδιάθετος/ζάλη/ναυτία!, **j** Έχω πυρετό/πονοκέφαλο/πονόλαιμο. **3 a** Αγάπησα την Ελλάδα. (aghápisa tin eláTHa), **b** Κολύμπησα πολύ. (kolímbisa polí), **c** Ήξερα Ελληνικά (íksera eliniká), **d** Έκανα γυμναστική (ékana ghimnastikí), **e** Έφαγα μουσακά (éfagha musaká)

UNIT 11

The weather in Greece

1 As mentioned before, the ending of nouns often indicates the gender. As a rule of thumb, the ending –ος is masculine, with some exceptions, but not here.

Vocabulary builder

3 Four alternative questions are: Τι καιρό κάνει σήμερα; What's the weather like today? Τι καιρό έχει στην Αθήνα; What's the weather like in Athens? Πώς είναι ο καιρός στο Λονδίνο; What's the weather like in London? Τι θερμοκρασία υπάρχει στη Βέροια σήμερα; What's the temperature in Veria today?

Four alternative answers are: Είναι αίθριος, είναι άστατος. It's fair, it's unsettled. Κάνει παγωνιά έξω. There's frost. Υπάρχει υγρασία σήμερα. It's humid today. Έχει 25 βαθμούς σήμερα. It's 25 degrees today. **4 a** έχει, **b** υπάρχει, **c** ρίχνει, **d** είναι, **e** κάνει

Conversation 1

1 No, they didn't have a good time. **2 a** They went to Lamia for three days. **b** Lamia is not that far from Athens. **c** The weather was very bad.

Language discovery 1

1 a Don't say these kind of things! Μη λες τέτοια λόγια! **b** What can I tell you? Τι να σας πω; **c** Why don't you tell us? Γιατί δε μας λες; **d** Come on, tell us! Έλα πες μας. **2 a** …you've sweated… έχεις βγάλει (την πίστη!) **b** …I have worried … έχω στεναχωρηθεί, **c** … we've called / telephoned … έχουμε τηλεφωνήσει, **d** …we have gone… έχουμε πάει, **e** …they have planned έχουν σχεδιάσει, **f** …it has not happened … δεν έχει ξανασυμβεί.

Conversation 2

1 Because they had to stay home all the time. **2 a** No, they did not want to watch TV. **b** They wanted to visit two museums and the Castle in Acrolamia. **c** No, they didn't go swimming.

Language discovery 2

1 a Έχει γυρίσματα ο τροχός! **b** Δε θέλαμε να φάμε του σκασμού! **c** Όλα ακούγονται μαύρα κι άραχνα! **d** Έβρεχε συνέχεια καρεκλοπόδαρα! **2 a** Didn't you see? Δεν είδατε; **b** We came back … επιστρέψαμε **c** Didn't you speak? Δε μιλήσατε; **d** We stayed … Μείναμε, **e** Didn't you eat? Δε φάγατε; **f** It rained … Έβρεξε **g** It didn't stop Δε σταμάτησε **h** What did they do? τι έκαναν;

Conversation 3

1 The weather was finally to blame. **2 a** They do not want to think about it. **b** It's sunny with a nice breeze. **c** He wanted to forget about rain, snow, cold, and frost.

Language discovery 3

1 a Αυτό να λέγεται! **b** Εκεί να δεις χειμώνες … **c** Μη μου μιλάτε για το Λονδίνο! **d** Γι'αυτό έχω έλθει στην Ελλάδα. **2 a** περίμενα, **b** Όλοι μας έλεγαν, **c** Ήθελα, **3** All three words are often in singular: rain, snow, and winter. The word 'snow' has no plural in English.

Practice

1 a Τι καιρό κάνει στην Ελλάδα; **b** Έχει συννεφιά συχνά. **c** Βρέχει πολλές φορές. **d** Χιονίζει το χειμώνα και κάνει πολύ κρύο. **e** Μου αρέσει όταν έχει λιακάδα και κάνει ψύχρα. **f** Ρίχνει χιόνι ή χαλάζι στην Ελλάδα; **g** In summer it is very hot in Greece, but it's not humid. **2 a** 2, **b** 4, **c** 5, **d** 1, **e** 3. **3** e, b, c, g, a, f, d, h. **4 a** Τι να σας πω; **b** Δεν ξέρω. Δεν έχω στεναχωρηθεί ποτέ άλλοτε έτσι. **c** Ο καιρός ήταν απαίσιος και πολύ άστατος. **d** Όχι. Όλοι μου έλεγαν ότι ο καιρός θα ήταν αίθριος και θαυμάσιος. Αντίθετα … **5 a** 6, **b** 3, **c** 9, **d** 1, **e** 8, **f** 2, **g** 5, **h** 7, **i** 4. **6 b** είδα-έβλεπα, **c** πήρα-έπαιρνα, **d** πήγα-πήγαινα, **e** ρώτησα-ρωτούσα, **f** τελείωσα-τελείωνα, **g** έφαγα-έτρωγα, **h** έφυγα-έφευγα. **7 a 1** φθινόπωρο, **2** χειμώνας, **3** άνοιξη, **4** καλοκαίρι. **b 1** Δεκέμβριος, **2** Ιανουάριος, **3** Φεβρουάριος, **4** Μάρτιος, **5** Απρίλιος, **6** Μάιος, **7** Ιούνιος, **8** Ιούλιος, **9** Αύγουστος, **10** Σεπτέμβριος, **11** Οκτώβριος, **12** Νοέμβριος. **8 a** Φαίνεσαι πολύ στεναχωρημένος. Τι συμβαίνει; **b** Έχεις πάει κι άλλες φορές (πολλές φορές) πριν στην Κέρκυρα. Έτσι δεν είναι; **c** Ο καιρός μάς χάλασε τα σχέδια. **d** Τι άσχημος καιρός! (Πω, πω παλιόκαιρος!) Δεν μου αρέσει καθόλου. **e** Είδες τηλεόραση; Έφαγες; Μίλησες; (or, είδατε φάγατε/μιλήσατε). **f** Θα έχεις την ευκαιρία να πας πίσω πάλι (ξανά). **g** Ναι, βέβαια! Του χρόνου, το πιο νωρίς! **9** Horizontal: Οριζόντια (in Greek!): ΛΙΑΚΑΔΑ, ΑΠΟΡΩ (I wonder), ΘΟΡΥΒΟΣ, ΒΡΟΧΗ, ΣΙΝΕΜΑ, ΑΓΩΝΙΑ (agony), ΠΑΓΩΝΙΑ (frost). Vertical: Κάθετα (in Greek): ΛΑΘΟΣ, ΒΙΑ (violence), ΚΡΥΟ, ΧΜ (Hm! When thinking!), ΔYO, AΣΣOΣ (ace). **10 a** αποφασίσει, **b** παραχρόνου, **c** Κοίτα, **d** βρέξει, **e** παρόμοιος, **f** δίκιο, **g** Προχτές, **h** επικίνδυνοι, **i** έλθει, **j** κρύο, **k** ήλιο, **l** σ' έστειλε, **m** χειμώνας, **n** περίμενα, **o** εποχή, **p** έλεγαν. **11 a** 3, **b** 4, **c** 6, **d** 5, **e** 1, **f** 2. **12 a** ✓, **b** ✗, **c** ✓, **d** ✓, **e** ✓, **f** ✓, **g** ✗, **h** ✗, **i** ✗, **j** ✓.

Test yourself

1 a νερό, **b** Ιούλιος, **c** ταξίδι/ταξείδι, **d** λιακάδα, **e** καιρός, **f** αεράκι, **g** στεναχωρημένος/η/ο, **h** βροχή, **i** Μάιος **j** χιόνι. **2 a** Έχω προγραμματίσει/τηλεφωνήσει, **b** (Δεν) Έχεις δίκιο, **c** Ακούγεσαι/φαίνεσαι …, **d** Είναι η καλύτερη εποχή στην Αθήνα, **e** Έβρεχε συνέχεια/Η βροχή δεν σταμάτησε ποτέ, **f** Δεν είναι χειμώνας τώρα, είναι άνοιξη!, **g** Έβρεξε καρεκλοπόδαρα!, **h** Πώς είναι ο καιρός;, **i** Θα έχετε την ευκαιρία να πάτε πίσω ξανά, **j** Είναι αίθριος/ άστατος/σχημος/θαυμάσιος. **3 a** Πήγα ταξίδι (pígha taksíΤΗi), **b** Ρώτησα στ' Αγγλικά (rótisa st'angliká), **c** Έφυγα νωρίς. (éfigha norís), **d** Πήρα τηλέφωνο (píra tiléfono), **e** Έκανε ζέστη (ékane zésti).

UNIT 12

Easter in Greece

1 The Greek for Easter is Πάσχα.

Vocabulary builder

1 a 1, 3, **b** 2, 3, **c** 1, 2, **d** 2, 3, **e** 1, 3, **f** 1, 2, **g** 1, 3, **h** 2, 3, **i** 1, 2, **j** 1, 3, **3 a** Καλό απόγευμα! **b** Στην υγειά σου! **c** Να' σαι καλά! **d** Η Παναγιά μαζί σου! **e** Καλές γιορτές! **f** Καλή όρεξη! **g** Καλό Πάσχα! **h** Καλή Ανάσταση! **i** Και του χρόνου! **j** Καλή σταδιοδρομία!

Conversation 1

1 Yes, they had a very good time. **2 a** They went to four places: Φισκάρδο, Ιθάκη, Δωδώνη, Γιάννενα. **b** They celebrated Easter: στο Φισκάρδο. **c** They ate fish.

Language discovery 1

1 a At first… Στην αρχή …, **b** Then … μετά, **c** Afterwards… κατόπιν…, **d** At the end … τέλος, **2 a** We ate… εμείς φάγαμε, **b** Where did you go? Πού πήγατε;, **c** we celebrated… κάναμε, **d** we met … γνωρίσαμε, **e** which withstand… άντεξε, **f** Where did you celebrate…? πού κάνατε…, **3** Αναστασία: Τι λες βρε παιδί μου; Τόσο καλό; What are you saying? Was it that good? Tim: Πού να σας λέμε. We have no words to describe that!

Conversation 2

1 She is impressed because Tim and Mary know so many wishes in Greek. **2 a** She forgot that Anastasia had her name day. **b** It is on Easter Sunday. **c** She promised her language teacher that she is going to learn Greek wishes and use them on the right occasion.

Language discovery 2

1 a Χρόνια (σου) πολλά! Many happy returns! **b** Να ζήσεις! Happy birthday! Happy Name Day! **c** Να χαίρεσαι τη γυναίκα σου! Best wishes to your wife! **d** Κι εσείς ό,τι επιθυμείτε! Likewise! Same to you! May your wishes come true! A verb is not often used in English compared to Greek. **2 a** I forgot it. Το ξέχασα! **b** Now I remembered. Τώρα θυμήθηκα. **c** I got you finally! Τελικά σ'έπιασα!

Conversation 3

1 They got to Yannena around 5:00 o'clock in the morning. **2 a** Dimitris did not know where Fiscardo is. **b** Because the oracle was closed the first time. **c** About 10 hours.

Language discovery 3

1 a Talking about it … Και που λέτε, **b** …later … έπειτα, **c** …and from there… απ' εκεί, **d** …before reaching … πριν να φτάσουμε, **2 a** before πριν, **b** yet ακόμα, **c** already κιόλας, **d** in a little while σε λίγο, **e** later έπειτα, **f** around γύρω

Conversation 4

1 This is the only Wax Museum in Greece. **2 a** They listen to local, traditional music and they saw people dancing to that music. **b** That was very interesting and captivating. **c** Tim is very excited about what Greece has to offer.

Language discovery 4

1 a we had read… είχαμε διαβάσει, **b** …they had promised us … μας είχαν υποσχεθεί, **c** …they had told us… μας είχαν πει, **d**…we had not heard … δεν είχα ξανακούσει!

Practice

1 a Πώς το λέτε στα Ελληνικά; **b** Γιορτάζεις; **c** Να σου ζήσει! Να σου ζήσει! Να σας ζήσει! **d** Ευχαριστώ/-ούμε, ό,τι επιθυμείς/ -είτε. **e** Χρόνια (σου/σας) πολλά Επίσης! **f** Πού πήγες/πήγατε; Τι έκανες/ κάνατε; **g** Πού αλλού πήγες/πήγατε; Τι άλλο έκανες/κάνατε; **2 a** 4, **b** 1, **c** 5, **d** 2, **e** 3. **3** d, f, e, b, a, c, g. **4 a** Είναι στο πιο βόρειο μέρος της Κεφαλονιάς. **b** Περάσαμε καλά. Σταματήσαμε εκεί όλο το Σαββατοκύριακο. **c** Υπήρχε ένα πανηγύρι και είχαμε την ευκαιρία να δούμε τοπικούς χορούς και ν' ακούσουμε τοπική παραδοσιακή μουσική. **d** Ήταν πολύ συναρπαστικό. Ειδικά για έναν ξένο. **e** Φυσικά ναι. Δεν θα με πείραζε να ξαναδώ οτιδήποτε είναι ωραίο. **5 a** 8, **b** 5, **c** 4, **d** 7, **e** 1, **f** 2, **g** 3, **h** 6 **6 a** Έφτασα, **b** γνώρισες, **c** είχες φάει, **d** σταματούσα, **e** είδες, **f** all three! **7 a** πότε, **b** πόσο, **c** πουθενά, **d** μεταξύ, **e** κοντά, **f** τουλάχιστον, **g** γύρω, **h** αμέσως, **i** πάλι, **j** μαζί. **8** Horizontal: ΠΟΤΕ, ΤΟΤΕ, ΟΣΑ/ΣΑΝ/ΑΝ, ΤΟ, ΚΟΝΤΑ, ΜΕΤΑΞΥ; Vertical: ΣΤΟ, ΠΟΣΟ, ΟΤΑΝ, ΤΕΝΤΑ (tent), ΕΦΤΑ, ΠΟΛΥ **9 a** πανηγύρι, **b** παραδοσιακή, **c** ενδιαφέρον, **d** υποσχεθεί, **e** συναρπαστικό, **f** γνωστοί, **g** τρομερό, **h** μυστικά, **i** χώρα, **j** παραπάνω, **k** χαίρομαι, **l** εντύπωση. **10** Έχει την παλιά πόλη, το Μαντράκι, το Ενυδρείο, το Μουσείο, αρχαιολογικούς χώρους, την Ακρόπολη στη Λίνδο. Δισκοθέκες, νάιτ κλαμπ, μπουάτ, μπυραρίες, μπαρ, εστιατόρια . **11 a** 6, **b** 8, **c** 12, **d** 9, **e** 10, **f** 1, **g** 11, **h** 2, **i** 4, **j** 5, **k** 7, **l** 3 **12 a** ✓, **b** ✗, **c** ✓, **d** ✗, **e** ✓, **f** ✗, **g** ✓, **h** ✗, **i** ✓, **j** ✓.

Test yourself

1 a (ε)φέτος, **b** άσκαλος/α, δάσκαλοι, δασκάλες, **c** φίλος/η, φίλοι/ες, **d** νησί, νησιά, **e** ζωή, **f** μουσική, **g** ιστιοφόρο/α, **h** βέβαια, φυσικά, **i** ψάρι, **j** μουσείο/α **2 a** Πού πήγες για Πάσχα πέρσι;, **b** Το είχαμε ακούσει πριν, **c** Φάγαμε πολύ ψάρι, **d** Γιόρταζες;/Είχες την γιορτή σου; **e** Χρόνια πολλά! **f** Να ζήσετε! **g** Ό,τι επιθυμείτε!, **h** Είχε ήδη μιλήσει σε μερικούς φίλους, **i** Δεν μας έχεις πει ακόμα … , **j** Ήταν πολύ ενδιαφέρον **3 a** Πού πήγατε; (pu píghate)?, **b** Ήταν συναρπαστικο. (ítan sinarpastikó), **c** Είχα την εντύπωση. (íha tin endíposi), **d** Το βάζο έπεσε. (to vázo épese), **e** Πώς πήγες; (pos píghes)?

REVISION TEST 3

1 a Να σου ζήσει – Να σου ζήσει – Να σας ζήσει. **b** Καλή βδομάδα! – Καλό μήνα! – Καλό χρόνο – Ευχαριστώ, επίσης. **c** For name days, birthdays but even during public or religious holidays (e.g. Christmas, New Year's, Easter etc.) – Επίσης, ό,τι επιθυμείτε (επιθυμείς)! **d** Πώς είναι ο καιρός στην Ελλάδα σήμερα; Πώς ήταν ο καιρός στην Ελλάδα (ε)χτές; Πώς θα είναι ο καιρός στην Ελλάδα αύριο; **e** Όχι, δεν ρίχνει πολλές βροχές και χαλάζι στην Αθήνα. **f** Είναι κρύος το χειμώνα με πολλές βροχές, χαλάζι και χιόνι. Το καλοκαίρι είναι ζεστός αλλά όχι όπως στην Ελλάδα. Η θερμοκρασία είναι γύρω ή κάτω από το 0° το χειμώνα και γύρω στους 15°–18° βαθμούς το καλοκαίρι. **g** Είσαι άρρωστος; Δεν φαίνεσαι (και) πολύ καλά. Να φωνάξω ένα γιατρό; **h** Έχω πολύ καιρό να σε δω. Πού ήσουν; Σ'έχασα Γιώργο. **i** Τι δουλειά κάνεις; – Εγώ είμαι τραπεζίτης/ζωγράφος/λογιστής/ νοσοκόμος/κτίστης/ δάσκαλος. For men only. If you are a woman you could say: Εγώ είμαι τραπεζίτης/ζωγράφος/

λογίστρια/ νοσοκόμα/κτίστρια/δασκάλα. **j** Τι σπορ σου αρέσουν; – Εμένα μου αρέσουν το κολύμΠι/η ποδηλασία/η ιππασία/το βόλεϋ/το τροχάδην/το ποδόσφαιρο. **2 a** Αα! Είσαι μάνατζερ (διευθυντής)! **b** Πώς λένε το ξενοδοχείο σας στα Ελληνικά; **c** Η Ρόδος είναι νησί. Έτσι δεν είναι; **d** Έχετε και εστιατόρια και διαμερίσματα; **e** Πού είναι το Φισκάρδο; **f** Μου δίνετε τον αριθμό τηλεφώνου σας, παρακαλώ; **3 a** €380. **b** Η πτήση του Δουβλίνου είναι ακριβότερη. **c** Η πτήση του Δουβλίνου – €500. **d** Είναι με επιστροφή. **e** Istanbul. **f** Ρώμη, Φλωρεντία, Βενετία, Μιλάνο. (Rome, Florence, Venice, Milan) **4 a** Λονδίνο – Δουβλίνο 620, **b** Φλωρεντία – Βενετία 600, **c** Μαδρίτη – Βαρκελώνη 500, **d** Βιέννη – Βερολίνο 575 **5 a** Έχει καλό καιρό με λιακάδα και μερικές συννεφιές. **b** Στη Μαδρίτη και τη Δαμασκό με 37 βαθμούς. **c** Στο Όσλο με 20 βαθμούς. **d** Atlantic Ocean. **e** Mediterranean Sea. **f** Πράγα, Μαύρη Θάλασσα, Λισσαβώνα, Βερολίνο, Βρυξέλλες. **g** Κοντά στη Μαδρίτη, Βαρσοβία και Δαμασκό. **6 a** Παρίσι, **b** Αθήνα, **c** Μαδρίτη, **d** Ρώμη, **e** Βερολίνο, **f** Όσλο **7 a** 100, **b** 199, **c** 166, 108 **d** 166, **e** 1571, **f** 11188, **8 a** Τον Αύγουστο, **b** Theatrical play – Θεατρικό έργο/Concert – κοντσέρτο or συναυλία, **c** Δύο ημέρες **d** Το Βράδυ – 9:00 μ.μ. **e** ENGLISH BACH FESTIVAL, **f** Probably the most popular Greek singer. By 2010 he had been singing many kinds of Greek and international music for over 40 years. **g** Το θεατρικό έργο, γιατί έχει εισιτήρια για φοιτητές (students) για €5. **9 a** Φοίβος: 22 Απριλίου, Ιούνιος, **b** Ορέστης: 5 Μαρτίου, Δεκέμβριος, **c** Ηρακλής: 8 Οκτωβρίου, Ιανουάριος, **d** Ελπίδα: 29 Μαΐου,Ιούλιος,, **e** Αγάπη: 5 Σεπτεμβρίου, Αύγουστος, **f** Ζωή: 13 Νοεμβρίου, Φεβρουάριος. **10 a** Months with 30 days: ο Απρίλιος, ο Ιούνιος, ο Σεπτέμβριος, ο Νοέμβριος, **b** Months with 31 days: ο Ιανουάριος, ο Μάρτιος, ο Μάιος, ο Ιούλιος, ο Αύγουστος, ο Οκτώβριος, ο Δεκέμβριος, **c** Days of the week: η Δευτέρα, η Τρίτη, η Τετάρτη, η Πέμπτη, η Παρασκευή, το Σάββατο, η Κυριακή **11 a** 2, **b** 5, **c** 3, **d** 7, **e** 1, **f** 6, **g** 4, **h** 8. **i** mobile phones κινητά, i-Pods, i-Pads, or lap tops φορητοί υπολογιστές and send SMS μυνήματα or emails. We usually chat μιλάμε or surf σερφάρουμε the Internet Ίντερνετ/διαδίκτυο. **12 a** ακούσει. **b** αλήθεια, **c** προσφέρει, **d** ζωή, **e** κοσμοπολίτικης, **f** δισκοθήκες, **g** κόσμος, **h** εύκολα, **i** πλοίο, **j** βιοτικό, **k** διασκεδάσεις, **l** τελικά, **m** μάλλον, **n** τύχη. **13 a** 4, **b** 1, **c** 2, **d** 3 **14 a** Θέλω να κάνω εμετό. **b** Κρυώνω πάρα πολύ. **c** Με πονάει το κεφάλι και ζαλίζομαι

Glossary of grammatical terms

The following explains, the most important grammatical terms, in a brief and simple way. Further explanations and examples in Greek are given in the **Grammar summary** section that follows. The **Index of grammatical terms and thematic vocabulary** includes the corresponding units in which these grammatical terms or thematic vocabulary are introduced.

adjective   Adjectives are words which describe people or things. They give more information about the noun they describe, e.g. a big car (big = adjective/car = noun). See also **comparative** and **superlative,** Grammar summary, section 3 and Unit 3.

adverb   Adverbs are words which usually give more information about the verbs they describe, e.g. move quickly (move = verb/quickly = adverb). See also Grammar summary, section 4 and Units 10 and 12.

article   There are two types of article: definite and indefinite. In English, 'the' is the definite article and 'a, an' are the indefinite articles. These words come before the noun they describe, e.g. a book/the book. In Greek, there are more than three words for these articles. See also Grammar summary, section 1 and Units 1 and 2.

case   This describes the different forms (inflections) taken by nouns, pronouns, and adjectives depending on their function in a sentence. English has four inflections and most words have no more than two forms. The following nouns and pronouns can show this: book/books and I/me, he/him. Greek, as a much more inflected language, uses usually three out of five existing cases especially nominative, genitive, and accusative, e.g. who, whose, and whom. See also **article**, **inflection**, **gender** and **noun** in this section and Unit 4.

comparative   We need the comparative form of the adjective when we make comparisons. In English this usually means adding '-er' to the adjective or putting the word 'more' before it. For example, 'cheap → cheaper' or 'expensive → more expensive'. Comparative works similarly in Greek. See also **adjective** and **superlative** and Unit 7.

demonstrative or **demonstrative pronouns**   Words like 'this', 'that', 'these' and 'those' are called demonstratives. See also Grammar summary, section 5 and Unit 11.

gender   Gender is one of the categories into which nouns are divided. In Greek, nouns are divided in masculine, feminine, and neuter categories, e.g. 'the man' **ο άνδρας** [o ánTHras] is of masculine gender, 'the woman' **η γυναίκα** [i ghinéka] is of feminine gender, and 'the child' **το παιδί** [to peTHí] is of neuter gender. See also **article**, **case**, **inflection**, and **noun** in this section, Grammar summary, section 1 and Units 1 and 3.

imperative   The imperative is the form of the verb used to give directions, instructions, orders, or commands, e.g. 'come here', 'go there', or 'get up'. See also Grammar summary, section 7 and Unit 5.

infinitive   The infinitive is the basic form of the verb. This is the form that you will find entered in a dictionary. In Greek, infinitives usually end in -ω [o], -αω/-ω [ao/o], -μαι [me], and -ει [i]. See also **verb**.

inflection or **inflexion**   This is an ending or other element in a word that shows its grammatical function (whether singular or plural, masculine, feminine, or neuter, subject or object, and so on). For example the 's' in 'books' or 'he walks'. Greek uses many more inflections compared to English. See also **case**.

interjections   Interjections are words that give flavour or emphasis in a statement or question, e.g. 'aha' for understanding, or 'hm' for uncertainty.

noun and **proper noun** (or **proper name**)   A noun is the name of a person, place or thing. Words like '*John*', '*Mary*', '*England*', '*Greece*', or '*table*' and '*house*' are all nouns. The names of persons or places are called *proper nouns* and are spelled with an initial capital letter. In English, most nouns can be used with an article, except the proper nouns, whereas in Greek all nouns, including proper names, will take an article. For example, England **η Αγγλία** [i anglía] is literally 'the England'! See also **gender**, **inflection**, **case**, and **article** and Grammar summary, section 2.

object   See **word order** for further explanation.

personal pronoun   As their name suggests, personal pronouns refer to persons, e.g. 'I, you, she, we, they'. In English, these pronouns are necessary to make a distinction between 'I speak' and 'we speak' whereas in Greek the verb ending will make that distinction. In Greek, personal pronouns are mostly used with a verb only for emphasis. See also **pronouns**, Grammar summary, section 5 and Units 2 and 6.

plural   See **singular** for further explanation and Unit 3.

possessive   Words like 'my, his, our, their' are called possessives, as are words such as 'mine, yours, ours', etc. See also **pronoun**, Grammar summary, section 5 and Unit 7.

preposition   Words like 'on, in, to', etc. are called prepositions. They usually show the position of something and normally precede a **noun** or **pronoun**. See also Grammar summary, section 6 and Unit 6.

pronoun   Important and frequent words like 'I/he', 'me/him', 'my/his', or 'mine/his' are pronouns. They often stand in the place of nouns which have already been mentioned. Pronouns are grouped in several sub-categories including **personal**, **reflexive**, **demonstrative**, and **possessive**.

proper name   See **noun**.

reflexive pronoun   Words like 'myself, yourself, ourselves' are called reflexive pronouns. See also **pronoun** and Grammar summary, section 5.

reflexive verb   A verb is reflexive when the subject and the object of that verb are one and the same, e.g. 'I shaved myself' instead of 'the barber shaved me'. Not all reflexive verbs in English happen to be reflexive in Greek. There are also some reflexive verbs in Greek, e.g. **κάθομαι** [káthome] (*to sit*) or **κοιμάμαι** [kimáme] (*to sleep*) which are not reflexive in English. See also **verb** and Unit 7.

singular   The terms **singular** and **plural** are used to make the contrast between 'one' and 'more than one thing' in nouns, e.g. 'book/books'.

subject   The term 'subject' expresses a relationship often between a noun or pronoun and the verb. See also **verb** and **word order**.

subjunctive or **subjunctive mood**   The subjunctive mood is rarely used in English today. In the example 'I insist that he come', 'he come' (not 'he comes') is in the subjunctive form of the verb. Greek uses the subjunctive much more frequently than English. See also **verb** and Unit 9.

superlative   The superlative is used for the most extreme version of a comparison. This usually means adding '-est' to the adjective or putting the word 'most' before it. For example, 'cheap → cheapest' or 'expensive → most expensive'. See also **adjective** and **comparative** and Summary in Unit 8.

tense   Most languages use change in the verb form to indicate an aspect of time. These changes in the verb are traditionally referred to as tense and the tenses may be past, present or future. This principle is carried out also in Greek verb forms expressing time in past, present, or future. See Units 10 and 12 for the simple past (I went), Unit 11 for the past continuous (I was going) and present perfect (I have gone), and Unit 12 for the past perfect (I had gone). See Units 1, 2, 4, 5, and 7 for the simple present (I go) and the present progressive (I am going). For the future tense, see Unit 8 (I will go). See also **imperative**, **reflexive verb**, **subjunctive** and **verb**.

verb   A verb denotes action, being, feeling, or sensation, e.g. 'I go, she is, we think, they exist'. The verb is always preceded by a single word or group of words usually either a noun or a pronoun, e.g. 'my mother cares' or 'she cares', which is often called the **subject** of the sentence. In this example for instance, the subject shows 'who' cares. English verbs cannot stand meaningfully without a subject, whereas Greek can do so more flexibly by changing the endings in the verb form. For example, **πάω** [páo] 'I go', **είναι** [íne] 'she is' or **νοιάζεται** [niázete] 'she cares'. See also **subject** and **tense** and Grammar summary, section 7.

word order   This refers to the correct sequence of words in a sentence. For example, in the sentence 'the book belongs to my father' there are two important points to note: first is the minimal word-units, which show which words belong together, in this case, 'the book', 'belongs' and 'to my father'; and second their inflexible sequence or rigid order in English, in this case the **subject** (the book) before the **verb** (belongs) and the verb before the **object** (to my father). In Greek, there is a similar notion about minimal word-units, but not about inflexible order of **subject–verb–object** sequence. The above example can be rendered in six different ways in Greek – the speaker places the part of the sentence that he/she would most like to emphasize at the beginning of the sentence. See also **subject**, **tense** and **verb** and Summary in Unit 4.

Grammar summary

This grammar summary is intended mainly to act as a reference guide to the language used in the course. It is by no means a complete grammar, although some elements in this section do not appear in the course and are included for learners who wish to progress a little further.

You can skim through this section before you start Unit 1 and you can always refer back whenever you meet a new grammatical point in a unit and compare it with the notes here. Grammatical explanations in the **Grammar** section in the course are somewhat short and to the point, with some examples for practical application. Here the approach is different and more organized and systematic in terms of grouping grammatical points together.

The most important grammatical groups outlined in this section are: **Articles**, **Nouns**, **Adjectives**, **Adverbs**, **Pronouns**, **Prepositions** and **Verbs**. In most instances you will find tables to which the different groups belong, along with a few examples and direct references back to units.

1 Articles

The words *a*, *an* and *the* are called **articles** in English. *A* and *an* are called **indefinite articles** and *the* is called the **definite article**. All articles come before a noun. Greek articles have a lot more than three forms! This is because the nouns they define are divided into three genders: masculine (m), feminine (f) and neuter (n). The Greek words for *a*, *an* and *the* are therefore different for each gender. This is one of the reasons that all nouns in the course are given with their gender, i.e. (m), (f) or (n). In addition, each noun group has further forms in the singular and plural, so the articles have to agree with these, too.

Greek also has different endings for **nouns** and their articles (and adjectives – see below) when nouns are used in different ways within a sentence – for example, if they are the subject or the object of the sentence. These different forms of nouns are called **cases**. There are three main cases: nominative (nom) – the subject of the sentence; genitive (gen) – this shows possession, that something belongs to someone; and accusative (acc) – the object of the sentence. English grammar has virtually lost all examples of case. The English word 'who' is perhaps the only one that can actually illustrate this idea. It is 'who' in the nominative case, 'whose' in the genitive case and 'whom' in the accusative case. The following tables show the different forms of Greek articles.

INDEFINITE ARTICLE *A/AN*

	Masculine	Feminine	Neuter
(nom)	ένας (énas)	μία (mía)	ένα (éna)
(gen)	ενός (enós)	μίας (mías)	ενός (enós)
(acc)	έναν (énan)	μία (mía)	ένα (éna)

DEFINITE ARTICLE *THE*

	Singular			Plural		
	Masculine	**Feminine**	**Neuter**	**Masculine**	**Feminine**	**Neuter**
(nom)	ο (o)	η (i)	το (to)	οι (i)	οι (i)	τα (ta)
(gen)	του (tu)	της (tis)	του (tu)	των (ton)	των (ton)	των (ton)
(acc)	το(ν) (to(n))	τη(ν) (ti(n))	το (to)	τους (tus)	τις (tis)	τα (ta)

Articles are often used with the preposition **σε** (se) *at, to, in, on,* creating compound definite articles in the genitive and accusative cases only. The words in the singular are: **στου** (stu), **στης** (stis), **στο(ν)** (sto(n)), **στη(ν)** (sti(n)), and in plural: **στων** (ston), **στους** (stus), **στις** (stis), **στα** (sta). These compound words cannot stand as two separate words, e.g. **σε + του** (se) **+** (tu).

2 Nouns

The names of people and things are called **nouns**. As stated above, Greek nouns are divided into three genders, and each gender has a singular and plural form, and changes according to the role it plays in the sentence (its case) – nominative, genitive, accusative. When you look up nouns in a dictionary you will find them in the nominative singular form. You can usually tell their gender by their endings. Most masculine nouns end in **-ας** (-as), **-ης** (-is) and **-ος** (-os), most feminine nouns in **-α** (-a) and **-η** (-i), and most neuter nouns in **-ι** (-i), **-ο** (-o) and **-μα** (-ma). The course has introduced most nouns in the nominative case either in singular or plural. Some genitive and accusative forms have appeared in a few dialogues without any special mention. As a rule of thumb, remember that nouns in the nominative case come before the verb and indicate the subject of the sentence, nouns in the accusative case come after the verb and indicate the object. The genitive case is used to show possession. The different forms are set out below:

MASCULINE NOUNS

	Singular	Plural
(nom)	ο φίλος (o fílos)	οι φίλοι (i fíli)
(gen)	του φίλου (tu fílu)	των φίλων (ton fílon)
(acc)	τον φίλο (ton fílo)	τους φίλους (tus fílus)

FEMININE NOUNS

	Singular	Plural
(nom)	η κουζίνα (i kuzína)	οι κουζίνες (i kuzínes)
(gen)	της κουζίνας (tis kuzínas)	των κουζινών (ton kuzinón)
(acc)	την κουζίνα (tin kuzína)	τις κουζίνες (tis kuzínes)

	Singular	Plural
(nom)	το βιβλίο (to vivlío)	τα βιβλία (ta vivlía)
(gen)	του βιβλίου (tu vivlíu)	των βιβλίων (ton vivlíon)
(acc)	το βιβλίο (to vivlío)	τα βιβλία (ta vivlía)

3 Adjectives

Adjectives are words which *describe* people or things. They give more information about the noun they describe. Note: a car (noun), a big car (adjective-noun), a big red car (adjective-adjective-noun). The endings of adjectives change according to the noun they describe, i.e. masculine, feminine or neuter endings, singular or plural, nominative, genitive, accusative. Most adjectives have the same endings as the word **μεγάλος** (meghálos) *big* below:

SINGULAR

	Masculine	Feminine	Neuter
(nom)	μεγάλος (meghálos)	μεγάλη (meghÁli)	μεγάλο (meghálo)
(gen)	μεγάλου (meghálu)	μεγάλης (meghÁlis)	μεγάλου (meghálu)
(acc)	μεγάλο (meghálo)	μεγάλη (meghÁli)	μεγάλο (meghálo)

PLURAL

	Masculine	Feminine	Neuter
(nom)	μεγάλοι (meghÁli)	μεγάλες (megháles)	μεγάλα (meghála)
(gen)	μεγάλων (meghálon)	μεγάλων (meghálon)	μεγάλων (meghálon)
(acc)	μεγάλους (meghálus)	μεγάλες (megháles)	μεγάλα (meghála)

4 Adverbs

Adverbs are words which usually describe *the way* things happen. Unlike adjectives, which give more information about the *nouns* they describe, adverbs give more information about the *verbs* they describe. Many Greek adverbs end in **-α** (-a) or **-ως** (-os), something similar to the English ending *-ly* for many English adverbs. Some examples include: **γρήγορα** (ghríghora) *quickly*, **καλά** (kalá) *well, nicely*, **βέβαια** (vévea) *of course/surely*.

Many Greek adverbs are formed from their corresponding adjective. Notice the changes below: **γρήγορος** (ghríghoros) *fast, quick* → **γρήγορα** (ghríghora) *quickly*, **καλός** (kalós) *good, nice* → **καλά** (kalá) *nicely*, **βέβαιος** (véveos) *certain, sure* → **βέβαια** (vévea) *surely*. Unlike adjectives, adverbs have only one form. An exception to this are a few adjectives which have two almost similar forms which are interchangeable in use. Some examples are **βέβαια** (vévea) and **βεβαίως** (vevéos) *of course, surely* and **σπάνια** (spánia) and **σπανίως** (spaníos) *rarely*.

Adverbs are often 'doubled up' for the purpose of emphasis, e.g. **γρήγορα – γρήγορα** (ghríghora – ghríghora) *very quickly* or **σπάνια – σπάνια** (spánia – spánia) *very rarely*.

5 Pronouns

Important and frequent words like *I*, *you*, *he* or *my*, *your*, *his* or *myself*, *yourself*, *himself* or *me*, *you*, *him* etc. are pronouns. Pronouns are grouped in several sub-categories: personal, reflexive, demonstrative, possessive, relative, interrogative and indefinite pronouns.

PERSONAL PRONOUNS

	Nominative		Genitive		Accusative	
	strong	**weak**	**strong**	**weak**	**strong**	**weak**
I	εγώ (eghó)	–	εμένα (eména)	μου (moo)	εμένα (eména)	με (me)
you	εσύ (esí)	–	εσένα (eséna)	σου (soo)	εσένα (eséna)	σε (se)
he	αυτός (aftós)	τος (tos)	αυτού (aftú)	του (tu)	αυτόν (aftón)	τον (ton)
she	αυτή (aftí)	τη (ti)	αυτής (aftís)	της (tis)	αυτή(ν) (aftí(n))	τη(ν) (ti(n))
it	αυτό (aftó)	το (to)	αυτού (aftú)	του (tu)	αυτό (aftó)	το (to)
we	εμείς (emís)	–	εμάς (emás)	μας (mas)	εμάς (emás)	μας (mas)
you (pl)	εσείς (esís)	–	εσάς (esás)	σας (sas)	εσάς (esás)	σας (sas)
they	αυτοί (aftí)	τοι (ti)	αυτών (aftón)	τους (tus)	αυτούς (aftús)	τους (tus)
	αυτές (aftés)	τες (tes)			αυτές (aftés)	τις/τες (tis/tes)
	αυτά (aftá)	τα (ta)			αυτά (aftá)	τα (ta)

The personal pronouns have both a strong and a weak form in the genitive and accusative cases.

Most Greek verbs like **έχω** (ého) *I have* take the nominative form of the personal pronoun, which is not absolutely necessary as it is in English, because the ending of the verb itself shows who is the subject. Some verbs like **μου αρέσει** (mu arési) I *like* or **με λένε** (me léne) *I am called* take the accusative form of the personal pronoun. All strong forms are used for the purpose of emphasis in Greek. Actually it is possible to use both the strong and weak form for extra emphasis. E.g. **εμένα μου αρέσει το ράδιο** (eména mu arési to ráTHio) *(I) like the radio* or **εμένα με λένε Δημήτρη** (eména me léne THimítri) *(I) am called Dimitri*.

REFLEXIVE PRONOUNS

Words like *myself*, *yourself*, etc. are reflexive pronouns. They are not as common in Greek as in English and they usually appear only in the accusative form with prepositions, e.g. **με τον εαυτό μου** (me ton eaftó mu) <u>with</u> *myself*, **για τον εαυτό της** (ya ton eaftó tis) <u>for</u> *herself*, **στον (σε+ τον) εαυτό τους** (ston eaftó tus) <u>to</u> *themselves*.

DEMONSTRATIVE PRONOUNS

	Masculine	Feminine	Neuter
this	αυτός (aftós)	αυτή (aftí)	αυτό (aftó)
these	αυτοί (aftí)	αυτές (aftés)	αυτά (aftá)
that	εκείνος (ekínos)	εκείνη (ekíni)	εκείνο (ekíno)
those	εκείνοι (ekíni)	εκείνες (ekínes)	εκείνα (ekína)
such a	τέτοιος (tétios)	τέτοια (tétia)	τέτοιο (tétio)
such + pl	τέτοιοι (tétyi)	τέτοιες (téties)	τέτοια (tétia)
so much	τόσος (tósos)	τόση (tósi)	τόσο (tóso)
so many	τόσοι (tósi)	τόσες (tóses)	τόσα (tósa)

▶ The different forms in the singular and plural for **αυτός, εκείνος** and **τόσος** are identical with the adjective **μεγάλος, -η, -ο** as shown in the previous paragraph in this section.

▶ The demonstrative pronouns **αυτός** and **εκείνος** need the corresponding article for the noun in use, e.g. **αυτός ο άντρας** (aftós o ándras) *this man*, **εκείνη η γυναίκα** (ekíni i ghinéka) *that woman*, **αυτά τα παιδιά** (aftá ta peTHiá) *these children*.

POSSESSIVE PRONOUNS

my	μου (mu)
your (sing/infml)	σου (su)
his	του (tu)
her	της (tis)
its	του (tu)
our	μας (mas)
your (pl/fml)	σας (sas)
their	τους (tus)

Possessive pronouns have only one form in Greek. They always come after the noun they modify, whereas in English they come before the noun. In Greek, the noun is accompanied by its corresponding article, e.g. **το σπίτι μου** (to spíti mu) *my house*, **τα σπίτια μας** (ta spítia mas) *our houses*, **ο φίλος της** (o fílos tis) *her friend*, **οι φίλοι τους** (i fíli tus) *their friends*.

These words are called possessive pronouns in Greek grammar and possessive adjectives in English grammar!

RELATIVE PRONOUNS

The words below are the most common relative pronouns in Greek.

who	που (pu)
which	που (pu)
that	που (pu)
whatever	ό,τι (óti)

INTERROGATIVE PRONOUNS

Question words like *what? who? how? where?* are interrogative pronouns. Some have only one form, some more than one for m/f/n use.

what?	τι; (ti)?
where?	πού; (pu)?
how?	πώς; (pos)?
why?	γιατί; (yiatí)?
when?	πότε; (póte)?

	Masculine	Feminine	Neuter
who? which?	ποιος; (pios)?	ποια; (pia)?	ποιο; (pio)?
how much?	πόσος; (pósos)?	πόση; (pósi)?	πόσο; (póso)?
which ones?	ποιοι; (pii)?	ποιες; (pies)?	ποια; (pia)?
how many?	πόσοι; (pósi)?	πόσες; (póses)?	πόσα; (pósa)?

INDEFINITE PRONOUNS

Words like *each one, everyone, someone, no-one,* etc. are indefinite pronouns. Some have only one form, some more than one for m/f/n use.

all, everything	όλα (óla) + plural
something, anything	κάτι (káti)
nothing, anything	τίποτε (típote)
every, each	κάθε (káthe)

	Masculine	Feminine	Neuter
everyone **(m/f/n)**	καθένας (kathénas)	καθεμία (kathemía)	καθένα (kath éna)
everybody **(m/f/n) + (pl)**	όλοι (óli)	όλες (óles)	όλα (óla)
some **(pl)**	μερικοί (merikí)	μερικές (merikés)	μερικά (meriká)
someone, something **(m/f/n)**	κάποιος (kápios)	κάποια (kápia)	κάποιο (kápio)
one, one (person) **(m/f/n)**	κανείς (kanís)	καμία (kamía)	κανένα (kanéna)
no-one, nothing **(m/f/n)**	κανένας (kanénas)	καμία (kamía)	κανένα (kanéna)

6 Prepositions

Prepositions in English are such words as *between, from, in, by, for, with,* etc. All corresponding Greek prepositions have only one form. The word following Greek prepositions will sometimes be followed by a noun in the genitive or more often in the accusative case. Some frequent prepositions are:

GENITIVE

εναντίον	(enandíon)	*against*
μεταξύ	(metaksí)	*between*
υπέρ	(ipér)	*in favour, for*

ACCUSATIVE

από	(apó)	*from*
για	(ya)	*for, to, over*
με	(me)	*with, by*
χωρίς	(horís)	*without*
μετά	(metá)	*after*
μέχρι	(méhri)	*until*
πριν	(prin)	*before*
προς	(pros)	*towards*
σε	(se)	*to, in, on, at (place)*
στις	(stis)	*at (time)*

There are also some two-word prepositions. All of them are followed by nouns in the accusative.

ACCUSATIVE

πάνω από	(páno apó)	*over, above*
κάτω από	(káto apó)	*underneath, below*
μπροστά από	(brostá apó)	*in front of*
πίσω από	(píso apó)	*behind*
κοντά σε	(kondá se)	*close to*
δίπλα σε	(THípla se)	*next to*
γύρω από	(ghíro apó)	*around from*
μέσα σε	(mésa se)	*inside*
έξω από	(ékso apó)	*outside, out of*

7 Verbs

Words that indicate action, being, or feeling are called verbs. **Κάνω** (káno) *I do*, **μιλάω** (miláo) *I speak* or **μένω** (méno) *I live* are three examples from the several verbs this course includes.

Remember that a dictionary will list these three verbs, and all others, using the *I* form of the verb in the present tense. This is the main form used for reference to Greek verbs (as the infinitive form in English – *to do, to speak, to live*, etc. – does not exist in Greek). Verb tenses refer to different points in time, such as the present, the future and the past. This course relies mostly on present tense, touches on the future and past tenses, and introduces some verb forms after the word **να** (na) *to* and imperatives.

Also, remember that personal pronouns, words like *I*, *he*, *they*, etc. in English, are not necessary in Greek because of the change in the verb ending. So, **κάνω** can be seen as **κάν-** (the verb stem which remains unchanged) and **-ω** (the verb ending which tells you whether *I*, *he*, *they*, etc. is performing the action). There are principally two verb endings in Greek for the I form: **-ω** (-o) and **μαι** (-me), e.g. **περιμένω** (periméno) *I wait* and **κάθομαι** (káthome) *I sit*. The course introduces you to the main verb groups (or conjugations – there are two main conjugations) in both the active voice (verbs ending in **-ω**) and the passive voice (verbs ending in **-ομαι/-αμαι**).

The present tense for the main verb groups found in the course are set out below. Once you memorize the different endings, you will be confident enough to use them in context. Remember that the majority of Greek verbs fall into the first conjugation.

Present tense

Active voice

1 Conjugation

έχω (ého)	I have	**θέλω** (thélo)	I want
έχεις (éhis)	you have	**θέλεις** (thélis)	you want
έχει (éhi)	he/she/it has	**θέλει** (théli)	he/she/it wants
έχουμε (éhume)	we have	**θέλουμε** (thélume)	we want
έχετε (éhete)	you have	**θέλετε** (thélete)	you want
έχουν (éhun)	they have	**θέλουν(ε)** (thélun(e))	they want

2 Conjugation

Group A		**Group B**	
πεινάω/πεινώ (pináo/pinó)	I am hungry	**μπορώ** (boró)	I can
πεινάς (pinás)	you are hungry	**μπορείς** (borís)	you can
πεινά(ει) (piná(i))	he/she/it is hungry	**μπορεί** (borí)	he/she/it can
πεινάμε (pináme)	we are hungry	**μπορούμε** (borúme)	we can
πεινάτε (pináte)	you are hungry	**μπορείτε** (boríte)	you can
πεινούν(ε) (pinún(e))	they are hungry	**μπορούν(ε)** (borún(e))	they can

Both groups in the second conjugation include verbs always stressed on the last syllable in their main form.

Passive voice

χαίρομαι (hérome)	*I am glad*	**λυπάμαι** (lipáme)	*I am sorry*
χαίρεσαι (hérese)	*you are glad*	**λυπάσαι** (lipáse)	*you are sorry*
χαίρεται (hérete)	*he/she/it is glad*	**λυπάται** (lipáte)	*he/she/ it is sorry*
χαιρόμαστε (herómaste)	*we are glad*	**λυπόμαστε** (lipómaste)	*we are sorry*
χαίρεστε (héreste)	*you are glad*	**λυπάστε** (lipáste)	*you are sorry*
χαίρονται (héronde)	*they are glad*	**λυπούνται** (lipúnde)	*they are sorry*

All verbs in the passive voice end in **-μαι** (me).

Future tense

The future tense in Greek is formed with the particle **θα** (tha) (equivalent to *will* in English) and the verb. Some verbs do not change their form in the future tense, but most do. Below you see a list of verbs belonging to both groups:

Verbs without any different form in the future

θα είμαι (tha íme) *I will be*, **θα έχω** (tha ého) *I will have*, **θα ξέρω** (tha kséro) *I will know* and **θα πάω** (tha páo) *I will go*.

Verbs with a different form in the future

Most verbs belong to this sub-group. Some are:

δίνω	→ **θα**	**δώσω**	(tha THóso)	*I will give*
θέλω	→ **θα**	**θελήσω**	(tha thelíso)	*I will want*
μένω	→ **θα**	**μείνω**	(tha míno)	*I will stay*
παίρνω	→ **θα**	**πάρω**	(tha páro)	*I will take*
στέλνω	→ **θα**	**στείλω**	(tha stílo)	*I will send*
φέρνω	→ **θα**	**φέρω**	(tha féro)	*I will bring*
φεύγω	→ **θα**	**φύγω**	(tha fígho)	*I will leave*

Verbs with an irregular form in the future

Some verbs have a completely new form in the future. Some are:

βλέπω	→ **θα**	**δω**	(tha THO)	*I will see*
έρχομαι	→ **θα**	**έρθω**	(tha értho)	*I will come*
ζω	→ **θα**	**ζήσω**	(tha zíso)	*I will live*
τρώω	→ **θα**	**φάω**	(tha fáo)	*I will eat*
χαίρομαι	→ **θα**	**χαρώ**	(tha haró)	*I will be glad*

The different endings for *I*, *he/she/it*, *you*, etc. are the same as those in the present tense. Below are two verbs **έχω** and **στέλνω** with their full forms in the future:

θα έχω (tha ého)	I will have	**θα στείλω** (tha stílo)	I will send
θα έχεις (tha échis)	you will have	**θα στείλεις** (tha stílis)	you will send
θα έχει (tha échi)	he/she it will have	**θα στείλει** (tha stíli)	he/she/it will send
θα έχουμε (tha éhume)	we will have	**θα στείλουμε** (tha stílume)	we will send
θα έχετε (tha éhete)	you will have	**θα στείλετε** (tha stílete)	you will send
θα έχουν (tha éhun)	they will have	**θα στείλουν** (tha stílun)	they will send

Here again is the future tense for **είμαι** (íme), the verb *to be*:

θα είμαι	(tha íme)	I will be
θα είσαι	(tha íse)	you will be
θα είναι	(tha íne)	he/she/it will be
θα είμαστε	(tha ímaste)	we will be
θα είσαστε/είστε	(tha ísaste)/(íste)	you will be
θα είναι	(tha íne)	they will be

Past tense

Unit 10 presented many aspects of the past tense in Greek. Here you are provided with the full conjugation of two frequent verbs in the past tense: **κάνω – έκανα** (káno – ékana) (*to do*) and **ξέρω – ήξερα** (kséro – íksera) (to know).

έκανα (ékana)	I did	**ήξερα** (íksera)	I knew
έκανες (ékanes)	you did	**ήξερες** (íkseres)	you knew
έκανε (ékane)	s/he/it did	**ήξερε** (íksere)	s/he/it knew
κάναμε (káname)	we did	**ξέραμε** (ksérame)	we knew
κάνατε (kánate)	you did	**ξέρατε** (ksérate)	you knew
έκαναν (ékanan)	they did	**ήξεραν** (íkseran)	they knew

The imperative form

The imperative is a form of the verb you can use to request, tell or order someone to do something, e.g. 'Come here!', 'Stop!', 'Don't speak!', 'Turn left!', 'Go now!'. This form is very frequent and important in everyday language. Remember that since Greek has two 'you' forms (informal–singular and formal–plural) like many other languages including German, French or Spanish, you need to learn two individual words for the imperatives.

(sing/infml)	(pl/fml)	
πήγαινε (píghene)!	πηγαίνετε (pighénete)!	*Go!*
στρίψε (strípse)!	στρίψτε (strípste)!	*Turn!*
βγες (vghes)!	βγείτε (vghíte)!	*Get off! Get out!*
συνέχισε (sinéchise)!	συνεχίστε (sinechíste)!	*Continue!*
σταμάτησε (stamátise)!	σταματήστε (stamatíste)!	*Stop!*
περπάτησε (perpátise)!	περπατήστε (perpatíste)!	*Walk!*
οδήγησε (oTHíghise)!	οδηγήστε (oTHighíste)!	*Drive!*

Index of grammatical terms and thematic vocabulary

Greek history timeline

Timeline	Events
3200 BC–2200 BC	Bronze Age in Cyclades and Crete
2000 BC–1700 BC	First Greek speakers; Golden Age and palaces in Crete
1600 BC–1200 BC	The beginning and end of the Mycenaean culture
776 BC	First Olympic Games
500 BC–400 BC	Parthenon was built; Golden Age under Pericles; drama flourishes with Aeschylus, Sophocles, and Euripedes
400 BC–300 BC	Plato's Academy was founded; time of Alexander the Great
200 BC–AD 300	The Roman Empire
AD 300–1200	Constantinople was built; Crusaders
1453–1821	Ottoman Empire; Greek independence
1912–1913	Balkan Wars
1914–1945	World Wars I and II
1945–1949	Civil War
1967–1974	Military junta in power
1974–present	Democracy returns to Greece
1982	Greece becomes a member of the European Union
2004	Olympic Games in Athens

Greek language timeline

Timeline	Events
2000 BC	**Ancient Greek.** Greek belongs to the large family of Indo-European or Indo-Hittite languages. It developed across the Balkan peninsula around 2000 BC. The language has undergone enormous phonological, morphological, lexical, and syntactical changes coming into contact with neighbouring and faraway nations and people speaking many different languages. The Greek alphabet is believed to have derived from the Semitic alphabet, specifically that of Phoenicians.
1100 BC	**Archaic Greek.** The Phoenician alphabet which was introduced to Greece around 1100 BC contained 22 separate signs for the consonants but none for the vowels. The Greeks innovated the letters, α, ε, ι, ο, υ, with the value of vowels as known today. Texts were written in syllabic script.
800 BC–500 BC	**Classical Greek.** The alphabet, which started replacing the syllabic script, continued to undergo many reforms and changes. The most notable change was the changing of the direction of writing from left to right instead of from right to left. City states had many different language variations at the time but the four main groups or dialects were the following: **Arcado-Cypriot, Doric, Aeolic,** and **Ionic-Attic.**
400 BC	**Hellenistic Greek.** The Ionic form of the alphabet was adopted by most city states, thus making a uniformed alphabet throughout the Greek world. During Hellenistic times the Greek alphabet has served as a model for the Latin and Cyrillic alphabet. The Attic dialect, actually an offspring of the Ionic, finally dominated the other dialects in the first century when philosophers such as Aristotle, Plato, and Socrates made Athens the centre of the Greek civilization.
100 BC–AD 337	In this period and especially close to AD 337, a new form of the Attic dialect appeared with simpler syntax and morphology, a stress accent, and loan words from Latin and Semitic origins. This was the Koine (the common) dialect also called the **Hellenistic Koine** or the **Alexandrian Koine.** Hellenistic Greek is the form also known as **New Testament Greek** (in which the Gospel and other books of the New Testament of the Bible were first written).
AD 337–1453	**Byzantine Greek**. This was both an imperial and an ecclesiastical language. It is still the ecclesiastical language of the Greek Orthodox church today.

1453 to present	**Modern Greek**. The majority of the foreign words in the Greek language are of Turkish origin because of the occupation from 1453–1821. After 1821, the language was principally divided into the general vernacular (**Demotiki**), and the language of education and literature (**Katharevousa**), which existed in parallel development for twenty centuries and competed for acceptance and establishment for about 150 years after the Turkish occupation. Demotic Greek prevailed as the everday spoken language whereas Katharevousa continued in government and scientific books. Demotic Greek was proclaimed the official language of Greece in 1977 and the use of one stress mark instead of five took place in 1982. Classical Greek word forms continue to have a great influence in the world's scientific and technical vocabulary, and make up a large part of the technical vocabulary of English.

Taking it further

This section gives you many suggestions of sources to help you develop your interest in Greek language and culture. It also provides you with a number of email addresses and Internet sites which can give a different dimension to your search. Some of the sites listed are bilingual but others are only in Greek. Good luck!

BOOKS

If you are in Athens, check out Eleftheroudakis bookshop at 16 Panepistimiou St. for the largest selection of books in English about Greek or Greece. (Their website is **www.books.gr**) The National Book Centre of Greece issues a bi-monthly magazine promoting Greek books in translation abroad. They can be found at 76 Emmanuil Benaki St. Stoa tou Bibliou, Pesmazoglou 5 or at **http://www.ekebi.gr.** The free *Travelling in Greece* brochure is very informative and available from any GNTO office in Greece or abroad. Their address is 2 Amerikis St. and their Internet address is below under the Travel heading. Check out **www.toubis.gr** for the largest selection of maps or travel books in English on Greece.

CULTURAL HERITAGE

www.greece.org is a sophisticated online magazine about Greece. **www.culture.gr** is the website of the Ministry of Culture and hosts many of the country's museums. **www.reconstructions.org** has fabulous 3-D models of the Parthenon. **www.fhr.gr** is the website of the Foundation of the Hellenic World. **www.pbs.org/empires/thegreeks** brings Ancient Greece alive. **www.sae.gr** is the site for the World Council of Hellenes Abroad.

TRANSPORT

www.gtp.gr gives ferry timetables. **www.ose.gr** offers train information. **ktelattikis.gr/** gives bus timetables and routes. **www.aia.gr** is the website for Athens airport. **www.olympicair.com, www.aegean.com,** and **www.airtickets.gr, www.airmanos.gr, www.cronus.gr, or www. airgreece.gr** offer flight information.

TRAVEL

The Greek National Tourism Organization can be found under **www.gnto.gr.** You can also access **www.travelling.gr** or **www.greekislands.gr** for travel agencies, tourist offices and tourist attractions. **www.ntua.gr/weather** offers frequently updated information on the weather. The site **www.allhotels.gr** offers hotel accommodation all over Greece.

GREEK LANGUAGE

Information about online Greek language courses can be obtained from **www.polyglot24. com.** If you are interested in Greek poetry in English, send an e-mail to **poetrygreece@ hotmail.com.** The site **www.greeklanguage.gr** will connect you to the Greek Language

Centre of the Ministry of Education which can offer valuable information about Greek classes or language examinations. An interesting site is also from the University of Thessaloniki at **www. smg.web.auth.gr**. **www.cyathens.org** is a study-abroad-programme of the College Year in Athens.

MISCELLANEOUS

www.greekcuisine.com offers an extensive array of Greek recipes. **www.greekwine.gr** lists several Greek wines from all over Greece. **www.athensnews.gr** is a daily newspaper in English. **www.in.gr** is a Greek portal on the web for Greek speakers. **www.athens.olympic.org** is an important site for everyone interested in the Olympic Games in Athens in 2004. Some sites for Greek music are: **www.e-radio.gr, www.babylon.gr**, **www.avpolis.gr** or **www.mad.gr**. Online auctions can be found at **www.fleamarket.gr**. Greek comics can be purchased at **www.arkas.gr**.

English–Greek glossary

(Note: m = masculine, f = feminine, n = neuter)

a.m.	(pi-mi)	π.μ.
a/an/one	(énas), (mía), (éna)	ένας, μία, ένα
about/approximately	(perípu)	περίπου
across/opposite	(apénandi)	απέναντι
adventure story/thriller	(peripétia)	περιπέτεια (f)
afterwards, later	(metá)	μετά
again	(páli) (ksaná)	πάλι/ξανά
agree	(simfonó)	συμφωνώ
aeroplane	(aeropláno)	αεοπλάνο (n)
airport	(aeroTHrómio)	αεροδρόμιο (n)
almost	(sheTHón)	σχεδόν
along/together	(mazí)	μαζί
always	(pánda)	πάντα
America	(amerikí)	Αμερική (f)
and	(ke)	και
angry	(thimoménos, -i, -o)	θυμωμένος, / -η/ -ο
another, more	(álos, -i, -o)	άλλος, / -η/ -ο
anything	(otiTHípote)	οτιδήποτε
anything?	(típota)?	τίποτα;
apartment building	(polikatikía)	πολυκατοικία (f)
apartment/flat	(THiamérizma)	διαμέρισμα (n)
appetizer, starter	(orektikó)	ορεκτικό (n)
April	(aprílios)	Απρίλιος (m)
architect	(architéktonas)	αρχιτέκτονας (m/f)
area	(hóros)	χώρος (m)
armchair	(polithróna)	πολυθρόνα (f)
around, about	(ghíro)	γύρω
arrive	(ftháno)	φθάνω
as	(ópos) (san)	όπως/σαν
Athens	(athína)	Αθήνα (f)
August	(ávghustos)	Αύγουστος (m)
Australia	(afstralía)	Αυστραλία (f)

autumn/fall	(fthinóporo)	φθινόπωρο (n)
availability	(THiathesimótita)	διαθεσιμότητα (f)
baby	(moró)	μωρό (n)
baby boy	(bébis)	μπέμπης (m)
baby girl	(béba)	μπέμπα (f)
balcony/porch	(balkóni)	μπαλκόνι (n)
banana	(banána)	μπανάνα (f)
bank	(trápeza)	τράπεζα (f)
basement	(ipóghio)	υπόγειο (n)
basketball	(básket)	μπάσκετ (n)
bass (fish)	(lavráki)	λαβράκι (n)
bathroom, bathtub	(bánio)	μπάνιο (n)
bathroom, toilet	(tualéta)	τουαλέτα (f)
be	(íme)	είμαι
be able	(boró)	μπορώ
be glad	(hérome)	χαίρομαι
be happy	(hérome)	χαίρομαι
be interested	(enTHiaférome)	ενδιαφέρομαι
be pleased	(hérome)	χαίρομαι
beach	(plaz)(paralía)	πλαζ, παραλία (f)
bean	(fasóli)	φασόλι (n)
beautiful, nice	(oréos/ -a/ -o)	ωραίος/ -α/ -ο
bed	(kreváti)	κρεβάτι (n)
bedroom	(krevatokámara)	κρεβατοκάμαρα (f)
bedroom	(ipnoTHomátio)	υπνοδωμάτιο (n)
beef	(mosharísios/ -a/ -o)	μοσχαρίσιος/ -α/ -ο
beefsteak	(biftéki)	φιλέτο βοδινό (n)
beer	(bíra)	μπύρα (f)
behind	(píso)	πίσω
beige	(bez)	μπεζ
bell	(kuTHúni)	κουδούνι (n)
between	(metaksí)	μεταξύ
beverage, drink	(potó)	ποτό (n)
big, large	(meghálos/ -i/ -o)	μεγάλος/ -η/ -ο
bill	(loghariazmós)	λογαριασμός (m)
black	(mávros/ -i/ -o)	μαύρος/ -η/ -ο

block/square	(tetrághono)	τετράγωνο (n)
blue	(ble)	μπλε
blues (music)	(bluz)	μπλουζ (n)
boat	(várka)	βάρκα (f)
book	(vivlío)	βιβλίο (n)
bookshop	(vivliopolío)	βιβλιοπωλείο (n)
booklet	(filáTHio)	φυλλάδιο (n)
bottle	(bukáli)	μπουκάλι (n)
bottled (mineral) water	(emfialoméno neró)	εμφιαλωμένο νερό (n)
bouzouki (instrument)	(buzúki)	μπουζούκι (n)
boy	(aghóri)	αγόρι (n)
bravo	(brávo)	μπράβο
bread	(psomí)	ψωμί (n)
breakfast	(proinó)	πρωινό (n)
bridge	(ghéfira)	γέφυρα (f)
brother	(aTHelfós)	αδελφός (m)
brown	(kafé)	καφέ
bus	(leoforío)	λεωφορείο (n)
bus station	(stathmós leoforíon)	σταθμός λεωφορείων (m)
bus stop	(stási leoforíon)	στάση λεωφορείων (f)
busy	(apasholiménos/ -i/ -o)	απασχολημένος/ -η/ -ο
but	(alá)	αλλά
but	(ma)	μα
butter	(vútiro)	βούτυρο (n)
café	(kafetéria)	καφετέρια (f)
can	(boró)	μπορώ
can/tin	(kutí)	κουτί (n)
car	(aftokínito)	αυτοκίνητο (n)
car park	(párking)	πάρκινγκ (n)
card	(kárta)	κάρτα (f)
carrot	(karóto)	καρότο (n)
cash desk	(tamío)	ταμείο (n)
celery	(sélino)	σέλινο (n)
central	(kendrikós/ -í/ -ó)	κεντρικός/ -ή/ -ό
centre	(kéndro)	κέντρο (n)
century	(eónas)	αιώνας (m)

cereal	(THimitriaká)	δημητριακά (n/pl)
chair	(karékla)	καρέκλα (f)
changing room	(THokimastírio)	δοκιμαστήριο (n)
cheap	(fthinós/ -í/ -ó)	φθηνός/ -ή/ -ό
check	(eksetázo)	εξετάζω
checked	(karó)	καρώ (m/f/n)
cheque	(epitaghí)	επιταγή (f)
child	(peTHí)	παιδί (n)
church	(eklisía)	εκκλησία (f)
cigarette	(tsigháro)	τσιγάρο (n)
cinema	(sinemá)	σινεμά (n)
close to	(kondá)	κοντά
closed	(klistós/ -í/ -ó)	κλειστός/ -ή/ -ό
closet/wardrobe	(dulápa)	ντουλάπα (f)
coca cola	(kóka kóla)	κόκα κόλα (f)
coffee	(kafés)	καφές (m)
coffee house	(kafenío)	καφενείο (n)
coffee (medium sweet)	(métrios)	μέτριος (m)
coffee (sweet)	(ghlikós)	γλυκός (m)
coffee (without sugar)	(skétos)	σκέτος (m)
comedy	(komoTHía)	κωμωδία (f)
company	(etería)	εταιρεία (f)
computer	(kompiúter)	κομπιούτερ (n)
conservatory	(tzamaría)	τζαμαρία (f)
contrast, antithesis	(antíthesi)	αντίθεση (f)
cook	(maghirévo)	μαγειρεύω
cooked foods	(maghireftá)	μαγειρευτά (n/pl)
corner	(ghonía)	γωνία (f)
counter	(pángos)	πάγκος (m)
courgette, zucchini	(kolokitháki)	κολοκυθάκι (n)
cousin	(ksaTHélfi)	ξαδέλφη (f)
cousin	(ksáTHelfos)	ξάδελφος (m)
credit card	(pistotikí kárta)	πιστωτική κάρτα (f)
crème caramel	(krem karamelé)	κρεμ καραμελέ (n)
croissant	(kruasán)	κρουασάν (n)
cucumber	(angúri)	αγγούρι (n)
cup	(flitzáni)	φλυτζάνι (n)

currency	(nómizma)	νόμισμα (n)
customs	(telonío)	τελωνείο (n)
cutlet	(brizóla)	μπριζόλα (f)
dance (verb, noun)	(horévo) (horós)	χορεύω, χορός (m)
dark	(skúros/ -a/ -o)	σκούρος/ -α/ -ο
date	(imerominía)	ημερομηνία (f)
daughter	(kóri)	κόρη (f)
day	((i)méra)	(η)μέρα (f)
December	(THekémvrios)	Δεκέμβριος (m)
deposit, down payment	(prokatavolí)	προκαταβολή (f)
dessert	(ghlikó)	γλυκό, επιδόρπιο (n)
dialogue	(THiáloghos)	διάλογος (m)
difficult	(THískolos/ -i/ -o)	δύσκολος/ -η/ -ο
dill	(ánithos)	άνιθος (m)
dining room	(trapezaría)	τραπεζαρία
dinner	(vraTHinó)	βραδινό (n)
disagree	(THiafonó)	διαφωνώ
discotheque	(THiskothíki)	δισκοθήκη (f)
dislike	(antipathó)	αντιπαθώ
doctor	(yatrós)	γιατρός (m/f)
door	(pórta)	πόρτα (f)
dorado or gilthead (fish)	(tsipúra)	τσιπούρα (f)
double room	(THíklino)	δίκλινο (n)
down	(káto)	κάτω
dress	(fórema)	φόρεμα (n)
dress myself	(dínome)	ντύνομαι
drink	(píno)	πίνω
early	(norís)	νωρίς
easy	(éfkolos/ -i/ -o)	εύκολος/ -η/ -ο
eat	(tró-o)	τρώω
eight	(októ)/(ohtó)	οκτώ/οχτώ
eight hundred	(oktakósia)/(ohtakósia)	οκτακόσια/οχτακόσια
eighteen	(THekaoktó)	δεκαοκτώ
eighty	(oghTHónda)	ογδόντα
eleven	(éndeka)	έντεκα

England	(anglía)	Αγγλία (f)
English (language)	(angliká)	αγγλικά (n/pl)
entrance	(ísoTHos)	είσοδος (f)
envelope	(fákelos)	φάκελος (m)
euro	(evró)	ευρώ
evening	(vráTHi)	βράδυ (n)
ever	(poté)	ποτέ
every	(káthe)	κάθε
everything/all	(óla)	όλα
everywhere	(pandú)	παντού
exactly	(akrivós)	ακριβώς
excuse me	(sighnómi)	συγνώμη
excuse me/pardon me	(me sinhoríte)	με συγχωρείτε (pl/fml)
exit	(éksoTHos)	έξοδος (f)
fall	(péfto)	πέφτω
family	(ikoghénia)	οικογένεια (f)
father	(patéras)	πατέρας (m)
February	(fevruários)	Φεβρουάριος (m)
ferry	(féribot)	φέρυμποτ (n)
fifteen	(THekapénde)	δεκαπέντε
fifth	(pémptos/ -i/ -o)	πέμπτος/ -η/ -ο
fifty	(penínda)	πενήντα
film (movie)	(érgho)	έργο (n)
film (camera)	(film)	φιλμ (n)
finally	(teliká)	τελικά
finish	(telióno)	τελειώνω
first	(prótos/ -i/ -o)	πρώτος/ -η/ -ο
fish	(psári)	ψάρι (n)
fish restaurant	(psarotavérna)	ψαροταβέρνα (f)
five	(pénde)	πέντε
five hundred	(pendakósia)	πεντακόσια
flat, apartment	(THiamérizma)	διαμέρισμα (n)
flight	(ptísi)	πτήση (f)
floor	(órofos)	όροφος (m)
flying dolphin, hydrofoil	(iptámeno)	ιπτάμενο (n)
football	(poTHósfero)	ποδόσφαιρο (n)

for	(ya)	για
fork	(pirúni)	πιρούνι (n)
fortnight	(THekapenthímero)	δεκαπενθήμερο (n)
forty	(saránda)	σαράντα
four	(téseris/ -is/ -a)	τέσσερις/ -ις/ -α
four hundred	(tetrakósia)	τετρακόσια
fourteen	(THekatéseris/ -is/ -a)	δεκατέσσερις/ -ις/-α
fourth	(tétartos/ -i/ -o)	τέταρτος/ -η/ -ο
France	(ghalía)	Γαλλία (f)
free	(eléftheros/ -i/ -o)	ελεύθερος/ -η/ -ο
French (language)	(ghaliká)	Γαλλικά (n/pl)
friend	(fílos) (fíli)	φίλος (m), φίλη (f)
from	(apó)	από
front	(brostá)	μπροστά
fruit	(frúto)	φρούτο (n)
fruit and vegetable market	(laikí aghorá)	λαϊκή αγορά (f)
garage	(garáz)	γκαράζ (n)
garlic	(skórTHo)	σκόρδο (n)
German (language)	(ghermaniká)	Γερμανικά (n/pl)
Germany	(ghermanía)	Γερμανία (f)
get up	(sikónome)	σηκώνομαι
girl	(korítsi)	κορίτσι (n)
glass	(potíri)	ποτήρι (n)
go	(páo)/(pighéno)	πάω/πηγαίνω
go for a walk	(páo vólta)	πάω βόλτα
good evening	(kalispéra)	καλησπέρα
good morning	(kaliméra)	καλημέρα
goodnight	(kaliníhta)	καληνύχτα
grandchild	(engóni)	εγγόνι (n)
granddaughter	(engoní)	εγγονή (f)
grandfather	(papús)	παππούς (m)
grandmother	(yayá)	γιαγιά (f)
grandson	(engonós)	εγγονός (m)
grape	(stafíli)	σταφύλι (n)
Greece	(eláTHa)	Ελλάδα (f)
Greek (language)	(eliniká)	Ελληνικά (n/pl)

Greek blues	(rebétika)	ρεμπέτικα (n/pl)
Greek coffee	(elinikós kafés)	ελληνικός καφές (m)
Greek pastry	(baklavás)	μπακλαβάς (m)
Greek pastry	(kantaífi)	κανταΐφι (n)
Greek restaurant/taverna	(tavérna)	ταβέρνα (f)
green	(prásinos/ -i/ -o)	πράσινος/ -η/ -ο
grilled foods	(psitá)	ψητά (n/pl)
ground floor	(isóghio)	ισόγειο (n)
half	(misós/ -í/ -ó)	μισός/ -ή/ -ό
hallway	(hol)	χωλ (n)
hand basin	(niptíras)	νιπτήρας (m)
happy	(eftihizménos/ -i/ -o)	ευτυχισμένος/ -η/ -ο
have	(ého)	έχω
he	(aftós)	αυτός
heating	(thérmansi)	θέρμανση (f)
hello/goodbye (pl/fml)	(hérete)	χαίρετε
hello/goodbye (pl/fml)	(yásas)	γεια σας
hello/see you (sing/infml)	(yásu)	γεια σου
her	(tis)	της
herb	(aromatikó fitó)	αρωματικό φυτό (n)
here	(eThó)	εδώ
here you are!	(oríste)	ορίστε
hi!	(yásu)	γεια σου
his	(tu)	του
hobby	(hóbi)	χόμπυ (n)
homemade	(spitikós/ -í/ -ó)	σπιτικός/ -ή/ -ό
hospital	(nosokomío)	νοσοκομείο (n)
hotel	(ksenoThohío)	ξενοδοχείο (n)
house/home	(spíti)	σπίτι (n)
how/what	(pos)	πώς
hungry	(pinazménos/ -i/ -o)	πεινασμένος/ -η/ -ο
husband/wife, spouse	(sízighos)	σύζυγος (m/f)
I	(eghó)	εγώ
I'm sorry/excuse me	(sighnómi)	συγνώμη/συγγνώμη
iced coffee/frappé	(frapé)	φραπές (m)

idea	(iTHéa)	ιδέα (f)
immediately	(amésos)	αμέσως
in	(se)	σε
information (piece of)	(pliroforía)	πληροφορία (f)
instant coffee	(nes kafés)	νες καφές (m)
interesting	(enTHiaféron)	ενδιαφέρον
introduce	(sistíno)	συστήνω
Ireland	(irlanTHía)	Ιρλανδία (f)
island music	(nisiótika)	νησιώτικα (n/pl)
it	(aftó)	αυτό
Italian (language)	(italiká)	Ιταλικά (n/pl)
Italy	(italía)	Ιταλία (f)
its	(tu)	του
January	(ianuários)	Ιανουάριος (m)
jazz music	(tzaz)	τζαζ (f)
job/work	(THuliá)	δουλειά (f)
juice	(chimós)	χυμός (m)
July	(iúlios)	Ιούλιος (m)
June	(iúnios)	Ιούνιος (m)
kilo	(kiló)	κιλό (n)
kiosk	(períptero)	περίπτερο (n)
kitchen	(kuzína)	κουζίνα (f)
knife	(mahéri)	μαχαίρι (n)
know	(kséro)	ξέρω
lamb	(arnáki)	αρνάκι (n)
late	(arghá)	αργά
later	(arghótera)	αργότερα
lawn/grass	(ghrasíTHi)	γρασίδι (n)
learn	(mathéno)	μαθαίνω
leave	(févgho)	φεύγω
left	(aristerá)	αριστερά
lemonade	(lemonáTHa)	λεμονάδα (f)
letter	(ghráma)	γράμμα (n)
lettuce	(marúli)	μαρούλι (n)

276

lift/elevator	(asansér)	ασανσέρ (n)
light (colour), *open*	(aniktós/ -í/ -ó)	ανοικτός/ -ή/ -ό
light	(fos)	φως (n)
light bulb	(ghlómbos)	γλόμπος (m)
(I) like	(marési)	μ᾽αρέσει
like (as if)	(san)/(ópos)	σαν/όπως
likely, probable	(pithanós/ -í/ -ó)	πιθανός/ -ή/ -ό (adj)
likely, probably	(pithanós)	πιθανώς (adv)
little	(líghos/ -i/ -o)	λίγος/ -η/ -ο
live	(méno)	μένω
living room	(salóni)	σαλόνι (f)
London	(lonTHíno)	Λονδίνο (n)
love	(aghápi)	αγάπη (f)
lucky	(tiherós/ -í/ -ó)	τυχερός/ -ή/ -ό
luggage	(aposkeví)	αποσκευή (f)
lunch	(mesimerianó)	μεσημεριανό (n)
lyre	(líra)	λύρα (f)

main	(kírios/ -a/ -o)	κύριος/ -α/ -ο
mainly	(kiríos)	κυρίως
man/husband	(ándras)/(sízighos)	άνδρας/σύζυγος (m)
map	(hártis)	χάρτης (m)
March	(mártios)	Μάρτιος (m)
market	(aghorá)	αγορά (f)
marmalade/jam	(marmeláTHa)	μαρμελάδα (f)
married (I'm . . .)	(pandreménos/-i)	παντρεμένος/-η
May	(máios)	Μάιος (m)
may/is possible to	(borí na)/(ísos na)	μπορεί να/ίσως να
me (after a preposition)	((e)ména)	(ε)μένα
me (after a verb)	(mu)	μου
medium, middle	(meséos/ -a/ -o)	μεσαίος/ -α/ -ο
melon	(pepóni)	πεπόνι (n)
mezzanine (floor)	(imiórofos)	ημιόροφος (m)
midday/afternoon	(mesiméri)	μεσημέρι (n)
middle	(mési)	μέση (f)
milk	(ghála)	γάλα (n)
mine	(THikó mu)	δικό μου

minute	(leptó)	λεπτό (n)
mirror	(kathréftis)	καθρέφτης (m)
Miss	(THespiníTHa)	δεσποινίδα
mixed Greek salad	(horiátiki saláta)	χωριάτικη σαλάτα (f)
moment	(stighmí)	στιγμή (f)
month	(mínas)	μήνας (m)
more	(pyo)	πιο
more	(perisóteros/ -i/ -o)	περισσότερος/ -η/ -ο
morning	(proí)	πρωί (n)
mother	(mitéra)	μητέρα (f)
motorcycle	(motosikléta)	μοτοσυκλέτα (f)
mountain	(vunó)	βουνό (n)
Mr/Sir	(kírios)	κύριος (m)
Mrs/Madam	(kiría)	κυρία (f)
much/very	(polís, polí, polí)	πολύς, πολλή, πολύ
museum	(musío)	μουσείο (n)
mushroom	(manitári)	μανιτάρι (n)
music	(musikí)	μουσική (f)
musician	(musikós)	μουσικός (m/f)
must/have to	(prépi na)	πρέπει να
my	(mu)	μου
name	(ónoma)	όνομα (n)
name (first)	(mikró ónoma)	μικρό όνομα
name (last)	(epítheto)	επίθετο
national	(ethnikós/ -í/ -ó)	εθνικός/ -ή/ -ό
naturally	(fisiká)	φυσικά
nought/zero	(miTHén)	μηδέν
near, close to	(kondá)	κοντά
need	(hriázome)	χρειάζομαι
neighbourhood	(ghitoniá)	γειτονιά (f)
never	(poté)	ποτέ
newspaper	(efimeríTHa)	εφημερίδα (f)
next to	(THípla)	δίπλα
nice, beautiful	(oréos/ -a/ -o)	ωραίος/ -α/ -ο
nice, beautiful	(ómorfos/ -i/ -o)	όμορφος/ -η/ -ο
nine	(enéa)/(eniá)	εννέα/εννιά

nine hundred	(eniakósia)	ενιακόσια
nineteen	(THekaeniá)	δεκαεννιά
ninety	(enenínda)	ενενήντα
no	(óchi)	όχι
not	(THen)	δεν
not (Do not…)	(min)/(mi)	μην/μη
nothing	(típota)	τίποτα
novel	(nuvéla)	νουβέλα (f)
novel	(mithistórima)	μυθιστόρημα (n)
November	(noémvrios)	Νοέμβριος (m)
now	(tóra)	τώρα
number, size (of clothes)	(número)	νούμερο (n)
nurse	(nosokóma)	νοσοκόμα (f)
nurse	(nosokómos)	νοσοκόμος (m)
October	(októvrios)	Οκτώβριος (m)
of course, naturally	(vévea)	βέβαια
often	(sihná)	συχνά
oh	(ah)	αχ
OK, all right	(kalá), (endáksi)	καλά, εντάξει
one	(énas), (mía), (éna)	ένας, μία, ένα
one hundred	(ekató)	εκατό
one thousand	(hílji),(hílies),(hília)	χίλιοι (m), χίλιες (f), χίλια (n)
one-family house	(monokatikía)	μονοκατοικία (f)
orange (colour)	(portokalí)	πορτοκαλί
orange (fruit)	(portokáli)	πορτοκάλι (n)
orangeade	(portokaláTHa)	πορτοκαλάδα (f)
our	(mas)	μας
out, outside	(ékso)	έξω
ouzo	(úzo)	ούζο (n)
oven	(fúrnos)	φούρνος (m)
over	(péra)/(páno apó)	πέρα/πάνω από
p.m.	(mi-mi)	μ.μ.
pair	(zevghári)	ζευγάρι (n)
parsley	(maidanós)	μαϊντανός (m)
passport	(THiavatírio)	διαβατήριο (n)

pear	(ahláTHi)	αχλάδι (n)
penthouse	(retiré)	ρετιρέ (n)
petrol/gas	(venzíni)	βενζίνη (f)
petrol/gas station	(pratírio venzínis)	πρατήριο βενζίνης (n)
pharmacy	(farmakío)	φαρμακείο (n)
pianist	(o pianístas)	ο πιανίστας (m),
	(i pianístria)	η πιανίστρια (f)
pineapple	(ananás)	ανανάς (m)
pink	(roz)	ροζ
plate	(piáto)	πιάτο (n)
play	(pézo)	παίζω
play (theatre)	(érgho)	έργο
please/you're welcome	(parakaló)	παρακαλώ
police	(astinomía)	αστυνομία (f)
pop music	(laiká)	λαϊκά (n/pl)
pork	(chirinó)	χοιρινό (n)
portion	(meríTHa)	μερίδα (f)
post office	(tachiTHromío)	ταχυδρομείο (n)
potato	(patáta)	πατάτα (f)
pound (sterling)	(líra)	λίρα (f)
pound (kilo)	(kiló)	κιλό
practical	(praktikós/ -í/ -ó)	πρακτικός/ -ή/ -ό
prefer	(protimó)	προτιμώ
prepare	(etimázo)	ετοιμάζω
price	(timí)	τιμή (f)
private	(iTHiotikós)/ (-í)/ (-ó)	ιδιωτικός/ -ή/ -ό
problem	(próvlima)	πρόβλημα (n)
prospectus	(prospéktus)	προσπέκτους (n)
purple	(mov)	μωβ
question	(erótisi)	ερώτηση (f)
radio	(raTHiófono)	ραδιόφωνο (n)
rain	(vrochí)	βροχή (f)
rarely	(spánia)	σπάνια
read	(THiavázo)	διαβάζω
realize, see	(vlépo) (katalavéno)	βλέπω/καταλαβαίνω

reception	(ipoTHochí)	υποδοχή (f)
red	(kókinos)/ (-i)/ (-o)	κόκκινος/ -η/ -ο
red mullet	(barbúni)	μπαρμπούνι (n)
reservation	(krátisi)	κράτηση (f)
residence	(katikía)	κατοικία (f)
restaurant	(estiatório)	εστιατόριο (n)
restaurant serving grilled meat	(psistariá)/ (hasapotavérna)	ψησταριά (f)/ χασαποταβέρνα (f)
restaurant serving fish	(psarotavérna)	ψαροταβέρνα (f)
return	(epistréfo)	επιστρέφω
return/round trip	(me epistrofí)	με επιστροφή (f)
right (direction)	(THeksiá)	δεξιά
right (you're right)	(THíkio) (éhis)	δίκιο (n) (έχεις/-ετε)
river	(potamós)	ποταμός (m)
rock	(vráhos)	βράχος
rock music	(rok)	ροκ (n)
room	(kámara)/(THomátio)	κάμαρα (f)/δωμάτιο (n)
round (in shape)	(strongilós/ -í/ -ó)	στρογγυλός/ -ή/ -ό
run	(trého)	τρέχω
running	(troháTHin)	τροχάδην (n)
sad	(lipiménos/ -i/ -o)	λυπημένος/ -η/ -ο
salad	(saláta)	σαλάτα (f)
sale/discount	(ékptosi)	έκπτωση (f)
same	(íTHios/ -a/ -o)	ίδιος/ -α/ -ο
Saturday	(sávato)	Σάββατο (n)
saucer	(piatáki)	πιατάκι (n)
school	(sholío)	σχολείο (n)
science	(epistími)	επιστήμη
Scotland	(skotía)	Σκωτία (f)
sea	(thálasa)	θάλασσα (f)
season	(epochí)	εποχή (f)
seat (to sit on)	(káthizma)	κάθισμα (n)
seat (class)	(thési)	θέση (f)
second	(THéfteros/ -i/ -o)	δεύτερος/ -η/ -ο
second (with time)	(THefterólepto)	δευτερόλεπτο (n)
second (Just a . . .)	(éna leptó)	ένα λεπτό

see	(vlépo)	βλέπω
see again	(ksanavlépo)	ξαναβλέπω
sell	(puló)	πουλώ
September	(septémvrios)	Σεπτέμβριος (m)
seven	(eptá)/(eftá)	επτά/εφτά
seven hundred	(eptakósia)/(eftakósia)	επτακόσια/εφτακόσια
seventeen	(THekaeftá)	δεκαεφτά
seventy	(evTHomínda)	εβδομήντα
shampoo	(sambuán)	σαμπουάν (n)
she	(aftí)	αυτή
ship	(plío) (karávi)	πλοίο (n)/καράβι (n)
shirt	(pukámiso)	πουκάμισο (n)
shoe	(papútsi)	παπούτσι (n)
shoe lace	(korTHóni)	κορδόνι (n)
shop window	(vitrína)	βιτρίνα (f)
shower	(duz)	ντους (n)
side	(plevrá)	πλευρά (f)
single (I'm …)	(eléftheros/-i)	ελεύθερος/-η (m/f)
single room	(monóklino)	μονόκλινο (n)
sister	(aTHelfí)	αδελφή (f)
sit	(káthome)	κάθομαι
sitting room	(kathistikó)	καθιστικό (n)
six	(éksi)	έξι
six hundred	(eksakósia)	εξακόσια
sixteen	(THekaéksi)	δεκαέξι
sixty	(eksínda)	εξήντα
size	(méghethos)	μέγεθος (n)
sky	(uranós)	ουρανός (m)
sky blue	(ghalázios/ -a/ -o)	γαλάζιος/ -α/ -ο
sleep	(kimáme)	κοιμάμαι
slip-ons (loafers)	(pandoflé)	παντοφλέ (n)
slipper	(pandófla)	παντόφλα (f)
small	(mikrós/ -í/ -ó)	μικρός/ -ή/ -ό
small bouzouki	(baghlamaTHáki)	μπαγλαμαδάκι (n)
small dishes/starters	(mezéTHes)	μεζέδες (m/pl)
smoke	(kapnízo)	καπνίζω
smoking	(kápnizma)	κάπνισμα (n)

so (therefore)	(étsi)	έτσι
so (to such an extent)	(tósos/ -i/ -o)	τόσος/ -η/ -ο
soap	(sapúni)	σαπούνι (n)
soda water	(sóTHa)	σόδα (f)
sofa	(kanapés)	καναπές (m)
soft	(malakós/-í/ó)	μαλακός/-ή/-ό
soft drink	(anapsiktiko)	αναψυκτικό
son	(yos)	γιος (m)
sorry	(sighnómi)	συγνώμη (m)
soup	(súpa)	σούπα
soup spoon	(kutáli)	κουτάλι (n)
space, area	(hóros)	χώρος (m)
Spain	(ispanía)	Ισπανία (f)
Spanish (language)	(ispaniká)	ισπανικά (n/pl)
speak	(miláo)	μιλάω
sport	(spor)	σπορ (n)
spring	(ániksi)	άνοιξη (f)
stamp	(ghramatósimo)	γραμματόσημο (n)
stay (verb)	(káthome)/(THiaméno)	κάθομαι/διαμένω
stay	(THiamoní)	διαμονή (f)
stay	(paramoní)	παραμονή (f)
sterling	(sterlína)	στερλίνα
still/yet	(akóma)	ακόμα
stool	(skambó)	σκαμπό (n)
story/history	(istoría)	ιστορία (f)
straight	(efthía)	ευθεία
straight ahead	(efthía brostá)	ευθεία μπροστά
straight ahead	(ísia)	ίσια
strawberry	(fráula)	φράουλα (f)
striped	(righé)	ριγέ (m/f/n)
studio/bedsit	(garsoniéra)	γκαρσονιέρα (f)
study	(THiavázo)	διαβάζω
study	(mathéno)	μαθαίνω
stuffed peppers/tomatoes	(ghemistá)	γεμιστά (n/pl)
suitcase	(valítsa)	βαλίτσα (f)
summer	(kalokéri)	καλοκαίρι (n)
Sunday	(kiriakí)	Κυριακή (f)

supermarket	(súpermarket)	σούπερμαρκετ (n)
sure!	(amé)! (vévea)!	αμέ! βέβαια!
surprised	(ékpliktos/ -i/ -o)	έκπληκτος/ -η/ -ο
sweet	(ghlikós/ -iá/ -ó)	γλυκός/ -ιά/ -ό
swim	(kolimbó)	κολυμπώ
swimming	(bánio)	μπάνιο
Sydney	(síTHnei)	Σίδνεϋ (n)
table	(trapézi)	τραπέζι (n)
table tennis	(ping pong)	πίνγκ πονγκ (n)
take	(pérno)	παίρνω
taverna/Greek restaurant	(tavérna)	ταβέρνα (f)
taxi	(taksí)	ταξί (n)
tea	(tsái)	τσάι (n)
teaspoon	(kutaláki)	κουταλάκι (n)
teacher	(THáskalos) (THaskála)	δάσκαλος (m), δασκάλα (f)
telephone booth	(tilefonikós thálamos)	τηλεφωνικός θάλαμος (m)
television	(tileórasi)	τηλεόραση (f)
ten	(THéka)	δέκα
tennis	(ténis)	τένις (n)
thanks (lit. I thank you)	(efharistó)	ευχαριστώ
thanks (lit. we thank you)	(efharistúme)	ευχαριστούμε
that/who (in statements)	(pu)	που
the	(o), (i), (to)	ο, η, το (m/f/n)
theatre (n)	(théatro)	θέατρο (n)
their	(tus)	τους
theirs	(THikó tus)	δικό τους
then, afterwards	(metá)	μετά
then/after that/later	(épita)	έπειτα
there	(ekí)	εκεί
Thessaloniki	(thesaloníki)	Θεσσαλονίκη (f)
they (f)	(aftés)	αυτές
they (m or m+f)	(aftí)	αυτοί
they (n)	(aftá)	αυτά
think	(nomízo)	νομίζω
third	(trítos/ -i/ -o)	τρίτος/ -η/ -ο
thirsty	(THipsazménos/ -i/ -o)	διψασμένος/ -η/ -ο

thirteen	(THekatrís/ -ís/ -ía)	δεκατρείς/ -είς/ -ία
thirty	(triánda)	τριάντα
though, although	(ómos)/(molonóti)	όμως/μολονότι
thought	(sképsi)	σκέψη (f)
three	(tris, tris, tría)	τρεις, τρεις, τρία
three hundred	(triakósia)	τριακόσια
thriller/horror (film)	(thríler)	θρίλερ (n)
ticket	(isitírio)	εισιτήριο (n)
time (what . . .)	(óra)	ώρα (f)
time (much . . .)	(hrónos)	χρόνος (m)
timetable	(pínakas THromologhíon)	πίνακας δρομολογίων (m)
tired	(kurazménos/ -i/ -o)	κουρασμένος/ -η/ -ο
tiring	(kurastikós/ -í/ -ó)	κουραστικός/ -ή/ -ό
to (used with verbs)	(na)	να
to/in/at the	(ston), (stin), (sto)	στον, στην, στο
to, until	(méhri)	μέχρι
today	(símera)	σήμερα (n)
toilet	(tualéta)	τουαλέτα (f)
tomato	(domáta)	ντομάτα (f)
toothbrush	(oTHondóvurtsa)	οδοντόβουρτσα (f)
toothpaste	(oTHondópasta)	οδοντόπαστα (f)
towel	(petséta)	πετσέτα (f)
town/city	(póli)	πόλη (f)
train	(tréno)	τρένο (n)
train station	(stathmós trénon)	σταθμός τρένων (m)
travel agency	(taksiTHiotikó ghrafío)	ταξιδιωτικό γραφείο (n)
trip	(taksíTHi)	ταξίδι (n)
triple room	(tríklino)	τρίκλινο (n)
trout	(péstrofa)	πέστροφα (f)
truth	(alíthia)	αλήθεια (f)
twelve	(THóTHeka)	δώδεκα
twenty	(íkosi)	είκοσι
two	(THío)	δύο
two hundred	(THiakósia)	διακόσια
tzatziki (yoghurt garlic dip)	(tzatzíki)	τζατζίκι (n)

underground	(metró)/(ilektrikós)	μετρό (n)/ηλεκτρικός (m)
understand, see, realize	(vlépo)	βλέπω
understand (language)	(katalavéno)	καταλαβαίνω
unfortunately	(THistihós)	δυστυχώς
until	(méhri)	μέχρι
until	(óspu)	ώσπου
up	(páno)	πάνω
upset	(taraghménos/ -i/ -o)	ταραγμένος/ -η/ -ο
up to	(méhri)	μέχρι
usually	(siníthos)	συνήθως
vegetable	(lahanikó)	λαχανικό (n)
view (opinion)	(ápopsi)	άποψη (f)
view (sight)	(théa)	θέα (f)
volleyball	(vólei)	βόλεϋ (n)
WC	(vesé)	W C (no Greek script) (n)
wait	(periméno)	περιμένω
waiter	(servitóros)	σερβιτόρος
waitress	(servitóra)	σερβιτόρα
wake up	(ksipnáo)	ξυπνάω
Wales	(ualía)	Ουαλία (f)
walk	(perpatáo/-ó)	περπατάω/-ώ
walk, stroll, car ride	(vólta)	βόλτα (f)
want	(thélo)	θέλω
watch	(vlépo)	βλέπω
water	(neró)	νερό (n)
we	(emís)	εμείς
weather	(kerós)	καιρός (m)
week	(evTHomáTHa)	εβδομάδα (f)
weekend	(savatokíriako)	Σαββατοκύριακο (n)
welcome (you're)	(parakaló)	παρακαλώ
welcome!	(kalosórises/-sate)!	καλωσόρισες/-σατε!
well (e.g. I'm well)	(kalá)	καλά
well (e.g. well, what?)	(lipón)	λοιπόν
what	(ti)	τι
when (in questions)	(póte)	πότε

when (within a sentence)	(ótan)	όταν
where	(pu)	πού
white	(áspros/ -i/ -o)	άσπρος/ -η/ -ο
white wine	(áspro krasí)	άσπρο κρασί (n)
why	(yatí)	γιατί
window	(paráthiro)	παράθυρο (n)
wine	(krasí)	κρασί (n)
winter	(chimónas)	χειμώνας (m)
woman/wife	(ghinéka)/(sízighos)	γυναίκα/σύζυγος (f)
work	(THulévo)	δουλεύω
work (noun)	(THuliá)	δουλειά (f)
world	(kózmos)	κόσμος (m)
write	(ghráfo)	γράφω
writer	(sighraféas)	συγγραφέας (m/f)
yard	(avlí)	αυλή (f)
year	(hrónos)	χρόνος (m)
yellow	(kítrinos/ -i/ -o)	κίτρινος/ -η/ -ο
yellow peach	(yiarmás)	γιαρμάς (m)
yes	(ne)	ναι
Yes, sure! Of course!	(málista)	μάλιστα
you (pl/fml)	(esís)	εσείς
you (pl/fml) (to you)	(sas)	σας
you (sing/infml)	(eséna)	εσένα
you (sing/infml)	(esí)	εσύ
your (pl/fml)	(sas)	σας
your (sing/infml)	(su)	σου
yours	(THikó su/sas)	δικό σου/σας

Greek–English glossary

Additional vocabulary can be found in the **Language notes** and **Grammar** sections.

Αα	*Aha (Oh, I get it!)*	**αμέσως**	*at once*
αγαπάω	*I love*	**αμμουδιά**	*sand (f)*
Αγγλία	*England (f)*	**αν**	*if*
Αγγλικά	*English (language)*	**ανακαινισμένος /-η /-ο**	*renovated*
αγγουράκι	*small cucumber (n)*		
αγορά	*market (f)*	**ανανάς**	*pineapple (m)*
αγροτικός /-ή /-ό	*agricultural*	**αναπαύομαι**	*I rest*
άγχος	*stress (n)*	**ανάπαυση**	*rest (f)*
αδιάθετος / -η /-ο	*sick*	**Ανάσταση**	*Resurrection (f)*
αεράκι	*wind (light), breeze (n)*	**ανατολικός /-ή /-ό**	*eastern*
αέρας	*wind (m)*	**αναψυκτικό**	*refreshment (n)*
αεροδρόμιο	*airport (n)*	**ανδρικός /-ή /-ό**	*male*
Αθήνα	*Athens (f)*	**ανεβαίνω**	*I go up*
Αθηναία	*Athenian (f)*	**άνεμος**	*wind (m)*
Αθηναίος	*Athenian (m)*	**ανηφόρα**	*uphill (f)*
αίθουσα	*room, hall (f)*	**άνιθος**	*dill (m)*
αιτία	*cause, reason (f)*	**ανοικτός /-ή /-ό**	*light/open*
ακόμα (η)	*still, yet*	**άνοιξη**	*spring (f)*
ακούγομαι	*I sound*	**αντέχω**	*I stand*
ακουστικό	*receiver (n)*	**αντί**	*instead*
ακούω	*I listen, I hear*	**αντιβιοτικό**	*antibiotic (n)*
ακριβά	*expensively*	**αντισηπτικό**	*antiseptic (n)*
ακριβός /-ή /-ό	*expensive*	**αντίστοιχος /-η /-ο**	*corresponding*
Αλεξάνδρα	*Alexandra (f)*	**αξιοθέατο**	*sight (n)*
αλήθεια	*truth (f)*	**απαισιόδοξος /-η /-ο**	*pessimist*
αλήθεια!	*really!, that's true*		
αλλά	*but*	**απαίσιος**	*awful*
αλλεργικός /-ή /-ό	*allergic*	**απλός /-ή /-ό**	*simple*
αλλιώς	*otherwise*	**απλά**	*simply*
άλλος /-η /-ο	*other, another*	**από**	*from*

απορρημένος /-η /-ο	confused	βοηθάω (-ώ)	I help
αποσκευή	luggage, suitcase (f)	βόλεϋ	volleyball (n)
αποφασίζω	I decide	βορειοανατολικός /-ή /-ό	north-eastern
Απρίλιος/Απρίλης	April (m)	βορειοδυτικός /-ή /ό	north-western
άρα	then	βόρειος /-α /-ο	northern
αρακάς	pea (m)	βοριάς	north wind
αριθμός	number (m)	βούτυρο	butter (n)
αριστερά	left	βρε	untranslated emphatic particle
αρκετά	enough		
αρκετός /-ή /-ό	several	βρεγμένος /-η /-ο	wet
αρνάκι	lamb (n)	βρίσκω	I find
άρρωστος	ill (m)	βροχή	rain (f)
αρχιτέκτονας	architect (m, f)	βυσσινής /-ή /-ί	burgundy
ασανσέρ	lift (n)	βύσσινο	morel
ασθενής /-ής /-ές	weak	γάλα	milk (n)
άσθμα	asthma (n)	γαλάζιο	sky blue, indigo
άσπρο	white	Γαλλία	France (f)
αστυνομικός	policeman (m)	Γαλλίδα	French woman (f)
άτομο	person (n)	γάμος	wedding (m)
Αύγουστος	August (m)	γάντι	glove (n)
αυξάνω	I increase	γεγονός	event, fact (n)
αύξηση	increase (f)	γέννηση	birth (f)
αύριο	tomorrow (n)	Γερμανίδα	German woman (f)
αυτοκίνητο	car (n)	γεύμα	meal (n)
αυτός /-ή /-ό	this, he, she, it	γεύση	taste (f)
		γιαρμάς	(kind of) peach (m)
βάδην	walking, jogging (n)	γιατί	because
βαθής /-ιά /-ύ	deep, dark	γιατί	why?
βαλίτσα	suitcase (f)	γιατρός	doctor (m, f)
βαριέμαι	I am bored	γιορτάζω	I celebrate
βάρκα	boat (f)	γιορτή	holiday (f), celebration
βγάζω	I take off, pull out	γιωτ	yacht (n)
βιβλίο	book (n)	γκαράζ	car park, garage (n)
βιοτικός /-ή /-ό	standard (of living)	γκοφρέτα	waffle (chocolate) (f)
βλέπω	I see		

γκρίζος /-α /-ο	grey	διασκεδάζω	I entertain (reflexive)
γκρινιάζω	I complain, I moan	διεύθυνση	address (f)
γκρουμ	porter (m)	δίκιο	right (n)
γλυκό	sweet (n), cake	δίκλινο	double room (n)
γλώσσα	language (f)	δίνω	I give
γνωστός /-ή /-ό	acquaintance, known	διπλός /-ή /-ό	double
γραβάτα	tie (f)	δισκοθήκη	disco, discotheque (f)
γραμματόσημο	stamp (n)	δίσκος	record (m)
γραμμή	line (f)	δόση	installment (f)
γραφείο	office (n)	δουλειά	work, job, employment (f)
γράφω	I write		
γρήγορα	fast	δουλεύω	I work
γρίππη	influenza (f)	δρομολόγιο	timetable (n)
γυμναστική	exercise (f) (gymnastics)	δρόμος	street (m)
		δροσερός /-ή /-ό	cool
γυναίκα	woman (f)	δυστυχώς	unfortunately, I am sorry but …
γύρος	gyros (m)		
γύρω	round	δυτικός /-ή /-ό	western
γωνία	corner (f)	δωμάτιο	room (n)
		δωρεάν	free
δάσκαλος	teacher (m)	δώρο	present (n)
δείχνω	I show		
Δεκέμβριος/ Δεκέμβρης	December (m)	εγκεφαλικός /-ή /-ό	of the brain cerebral (adj.)
δέντρο	tree (n)	εγώ	I
δεξιά	right	εδώ	here
Δευτέρα	Monday (f)	εθνικός /-ή /-ό	national
δέχομαι	I accept	ειδικά	especially
δηλαδή	in other words, that is to say	ειδικός /-ή /-ό	specialist (m, f)
		εικόνα	picture (f)
δηλητηρίαση	poisoning (f)	είμαι	I am
διαβατήριο	passport (n)	είσοδος	entrance (f)
διακοπές	vacation	εκεί	there
διάδρομος	corridor (m)	εκείνος /-η /-ο	that man, woman, thing
διανυκτέρευση	(staying) overnight (f)		
διάρροια	diarrhoea (f)	εκπλήσσω	I surprise

εκπτωτικός /-ή /-ό	discount(ed)	έτσι	so, like that
Ελληνικά	Greek (language)	ευκαιρία	chance (f)
ελπίζω	I hope	εύκολα	easily
εμπορικός /-ή /-ό	commercial	εύκολος /-η /-ο	easy
εντάξει	OK, all right	Ευρώπη	Europe (f)
ενδιαφέρον	interest (n)	ευχαριστώ	(I) thank you
ενοικίαση	rent (f)	ευχή	wish (f)
εντύπωση	impression (f)	εύχομαι	I wish/I hope
ενυδρείο	aquarium (n)	εφημερίδα	newspaper (f)
ενώ	while	εφιάλτης	nightmare (m)
εξέταση	examination (f)	εχθές	yesterday
έξω	out, outside	έχω	I have
εξωτερικό	abroad (n)		
επάνω	up, above	ζάλη	dizziness (f)
έπειτα	afterwards, then	ζαμπόν	ham (n)
επιθυμώ	I wish, I desire	ζαχαροπλαστείο	pastry shop (n)
επίπεδο	level (n)	ζηλεύω	I become/am jealous
επικίνδυνος /-η /-ο	dangerous	ζωγράφος	painter (m, f)
επίσης	too, also	ζωή	life (f)
επιστρέφω	I return		
επιστροφή	return, round-trip (f)	η	the (f)
επιτέλους!	at last!	ή	or
επιτόκιο	interest (n)	ήδη	already
εποχή	season (f)	ήλιος	sun (m)
εργασία	job, work (f)	ημικρανία	migraine (f)
εργάτης	employee, worker (m)	ήρεμος /-η /-ο	tranquil, quiet
έρχομαι	I come	ήσυχος /-η /-ο	quiet
εσείς	you (pl., pol.)		
εσένα	you	θαλαμηγός	yacht (f)
εσύ	you (sing. and fam.)	θάλασσα	sea (f)
εσώρουχο	underwear (n)	θαλασσής /-ή /-ί	sea blue (f)
εσωτερικός /-ή /-ό	inner, inside	θάνατος	death (m)
εταιρία	company (f)	θαυμάσιος /-α /-ο	marvellous
ετήσιος /-α /-ο	annual	θεά	goddess (f)
έτοιμος /-η /-ο	ready	θέα	view (f)
		θέλω	I want/like
		Θεός	God (m)

θεραπεία	treatment (f)	καιρός	time/weather (m)
θέρετρο	resort (n)	καλά	well, fine, good, OK
θερμοκρασία	temperature (f)	καλαμπόκι	corn (n)
Θερμοπύλες	Thermopiles, an archeological site	καλλυντικά	cosmetics (pl.)
		κάλτσα	sock (f)
θερμότερος /-η /-ο	warmer	καλύτερος /-η /-ο	better
Θεσσαλονίκη	Thessaloniki/ Salonica (f)	καλώς ορίσατε!	welcome!
		καμαριέρα	maid (f)
θέση	class, seat (f)	κανέλα	cinnamon (colour) (f)
θύελλα	storm, hurricane (f)	κανελής /ή /-ί	cinnamon
θυμάμαι	I remember (f)	κανένας /καμία / κανένα	nobody (m, f, n)
ιδιωτικός /-ή /-ό	private		
Ιανουάριος/Γενάρης	January (m)	κανό	canoe (n)
ίδιος /-α /-ο	similar	κάνω	I do/make
ιδίως	especially	καλοκαίρι	summer (n)
Ιονικός /-ή /-ό	Ionian	καπετάνιος	captain (m)
Ιούλιος /Ιούλης	July (m)	καράβι	ship (n)
Ιούνιος /Ιούνης	June (m)	καραβοκύρης	skipper (m)
ιππασία	riding (f)	καραμέλα	candy (f)
ισόγειο	ground floor (n)	καραφάκι	small bottle of ouzo (n)
ιστιοπλοΐα	sailing (f)		
ιστιοφόρο	sailing boat (n)	καρδιακός /-ή /-ό	cardiac
ιστορία	story, history (f)	καρεκλοπόδαρο	chair leg (n)
ισχυρός /-ή /-ό	strong	καρκίνος	cancer (m)
ίσως	maybe, perhaps	καρό	chequered
Ιταλικά	Italian (language)	καρότο	carrot (n)
Ιταλός	Italian (m)	καρπούζι	watermelon (n)
ιώδες	violet	κάρτα	card (f)
		καρύδα	coconut (f)
κτίριο	building (n)	κάστρο	castle (n)
καθηγητής	teacher, tutor (m)	καταιγίδα	(thunder) storm (f)
καθόλου	not at all	καταλαβαίνω	I understand
κάθομαι	I sit/stay	κατάλογος	menu (m), catalogue, list
και	and		
και τα δύο	both	κάτοικος	inhabitant, resident (m, f)
καινούργιος /-α /-ο	new		

κατσικάκι	kid, goat (n)	κοσμοπολίτικος	cosmopolitan
κάτω	down, under	κόσμος	people, crowd (m)
καφέ	brown	κοσμοσυρροή	crowd, throng (f)
καφένειο	coffee shop (n)	κότ(τ)ερο	cutter (n)
καφές	coffee (m)	κουνουπίδι	cauliflower (n)
καφετής /-ή /-ί	coffee brown	κουρασμένος /-η /-ο	tired
κεραμιδής /-ή /-ί	brick red		
κεραμίδι	tile (n)	κουρτίνα	curtain (f)
κεράσι	cherry (n)	κουστούμι	suit (n)
κέρινος /-η /-ο	wax	κρατάω(ώ)	I keep
κεφάλι	head (n)	κράτηση	reservation (f)
κιλό	kilo (n)	κρατικός /-ή /-ό	state
κίνηση	traffic (f)	κρέας	meat (n)
κιόλας	already	κρέμα	cream (f)
κίτρινο	yellow	κρεμμύδι	onion (n)
κλασικός /-ή /-ό	classic	κρουαζιερόπλοιο	cruise ship (n)
κλειδί	key (n)	κρύο	cold (n)
κλειστοφοβία	claustrophobia (f)	κρύωμα	cold (n)
κλιματιζόμενος /-η /-ο	air-conditioned	κτηνίατρος	vet (m, f)
		κτίριο	building (n)
κόβω	I cut	κτίστης	builder (m)
κοιλιά	belly (f)	κτυπώ	I hit
κοιλόπονος	stomach-ache (m)	κυλιόμενος /-η /-ο	rolling, on rollers
κόκκινο	red	κυπαρισσής /ή /-ί	cypress green
κολοκύθι	squash (n)	κυπαρίσσι	cypress (n)
κολόνια	perfume (f)	κυρ	Mr
κολυμπώ	I swim	Κυριακή	Sunday (f)
κολύμπι	swimming (n)	κύριε	Mr
Κολωνάκι	Kolonaki, neighbourhood in central Athens	κυρίως	mainly
		κωπηλασία	rowing (f)
κοντά	near/close to	λέω	I say
κοντινένταλ	continental	λάθος	mistake (n), false
κόπωση	exhaustion (f)	λαϊκός /-ή /-ό	popular
κορτιζόνη	cortisone (f)	λαιμός	throat (m)
		λάμπα	lamp (f)

λαχανής /-ή /-ί	cabbage green	Μαντράκι	Mantraki, the harbour for yachts, sailing and fishing boats in Rhodes (n)
λαχανικό	vegetable (n)		
λάχανο	cabbage (n)		
λέγομαι	my name is		
λεμονάδα	lemonade (f)	μαρμελάδα	marmalade/jam (f)
λεμόνι	lemon (n)	μαρούλι	lettuce (n)
λεπτό	minute (n)	Μάρτιος/Μάρτης	March (m)
λέσχη	club (f)	μας	our
Λευκωσία	Nicosia (Cyprus) (f)	ματώνω	I bleed
λεφτά	money (pl.)	μαύρο	black
λιακάδα	sunshine (f)	μαχαιρώνω	I knife, stab
Λίβερπουλ	Liverpool (n)	με	with
λίγο	some, little	Μεγάλη (Ε) βδομάδα	Holy Week (f)
λιμένας	port (m)	μεγάλος /-η /-ο	large
Λίνδος	Lindos, a village 54 km south of Rhodes City	μεγαλύτερος /-η /-ο	larger
λογιστής	book keeper (m)	Μέγαρο Μουσικής	Music Hall (n)
λοιπόν	then, well	μέγεθος	size (n)
λόμπυ	lobby (n)	μεζεδοπωλείο	tavern with a selection of appetizers (n)
Λονδίνο	London (n)		
λουλουδάτο	flowery, floral	μεζές	appetizer, snacks (m)
Λυκαβηττός	a hill in the centre of Athens (m)	μεθαύριο	the day after tomorrow
		μειώνω	I reduce
μάγειρας	cook (m)	μελιτζάνα	aubergine, eggplant (f)
μαζί	together, with	μελιτζανοσαλάτα	aubergine, eggplant dip (f)
μαθαίνω	I learn		
μαθητής	student (m)	μένω	I live, I stay
μαϊντανός	parsley (m)	μερικά	some
Μάιος/Μάης	May (m)	μέρλι(ν)	extremely sweet
μακάρι	I wish, would that, if only, may	μέρος	place (n)
		μέσα	in, inside
μακριά	far	μεσαίος /-α /-ο	medium
μάλλον	rather, probably	μετάβαση	going (f)
μάνατζερ	manager (m, f)	μετακίνηση	transport (f)

μεταξύ	between	μπουάτ	night club (with Greek music) (f)
μέτρο	metre (n)	μπουκάλι	bottle (n)
μετρό	metro (n)	μπουφές	buffet (m)
μέχρι	until	μπροστά	in front
μήλο	apple (n)	μπύρα	beer (f)
μηχανή	machine (f)	μπυραρία	pub (f)
μία/μια	one, a	μυστικό	secret (n)
μικρό	small	μωβ	violet
μικρός/-ή /-ό	small	μώλος	pier (m)
Μιλάνο	Milan (n)	νοικοκυρά	housewife (f)
μιλάω(-ώ)	I speak	να	to (verb participle)
μίνι-μπαρ	mini-bar (n)	να!	there!
μινιόν	minion	ναι!	hello (on the phone), yes
μ.μ. = μετά μεσημβρίας	p.m. = post meridiem	νάιτ κλαμπ	night club (n)
μόλις	just	να το!	here it is!
μολύβι	pencil (n)	ναύτης	sailor (m)
μόνο	only	ναυτία	sea-sickness, nausea (f)
μονόκλινο	one bed, single room (f)		
μονόχρωμο	single colour	νερό	water (n)
μου	my	νεφελώδης /-ης /-ες	cloudy, overcast
μουσακάς	moussaka (m)	νέφος	cloud, smog (n)
μουστάρδα	mustard (f)	νησί	island (n)
μουσταρδής /-ή /-ί	mustard yellow	Νοέμβριος/ Νοέμβρης	November
μπα!	wow! (surprise)		
μπαλκόνι	balcony (n)	νομίζω	I think
μπανάνα	banana (f)	νορμάλ	normally
μπανιέρα	bathtub (f)	νοσοκόμα	nurse (f)
μπάνιο	swimming (n)/bath	νοσοκομείο	hospital (n)
μπαρ	bar, pub (n)	νοσοκόμος	nurse (m, f)
μπάρμπεκιου	barbecue (n)	νόστιμος /-η /-ο	delicious
μπάσκετ	basketball (n)	νοστιμότατος /-η /-ο	most delicious
μπερδεύω	I mix up		
μπλέ	blue	νούμερο	number, size (n)
μπορώ	I can	ντολμαδάκια	dolmadakia

ντομάτα	tomato (f)	όσο	as much as
ντόπιος /-α /-ο	local	ό,τι	whatever, that
ντους	shower (n)	ουζερί	ouzeri (n)
ξανά	again	ουίσκι	whisky (n)
ξαναβλέπω	I see again	ουρανής /-ή /-ί	sky blue
ξεκινώ	I start	ουρανός	sky (m)
ξενοδοχείο	hotel (n)	ούτε . . . ούτε . . .	neither . . . nor
ξένος /-η /-ο	foreign	ουφ!	Phew!
ξέρω	I know	οφείλω	I owe
ξεχνώ	I forget	όχι	no
ξηρά	ashore (f)		
ξιφασκία	fencing (f)	παγάκι	ice cube (n)
ξυράφι	razor (n)	πάγκος	counter (m)
ο	the (m)	παγωνιά	frost (f)
οδηγός	driver (m, f)	παγωτό	ice-cream (n)
οδοντογιατρός	dentist (m, f)	παθαίνω	I suffer
οικισμός	settlement (m)	παιδί	child (n)
Οκτώβριος/ Οκτώβρης	October (m)	παίρνω	I take
		πάλι	again
όλοι	everyone [people]	παλιόκαιρος	awful weather (m)
όλος /-η /-ο	everything, whole	παλτό	coat (n)
ομελέτα	omelette (f)	Παναθήναια	a name of a park in Athens
ομοιότητα	resemblance (f)		
ομοίωμα	model (n), image, figure	πανηγύρι	(religious) fair (n)
όμορφος /-η /-ο	beautiful	πάντα	always
ομπρέλα	umbrella (f)	παντού	everywhere
όμως	but, though	πάνω	on the top/on/over
ονομάζομαι	my name is	παραδοσιακός /-ή /ό	traditional
όπως	as, like		
οπωσδήποτε	definitely	παρακαλώ	please/you're welcome
ορίστε!	Here you are! Here you go!	παραλία	beach (f)
		παραμονή	stay (f)
όροφος	floor (m)	παραπάνω	more than
ΟΣΕ Οργανισμός Σιδηροδρόμων Ελλάδας	Greek Railway Organization (Greek Interail)	Παρασκευή	Friday (f)
		παράσταση	performace (f)
		παραχρόνου	the year after next

παρέα	company (f)	πληθυντικός	plural (m)
Παρίσι	Paris (n)	πλήρης/-ης/-ες	complete
πάρκο	park (n)	πληροφορία	information (f)
παρόμοιος /-α /-ο	similar	πλοίο	ship (n)
πατάτα	potato (f)	π.μ. = προ	a.m. = ante
πατινάζ	ice-skating (n)	μεσηβρίας	meridiem
πάω	I go	πνευμονία	pneumonia (f)
Πέμπτη	Thursday (f)	ποδηλασία	cycling (f)
πενήντα	50	ποδόφαιρο	soccer (n)
πέντε	five	ποικιλία	selection (f)
πεπόνι	melon (n)	ποιος /-α /-ο	who, which
περαστικός	passer-by (m)	ποιότητα	quality (f)
περιοδικά	periodically	πόλη	town (f)
περιοδικό	magazine (n)	πολύ	much, very
περίπου	about, approximately	πολυκατάστημα	department store (n)
περίπτερο	kiosk, news stand (n)	πονάω	I hurt
περνώ	I spend	πονοκέφαλος	headache (m)
περπατάω (-ώ)	I walk	πονόλαιμος	sore throat (m)
πέρσι	last year	πόνος	pain (m)
πετάω (-ώ)	I fly, I throw	πορτοκαλής/-ή /-ί	orange
πέφτω	I fall	πορτοκάλι	orange (n)
πηγαίνω	I go	πόσο;	how much?
πια	already	ποτέ	never
πιανίστας	pianist (m)	πότε;	when?
πιάνω	I catch, I hold	που	that
πίκλα	pickle (f)	πού;	where?
πιλότος	pilot (m, f)	πουά	spotted, dotted
πίνακας	statistical table (m)	πουθενά	nowhere, anywhere
πιο	more	πουκάμισο	shirt (n)
πιστεύω	I believe	πουλόβερ	sweater (n)
πιστωτικός /-ή /-ό	credit	πράγματι	indeed
πίσω από	behind	πράσινο	green
πίτα/πίττα	pitta bread	πριν	before
Πλ. = πλατεία	sq. = square	πρόγραμμα	schedule (n)
πλατεία	square (f)	πρόπερσι	the year before last

προς	to, towards	σερβιτόρος	waiter (m, f)
προσπαθώ	I try	σέρβις δωματίου	room service (n)
προσφέρω	I offer	σήμερα	today
προσφορά	offer (f)	σιγά	slowly
πρόσωπο	face (n)	σίγουρος /-η /-ο	sure
προχθές	the day before yesterday	σιέλ	sky blue
πρωινό	breakfast (n)	σινεμά	the cinema (n)
πρώτος /-η /-ο	first	σκάλα	staircase (f)
πτήση	flight (f)	σκαλοπάτι	step (n)
πτώση	decrease (f)	σκάφος	motor boat (n)
πω! πω!	Wow!	σκέπτομαι	I think, I plan
πώς!	of course!	σκέτο	straight
πώς;	how?/what?	σκι	skiing (n)
ράδιο	radio (n)	σκοντάφτω	I trip over
ραντεβού	appointment (n)	σκούρος /-α /-ο	dark
ρεσεψιόν	reception desk (f)	σοβαρός /-ή /-ό	serious
ρεσεψιονίστας	receptionist (m)	σοκολάτα	chocolate (f)
ρετσίνα	retsina (Greek wine) (f)	σοκολατής /-ή /-ί	chocolate brown
ριγέ	striped	σου	to you/you (sing.)
ροδάκινο	peach (n)	σου	your
ρολόι	watch, clock (n)	σουβλάκι	souvlaki (n)
Ρόμπερτ	Robert (m)	σουίτα	suite (f)
ρωτάω (-ώ)	I ask	σουτζουκάκια	spicy meat balls in tomato sauce
στην	into, to the	σπάνια	rarely, seldom
Σάββατο	Saturday (n)	σπάω	I break
Σαββατοκύριακο	weekend (n)	σπίτι	house (n)
σαν	as, like	στατιστικός /-ή /-ό	statistical
σάντουϊτς	sandwich (n)	σταφύλι	grape (n)
σας	your	στάχτη	ash (f)
σεισμός	earthquake (m)	σταχτής /-ή /ί	ash grey
σέλινο	celery (n)	στεγνώνω	I dry up
σεμινάριο	seminar (n)	στεναχωριέμαι	I worry
Σεπτέμβριος, Σεπτέμβρης	September (m)	στεναχωρημένος /-η /-ο	worried, troubled

στης	at (the)	τέσσερις	four
στο	at (the)	Τετάρτη	Wednesday (f)
στοιχεία	data	τέτοιος /-α /-ο	such (a), of such a kind
στυλό	pen (n)	τετράκλινο	four beds (n)
συγγνώμη	excuse me	τζατζίκι	yoghurt, cucumber, and garlic dip (n)
συμβουλή	advice (f)		
συμπληρώνω	fill out	τζούντο	judo (n)
συνάδελφος	colleague (m, f)	τη(ν)	the
συνάλλαγμα	exchange (n)	τηλεφωνητής	telephone operator (m)
συναρπαστικός /-ή /-ό	unique, exciting	τηλέφωνο	telephone (n)
		την	her
συνέδριο	conference (n)	της	her
συνεργασία	co-operation, collaboration (f)	τι	what, how
		τιμή	price (f)
συνέχεια	continually	τίποτα	not at all, don't mention it!
συνηθίζω	I get used to		
συνήθως	usually	τμήμα	section (n)
σύννεφο	cloud (n)	το	the (n)
συνταγή	prescription (f)	Τόνια	Tonia, Antonia (f. name)
συνταξιούχος	retired person (m, f)		
σύντομα	shortly, soon	τοπικός /-ή /-ό	local
σύστημα	system (n)	τόσος /-η /-ο	so, so much, so big, so many
συχνά	often, frequently		
σφαιροβολία	shot put (f)	τότε	then
σχεδιάζω	I plan	του	his (m), its (n)
σχεδόν	almost	τουαλέτα	toilet (f)
σχεδόν ποτέ	hardly ever	τουλάχιστο(ν)	at least
		τουρτουρίζω	I am shaking
ταβέρνα	taverna (f)	τους	their
ταραγμένος /-η /-ο	rough	τράπεζα	bank (f)
ταραμοσαλάτα	egg-fish salad, taramosalata (f)	τραπεζικός /-ή /-ό	banking
		τρέμω	I shiver
τελειώνω	I complete, I end, I run out	τρέχω	I run
		τριανταφυλλής /-ιά /-ί	pink
τελικά	at the end, finally		
τέλος	end (n)	τριαντάφυλλο	rose (n)

τριήμερο	long weekend	φανταστικό!	fantastic!
τρίκλινο	three beds (n)	φαρδύς /-ιά /-ύ	wide
τρικυμία	storm, tempest (f)	φαρμακείο	chemist's (n)
Τρίπολη	Tripolis (Greek town) (f)	φάρμακο	medicine (n)
Τρίτη	Tuesday (f)	φαρμακοποιός	chemist (m, f)
τρομερό!	awesome!/awful!	Φεβρουάριος/ Φλεβάρης	February (n)
τρομερός /-ή /-ό	awful, terrible		
τροφικός /-ή /ό	food	φεύγω	I leave
τροχάδην	running (n)	φημισμένος /-η /-ο	famous
τροχός	wheel (m)	φθινόπωρο	fall, autumn (n)
τρώω	I eat	φιλικότερος /-η /-ο	friendlier
τσάι	tea (n)	φοράω(-ώ)	I wear
τσάντα	bag (f)	φόρεμα	dress (n)
τσίκλα	chewing gum (f)	φουαγιέ	foyer (n)
τυρί	cheese (n)	φούστα	skirt (f)
τώρα	now	ΦΠΑ	VAT
υπάλληλος	officer, clerk, employee (m, f)	φράουλα	strawberry (f)
		φρούτο	fruit (n)
υπάλληλος	receptionist (m, f)	φρυγανιά	rusk (f)
		φτηνός /-ή /-ό	cheap
υπάρχει	there is	φυλασσόμενος /-η /-ο	guarded
υγεία	health (f)		
υγρασία	humidity (f)	φυσικά	of course, naturally, physically
υπεραστικός /-ή /-ό	distance		
υπερκόπωση	over-exhaustion (f)	φωνάζω	I call
υπέροχος /-η /-ο	excellent	φωτογραφική μηχανή	camera (f)
υπόγειο	cellar (n)		
υπόλοιπος /-η /-ο	rest		
ύστερα	later on, after, afterwards	χαίρετε	hello (formal)
		χαιρετίσματα	greetings, regards
υψηλός /-ή /-ό	high	χαίρομαι	I am glad
		χαλάζι	hail (n)
φαίνομαι	I look	χαρτοφύλακας	briefcase (m)
φάκελος	envelope (m)	χαλασμένος /-η /-ο	out of order
φανάρι	traffic lights (n)	χάμπουργκερ	hamburger (n)

χάντμπολ	handball (n)	χτες	yesterday
χάνω	I miss	χυμός	juice (m)
χάπι	pill (n)	χώρα	country (f)
χάρτης	map (m)	χώρος	site (m), space, area (m)
χειμώνας	winter (m)		
χθες	yesterday	ψαράς	fisherman (m)
χιόνι	snow (n)	ψάρι	fish (n)
χλωμός /-ή /-ό	pale	ψαρόβαρκα	fishing boat (f)
χμ!	hm!	ψαροταβέρνα	fish taverna (f)
χορεύω	I dance	ψάχνω	I look for
χόρτα	greens	ψιχάλα	drizzle (f)
χουρμάς	date (m)	ψυγείο	refrigerator (n)
χρειάζομαι	I need	ψωμί	bread (n)
χρυσαφικά	jewellery	ψώνια	shopping (pl.)
χρησιμοποιώ	I use		
χρόνος	year (m)	ωραία	nice, wonderful
χρώμα	colour (n)	ωραίος /-α/-ο	beautiful

Credits

Voice Credits:

Recorded at Alchemy Studios, London

Cast: Melina Theocharidou, Manolis Stavrakakis, Emma West